ƒP

JOSEPH McCARTHY

Reexamining the Life and Legacy of America's Most Hated Senator

Arthur Herman

The Free Press

*f*P

THE FREE PRESS
A Division of Simon & Schuster Inc.
1230 Avenue of the Americas
New York, NY 10020

Designed by Carla Bolte

Manufactured in the United States of America

10   9   8   7   6   5   4   3   2   1

Library of Congress Cataloging-in-Publication Data

Herman, Arthur, 1956–
   Joseph McCarthy : reexamining the life and legacy of America's most hated
senator / Arthur Herman.
      p.   cm.
   Includes bibliographical references and index.
      1. McCarthy, Joseph, 1908–1957.   2. Legislators—United States.
Biography.   3. United States. Congress. Senate Biography.
4. Anti-communist movements—United States—History—20th century.
5. Internal security—United States—History—20th century.   I. Title.
E748.M143 H47 2000
973.921 '092—dc21
[B]
                                                      99-37011
                                                        CIP

ISBN 0–684–83625–4

Contents

Introduction

When I walked into the mall in downtown Appleton, Wisconsin, on a late and lazy Sunday morning, I had no address for the place I was going. I didn't even know the name of the cemetery. The idea for doing this had come to me while my wife and I were flying to Wisconsin to visit my parents. Sitting in Chicago's O'Hare Airport during those heavy, boring moments before boarding our plane, I had suddenly decided that while I was out here, I should visit Joe McCarthy's grave.

Since I was writing a book on him, it seemed only fitting to pay a visit. It was also the fortieth anniversary of his death—a lifetime ago in my case. I was barely five months old when McCarthy had been buried on May 7, 1957, in his home town of Appleton. In one sense he has never been laid to rest. Joe McCarthy was and remains the single most despised man in American political memory—far more reviled than Aaron Burr or Richard Nixon or even George Wallace. Yet I knew that some people treat his grave as a kind of shrine. The John Birch Society, the final word in right-wing extremism and anti-Communist paranoia, made its home in Appleton—keeping vigil, as it were, beside the fallen hero's tomb (although their offices are actually in a strip mall on the other side of town). One biographer, David Oshinsky, had published a picture of McCarthy's grave strewn with flowers from well-wishers. Thanks to the Oshinsky photo, I had an idea what the headstone looked like. My problem, since I hadn't brought any of my notes with me, was to find out exactly where it was.

McCarthy's grave. A shrine to die-hard supporters. A milestone of justice to his enemies. ("Joe McCarthy's death," Daniel Boorstin had growled to me when we had had lunch at the Cosmos Club a few weeks earlier, "isn't that the fifth proof for the existence of God?") The term *enemies* seems harsh for describing McCarthy's detractors and critics more than forty years after his death. But the bald truth is that the term does capture the spirit of their attacks,

1

both then and now. "Senator McCarthy died yesterday in Washington," wrote the English newspaper *News Chronicle* in May 1957. "America was the cleaner by his fall, and is cleaner by his death." When Richard Rovere would publish his dark masterpiece, *Senator Joe McCarthy*, two years later, he asserted that, "like Hitler, McCarthy was a screamer, a political thug, a master of the mob," and that he "usurped executive and judicial authority whenever the fancy struck him." As for McCarthy's supporters, "the bat-haunted Minute Women of the U.S.A., to the Texas millionaires, to the China Lobby, to the 'hard' anti-Communist intelligentsia of New York," they came to McCarthy "from the outmost fringes, where grievances and anxieties were the strongest and the least grounded in reason; where the passion for authoritarian leadership was greatest; where the will to hate and condemn and punish could most easily be transformed into political action."[1]

Rovere was a journalist and the quintessential liberal anti-Communist of that era. He despised the vicious and narrow-minded totalitarian spirit communism represented, but he and other liberals thought they saw the same spirit among their fellow Americans on the political right. McCarthyism was part of "a popular revolt against the upper classes," as Harvard sociologist Talcott Parsons put it, and Rovere for one had no doubt about which side he himself was on. He had written a series of devastating pieces on McCarthy for the *New Yorker* and had crossed swords with him more than once. Yet he did not for a moment believe that his own personal involvement in those events disqualified him from passing historical judgment on the era or the man. Joe McCarthy, Rovere concluded, had never actually believed in the monstrous crusade he had set in motion; anticommunism, patriotism, the Catholic church, were all tools for self-promotion, never sacred causes. "To McCarthy, everything was profane." He had some decent instincts—"who doesn't?" Rovere had to add—but "in the mirror, McCarthy must have seen and recognized a fraud."[2]

Have more recent commentators changed their perspective? Try William O'Neill (in *American High: The Years of Confidence 1945–1960*): "Dishonesty was the best policy to McCarthy until the bitter end." Or John Patrick Diggins: "A consummate demagogue, McCarthy played upon cold war emotions and made charges so fantastic that frightened people believed the worst." Or Michael Barone: "McCarthy was a pathological liar, an uninformed and obscure politician with certain demagogic gifts" (that classic word again, the favorite for describing McCarthy's rapport with his constituents). Or Paul Johnson (in *Modern Times*): "He was not a serious politician but an adventurer, who treated politics as a game." Or, David Halberstam (in *The Fifties*): "He instinctively knew how to brush aside the protests of his witnesses, how to humiliate vulnerable, scared people. In the end, he produced little beyond fear and headlines."[3]

Even those who have belatedly recognized that some of what McCarthy said and did had genuine merit cannot resist joining in. In a 1996 piece that appeared in the *Washington Post*, provocatively titled "Was McCarthy Right About the Left," Nicholas von Hoffman acknowledged that McCarthy's charges did rest against a background of genuine Communist subversion and of liberal excuses for it, but still felt it necessary to add that he was "a loutish, duplicitous bully, who carried, not the names of Reds but bottles of hootch in his briefcase."[4] And in their careful, painstaking summary of new evidence about the Communist Party of the United States taken from Soviet archives, which definitively shows that it was secretly financed by the Soviet Union and helped to support the KGB's espionage activities, historians John Earl Haynes and Harvey Klehr were quick to add, "None of this, however, offers any vindication for Senator McCarthy, or McCarthyism"—a judgment I will leave to readers to assess by the time they finish this book.[5]

In short, McCarthy remains what the Germans would call *vogelfrei*—the "free bird" everyone and anyone is free to take a shot at, even forty years after his death. Today he exists in most people's imagination almost solely as an established icon of evil. In fact, when people learned that I was doing a biography of McCarthy, a standard response was, "Who are you going to write about next? Adolf Hitler?"

In retrospect, McCarthy's disgrace and obloquy has come at a certain price to historical truth. He has become so taboo a figure, someone presented only in Rovere-style caricature rather than flesh and blood, that confusion and ignorance about what he did and the times in which he operated are widespread. Books like David Caute's *The Great Fear*, which implicitly compared the anti-Communist crusade of the fifties to Stalin's Great Terror, or Ellen Schrecker's *Many Are the Crimes: McCarthyism in America*, can portray the entire period in the most terrifyingly nightmarish colors, and be believed. So part of dispelling the myths about Joe McCarthy has to include dispelling the myths about the 1950s and the so-called red scare.

We need to remember that during the entire period, from 1947 to 1958, no American citizens were interrogated without benefit of legal counsel, none was arrested or detained without due judicial process, and no one went to jail without trial. As George Kennan, no admirer of the investigations, stated, "Whoever could get his case before a court was generally assured of meeting there with a level of justice no smaller than at any time in recent American history."[6] All through the "worst" of the McCarthy period, the Communist

Party itself was never outlawed, membership in the party was never declared a crime, and it continued to maintain public offices, publish books and the *Daily Worker*, and recruit new members (admittedly a tough sell by then).

In fact, most of what people ordinarily mean when they talk about the "red scare"—the House Un-American Activities Committee; anti-Communist probes into Hollywood, labor unions, and America's schools and universities; the Rosenberg trial; blacklisting in the media and schoolteachers fired for disloyalty—had nothing to do with McCarthy and he had nothing to do with them (although when asked, he generally approved of them, as most other Americans did). McCarthy's own committee in the Senate, the Permanent Subcommittee on Investigations, which he chaired for less than two years, had a specific duty to investigate communism in the federal government and *among government employees*. It had done so before he became chairman, and it did so after he left, under Senator John McClellan and Bobby Kennedy. The men and women McCarthy targeted, rightly or wrongly, as Communists or Communist sympathizers all shared that single characteristic: they were federal employees and public servants, and therefore, McCarthy and his supporters argued, they ought be held accountable to a higher standard than other American citizens.

That fact tends to get lost when historians dwell exclusively on the stories of harassment, professional disgrace, and other indignities suffered as a result of McCarthy's and other anti-Communist investigations. Dalton Trumbo, Dashiell Hammett, Howard Fast, Paul Robeson, Steve Nelson, Frances Farmer, and Lillian Hellman appear in standard treatments of the period in the same way in which the names of martyrs grace the pages of histories of the early church. Their personal ordeals are constantly presented as proof that America in those days must have been in the grip of an anti-Communist hysteria and a "witch-hunt." (In order not to be left out, Hellman told her own tale of woe in a short book of breathtaking dishonesty, entitled *Scoundrel Time*.) The best and most generous estimate is that during the entire decade of the red scare, ten thousand Americans lost their jobs because of their past or present affiliation with the Communist Party or one of its auxiliary organizations.[7] Of those who lost their jobs, two thousand worked in the government, and in perhaps forty cases McCarthy himself was directly or indirectly responsible for their being fired. In only one case—that of Owen Lattimore—can anyone make the argument that McCarthy's allegations led to any actual legal proceedings, and there a judge eventually threw out most of the indictment. Paradoxically, the fact that McCarthy never sent anyone to prison is also turned against him; opponents claimed that during his entire career, he never actually exposed a single spy or Communist—a claim that is manifestly untrue, as we will see.[8]

4

In fact, the number of people who did spend time in prison remained small. A grand total of 108 Communist Party members were convicted under the antisubversion provisions of the Smith Act, which Congress passed in 1941 (long before McCarthy was a member) and applied as equally to Nazi and fascist organizations as it did to Communists. Another twenty Communist Party members were imprisoned under state and local laws.[9] Fewer than a dozen Americans went to jail for espionage activities (one of them being Alger Hiss, who was convicted of perjury). Exactly two were sentenced to death for conspiracy to commit espionage: Julius and Ethel Rosenberg.

We need to contrast all this with the *three and a half million* people who, according to the KGB's own official numbers, were arrested and sent to the gulag during the six years of Stalin's Great Terror, from 1935 to 1941. None had the benefit of any genuine legal protection; Stalin's secret police seized, interrogated, and sentenced the lot. The KGB states that of that number, 681,692 were executed in 1937–1938 alone. Taken with the four or five million people who died in Stalin's Great Famine of 1932–1933, the total number of human beings executed, exiled, imprisoned, or starved to death in those years comes to ten to eleven million.[10] These are official KGB numbers released at the end of the cold war. They are almost certainly low. And during all the years when this was taking place, men and women like Trumbo, Robeson, and Hellman insisted that Stalin was the just and compassionate father of his people, asserted that Soviet citizens enjoyed a freedom and happiness unknown in American society, and celebrated the Soviet Union as the model society for the future. Others, such as Julius Rosenberg, Alger Hiss, Judith Coplon, Martin Sobell, and Steve Nelson, willingly served the Stalinist regime, as other espionage agents or as part of the Communist underground apparatus.

In the 1970s, it became fashionable to deny or at least avoid mentioning this part of the historical context in which McCarthy lived and breathed. If McCarthy was guilty, the reasoning goes, then those he tormented must be innocent. David Oshinsky could publish a 597-page biography of McCarthy that contained exactly one and a half pages on the Communist Party. As late as 1994, in *The Era of McCarthyism*, Ellen Schrecker could dismiss the charge that Julius Rosenberg gave atomic secrets to the Soviets as "uncertain," and present the Rosenbergs' conviction and execution in 1951 as just another example of anti-Communist hysteria.[11]

Today we know better. Archival materials from the former Soviet Union have revealed that Stalin's intentions were aggressively malign and expansionist, just as America's coldest cold warriors had believed. We now know that Mao Tse-tung was not a progressive nationalist forced into the Soviet camp by American hostility and incomprehension, as revisionist scholars in the seventies like to pretend, but was a brutal and dedicated Communist who enthusiastically embraced Stalin from the beginning. Historians J. E. Haynes, Harvey Klehr, Ronald Radosh, Allan Weinstein, and Alexander Vassiliev have used new declassified American materials as well as Soviet sources to lay to rest any doubts about the Soviet Union's espionage activities, as well as the Communist Party's active support of it.

The declassified Venona decrypts have revealed to the public the full extent and depth of Soviet spying in America and proved that fears of Russian espionage networks at work in the highest reaches of the government were not fantasy but sober fact. Meanwhile, independent sources from iron curtain Hungary have confirmed Alger Hiss's role as a Soviet spy, just as Russian sources (including his former KGB case officer) have finally definitively established that Julius Rosenberg was a central figure in the Soviet spy network (although the importance of the material he provided on the atomic bomb, and the degree of his wife Ethel's involvement, is still under debate). Even the truth about Owen Lattimore, the most famous of McCarthy's "victims," has finally come out, thanks to a former Chinese espionage agent's memoirs and declassified FBI files, which go a long way to vindicate McCarthy's original charges. In retrospect, the cause McCarthy made his own— anticommunism—has proved to be more valid and durable than the basic assumptions of his *anti*-anti-Communist critics.[12]

So in the midst of all this revision and reevaluation of the period and the issues at stake, what has happened to McCarthy himself? Virtually nothing. Even the professional historians who know better have shied away from attempting any major reassessment of McCarthy's place in the history of the cold war. The result is that his real role in the story of cold war anticommunism, and his place in the making of modern American political culture, remains unexplored and unexplained. In spite of everything, the old taboos and the old myths still hold.

I first encountered them growing up as a teenager in Wisconsin. Joe McCarthy was the Dairy State's dirty little secret. How could one of the most progressive states in the union, the original home of "Fighting Bob" La Follette, have sent *that man* to the U.S. Senate not once but twice, and by substantial margins? There were vague dark hints about his support among Wisconsin's German-American farmers, who had rallied around him when he defended Nazi war criminals early in his senate career—which helped to feed the notion that McCarthy and his supporters were cryptofascists with neo-Nazi leanings. But presumably that same Wisconsin voter base which sent McCarthy to the Senate also voted for his predecessor, Robert La Follette, Jr., and then for his successor, William Proxmire. Hardly radical right-wingers. What had happened? Again, no one seemed inclined to supply me with any answers.

Now, two decades later, visiting Appleton, and McCarthy's grave, seemed a good place to start.

I went over to a phone booth near the mall entrance and glanced at the telephone directory. It listed two Catholic cemeteries. Which one: St. Joseph's or St. Mary's? I decided to try St. Joseph's and asked the elderly concierge sitting forlornly at the information desk (the mall shops were not open yet). He was heavyset, with a slow, shy manner typical of midwestern males.

"How do I get to St. Joseph's cemetery?" It turned out he knew but didn't really know. It was the sort of encounter you often have when traveling: natives who try to be helpful without being forthcoming. So after a minute or two, I decided on a different tack.

"I'm looking for the cemetery where Joe McCarthy is buried."

At first, there was no expression. Then a slow, sly smile started from the corner of his mouth and spread across his face. He leaned forward and actually got out of his chair with excitement—clearly this was going to make his weekend. I had instantly acquired a gleeful ally.

"Lemme call my wife," he said with the same complicitous smile. "She'll know." He was dialing the number as my wife came back after looking in the mall window shops. I turned to her, barely containing my pleasure. "He's calling his wife. She knows where the grave is." Beth's eyes opened wide. I don't know what she expected from this impromptu pilgrimage—certainly not this kind of instant service.

He hung up. His wife wasn't home. But now he was involved in the hunt too, so he asked: "You gonna be around for a while? Lemme find out for you."

When we came back ten minutes later, he had two numbers for me but nothing else. He had called St. Joseph's cemetery and the parish house. No answer. He was as crestfallen as I was. Then he glanced behind me and said, "Hey!"

He had stopped a slight man in his sixties wearing a straw hat who was on his way to McDonald's for an early lunch (it was now 11:30). "Where's Joe McCarthy buried?" he called out. The other man said without hesitation, "In St. Mary's cemetery," and then looked at me.

"You sure? Not St. Joseph's?" the concierge asked.

"Yeah, I'm sure—I been out there a couple times. Right down near the river. Real pretty spot."

Getting directions turned out to be long, and involved, with each man

7

describing the route to St. Mary's from a slightly different starting point, while I was trying to introduce a third starting point, namely, where our car was parked. Finally the concierge asked me, not unkindly, to be quiet for a minute and he turned to get his bearings straight with the man in the straw hat. I had no idea who this other man was, except that he was an old Appleton resident, obviously a McCarthy fan ("I go down there every year or so," he confided to me), and like the concierge, a Roman Catholic. Because Joe McCarthy, for better or worse, was one of their own.

I had grown up in a different midwestern tradition. Mine was Minnesota Scandinavian, either Lutheran or freethinking and sometimes both, and politically progressive. When my Lutheran grandmother had learned that I was studying Latin at college, she began to worry that I had fallen in with the wrong crowd—meaning Catholics, possibly even Jesuits, who might try to woo me into the arms of the Scarlet Woman. I had been taught to think of the Roman Catholic church as a reactionary and authoritarian institution—as witness the Middle Ages, the Spanish Inquisition, Cardinal Francis Spellman (deeply detested in our house), William F. Buckley, Jr.—and Joe McCarthy.

But central Wisconsin, where I grew up, had a large Polish population, and although I didn't realize it at the time, it gave me my first clues for understanding the McCarthy phenomenon. At school I met the sort of working-class Catholics whose fathers and mothers had been McCarthy's bedrock of support. It became a familiar yet always foreign world: the world of Knights of Columbus and the Holy Name Society for Catholic men, and rosary groups for the women. It was a world of strange foods (kielbasa, golabki, and punchkas), of huge and elaborate weddings at churches illuminated by stained glass windows and topped by onion-shaped domes, with polka bands that played songs with titles like "Oj nasza Kasia" (O My Katy) and "Hupi Shupi Polka." There were classmates who had eight or nine brothers and sisters, some of whom attended church schools they called "St. Joe's" or "St. Pete's," and whose father worked for the paper mill and whose grandfather was named Roman or Casimir. Later those classmates went to the Catholic high school, with the very unmidwestern name of Pacelli, while still later one of their sisters might very occasionally take vows at the convent at the north end of town on Maria Drive.

In 1950, the year McCarthy gave his Wheeling, West Virginia, speech and launched himself into national prominence, nearly half of all churchgoers in Wisconsin were Catholics. His neighbors in the township of Grand Chute where he was born were Dutch Catholics, rather than Polish or Irish. Irishmen were rare in eastern Wisconsin—neighbors called the McCarthy family "the Irish settlement"—but there was a strong bond that drew them together, as fellow Catholics in a Protestant country that viewed them with fear and suspicion. Since the Irish were the first large-scale Catholic immigrants, they served as principal targets of American antipopery.

Unlike America's Jewish immigrants, of whom more than three-quarters were skilled workers, the Irish came from an overwhelmingly rural background. In the nineteenth century they had had to take jobs at the very bottom of the economic ladder and became caught up in urban political machines such as New York's Tammany Hall. To high-minded Anglo-Saxon Protestant observers, Irish politics was synonymous with corruption. "A more improvident, heedless, and dishonest class of people never defiled the fair face of the earth."[13] Antebellum New Orleans even made up a rhyme about the Irish:

> *Ten thousand micks*
> *Swung their picks*
> *To dig the New Canal.*
> *But the choleray*
> *Was stronger'n they.*
> *An' twice it killed them all.*

"What ought to be surprising about the American Irish," writes Andrew Greeley, "is not that they have not been quite as socially and financially successful as the Jews, but that they have been successful at all."[14] They did it by embracing what John Courtney Murray called "the American proposition," the principles of religious and economic liberty, of science and technological progress, and of democracy and the separation of church and state. For Irish Catholics of McCarthy's generation, anticommunism became one more way of erasing an ancient stigma. Having been unjustly accused of serving one secret conspiracy against America, they would dedicate themselves to rooting out another.[15]

That determination to succeed in a hostile environment was one of the bonds that drew together Joe McCarthy and another prominent Irish Catholic family in the fifties, the Kennedys. Robert Kennedy had joined McCarthy's staff in 1953 at the behest of his father, the senator's keen admirer. Like McCarthy, Joseph Kennedy was a former Roosevelt Democrat and a fervent anti-Communist. He often invited McCarthy to stop by for drinks at the Kennedy house at Palm Beach and to stay at the family compound at Hyannis Port. The senior Kennedy's view of politics, and of life, was much like McCarthy's: "It's not what you are that counts, but what people think you are."[16] McCarthy became a minor figure in the Kennedy circle. To the ex-ambassador's delight, he dated two of the Kennedy daughters, Patricia and Eunice, who discovered "he had a certain raw wit and charm when he had not had too much to drink," as Eunice later put it.[17] Joe also played shortstop in family softball games (he did so badly that the Kennedys eventually had to bench him).

Robert Kennedy served McCarthy loyally as assistant counsel for his Subcommittee on Investigations, until a personal quarrel with the chief counsel, Roy Cohn, forced him to quit. But he and Joe remained close, and Joe McCarthy stood as godfather for Bobby and Ethel's first child. One day after McCarthy's censure by the Senate in 1954, Bobby was sailing on the Potomac with a group of reporters. He started defending McCarthy against their criticisms. "Why do you reporters . . . feel the way you do?" he wanted to know. "OK, Joe's methods may be a little rough, but after all, his goal was to expose Communists in government—a worthy goal. So why are you reporters so critical of his methods?" Even after his own conversion to left-to-center liberalism, he refused to disown or even criticize his old boss. "A very complicated character," he would muse to himself years later. Robert Kennedy had seen in America's Grand Inquisitor a man who, for all his glaring faults, had "wanted so desperately to be liked."[18]

John Kennedy's views, on communism and the Soviet threat, were not so different from McCarthy's either. Although a loyal Democrat, Kennedy had also bashed the Truman administration for its dismal China record. One night in February 1952 he heard a speaker at Harvard's Spree Club denounce McCarthy in the same breath as Alger Hiss. Kennedy shot back, "How dare you couple the name of a great American patriot with that of a traitor!"[19] Later he would back the Communist Control Act, a measure that went far beyond anything McCarthy had ever proposed, by virtually outlawing the Communist Party in the United States. During the debate on McCarthy's censure in 1954, while most Democrats lined up against him Kennedy warned that censure might have serious repercussions for "the social fabric of this country." And when the actual censure vote came, John Kennedy carefully contrived to be in the hospital for a back operation, so that he would not have to cast a vote against a man who was wildly popular with not only his father but his Irish and Italian constituents.

In many ways, McCarthy and John Kennedy represented the two divergent paths available to Irish Catholic politicians for success in what was still a predominantly Anglo-Saxon and Protestant nation. McCarthy never lost track of his roots. He attended mass every Sunday, built strong friendships with priests and clerics, and remained a strict Catholic. John Kennedy, by contrast, was embarrassed by the presence of priests and the outward trappings of Catholicism.[20] He had attended Choate and Harvard rather than Catholic schools, while McCarthy was a graduate of the Jesuit university at Marquette. Kennedy avoided doing or saying anything in public that would make him identifiably or stereotypically

"Irish" (although in private he enjoyed sitting at the piano and singing traditional Irish ballads with his sisters). Early on he had decided his destiny lay
with the dominant eastern political establishment. He forged links to its key
institutions: Harvard, the mainstream press, and groups like the Council on
Foreign Relations and Americans for Democratic Action. Six years after Mc-
Carthy's censure, Kennedy ran for president as the standard-bearer for that
establishment liberalism. He surrounded himself with its "best and brightest"—some of the same men, as it happened, Joe McCarthy had spent his
career attacking.

By contrast, Joe McCarthy was what a knowing observer would call
"shanty Irish," as opposed to "lace curtain Irish," which John Kennedy's
mother Rose Fitzgerald epitomized. McCarthy was authentic working class.
His eldest brother, Steve, was a factory worker; another a local auctioneer;
the third a truck driver. It was only in law school that he finally shed his
broad Irish brogue. The grandiloquent gesture, the blarney, the do-or-die
bravado, the inability to forget slights and humiliations, as well as the drinking and affinity for lost causes: it is not possible to understand McCarthy's career without this ethnic component.

The other side of that Catholic and Irish-American experience, however,
was the desperate need for assimilation. The Irish wanted above all to be part
of the mainstream of American life and to enjoy its most dazzling promise,
that of personal success. Success was the best revenge on one's supposed social betters. That too was part of the McCarthy reality.

If Joe McCarthy had ever paused to consider his life as a whole, he
would have looked at it as a typical American success story: son of a poor
Wisconsin dirt farmer—"I'm just a farm boy," he disarmingly told the audience at a debate in his first successful statewide campaign—to U.S. senator.
It engendered in him a deep emotional commitment to the nation that had
enabled him to rise up from obscurity and a sense of pride, even hubris, that
blinded him to the downside of his success. When talking about him, Robert
Kennedy used to compare McCarthy's career to a toboggan ride: "It was so
exciting and exhilarating as he went downhill that it didn't matter to him if he
hit a tree at the bottom."[21]

Here the better comparison is not with John Kennedy (or even Richard
Nixon, whom he resembled in certain other ways), but with another Senate
colleague, Lyndon Baines Johnson. It was Johnson who arranged for the
Senate to censure McCarthy in December 1954, the move that effectively
ended McCarthy's career. But in the end they shared more than they differed.

They were both big men, homely, even ugly, in appearance, with an intense physicality that some people found reassuring, but others intimidating
and even repulsive. Both had a capacity for generosity, and for an explosive

temper and incredible bullying. Both drank to excess. Both did not hesitate to lie for political effect. Both, in fact, did lie about their war record because it had been good politics to do so, and for both success in politics was their final measure of themselves as human beings.

Johnson and McCarthy reflected the degree to which politics in post–New Deal America had become a form of self-fashioning. By devoting himself to electoral politics, a man from a poor or provincial background could transform himself into someone new, and even become a substantial player on the national stage. McCarthy had risen from county circuit judge to the Senate at age thirty-eight; LBJ became minority leader at age forty-six. In terms of their origins, they stood at the opposite pole from what was then called ESA—Eastern Socially Attractive types who normally ran Washington.* Yet through simple command of majorities at the ballot box, McCarthy and Johnson made themselves their equals and earned their respect—and in McCarthy's case, their fear. Like Johnson, McCarthy had had to rely on powerful local patrons in order to get launched in the political arena. In McCarthy's case, it was Wisconsin political boss Tom Coleman and various wealthy Milwaukee businessmen; in Johnson's case, it was the millionaire Brown Brothers of Texas. Like Johnson, McCarthy had lost his first run at the Senate, and in the same year: 1944. Like Johnson, he then won office by upsetting a major figure in their state's political establishment. For Johnson, this was former governor Coke Stevenson; for McCarthy, Robert La Follette, Jr.

Both men would also be haunted by their ruthless, single-minded pursuit of their ambitions. Johnson's razor-thin victory over Stevenson (by only eighty-three votes) was almost certainly fraudulent and earned him the derisive nickname "Landslide Lyndon." McCarthy became the "Pepsi-Cola Kid" because of his cozy relationship with the soft drink company, and his use of the anti-Communist issue for personal publicity earned him as many dedicated enemies as it did fanatical supporters.

Both men judged the world according to a harsh masculine standard. The world was divided into boys and men, and they knew to which category they wanted to belong. There were men who fought for what they believed and didn't back down, and those who did back down. There were those who were soft on issues like communism, and those who were not. That standard was reflected in McCarthy's fight against the "silk handkerchief liberals" who frustrated his efforts to ferret out Communists in government, and his push to get the "queers" as well as the "reds" out of the State Department and

---

*Harry Truman might seem another example. But the establishment's view of Truman always remained condescending; even when he was president, men like Dean Acheson and Averell Harriman treated him as their inferior, as if his chief virtue was that he was willing to have them as his principal advisers.

other government agencies. It turned up in Johnson's later campaign against Communist aggression abroad, in Southeast Asia. In the face of opposition, you stood tough and hit back, whether you were fighting the State Department or Ho Chi Minh. You accepted the rules of engagement (as did McCarthy, the former boxer) and fought with all your heart.

In the end, the cold war proved to be a point of no return for both. How strange, yet appropriate, how ironic that the man who had destroyed Joe McCarthy over domestic communism would himself be destroyed in less than fifteen years, over Vietnam. However, the wreckers in this case came not from the right but the left, and from within the ranks of his beloved Senate. The very people who had urged him on in the McCarthy censure, like William Fulbright and Wayne Morse and Mike Mansfield, would then turn against *him* and condemn him for his war against communism in Southeast Asia. Ironic, too, that another Irish Catholic senator, Eugene J. McCarthy of Minnesota, would be instrumental in his destruction, while Joe McCarthy's own successor, William Proxmire, became one of President Johnson's most bitter and effective critics.

Less than a decade after Joe McCarthy had been interred in St. Mary's cemetery, Lyndon Johnson would learn what it was like to be the target of hostile liberals and an unsympathetic national press. People would regularly attack him as a murderer, a tyrant, and a psychopath, and compare him to Hitler, much as they had McCarthy. A popular Broadway play, *MacBird*, by Barbara Garson, even implied that Johnson had murdered John Kennedy in order to seize power, a theme later picked up by various conspiracy theorists and exploited in Oliver Stone's film *JFK*.

In 1968 cartoonist Jules Feiffer published *LBJ Lampooned*. In the introduction to his grotesque caricatures, Feiffer revealed a great deal about not just liberal attacks on Johnson, but the earlier campaign against McCarthy as well. The "secret ingredient" to good cartooning, Feiffer said, was hate—"not personal hate," he added, "but professional hate: the intensity of conviction that comes to a craftsman's work when he has made the decision to kill; a commitment to shun all political and behavioral complexities, so that the subject becomes . . . purely and simply, a demon."[22]

Finally, the directions got settled and the man in the straw hat got back to the business of finding lunch. People were beginning to filter in as the shops began to get ready to open. My new-found friend was reluctant to see me go. I had obviously brightened up his otherwise routine day, and he took the opportunity to ask some questions of his own, and to reminisce.

"So are you studying him in school?" I explained that I was writing a book on McCarthy for The Free Press. Then I asked him if he remembered McCarthy at all.

"Sure, I remember him," he laughed. I didn't ask if he had voted for him. The concierge would have to be at least sixty-five (or born in 1931) to have done so, since the last time McCarthy last faced the voters was in 1952.

"Drank a lot, didn't he?" he asked. Yes, I said, he did, and I added that in my opinion his alcoholism was the principal cause of his downfall.

"But he married a pretty woman." That was a reference to Jean Kerr, who had buried her husband down by the river in May 1957. Smart, attractive, ambitious, and twenty years younger than her husband, she had come from a well-to-do Washington family, conservative and upright, and she had helped to steer the man who had voted for Roosevelt not twice, not thrice, but four times, into the conservative Republican camp. To the farm boy from Grand Chute township, with his five o'clock shadow and preference for working in sweat-stained shirt sleeves, she added a touch of class, even glamor. George Washington University had voted her the most beautiful girl on campus in 1945.[23] Unlike her husband, she was remarkably photogenic, even on the day she attended her husband's memorial service at the Capitol, when his body lay in state in the Senate chamber and his colleagues paid him their belated respects.

As I discovered, the real story of Joe McCarthy is also Jean Kerr's story. When I told a friend, a member of Washington's old social establishment (she had been a bridesmaid at Margaret Truman's wedding), that I was writing a book on Joe McCarthy, she amazed me by telling me that Jean had been a sorority sister. Everyone, she said, had liked and admired her. None of her old Washington friends could understand why she had married a man they all regarded as a monster. But Jean's reasons had been as much political as personal. She was more than just a pretty face. She served as his chief staffer, wrote speeches for him, and even a book: his 1952 apologia, *McCarthyism, The Fight for America*, is largely her composition, with the help of friends J.B. and Ruth Matthews. She also had a hand in McCarthy's notorious attack on General George Marshall.

Jean believed in playing hardball, harder at times than Joe himself. She, not Joe, was responsible for the infamous "composite" photo showing Senator Millard Tydings cozying up to Communist Party boss Earl Browder, and while McCarthy admitted the attempt to smear his old nemesis from Maryland had gone too far, Jean was unapologetic. Joe's enemies were her enemies. They managed to pay her back with interest, since she had to endure constant rumors that her husband was a secret homosexual, and Herblock cartoons that ridiculed her husband so cruelly they left her in tears. Later she had to shield him from public scrutiny as his drinking ran out of control and his health declined. As in so many similar cases, in trying to prevent her husband from becoming an alcoholic, she became one herself. She would also act as the careful guardian of his memory, even long after his death and after she had remarried, declaring his papers off limits to snoopy and usually unsympathetic biographers and historians.

But my concierge friend was still reminiscing. "That senator from Arkansas. Tall and gravely voice. He really went after him, didn't he?" After a moment, I realized he was talking about J. William Fulbright, Democratic senator, chairman of the Foreign Relations Committee, and nearly secretary of state under Kennedy. He and Joe McCarthy were long-standing adversaries. Articulate, erratic, complex, Fulbright was precisely the sort of cerebral, self-doubting liberal the brash and macho McCarthy despised, just as McCarthy represented a side of America that Fulbright could not stomach. Fulbright was a disciple of Dean Acheson, McCarthy's chief *bête noire*, and member of the Metropolitan Club. As David Halberstam later observed, "He was a public official, publicly elected, and yet he seemed to be an ally of the elitists, sharing their view of the private nature of national security."[24] McCarthy used to ridicule him by calling him "Senator Halfbright." Once a senate employee caught Fulbright in a rage about McCarthy: "that SOB's referred to me so often as Halfbright, that the country is partially beginning to believe it!" Yet one day Fulbright astonished one of his own staffers, by remarking, "You know, considering McCarthy is such an SOB, he's a very interesting personality. You know, I enjoy him in the locker room."[25]

And liberal though he was on most matters, on the matter of race Fulbright was a stalwart segregationist and an ardent opponent of civil rights for black Americans. McCarthy took the opposite view. His position on race and ethnicity was recognizably "liberal" in a fifties sense and even in a later sense (associates recalled him campaigning as vigorously in black neighborhoods in Milwaukee and other Wisconsin cities as in white ones), although he was dead before the issue really became part of the nation's agenda.

Fulbright the liberal segregationist versus McCarthy the color-blind Republican—a strange juxtaposition, but perhaps not so strange. Most Republicans in the fifties, including Taftites, were aware that theirs was the party of Lincoln and Reconstruction, while Fulbright had learned to support his fellow Southern Democrats on Jim Crow in order to consolidate his position on the Senate Foreign Relations Committee.

Afterward, with America mired in Vietnam and Fulbright now leading the charge to get the country out, he challenged Joseph Rauh of the Americans for Democratic Action (who had opposed Fulbright's hopes of heading the Department of State) to admit that he had done the right thing by his devil's bargain on Jim Crow, in order to secure the Foreign Relations Committee. Rauh felt it was an unanswerable proposition—"to do wrong in order to do right."[26] Yet that was precisely what McCarthy had done in overstepping the bounds of truth in his fight against communism—and what Rauh himself had done, as we will see, in the Paul Hughes case.

The battle between McCarthy and his adversaries was not a simplistic confrontation between right and wrong, or good and evil, or even between the righteous and the damned. It was a complex struggle, with strange twists and ambiguities, and at its heart lay two very different visions of what the cold war meant and how it should be fought.

For Joe McCarthy, the struggle with Soviet communism was a matter of victory or defeat. There could be no middle ground. Fulbright, like so many fellow liberals, could not and would not see it in such forthright terms. Fulbright himself nourished secret doubts about whether the United States could really resist what seemed to him an inevitable tide of historical decline, of which the rise of communism was only one part. Those doubts about America's ability to fulfill its self-imposed global mission would eventually spill over into his opposition to the Vietnam War, and filled the pages of his book on American foreign policy, *The Arrogance of Power*. Both McCarthy and Fulbright agreed that the fate of civilization hung in the balance in the cold war. McCarthy believed that in the end, it and America would survive; Fulbright, in his own sardonic, cynical way, did not.

In this sense, politics was *not* a game to Joe McCarthy. In the glare of the cold war, the stakes seemed vast. He was convinced that the "liberals" of his day—the heirs to progressivism and New Deal Democracy—had failed in that fight. He believed in many of the things they did. Unlike some of his right-wing Republican colleagues, he saw no problem with an activist government and never challenged the New Deal's social welfare programs; he took a broad view on civil rights and race. In fact, when he came to the Senate in 1947, newspapers had originally described him as a moderate, until he took up the domestic communism issue. But it was on precisely that issue that Democrats and liberals had failed the American people, McCarthy believed, and had revealed their true colors, and he was going to prove it. In trying to do so, he sealed his own doom, as both a man and a historical figure. In the end, the principal and most pathetic victim of McCarthyism would be—McCarthy himself.

I thanked my friend the concierge and got ready to set off. He wished me well, and gave a last smile: "That Joe McCarthy—he sure shook things up, didn't he?"

Yes, I had to admit, he certainly did.

A fter lunch, my wife and I were ready to make our way to St. Mary's cemetery. On the way we drove through East Appleton, which had been the affluent part of town in McCarthy's day and is still studded with large Victorian
houses and beautifully manicured lawns and shrubs. The elegant turreted
and porticoed homes stand in striking contrast to the shabby clapboard farm-
houses and dirt roads of Grand Chute township, where McCarthy was born
and raised. East Appleton is also the town's intellectual center. Lawrence
University, founded in 1847, sits quietly and confidently in its midst, a pic-
ture-perfect image of a liberal arts college. Its disdain, like that of East Appleton, for Senator Joe McCarthy, home town boy, was legendary. Lawrence's
president, Nathan Pusey, sponsored one of the very first anti-McCarthy
books, entitled *The McCarthy Record*, and helped to spread the rumor (which
had no foundation) that McCarthy liked to carry around a copy of *Mein
Kampf*.[27]*

Needless to say, McCarthy did not attend Lawrence College. He left
school at fourteen to start his own business, raising chickens and buying a
truck to drive the eggs to market. Years later, Edwin Bayley remembered how
he and his East Appleton friends spent their leisurely Saturday mornings at
the downtown YMCA. As they went home for lunch, they regularly passed Joe
McCarthy (who had been up before dawn) with his bib overalls and his Irish
brogue—"a hick," as Bayley would recall—and would yell good-natured insults at him as they rode by on their bikes. Joe would yell back in the same
spirit, and chase them as they circled him. Big, burly, with a hearty, energetic
manner, Joe McCarthy was someone people noticed: "I can't remember how
we knew his name, but we did." Later, as editor of the *Milwaukee Journal*,
Bayley would become one of McCarthy's bitterest opponents.[28]

St. Mary's turned out to be a surprisingly small cemetery, a strip of level
land running along the bluffs overlooking the Fox River. My wife and I got
out of the car, Beth carrying the camera, and we began reading the headstones. Many, I noticed, had Dutch names—the names of McCarthy's father's
and mother's neighbors in Grand Chute, descendants of the Dutch Catholic
settlers who had arrived in eastern Wisconsin in the 1840s and carved out
their farms from the surrounding wilderness just as Joe's grandfather had
done. Many of the other names were Polish, German, or Irish. In fact, it took
some time to sort through all the headstones bearing the name McCARTHY,
and there were several false starts. We even found a "Joseph T. McCarthy,"

---

*Later McCarthy got his revenge. When Pusey left Lawrence for Harvard, McCarthy wrote
an angry letter to a Boston newspaper calling Pusey "a rabid anti-anti-Communist . . . [who]
appears to hide a combination of bigotry and intolerance behind a cloak of phony, hypocriti-
cal liberalism." He added that "Harvard's loss was Wisconsin's gain."

whose birth and death dates were near to Joe's own . . . until I realized he must be a cousin, the child of one of grandfather Stephen McCarthy's other sons. The McCarthys' "Irish settlement" had reproduced itself here in St. Mary's. Next came Joe's father's grave, and his mother's—with BRIDGET TIERNEY MCCARTHY in large letters.

Then I saw it. Sitting by itself in the warm sunshine, flanked by marble urns and a pair of evergreen bushes—these are vandalized from time to time but today they looked plain and unremarkable. We walked up to the dark gray cenotaph. It stood almost waist high, reading in large block letters, JOSEPH R. MCCARTHY, and underneath UNITED STATES SENATOR, with the dates below, *Nov. 14, 1908* and *May 2, 1957*. There was nothing else, no flowers or any other special votive offering. Not the martyr's shrine today. The view from the 50-foot bluff was now largely overgrown with trees and shrubs, but the man in the straw hat had been right, it was a pretty spot. McCarthy occupied it alone. No other grave, not even Jean's, interfered with its silent, almost eerie, isolation.

We paused for a moment, my wife took pictures, and she said something about the visit being a good omen. I turned for one last look and then headed for the car. Afterwards I thought about the words from the prayer said at the unveiling of McCarthy's memorial in 1959: "death is only a horizon, and a horizon is nothing save the limit of our sight." I realized that was true in an historical as well as a religious sense. It is now possible, forty years on, to set McCarthy's life and career against a broader and somewhat different horizon from the one he and his contemporaries had been limited to. The dark and uncertain future over which he and opponents like Rovere and Fulbright fought is now our present. Maybe it is time to try to understand what happened.

I

ORIGINS

Democracies are turbulent.

—David Hume, *Idea of a Perfect Commonwealth* (1752)

Chapter 1

Wisconsin and the Wider World

G rand Chute was a rural township made up of the wheat and dairy farms that encircled Appleton. Joseph Raymond McCarthy was born there on his father's farm on November 14, 1908. His grandfather had come from Ireland to eastern Wisconsin in 1858, and carved a farm and a life for himself and his family out of the wilderness. Stephen McCarthy's son, Tim, cleared another 142 acres in Grand Chute, married an Irish girl named Bridget Tierney, and raised a family of seven children. Joseph was the fifth child and the third boy.

Since relationships with parents determine so much of what happens in later life, McCarthy biographers have spent much time and energy speculating on Joe's. Some have suggested that while his father was inordinately hard and strict, his mother pampered and spoiled him, taking this "ugly duckling" under her protective wing. Others have proposed seeing McCarthy as a boy who was viciously abused and bullied as a child, and who buried his resentments and aggression until he could take them out on the world at large. There doesn't seem to be much truth to either version. After looking at all the available evidence, McCarthy's best recent biographer, Thomas Reeves, had to conclude that "the McCarthys were a close, happy family," in which both father and mother shared domestic authority and urged all their children to make the most of themselves. In fact, nothing really distinguished the McCarthys from any of the other families who lived along the strip of farms that their Dutch neighbors called "the Irish settlement."[1]

It was a simple, hard life. The family lived in an house made from trees

Tim McCarthy had cut down clearing the land, making Joe McCarthy the last major American political figure who could trace his beginnings to a log cabin.[2] Like the other McCarthy boys, Joe grew up rising before dawn and spending the day in the fields, planting and then harvesting corn, barley, oats, and cabbage and tending the family dairy cows. One thing he does seem to have inherited from his father was his incessant, restless energy. Everyone remembered him as the boy who couldn't sit still. He ran rather than walked from room to room, bolted his food at the dinner table before rushing outdoors, and needed far less sleep than his brothers and sisters to do a good day's work. Today psychologists would label him a hyperactive child and could point to much of his later behavior—his nervous twitchy manner, his ability to skip a night's sleep without losing any focus or energy, his manic impatience—as indicators of a hypomanic tension condition.[3] At the time, of course, it simply meant that Joe McCarthy impressed everyone with his tireless capacity for hard work and infectious enthusiasm for whatever came to hand.

Tim McCarthy was also a strict Roman Catholic, leading the family in praying the Rosary every evening and taking them to church every Sunday. If first-generation Irish families were rare in the Fox River valley, Catholics were not. Dutch Catholics had been moving into the eastern part of the state since the 1840s, and some of McCarthy's earliest political associates, such as Henry Van Stratten and Urban Van Susteren, came from this Dutch Catholic stock.

Thus, between 1870 and 1910 Wisconsin had absorbed a steady influx of other European immigrants—Germans, Poles, Czechs, and Croats. By 1930, the year McCarthy graduated from high school, persons of foreign or mixed origin made up 50 percent of the state's population. Almost a quarter of them were Catholic.[4] They settled on the land in southern and eastern Wisconsin, and in the more northern counties of Portage, Adams, Juneau, Taylor, and Marinette. They would provide McCarthy with his original bedrock political base. With recent roots in the old country, Wisconsin's Catholics had strong feelings on foreign policy issues and on communism. Through their diocesan bulletins and in meetings of groups like the Knights of Columbus and the Holy Name Society, they kept track of the persecution of Catholics in Soviet-occupied territory and the trial of Cardinal Mindszenty in Hungary in 1948. The key events of the cold war—the Yalta conference, the partition of Germany, the Soviet conquest of Eastern Europe, the mobilization of young men to fight in Korea and later Vietnam—all directly affected these Wisconsin families and communities. To them, McCarthy's anti-Communist crusade was not an abstract, but a deeply personal, issue.

Their homey, rural values were also McCarthy's. He would remain a strong Roman Catholic, although he was never an ostentatiously devout, or as he put it, "a candle-lighting" Catholic.[5] Like his neighbors, he believed that success was a matter of hard, physical work and that people who grew up on farms had a built-in advantage over those who didn't. McCarthy was fond of drawing on farm life for lessons in his political speeches. He would often say that political opponents "sucked eggs," a reference to weasels, skunks, and other vermin raiding the chicken house, and liked to compare his own efforts as a Communist baiter to "skunk-hunting." "Digging out a skunk," he used to say, "is a dirty, smelly business. No one wants to be near you when you're done—but someone's got to do it." A man willing to do the dirty work, and stand the smell, was a real man, just like the man who stood up for what he believed, regardless of the consequences.[6]

Since money was tight, Tim McCarthy encouraged his children to start out on their own early. This is what led Joe to start his chicken farm and make ends meet by selling eggs to grocery stores in Appleton. After his chickens died, McCarthy took on a series of unsatisfactory jobs until 1929, when he decided to enroll at Little Wolf High School in Manawa. Joe, almost twenty-one, would be sharing a classroom, doing the same homework, and submitting to the same discipline as fourteen- and fifteen-year-olds. "The day I first walked into that classroom and sat down with those kids," he later told a friend, "I would have sold out for two cents on the dollar." But he somehow persuaded the school's principal to let him take more than twice the normal load. Even though he had to work a night job, he finished four years of study in nine months. He did so well that he made the honor roll every quarter, and so impressed his classmates that they voted him vice president of the freshman class (although at his breakneck pace McCarthy stayed in ninth grade for only two months). In June 1930 he left Little Wolf with a high school diploma, the first McCarthy ever to do so.

The experience changed his life. It opened up the possibility of going to college—although Joe had some difficulty convincing college admissions boards that he had managed to get a genuine high school education so quickly. It also proved that Joe McCarthy had brains as well as brawn: that he could memorize numbers and information at a quick glance, and put together an easy command of any subject that came to his attention. Even more, he had watched the attitude of his principal, teachers, and fellow students change from scorn and skepticism to respect and admiration. It taught McCarthy a basic lesson for life: that if he applied the right amount of grit, charm, and sheer determination, there was nothing he could not accomplish and no barrier, even the hostility of others, he could not overcome.

The same lesson applied to college. When the application to Marquette University in Milwaukee arrived it asked, "Did you complete four years of high school?" His high school principal, acting as Joe's adviser, decided to mark the answer yes, and McCarthy was admitted in the fall of 1930. Critics and admirers alike would later paint vivid images of Joe McCarthy's "education by Jesuit fathers" at the traditional Catholic college in Milwaukee; but for Joe McCarthy, Marquette represented not continuity with his family and his heritage, but a drastic and necessary break.

At first, like other smart, upwardly mobile young men, he assumed technology was the path to success and took up electrical engineering. But after finding that the math was too difficult and tedious, he gave up engineering for the study of law. In 1932 he switched as a junior to the law school. He was a mediocre law student. Working full time at a gas station to pay the bills, taking over the Marquette boxing team when its regular coach resigned (McCarthy was the school's heavyweight champion), participating in the college debate club, and enjoying late-night poker games with beer-drinking cronies cut into his studies. He managed to get his degree and pass the bar in 1935, and he hung out his shingle in the nearby town of Shawano. Yet he knew that any real future for a self-made lawyer lay in politics.

Like his father, Joe McCarthy was a staunch Democrat. In 1932 Roosevelt won 67 percent of the vote in Wisconsin. Most rural Wisconsinites admired Franklin Roosevelt and the New Deal, which was busily transforming the politics of the state, and the rest of the nation. McCarthy's neighbors, like other recent immigrants and working-class families in cities like Milwaukee, had benefited from the economic prosperity of the twenties. They had watched their standard of living advance more rapidly than they had ever imagined possible. The Depression had stopped them in their tracks. Despite our stereotyped image of the period from books like *The Grapes of Wrath*, the most typical victims of the Great Depression, as Michael Barone points out, "were not so much people mired in poverty as people suddenly and cruelly checked in upward mobility."[7] From New York City to Wisconsin and from Texas to California, Roosevelt managed to restore their faith in the American system and gave them a sense that the national government was there to protect them. New Deal Democracy made them feel part of a larger community. They were no longer just ignorant Irish micks or Brooklyn Jews, or southern "white trash," or backwoods hillbillies, but American citizens living in the modern world.

In the South, the New Deal helped to restructure southern agriculture, winning over poor blacks to the Democrats even as it solidified the lines of racial segregation.[8] In the West and Midwest, the New Deal satisfied the urgings of two generations of Populists and Progressives for an activist federal government with a concern with social justice, defined as government help for the "little guy" and constraints on big business and the rich. Among those who jumped on the Roosevelt bandwagon were the La Follette family, who had dominated state politics for more than twenty years.

In 1900 "Fighting Bob" La Follette had decided to launch his Progressive campaign under the Republican banner, which was at that time the party of the big business–hating, activist government–loving Theodore Roosevelt. Within a decade La Follette had created the same thing Democrats achieved across the Jim Crow South: one-party rule. The Republican primary became more important than the general contest, and since in 1906 La Follette had instituted open rules for primaries, it was not unusual to have larger turnout for the primary than for the general election. Republican candidates, including the future Joe McCarthy, learned to direct their campaign at general voters, not just party regulars.

One-party politics was also one-family politics. When Fighting Bob died in 1924, his sons Philip and Robert Jr. inherited their father's political power and Progressive mantle. They divided the state's key offices between them, with Robert sitting in the U.S. Senate and Philip in the governor's mansion in Madison. The La Follette alliance with the New Deal forced some modifications to this picture. In presidential elections, Wisconsin would vote Democratic—from 1932 to 1948, it turned to the Republican nominee only once, in 1944.[9] At the state level, Robert Jr. won FDR's personal endorsement in 1934, and Philip secured at least Democratic neutrality in the gubernatorial contest that same year. The La Follette sons also decided to capitalize on the new liberal mood by leaving the GOP and setting up their own Progressive Party, which drew on the same urban voters and poorer rural farmers who put their trust in FDR.

Their decisions left Wisconsin Democrats high and dry. Ironically, even as Roosevelt the Democrat racked up large majorities at Wisconsin polls, the state's party was starved of funds, leadership, and a base for local political patronage. When McCarthy decided to get involved in Democratic politics, he was gambling that he would stand out from an otherwise sorry field, and even if he couldn't win, he would at least make a name for himself. So he resisted pressure to join the state GOP (his law firm mentor was a leading anti–La Follette Republican) and ran for district attorney of Shawano County in 1936.

McCarthy turned out to be the best candidate, and the most effective organizer, Shawano Democrats had had for years.[10] He lambasted the national Republican ticket as reactionary and called its presidential candidate, Alfred Landon, the "puppet" of conservative business interests like William Randolph Hearst. Since he was a political nonentity and had no chance of winning without a sensational issue, he launched a harsh attack on the Progressive Party incumbent, accusing him of maintaining a private practice even though it was forbidden by state law. The incumbent published a large ad denouncing McCarthy's charge as "unfair" and dirty politics—a foretaste of the McCarthy to come, it seemed, except that McCarthy had been technically correct.

A more serious example of distortion and lying on the campaign trail came when he ran for judge in Wisconsin's Tenth Judicial Circuit. Borrowing an idea from a Shawano County judge who had run against and defeated an opponent by making age an issue, McCarthy decided to tell the voters that his opponent, the sixty-six-year-old Edgar Werner, was seven years older than he was. Judge Werner angrily denied the story, but the truth was that Werner *looked* seventy-three, and acted like it. He commanded little respect from lawyers in his circuit, while McCarthy seemed active and energetic; as the Swedish janitor in Shawano County courthouse put it, "Joe McCarthy he get older. Judge Werner, he never get any younger." The newspapers never bothered to check McCarthy's allegation, and the claim that Werner was too old to serve stuck. McCarthy won handily, with 43 percent to Werner's 31.7 percent and Whiting's, the other challenger, 25.5 percent. However, he had also deliberately lied about his opponent and distorted the record—and had learned it could work.

Richard Rovere and others would later solemnly shake their heads over the Werner case and claim it revealed McCarthy to be someone who, as Rovere said, "would unashamedly persist in misrepresenting a simple truth even when the truth was accessible to everyone and when everyone could see what he was doing."[11] But local politics is often a rough-and-tumble business and crude insults and egregious tactics are soon forgotten in the wake of victory. If Werner hadn't acted the part, or if the local papers had done their job and forced McCarthy to retract the fib, he probably would have dropped it and gone on to something else. The real point was that McCarthy didn't need the lie. He proved an able and energetic campaigner, assembling poll lists and telephone directories from three neighboring counties and personally visiting everyone he thought might vote for him. "He didn't know me from Adam," one farmer recalled about that campaign, "but somehow he had learned my name. When I first noticed him, he was outside petting the dog. By the time I got to the front door, he was handing my daughter a lollipop, and then Indian-wrestling with my boy."[12]

Like most other politicians, McCarthy discovered that winning the attention and admiration of people he didn't know made up for whatever lack of security or intimacy he experienced with those he did. McCarthy would remain a bachelor until his early forties; when he married, he chose a member of his Senate staff. Their house on Capitol Hill served more as an extension of his office than a haven from it. Beginning in Shawano, politics, and politics alone, ran his life: losing that attention and retiring from the limelight became the thing Joe McCarthy dreaded more than anything else.

Critics would later circulate dark tales about McCarthy's malfeasance as a circuit judge in Shawano, just as they would dwell on his behavior in the Werner case—or claim that he had never really finished law school (Arthur Watkins was still repeating that falsehood more than ten years after McCarthy's death), or cheated on exams to get his high school diploma.[13] The truth was, in each and every case, very different. McCarthy proved to be a fair, shrewd, and hardworking (if not particularly knowledgeable) judge, and local attorneys enjoyed practicing in his courtroom. The atmosphere was relaxed and informal, with plenty of wisecracking from the bench, although he forbade lawyers to smoke in his presence (he was allergic to tobacco). Once he told a defense attorney, "Bill, if you want to win a case in this court, put out that cigar!" But another time he gave ten dollars to a female prisoner who was accused of attempting to kill her husband so that she could buy cigarettes. Her husband was a louse and deserved to die anyway, McCarthy said.[14]

His ignorance of the finer points of the law landed him into trouble only once, when he precipitously set aside an injunction the Department of Agriculture had filed against a local dairy company for artificially lowering the price of milk in the county. His action won him a stinging rebuke from the Wisconsin Supreme Court, which called his action "an abuse of judicial power" and ordered him to hear the case again. McCarthy managed to save the day by pointing out that he had acted in the best interests of consumers (which was true) and to make sure Quaker Dairy made milk affordable to everyone. Joe McCarthy the judicial activist became a hero in the local newspapers—an example of how bad law can sometimes be good politics.

McCarthy heard the Quaker Dairy case in June 1941. By then the Democratic-Progressive condominium that had run state politics for seven years was breaking apart, thanks to one issue: isolationism.

The term is actually a misnomer. Those who wanted America to play a more active role in world affairs (which in those days meant European affairs) coined it to suggest that their opponents were narrow-minded, head-in-the-sand curmudgeons—just as they would also imply that they were secret sympathizers with Hitler and Mussolini. In fact, most so-called isolationists believed in strong trade links with both Europe and Asia and had no problems with a foreign policy that pursued legitimate American interests overseas. Their difficulty was with how one defined legitimate. Back in 1796, George Washington had warned his fellow citizens of the dangers of "foreign entanglements." He worried less about formal alliances or treaties than an unhealthy involvement in the destinies of others. "The Nation which indulges towards another an habitual hatred," he said, "or an habitual fondness, is in some degree a slave." It was a warning that generations of Americans would solemnly take to heart and would help to shape American foreign policy for a century and a half.[15]

Isolationism, or more accurately, noninterventionism, partly reflected a typical American diffidence regarding Europe, which seemed both a source of corruption and a potential competitor in the eternal struggle for markets and resources. It partly reflected the tastes of American ethnic voting blocs, such as German-Americans who were still smarting from American involvement in World War I and anti-British Irish voters in New York, Illinois, and Massachusetts.[16] Part of it also sprang from an instinctive distaste for traditional, balance-of-power diplomacy and realpolitik, and a hatred of European colonialism and its practitioners, particularly Great Britain. That same hatred of nations that tried to subjugate helpless peoples at long distances, and to exploit them for their own gain, would later focus on the Soviet Union, one reason that so many former "isolationists" would become formidable cold warriors.

But at its heart noninterventionism was a fear of empire, and of America's becoming an imperial presence in the world. The noninterventionist worried that "foreign entanglements" would bring a double-edged corruption. By learning to compete for dominion over others, America would assume the same historical fate of Rome and other great empires: a vast militarized superstate abroad and at home, diverting resources and energies to serve the interests of the few (big business, munitions makers, and corrupt politicians and diplomats) at the expense of the many. But it would also lead to a deadening of our moral sensibilities. By playing the game of international power politics, America would lose its unique identity as the moral standard-bearer of the world. It would, as one noninterventionist senator put it, "slit the throat of the last Democracy still living."

By the thirties noninterventionism found support from every class background and political camp. It included old-fashioned Progressives and New Dealers like Burton K. Wheeler and Hiram Johnson, conservatives like Arthur Vandenberg and Robert Taft, and modern up-to-date liberals like McGeorge Bundy and Robert M. Hutchins. A wide range of Americans worried that the United States would be dragged into another bloody and unnecessary war in Europe. In December 1939 47 percent of Americans wanted to stay out of the war boiling over in Europe, and more than two-thirds believed that U.S. involvement in the previous war was a mistake.[17] McCarthy and his Shawano neighbors were among them. Young Judge McCarthy gave the Fourth of July speech at a picnic in Appleton in 1939, warning his neighbors about the "damnable flow of war propaganda" sweeping the nation. "We would like to see all the peoples of the world enjoying the liberty and freedom that we have," he said. "But it is written in history that when an autocracy is removed by powers other than the people themselves, that autocracy will be replaced by an autocracy even more vicious. Democracy," he concluded, "has never been bestowed upon a people by a paternal outside hand."[18]

Hence, the strange paradox of opposing support for Britain against Hitler's Germany on *moral* grounds. By evoking the cause of democracy abroad, many Americans worried, Washington policymakers would destroy it at home. Roosevelt's stealthy moves toward support of Britain deeply disturbed progressive but noninterventionist allies. War, they feared, would mean a compulsory draft, regimentation of the economy and society, and a huge expansion of the army and navy—the latter being the classic instrument for acquisition of empire. Some even worried that in the event of war, Roosevelt might cancel congressional elections for 1942. At stake, said Senator Burton K. Wheeler in a national radio address, "is the preservation of our way of life here in America."

The Senate had passed the official Neutrality Act, which both members of the Wisconsin delegation supported. Like most other members of the noninterventionist organization America First, Bob La Follette, Jr., detested National Socialism and felt strong sympathy for the suffering of Germany's Jews (this was long before anyone had an idea what the Nazis were really planning). But he also believed that the Anglophile Roosevelt and his advisers were more concerned about propping up a failing, declining Great Britain at America's expense. La Follette promised his constituents, "I will never give my vote to sending American boys to fight and die on the foreign battlefields of the Old World."[19]

Neither the fall of France in June 1940 nor Hitler's invasion of Russia in June 1941 could sway him. On the contrary, he hoped that Hitler and Stalin would finish each other off in a general conflagration, thus sparing the world of two evil dictators rather than just one. Then America First's Charles Lindbergh made his disastrous speech in Des Moines, Iowa, in which he spoke of the "dangerous influence" of Jews on American policy. A public uproar followed as Roosevelt and others accused America First of being pro-Nazi and "appeasement fifth columnists." The isolationist cause began to fall apart. In August 1941 the House of Representatives approved Roosevelt's Atlantic Charter by a single vote. In November both houses of Congress made modifications to the Neutrality Act to permit Roosevelt to send direct military aid to Britain. One month before Pearl Harbor, the vice chairman of America First announced that the organization had reached "the end of the road."

Isolationism proved to be the death knell of Wisconsin progressivism, just as it almost destroyed the Republican Party. La Follette watched a steady defection of his supporters to the triumphant Democrats, which turned into a flood after Pearl Harbor. However, the concerns that underlay noninterventionism did not go away. A fear that political leaders might willingly exchange America's highest moral ideals for power on the international stage remained rooted in American political culture. It would reemerge in the face of the new Soviet threat. In fact, one can trace a direct line from La Follette's conclusion that interventionism is merely "a cloak" for empire building and the corruption of American life to the national sense of betrayal after Yalta. The feeling was widespread that in destroying one evil empire, Roosevelt's war had spawned another.

World War II completed what the New Deal had begun: the transformation of the United States into a unified modern nation. As historian John M. Blum points out, the war made size and abundance the chief facts of American economic life. But they were key characteristics of its new cultural life as well.[20] Against all expectations, the war changed life for the better for most Americans. Among them was Joe McCarthy.

As a judge McCarthy was exempt from the draft, but he joined the Marines anyway on July 29, 1942. By all accounts, McCarthy chose the Marines on the advice of a friend, who told him that the Marines' tough reputation would serve him well politically after the war—assuming he survived it. McCarthy took steps to make sure he did. His status as a judge qualified him for an automatic commission, and he arrived at Quantico for basic training as a second lieutenant (not as a buck private, as he liked to claim later). He trained as an intelligence officer and was assigned in March 1943 to a desk job with a dive bomber squadron, VMSB-235, which was departing for Guadalcanal.

McCarthy made the most of his war service then and later, just as other ambitious politicians of his generation did. When his unit sailed for the South Pacific, McCarthy broke his leg during his "shellback" ceremony, the initiation rite for sailors who crossed the equator for the first time. That November, he sent out a press release telling Wisconsin newspapers that he had been wounded in action. Years later, he told friends and audiences various stories about how he had obtained his "war wound": how his Helldiver had overturned on the runway and burned, or how he had been hit by antiaircraft fire and was still carrying "ten pounds of shrapnel" in his leg. McCarthy even developed a limp to go with the story—all of which impressed audiences whom, he knew, would have been disappointed by the truth.[21]

In 1951 a reporter looking for dirt on McCarthy unearthed the basic outline of his real war record. McCarthy claimed that he had regularly flown missions with the dive bombers as a gunner-observer—hence the nickname "Tail Gunner Joe." The reporter learned that McCarthy had actually flown with the squadron only twelve times in seven months of frontline duty, although he had claimed thirty-two combat missions in order to qualify for a Distinguished Flying Cross (which the Marine Corps decided in 1952, for obvious political reasons, to give him). McCarthy pointed to a letter praising his combat service signed by his commanding officer and countersigned by Admiral Nimitz. It turned out that McCarthy had written the letter himself, in his capacity as unit intelligence officer.[22] By the time the media had finished, very little of McCarthy's reputation as a Marine war hero remained (although the Marines decided not to rescind the Distinguished Flying Cross).

The experience of another politician "war hero," Lieutenant Commander Lyndon Baines Johnson, serves as a useful standard of comparison. In 1940 the two-term congressman from Texas used his political connections to get a commission in the Navy Reserve, knowing, like McCarthy, that a military service record would come in handy if and when war broke out. When it did, he asked his mentor FDR to get him a posting on "active duty with the Fleet." The fleet took one look at his lack of naval training and refused. Instead, Roosevelt sent him in 1942 on a fact-finding mission to Douglas MacArthur's command in Australia and New Guinea.

MacArthur told his staff that they were to extend every courtesy to "Congressman—*not* Lieutenant Commander Johnson," but Johnson had other plans. He inveigled himself onto a bombing raid over New Guinea, and the plane was struck by shrapnel. After they were safely back at base, Johnson told the crew the trip had been "very interesting." However, he did not leave Australia until he had secured a citation for a Silver Star—as David Halberstam later put it, "the least deserved but most often displayed Silver Star in American military history." Johnson enjoyed telling intimates and visitors different versions of the exploits he had performed to earn the medal. He even told historian Henry Graff he won it for shooting down twenty Zeros.[23]

Reporters and historians generally treated Johnson's deceitful boasting with amused tolerance, while treating McCarthy's with revulsion and disapproval. But they have been so determined to cast him as a shameless liar that they have overlooked what McCarthy *did* do. Although being an intelligence officer was officially a desk job, McCarthy insisted on learning how to operate the Helldiver's rear guns and did participate in eleven combat missions (although his gunnery instructor later described most of them as local strikes and "milk runs"). McCarthy flew one mission after he had complained about the quality of the photographs crews were taking of their bombing runs. His commanding officer, Major Todd, told him to go up and try taking photographs himself. McCarthy did—"I was the most involuntary volunteer you ever saw," McCarthy recalled later—and narrowly missed being hit when the bomber he was flying got caught in tracer fire. McCarthy was too busy firing back to stop to think what was happening, so the legend of Tail Gunner Joe had a shadow of reality behind it after all.[24]

The incident served McCarthy in the same way as Johnson's impromptu mission over New Guinea: an opportunity to get a taste of combat with a minimum of danger and maximum of publicity, in order to impress the voters back home. When Joe's name appeared in a press release on a big raid on Bougainville, he told a fellow officer, "That's worth 50,000 votes to me," and bought him a drink to celebrate.

Beyond that, McCarthy performed the job he was assigned—debriefing fliers after missions and assessing damage to bombed targets—with skill and distinction. Even after he learned about McCarthy's exaggerated claims about his war record, Major Todd could still rebuke critics by stating that "he was a sincere, patriotic, excellent Marine Corps officer and as brave as the rest of us." McCarthy proved to be a popular officer. The Marines were the sort of brash, rowdy but disciplined, masculine environment in which McCarthy excelled. Plenty of hard drinking, all-night poker sessions with a stand-to at dawn, practical jokes, smuggling in canned goods and contraband liquor to deliver to his men: much of McCarthy's service record reads like an episode of *Sergeant Bilko*.

But at the same time he never lost sight of his main goal. In 1943 he told his astonished gunnery instructor that he was going to run for senator the following year. This time he would run not as a Democrat but a Republican, in the primary against Senator Alexander Wiley who was up for reelection. McCarthy filed his candidacy by mail in March 1944 and formally entered the race in April, although he would not be able to get leave to campaign in person until a few weeks before the election.

To his fellow Marines it must have seemed a harebrained scheme—running for national office against a senior and popular senator seven thousand miles away. But McCarthy knew what he was doing. A statewide run like this would make his reputation and start the political networking he would need for a serious race when the war ended. He also had a windfall of money on hand—$46,000 from a lucky investment tip, a large sum in those days and a generous war chest for his campaign. And since state campaign law forbade personal use of funds more than $5,000, McCarthy in effect laundered the money through various friends and associates, four and five thousand dollars at a time. Judge McCarthy also decided not to file his state income tax that year in order to protect the entire sum from the government's prying eyes. Both decisions came back to haunt him later.[25]

It seemed like a good idea at the time, however, and so McCarthy launched his campaign from the Solomon Islands in typical flamboyant style. He and some friends mounted huge signs reading JOE MCCARTHY FOR US SENATOR on jeeps and he made sure to visit every Wisconsin serviceman in the area to ask him to vote for him. The primary vote went as expected. Republicans rallied around the old stalwart Wiley, who denounced McCarthy as a typical New Deal Democrat, and gave him 60 percent of the vote to McCarthy's 28 percent. But McCarthy was already planning his departure from the Marines and the war to resume his life in Wisconsin.

McCarthy returned to Shawano a conquering hero. He even sat on the circuit bench in his uniform. If the other judges resented having to handle his case load as well as their own during his three-year absence, they said nothing about it. People had kept up with his war exploits in the *Appleton Post-Crescent*. (One story described him conducting his debriefing of pilots and asking them, "What kind of hell did you give the Japs today?") Shawano's mayor had endorsed his senatorial bid in 1944, as did other local politicians and attorneys. In fact, McCarthy had received the majority of votes in his own county and neighboring Outagamie and Langlade counties, and 41 percent of the Republican vote in the Fox River valley. Columnist John Wyngaard praised him in the *Wisconsin State Journal* as "a political Horatio Alger" and predicted he would be "the first in a long caravan of soldier candidates." He won reelection as a judge without opposition in April 1945, and Wyngaard and others believed McCarthy was in a strong position for a run at the Senate again the next year.[26]

When peace came in August, McCarthy was steadily working to extend his political base. Urban Van Susteren returned from the army that summer and was amazed to learn that his old friend was already planning electoral strategy for 1946. "Van," he said, "you're going to be my campaign manager." In addition to regular political helpmates like Van Susteren; his brother Howard and sister Olive; and Ray Kiermas, owner of a large hardware store and other businesses in Stephensville, McCarthy was reaching out to wealthier and more influential Republicans in Milwaukee. Then as now, money was the mother's milk of politics, and McCarthy built up a circle of business supporters who could bankroll any future statewide campaign. He became friends with Milwaukee attorney Charles Kersten and with James Colby of the *Milwaukee Sentinel*, a Hearst publication. The Hearst newspaper syndicate, which McCarthy had denounced when he was a Democrat, would become his most important media supporter.

A photograph taken a bit later shows him at a GOP picnic in Shawano County Park standing in the sunlight with five of his constituents. He smiles, and they smile back. He wears what appear to be old Marine khakis, with his arms resting easily around two of his fellow Republicans. Warm: friends noted that McCarthy always threw an arm around a person's shoulder when they shook hands. Ingratiating. Funny in a down-home, back-slapping sort of way. "Magnetic personality" and "a good natured Irishman" were the sort of comments he elicited from voters and GOP officials. He also had a politician's memory for faces and names. Once he left the podium at a rally in Racine to go down into the audience and shake hands with a fellow soldier he had last seen in Bougainville eight years earlier.[27]

The Marines accepted McCarthy's resignation in January 1945. At about the same time, an officer in the Office of Strategic Services (OSS) in Washington named Kenneth Wells was glancing through the current issue of *Amerasia*, a left-leaning journal on Asian policy, and came across an anonymous article on "British Imperial Policy in Asia." To his amazement, Wells realized he was reading one of his own reports—a highly classified "For Your Eyes Only" briefing on British-American relations he had written for top Asian hands in the State Department and the OSS. The report had contained sensitive information about an anti-Japanese resistance group still operating in Thailand—and here it was, reproduced word for word for anyone to see.

Wells alerted his superiors to this serious breach of security, and the OSS sent a team of investigators to the offices of *Amerasia* in New York, at 225 East Fifth Street. The five-man team entered the modest brownstone on a Saturday, March 11, and picked the lock to the *Amerasia* suite. At the end of the corridor they found a large darkroom (even though *Amerasia* carried no pictures or photographs) with curled-up photographs of documents marked TOP SECRET. Opening the other desks and drawers, they discovered thousands of documents from the War and State Departments, from the OSS and Office of Naval Intelligence (ONI) and other government agencies—many of them highly classified and top secret.

Agents kept the *Amerasia* office under surveillance for another two months, until June 7. They then arrested the journal's publisher and editor, Philip Jaffee; his coeditor, Kate Mitchell; a journalist named Mark Gayn; and three government employees: Emmanuel Larsen and John Stewart Service, both of whom worked at the State Department, and a naval reserve officer named Andrew Roth. By then the FBI had discovered that Service, Larsen, and Roth were regularly passing documents to Jaffee, who was closely linked to the American Communist Party and the associate of a Soviet espionage agent named Joseph Bernstein. Roth had also had meetings with an operative of the Chinese Communist Party living in New York.[28]

The FBI had stumbled on the leading edge of an active Soviet espionage ring operating in the United States, with the covert help and support of the Communist Party and its sympathizers. The full implications would become clear only later—but taken together with the outbreak of civil war in China that same month, the *Amerasia* spy ring indicated that the world stage was heating up for yet another major conflict, even before the final shots were fired from the last one.

For men like Franklin Roosevelt, Secretary of War Henry L. Stimson, and the coterie of younger men (such as Dean Acheson and John J. McCloy) who would form the core of America's foreign policy establishment—"the Wise Men"—the war represented an essential continuity of values and experiences. For the rest of the country, it was a cultural transformation. It mobilized millions of men and women who otherwise would never had left their home towns or met a single foreigner. Twelve million Americans put on uniforms and traveled to places like Quantico in Virginia, Fort Bragg in Georgia, the Air Corps Tactical School in Texas, and Pearl Harbor in Hawaii. From there they went to live on air bases in rural England and naval depots in Australia, to fight for remote hill towns in Sicily and jungle villages in New Guinea, or fly over the Himalayas into Burma or sail across the top of the world to Murmansk in Russia. Another twenty million Americans left their homes to find work in war industries. Cities like Detroit, Chicago, San Francisco, Washington, Mobile, and Norfolk became magnets for people filling the increasing demand for factory workers, longshoremen, secretaries, clerks, and a myriad other jobs the war effort and the burgeoning economy had created. It was "the largest internal immigration in American history," and people found their normal sense of place profoundly altered.[29]

For most Americans the war was a broadening experience. As someone remarked to historian Roy Hoopes when reminiscing about the home front many years later, "The war tended to magnify everything," including people's individual ambitions and desires.[30] Los Angeles or Washington, D.C., no longer appeared as just dots on a map but as future destinations within any American's grasp. The war put Americans on speaking terms with their own country and the rest of the world, and allowed them to talk about China or Japan or Russia or Iran or the Philippines with an ease of familiarity and a relative sense of scale. And in reference to that outside world, being a southerner, or a New Yorker, or a Jew, or an Irish Catholic, or a Mormon counted for less than being an American.

We make a huge mistake if we don't see Joe McCarthy's career as part of that same transformation. He was part and parcel of a generation of what Tom Brokaw has called "the best generation," who learned that America was part of a larger world, but that that world was also a dangerous place. Ordinary Americans had taken leading parts in "the great crusade," and had saved the planet from the twin menaces of an imperial Japan and Nazi tyranny. But unlike many of their cultural and social superiors, they had few illusions about what was to follow. In 1942 a Gallup poll revealed that only 45 percent of Americans expected any serious form of postwar cooperation with the Soviets (by contrast, 83 percent expected close ties with China). Two-thirds wanted the United States to act to keep Stalin's Russia in check after the war.

Later, leftist revisionist historians would pretend that it was ordinary Americans who wanted friendship with the Soviet Union, and that the cold war was a plot organized from the top by a reactionary political establishment and business interests.[31] The exact opposite was the case. However favorable their view of Roosevelt and the New Deal during or after the war, Americans were in no mood to be taken advantage of. If they resisted hasty integration into the larger world they had encountered, and worried whether the postwar struggle for "permanent peace" might mean "a permanent war for America," they also saw no reason that their nation shouldn't flex its muscles to make sure nothing like it happened again.

It is also true that mobilization for World War II helped to prepare American attitudes for the cold war, but we make another mistake if we assume that those attitudes were rigid or artificial, or sprang from a xenophobic rejection of outsiders or difference. After all, the newly affluent postwar America that McCarthy epitomized descended from outsiders, as sons and daughters of immigrants, and poor farmers and laborers from Texas, Oklahoma, and the South. They understood that "being an American," as sociologist Seymour Martin Lipset later put it, "is an ideological commitment."[32] America could assimilate anyone, from any background or any ethnic origin or geographic region, but it required a submission to the values of individual success and social mobility that made America distinct. Americans of McCarthy's generation recognized in Soviet communism an overwhelming threat to those values, which had been central to their own lives and families.

The war had also left the Wisconsin political scene in a state of flux. The collapse of the Progressive-Democrat condominium put the Republican Party in charge of state politics by default. Robert La Follette, Jr., himself was in poor health. Embittered by the war and alarmed by the growing Communist presence in labor unions that had once been his source of strength, La Follette at one point even announced that he would not run for reelection in 1946. But then he changed his mind and decided to run—to the amazement of observers—in the Republican primary.

La Follette's weakness turned out to be McCarthy's opportunity. He turned first to Wisconsin's Young Republicans, which he had helped to reorganize and was led by a McCarthy ally with the astonishingly appropriate name of Loyal Eddy. McCarthy gave a rousing speech at the Young Republicans' convention in Milwaukee and won their support. The operative word was *young*. To his supporters and other Republican campaign workers, McCarthy came across as a youthful alternative to a tired generation of New Dealers and La Follette hangers-on: a fresh face, an American veteran who had come home to sweep out the old and begin the new.

The party's most important political boss, Tom Coleman, was at first suspicious of McCarthy's Democratic past. McCarthy's physical energy, personal warmth, and stamina (he could skip a night's sleep without a thought) impressed Coleman, although he had doubts about his lack of sophistication and hick manners.[33] But he became convinced when he heard the young ex-Marine denounce the Truman administration's foreign policy and accuse its bureaucrats of trying to "kill off the farmer." When the Republican Volunteer Committee met on May 4 and 5 to endorse a candidate before the primary, McCarthy had no serious rivals.

If La Follette ran a lackluster campaign for the Republican primary, counting on his family prestige to see him through, McCarthy ran a sensational one. He crisscrossed the state several times (later his driver estimated they had traveled thirty-three thousand miles and worn out two automobiles). He insisted on meeting everyone in every little town, crossing the street to greet someone sitting on a bench with, "My name's McCarthy, I'm running for the United States Senate—against Bob La Follette, you know." He mailed out 750,000 postcards to resident voters, with a picture of him in his Marine uniform on one side and a handwritten note asking them personally to give him their support (most were actually written by campaign volunteers and students).

The former New Deal Democrat had turned himself into a conservative Republican stalwart. He campaigned on issues close to the pocketbooks of Wisconsin voters, such as taxes and federal farm policy, much as one might expect. He called the government in Washington a "bureaucratic nightmare," which "in most cases hindered the normal functioning of a free and prosperous America." He hammered hard on foreign policy issues. The Truman administration, he charged, had squandered all the gains the United States had made since the end of the war. Roosevelt's Four Freedoms had become a "hollow mockery," McCarthy charged. "We retreated mentally and morally in Austria, in Poland, in the Baltic states, and there is no reason to believe that tomorrow we shall not do the same thing" in other parts of the world. The time had come for fresh faces in Washington, so that "the curtain that is hiding the graft and corruption of war days can be torn away."

He slammed Bob La Follette for "playing into the hands of the Communists" by encouraging their spread into Wisconsin unions (which was untrue—the Communists hated La Follette almost as much as they would later hate McCarthy) and accused him of profiting from the licensing of a

Milwaukee radio station he owned. In late July, two weeks before the primary, McCarthy renewed the anti-Communist theme in a radio speech in Appleton: "Doesn't the Progressive New Dealer realize what it would mean for the future of human liberty if the Communists move in, or doesn't he care? Doesn't he realize what it would mean for the rank and file of the people of all the nations of Europe?"[34]

La Follette had had a commanding lead in the polls and rejected the idea of debating McCarthy. "I don't see why I should help him draw a crowd," he said. So on August 13, Election Day, he and his supporters were astonished when McCarthy beat him by 5,300 votes, 41 percent to 40 percent. La Follette blamed his defeat on a vicious smear campaign—conducted not by McCarthy, as it happened, but by the Wisconsin Communist Party and its allies in the CIO. They had never forgiven La Follette for his refusal to help the Soviet Union fight Hitler and had undermined his labor support in cities like Milwaukee by branding him profascist. McCarthy carried Milwaukee by 10,000 votes, the first and last time he ever took that nominally progressive, even socialist, city. In retrospect, the campaign takes on a strange irony. La Follette blasted the Communists for using "the big lie, the big smear, and the wholesale impugning of motives and character," much as McCarthy's critics would later accuse him of doing, and called their involvement in union activity "a serious menace to our democracy."[35] But the simple truth was that La Follette had underestimated his opponent while McCarthy had outspent and outcampaigned the older man.

After McCarthy's victory in the crucial general primary, the November election was an anticlimax. The personal abuse and attacks, or what a later, more thin-skinned generation would call negative campaigning, continued as before. His Democratic opponent gamely struck at McCarthy as "two-job Joe" for his decision to run for public office while still a circuit judge, which was technically illegal under the state constitution. He tried to brand him an ultrareactionary when a group sponsored by Chicago newspaper magnate Robert McCormick called America Action, Inc. endorsed the ex-Marine.[36] Unfortunately, the Democrats' candidate had shot off most of his negative ammunition earlier in the general primary against La Follette, accusing *him* of being pro-Nazi and of spending five years in the Senate "voting for Hitler." Next to these sorts of accusations, McCarthy's suggestion that his opponent was "communistically inclined" seems mild enough (some of the newspapers that endorsed McCarthy were harsher—one called the man "a friend to the enemies of this country"). But McCarthy already knew that his liberal opponent, a diffident, rather pompous college professor, didn't have a chance.

Across the nation, confidence in the Democrats was fading. Americans were fed up with wartime austerity, gas rationing, meat rationing, and end-less federal regulations. The GOP campaign slogan in 1946 was: "Had enough?" Republicans ran an aggressively antistatist, anti–New Deal campaign, asserting that "the welfare state" leads to "the police state." They capitalized on the fact that many of their candidates were returning veterans, and for the first time ran a campaign that linked their liberal Democratic opponents directly to the ideals and principles of communism.* The party's chief spokesman, Robert Taft of Ohio, told voters the Democrats appeased the Russians abroad and fostered communism at home. Congressman Carroll Reece of Tennessee said that the Democrats' domestic policies "bore a definite made-in-Moscow label" and that the choice in 1946 was between "Communism and Republicanism."[37] In California's Twelfth Congressional District, ex–Navy Lieutenant Commander Richard Nixon ran a campaign against incumbent Jerry Voorhis that established Nixon's reputation as a tough red baiter.

House minority leader Joe Martin of Massachusetts promised that if the Republicans won, "Congress will ferret out all those who sought to destroy the American way of life." His anti-Communist theme fit in with the current Republican theme of a general housecleaning of government. It was reflected in Joe McCarthy's vow to Wisconsin voters that he would "make every effort toward removing the vast number of Communists from the public payroll"—his 1950 speech at Wheeling being in that sense the fulfillment of an earlier campaign promise.

Republicans campaigned against big government, big labor, big regulation, and the New Deal's links to communism. The response was overwhelming. Over thirty-four million voters turned out for the 1946 congressional election, and more than half voted Republican. Before morning, Republicans knew they had won control of both the Senate and the House, where they captured fifty-four seats. In the Senate, it was the Republicans' biggest midterm win since 1894.

The 1946 election shattered the left-laborite wing of the Democratic Party. Of the sixty-nine most liberal Democrats in Congress (by the estimation of the *New Republic*), thirty-seven had been turned out of office. Since the New Deal, Republicans' strength had been in rural areas and small towns, while Democrats dominated the vote in urban areas. With the rise of the new affluent, suburban voter in the Northeast, Michigan, and Illinois, that trend now came to a halt. In Connecticut, the growing haven for

*They were helped by the fact that the Political Action Committee of the CIO, which was Communist dominated, had endorsed many Democratic candidates, including McCarthy's opponent.

commuters to New York City, the Democrats lost every congressional seat.[38] The only place where Democrats could still count on rural voters and nonunion support was in the South.

It was the same story in Wisconsin. The Democrats lost every seat in Congress. McCarthy took seventy of seventy-three counties and won by nearly a quarter of a million votes, although analysts later pointed out he trailed other Wisconsin Republicans by an average of 4.2 percent.[39] A tired but exultant McCarthy celebrated his victory. He calculated that he had driven over eighty thousand miles across the state since April 1945 on the campaign trail. He told one reporter, "I don't claim to be any smarter than the next fellow, but I do claim that I work twice as hard and that's what I intend to do in Washington the next six years."[40] The *Milwaukee Journal*, which had refused to endorse him and ran a series of highly critical stories about him during the campaign, swallowed its pride afterward and predicted: "We think he has it in him to be a good senator and a good representative for his state."

In fact, it was an amazing success story for the Irish farm boy. To voters and reporters alike, McCarthy seemed to be a living Horatio Alger: the son of rural poverty who finished high school and gone on to college, then judge, Marine officer, and now U.S. senator. At age thirty-eight he was the Senate's youngest member, fully a decade younger than the average incumbent. He was entering a world that he and his peers only dimly understood and knew, but it was one on which they were determined to leave their mark.

Chapter 2

The Class of '46

McCarthy arrived at Union Station in Washington, D.C., on December 1, 1946. He had traveled from Wisconsin with campaign aide Victor Johnston, who would become his administrative assistant. McCarthy was now the nation's youngest senator (a point he emphasized by knocking another year off his birthdate for his official biography). Johnston half-jokingly asked him if he wanted to say anything quotable as his train pulled into the nation's capital. McCarthy grimaced and looked out the window. "Shit. It's raining."

He stepped out into a city that was still in many ways a conservative, slow-moving southern town. For one thing, it was still segregated. Blacks living in the District of Columbia had to use separate hotels, separate restaurants, even separate movie theaters and taxicabs. They could buy clothes in a white-owned store but could not try them on there. They could ride in the front of streetcars and buses—until they crossed the Potomac into even more segregationist Virginia, when they were obliged to move to the back.[1]

To northerners, Washington was a southern town. But to real born and bred southerners, like the young Harry McPherson who came from Texas to work as a Senate aide (later he would be Lyndon Johnson's aide), it seemed a foreign city, as strange—and almost as menacing—as New York City. Washington could project a gleaming, imperial presence to the first-time visitor. Driving from the Capitol to the White House, McPherson had traveled past the new Supreme Court building (completed in 1935) and the Department of Labor, the temple that the New Deal had built to its most important

41

supporters, America's unions. The White House itself was flanked by twin relics of the past: the corinthian-pillared Treasury and the Old Executive Office Building, home to the State Department, where Negro servants wearing white gloves silently carried messages from one oak-paneled office to the other. Across the river, beyond Arlington cemetery, stood the starkly functional Pentagon, soon to be the home of the newly consolidated Defense Department. In 1946, very much against its will, Washington had become the nerve center of the free world and was straining to bear the burden.[2]

The biggest change had come to the executive branch. It came in two waves. First, the New Dealers had descended on the city in the 1930s, invading the precincts of the old elite, and pushing them out to their preserves in Chevy Chase and Silver Spring, Maryland.

Then came the war. In 1939 the federal government had 953,891 employees. In 1942 that number more than doubled. When McCarthy arrived, it was less than its peak but still almost three million—more than three and a half times the number in the last year of the Hoover administration. One-quarter of a million federal employees now lived in the Washington area—versus 73,455 in 1932.[3] One result was Washington's famous wartime housing shortage, which meant that McCarthy had to share an apartment with friends during his first term as senator.

The war and the huge expansion of the executive branch and its agencies had brought another momentous, unforeseen change to the Washington scene. In 1943 the KGB's chief of its New York residency, General Vassili Zarubin (cover name Zubilin), moved to the American capital to take over the important espionage networks the Soviets had established there. By 1945 the volume of secret cable traffic was almost twice that of the New York residency, which spent most of its energy gathering information from the Manhattan Project and, through Joseph Bernstein, its *Amerasia* contacts. Most of the agents and sources Zubilin and the KGB had recruited in Washington came from this enormous pool of new federal employees, and spied on a range of government agencies, running from the army and the OSS to the Treasury and Labor departments.[4]

To this day no one knows exactly how many federal employees were secretly working for the Soviet Union. But in 1945 one of Zarubin's principal couriers, Elizabeth Bentley, defected to the FBI and confessed that her network alone had contained twenty members and that she knew about at least twenty others working for other clandestine networks. It was clear that many had had long-standing Communist affiliations that no one, in the heat of the war effort, had bothered to check or even cared about. In other words, the Democrats' rapid expansion of the federal government had also spurred the expansion of Soviet espionage activities. Framed in this way, the executive branch sat on a political time bomb, waiting to go off once anyone discovered the truth.

By contrast, the war had added fewer than a thousand employees to the entire legislative branch. They clustered in the rabbit warrens of offices in the Capitol and in the Senate and House office buildings, which had been built during the presidency of William Howard Taft. The only significant change to Congress since the last century had been the installation of air-conditioning in 1938, which enabled the House and Senate to remain in session, and members to speak for hours without discomfort, even when the summer heat was at its height, and tourists flooded the simmering sidewalks and streetcars.

Yet change was gradually forcing itself on Congress. It had had to abandon its traditional calendar, when all of the nation's business was conducted in a space of exactly four months, from March 4 to July 4, and had begun to adopt a more burdensome schedule, running from January through August (the air-conditioning helped). This meant more work for senators and for their staffs. The Legislative Reorganization Act of 1946* reflected the attempt to catch up. It had cut the number of congressional committees by more than half. In order to take up the slack, both the House and Senate had had to expand their staffs. The result was a whole new postwar generation of Senate employees, who reflected the changes that were taking place in the country at large.

A good example was Ruth Watt. She had been born in Maine in 1910, in the small town of Brooks—"a wide place in the road," as she put it. When she was thirteen the family moved to Yarmouth, where her father worked in a shipbuilding yard during World War I. When she finished high school, her father told her, much as Tim McCarthy had told his son Joe, "You're on your own." Her brothers found careers nearby, and married and settled down. Ruth was more adventurous; she went to Poland Springs, Maine, to wait on tables at the health spa, and then to Atlantic City, New Jersey, to save money for college.

In 1930 she had saved enough to get into George Washington University at the start of the depression. While she studied at the business school, she waited on tables for thirty-five cents an hour plus breakfast and dinner. Lunch she took at the counter at People's Drug Store, where a milkshake and

---

*This passed in the last days of the Seventy-ninth Congress, and was sponsored by two men who, coincidentally, would play key roles in the McCarthy story: Bob La Follette, Jr., in the Senate and Mike Monroney of the House (on Monroney, see Chapter 11).

grilled cheese sandwich cost a quarter. At graduation she took a job as secretary to the director of Washington Children's Hospital, for eighty dollars a month. It was good pay in the thirties, but came without social security or a pension, and not much of a future.

Then in February 1947 her next door neighbor, who was superintendent of the Senate press gallery, told her about new job openings on Capitol Hill. He said, "The Republicans have just won the Senate and House, and you're from Maine and Senators [Owen] Brewster and [Wallace] White both are going to have chairmanships of committees. . . . Why don't you go see them?" She took his advice and found a spot on the Senate's Special Committee for Investigating the National Defense Program, known as the Truman Committee, after its first chairman, Harry S. Truman of Missouri. Truman had conducted a series of famous investigations into fraud and profiteering on government military contracts before leaving to become FDR's running mate in 1944. Now Owen Brewster and the Republicans were taking over. Senator Brewster warned her that the committee was being shut down in a year because of the Legislative Reorganization Act, but she did not care; the work sounded interesting.[5]

In fact, the committee did not shut down. Instead, it became one of the sharper arrows in the quiver of a reform-minded Eightieth Congress. It took pride of place beside the Appropriations Committee and the Un-American Activities Committee in the House and the Committee for Expenditures in the Executive Department in the Senate. Eventually the two Senate investigative groups merged, and Truman's old committee now became the Permanent Subcommittee on Investigations—PSI for short.

One of its new Republican members was Joseph McCarthy. Ruth Watt would serve as chief clerk of PSI for the next two and half decades; her young assistant that summer, Jean Kerr, would eventually became Joe McCarthy's wife. Ruth Watt would remember the freshman Joe McCarthy as "charming" and "a gay blade about town" (which had a slightly different meaning then than it does now). He was only one of a huge crop of freshman Republicans. The 1946 election had forced a sharp redistribution of power. The previous Senate had had 56 Democrats and 40 Republicans; now the Republicans numbered 51, with only 45 Democrats. The same redistribution had happened in the House. In 1944 there had been 241 Democrats and 193 Republicans; now the numbers were almost exactly reversed. The new Republican Speaker, Joe Martin of Massachusetts, commanded a 58-seat majority, while the Democrats had shrunk to only 188 seats. The press labeled the new Republican freshmen "the class of '46."

It was a Congress of distinctly conservative principles. As influential editor and columnist David Lawrence of U.S. News and World Report put it, "The hand out era is over." The Eightieth Congress was "opposed to large-scale foreign lending; to regulation of business, to expensive public works, to strikes, and the power of union leaders." It represented not so much a swing to the right, Lawrence said, but away from a runaway New Deal and its "revolutionary concept that the end justifies the means"— meaning governance by bureaucratic fiat. The GOP would act not as a party of reaction but as "a party of young men and women—lots of them veterans who have come back to demand that America find a way to govern herself fairly and effectively."[6] Above all, power would shift away from the executive branch and the White House, and back to the legislative.

This devolution of power became a centerpiece of the Republican agenda. As he was sworn in, House Speaker Martin stated, "Our American concept of government rests upon the idea of a dominant Congress. Congress is the people's special instrument of control over their government." He vowed to expose how New Deal Democrats had abused their monopoly of power for the past fourteen years and "how public funds were used to enrich contractors and political lobbyists." Finally, the American people would learn "what has been done under the cloak of official secrecy." As Representative Clarence Brown told reporters, "We will open with a prayer, and close with a probe."[7]

That sort of forthright language was more typical of congressmen than members of the more genteel Senate. One has to wonder how history might have been different if Joseph McCarthy had originally been elected to the House, where his sometimes crude behavior and demeanor would have been less conspicuous because it was more the norm, and where he could have learned the skills of being a legislator in a less exacting, and more forgiving, school. But fate had directed him to the upper chamber instead, where he found himself subject to its strange and anachronistic customs.

The Senate in which McCarthy lived and worked had come into existence in the years between 1896 and 1910, when for the first time being a senator or congressman became a full-time career and being in one of the two major parties the key to political success. Prior to 1910, senators were chosen by their state legislatures. They were creatures of their party and its legendary leaders—giants like John Sherman of Ohio and Nelson Aldrich of Rhode Island, who for thirty years wrote most of the nation's economic legislation but never bothered to give a speech outside the Senate.

Then had come direct popular election. Like Gulliver, the Senate giants watched helplessly as the pygmies stripped them of their privileges. Power devolved to the standing committees and their chairmen. The result was a Senate dominated by the iron-clad law of seniority and the all-important farm bloc, made up of midwestern and southern senators of both parties. They provided the institution with its internal ballast, or what was known as "the sense of the Senate." Legislation became the product of compromise, not command, as men of both parties learned to come together to create majorities and make decisions.

A set of informal rules governed the distribution of power, which every senator had to learn in order to get ahead. The first was control by seniority. The second was "stick to your knitting," meaning committee assignments. A freshman senator on the Banking Committee built his career by mastering the minutiae of the money supply; a senator on the Interior Committee would turn himself into the nation's watchdog on salmon fisheries. This reflected the third rule: be a work horse, not a show horse. The reward for such humble labors, and obeying one's elders, was advancement. One moved up to membership on one of the prestigious Senate committees, such as Finance, Foreign Relations, Armed Services, or Appropriations; then a subcommittee chairmanship; and then, finally and eventually, chairmanship of a permanent or standing committee.[8]

Unfortunately, this system meant that senators learned to stick to issues that the Senate, not the general public, deemed important. The same "sense of the Senate" also discouraged taking political disagreements outside the chamber. In 1947, using one's seat to gain publicity or personal advantage over one's colleagues was strongly frowned on.

In its style, sense of collegiality, and underlying attitudes, the Senate exuded the atmosphere of the nineteenth century. It was also overwhelmingly male and Northern European Protestant in its membership. Most senators were college educated, but not all had finished, and fourteen had no formal education beyond high school. The Senate of the Eightieth Congress included lots of lawyers (sixty-eight in all), more than before but not as many as there would be.

The Democrats were predominantly the party of social mobility, especially in the cities of the Northeast. They were also the party of professional politicians. Republicans tended to include more amateurs and men with other full-time careers. In 1947, the GOP was the party of small-town Protestantism, farmers, and local businessmen. An Irish Catholic like McCarthy was a rare bird in the Senate in any case, but especially in the GOP.[9] If Republicans tended to be less skilled in understanding the ins and outs of government and were at a disadvantage in dealing with an executive branch that had been exclusively Democratic for nearly a decade and a half, they also enjoyed richer and more varied contacts beyond the world of government and the Washington press corps (or what would later be termed "inside the Beltway"). They prided themselves on understanding what ordinary Americans were thinking and feeling. Men like Robert Taft, and Kenneth Wherry, and Homer Ferguson, not to mention Joe McCarthy, spoke and acted with a self-confident sense that they were speaking for the nation as a whole.

As an institution, the Senate tended to deaden the sounds emanating from that outside world. Most observers compared the Senate to a gentleman's club. A more accurate image might be of two concentric rings, with an inner and an outer circle. In a formal sense the Senate's leaders were Wallace White for the Republicans and Tom Connally for the Democrats. But real power belonged to a cluster of senators, both Democrats and Republicans, who occupied that inner circle. These were men like Walter George of Georgia, Carl Hatch of New Mexico, Harry Byrd of Virginia, Warren Magnuson of Washington, Robert Taft of Ohio, and Millard Tydings of Maryland. Membership was based primarily on seniority, but also on the number and quality of committee chairmanships, a devotion to process over substance, and a parliamentary command over resources that other senators wanted and needed. This was particularly true of the Interior Committee, with its control over access to government-owned land, the Finance Committee headed by Walter George, and the Armed Services Committee under Millard Tydings.

In short, a handful of Senate elders dominated the workings of the whole, and they used their formal position of power and the informal rules of the Senate to bring the rest into line. Freshmen senators were exposed to this system on their very first day. Once an eager newcomer accosted elderly Senator George on the floor and respectfully asked what was the biggest change he had seen in the upper chamber after some forty years of service to the Senate. George looked at him and said, "Freshmen didn't used to talk so much," and walked away. Even a nationally known figure like Robert Taft never forgot that he was a Republican spokesman *in the Senate*, and had to include Democrats to get anything done.[10]

"A Senator whose emotional commitment to Senate ways appears less than total is suspect."[11] They were relegated to the outer circle, with whom the inner circle cooperated but never fully trusted. The outer ring included Republican mavericks like the unregenerate isolationist William Langer and the radical Wayne Morse; it included liberal Democrats like Herbert Lehman and (a little later) Hubert Humphrey, who refused to cooperate with the party's large southern contingent. Some members of the outer circle, like McCarthy, never really understood the nature of the rules; others, like William Fulbright, did but preferred not to play. However, before the Eightieth Congress had adjourned, the nonconformists from the outer circle were developing weapons of their own. They learned to use the Senate floor rather than the committee room as their lever for influencing the nation's business by making speeches and offering floor amendments to pending bills.

McCarthy caught on quickly. His second day in Washington he called a press conference to issue a statement on the current United Mine Workers strike and was gratified to see that the *New York Times* quoted him. He realized how easy it was for a senator to generate news stories on his own, and once he mastered the art of shaping public debate by making the headlines, he never looked back. But he ignored Machiavelli's key admonition to any ambitious politician: build a secure base. For all his skill at generating publicity and his pushful ambition and supposed influence, McCarthy was never allowed to chair a major standing committee or hold a leadership position.* Throughout his career, the real reins of power belonged to others above him.

Deprived of a strong base, McCarthy came to rely on his talent for generating publicity even more, which undermined his base in the Senate even further. In the end it exposed him to the worst of both worlds. Senators who disliked him were free to take whatever liberties they wished in attacking him, those who agreed with him were reluctant to take a public stand on his behalf. A sense of collegiality was particularly crucial for inner-circle southern Democrats like John McClellan, Walter George, and Richard Russell, who were more willing to support Republicans on cold war issues than they were their fellow Democrats. But when push came to shove they loved the Senate more than they loved anticommunism, and in the event they would to a man vote for censure of someone whose political views were (with the exception of race and civil rights) not much different from theirs. If it was the liberals who provided the dagger for McCarthy's destruction and the Eisenhower White House who unsheathed and sharpened it, then it was the Old Guard southern Democrats who would plunge it into McCarthy's heart.

One final thing separated the newcomer McCarthy from the men who dominated the Senate's inner circle. This was their devotion to process over substance. The Senate was run by men who understood the skeptical principles of government laid out in the *Federalist Papers*—understood them at least as much by instinct as by design. They understood that modern representative government is about the slow interplay of interests over time. Consensus, compromise, and incrementalism were not just desirable but

---

*His one chairmanship was that of Government Operations, which was significant only because McCarthy made it so, through his work on its Permanent Subcommittee on Investigations. Compared to similar committees, the Judiciary or the Internal Security subcommittee, it was in Senate terms a marginal post.

inevitable; impatience and passion occupied no place on their political horizon. Yet they also paid a price for it. Author and United Press reporter Allen Drury, who in his diary referred to Senate business as "mountainous labors that bring forth mice," also wrote of the "inertia" and "subtle apathy" that crept over those who did business on the Hill. To the young and ambitious, it brought a gradual "desiccation of ambition, force, and will."[12] The men in the inner circle preferred it that way. The contrast between the hustling, striving McCarthy and old Senator George gently rebuking a freshman senator for daring to ask a question sums up two irreconcilable visions of how self-government works best.

McCarthy was by no means alone in his impatience with the old order. Here he reflected the general attitude of the class of '46. As David Lawrence had pointed out, many others of that freshman crop, including Democrats, owed their new status to the war. John F. Kennedy had campaigned for his congressional seat in his Navy uniform. His fellow Democrat George Smathers had spent three years with the Marines, and freshman Carl Albert of Oklahoma won a Bronze Star and a lieutenant-colonelcy for his service in the Pacific theater.

For Republicans even more than Democrats, the experience of war and military service seemed to reinforce a sense of populist mission and a forthright attitude toward foreign enemies that would crystallize in a hatred for international communism. The Republican freshmen of the class of '46, both House and Senate, were an interesting collection of amateurs and outsiders. With one or two exceptions,[13] they had little interest in sponsoring elaborate government programs, organizing international conferences, or building a strong support network among Washington insiders. They wanted to trim back the government, cut taxes, and then go home. That alone was enough to make professional "experts" ridicule and condemn them, just as they did Robert Taft and his conservative allies in the 1930s. When *Redbook* did a story on "the worst Congressmen in Washington" in October 1952, as judged by congressional insiders and political reporters, it naturally listed a large number of the class of '46.

They were men in many cases with strong local roots. William Jenner had served in the Indiana Senate for almost a decade when he entered the Army Air Corps at age thirty-four. Jenner was discharged two years later after suffering a serious injury and ran for the U.S. Senate. Tough, tenacious, and deeply, almost bitterly, conservative, he would become McCarthy's closest friend in the Senate and its most ferocious anti-Communist next to McCarthy himself.

William Knowland, the scion of a rich California newspaper dynasty, had served in France, Belgium, and Germany with the Army. He was still in uniform when Senator Hiram Johnson had died and the governor appointed Knowland to fill his seat. He won election to a full term as senator in November and would become one of the anchors of the anti-Communist China Lobby and another strong McCarthy supporter.

Harry Cain was originally considered to be a liberal, but he also turned out to be a McCarthy ally. He had been a banker and newspaper publisher in Washington State and was mayor of Tacoma when the war began. He took a leave of absence from office to enter the Army, serving in North Africa and the Italian theater before being assigned as assistant chief of staff to the 18th Airborne Corps during the Normandy invasion. Like McCarthy, Cain had originally run for the Senate while serving overseas and, like McCarthy, had lost to the incumbent. However, Cain returned a hero to Tacoma, with a Bronze Star, the Legion of Merit, and the Croix de Guerre. This time when he ran for the Senate, he won. Cain's most important service to McCarthy would be a ringing speech he would deliver on the Senate floor defending McCarthy's war record against its critics. Later he would serve on the Subversive Activities Control Board under President Eisenhower.

Bronze Star holder John Sherman Cooper of Kentucky had served with General George Patton from the invasion of Normandy to the Rhine crossing. In the House there were New York's Greg McMahon, veteran of thirty-three naval engagements and wearer of fifteen battle stars, and Wisconsin's Glenn Davis, who also served in the Pacific and was discharged as a lieutenant with nine battle stars. Davis became a close McCarthy supporter and a fervent anti-Communist, along with Richard Nixon of California, who had served in the Navy in New Guinea at about the same time as McCarthy.[14]

Other freshman Republican senators, like Zale Ecton, James P. Kem, George Malone, and John Bricker, were not so young or inexperienced in Washington's ways (Bricker had been governor of Ohio and the Republican vice presidential candidate in 1944). They were men who were proud of being considered outsiders. Their enemy was Big Government, which Roosevelt's New Deal had set in motion and the war extended. Their hero was Robert Taft, who had fought an often lonely fight against that expansion of government power for nearly a decade. Like Taft, they saw the New Deal's record as one of a continuous assault on individual freedom under the guise of social welfare. The Democrats, John Bricker had said on the 1946 campaign trail, "have presumed to tell us where we will work, what we will be paid, the clothing we shall wear, and the food we shall eat." He termed the New Deal "the most reactionary force in history" and warned that the welfare state was only one step on the way to the police state.[15]

Now it was time for a fresh start. In November, according to *Time* magazine, the American public had voted for "a climate for freedom." It was exemplified by a publicity photo of Congressman Nixon with his wife, Pat, on bicycles and their daughter, Tricia, strapped to the baby seat behind, posing under the cherry blossoms on the Mall. Fit, relaxed, and informal, they seemed ready to challenge the established rules and conventions. The class of '46 was distrustful of accepted shibboleths and sacred cows, and the "official story." To them, Washington and its resident governing class were the enemy, and the power the federal government had accrued for itself since the New Deal a dangerous source of corruption. George "Molly" Malone of Nevada, another close McCarthy supporter, summarized their attitude. "What happens to a representative or a Senator when he is elected to Congress?" he once mused in a speech on the Senate floor. "What happens to make him seem to vote with a wet finger, and makes him think that the sentiment of the country is formed in Washington? There is no public sentiment in Washington." Malone added grimly, "The only city that approaches Washington in its danger to the welfare of the country is the city of New York. It is a close second."[16]

Yet McCarthy and his colleagues had a certain pride in being in the belly of the beast. One day McCarthy attended a smart Georgetown cocktail party, and as he watched the mink stoles and sleek tuxedos gracefully floating by, he laughed out loud. "I wonder," he remarked to the man standing next to him, "what these people would think if they knew I once raised chickens."[17]

There are two different versions of McCarthy's early years in the Senate. The first, and more popular, version is that he was a flop. By 1950 he had been "voted the worst U.S. Senator in one poll of the press corps," chroniclers Evan Thomas and Walter Isaacson tell us, and was "more visible to Washington barflies than to his Wisconsin constituents."[18] According to this view, McCarthy finally and desperately seized on the anti-Communist crusade as a way to salvage his disastrous do-nothing career.

The other version is that McCarthy was one of the brightest and popular members of the freshman class, charming and "handsome in a dark, square-jawed way" who set Georgetown hostesses "scratching for the decorative McCarthy's presence at dinners and cocktail parties."[19] In fact, both versions contain something of the truth. McCarthy was a crowd pleaser with a flair for getting himself noticed and admired. He sent huge wheels of Wisconsin cheese to the National Press Club for its luncheons and once gave a party for a group of female Senate reporters, charming them by appearing at the door in an apron and whipping up a batch of homemade fried chicken. Yet for all his jaunty self-confidence and unstoppable drive, McCarthy was over-whelmed by his new job.

For one thing, Robert La Follette, Jr., had been highly popular in the Senate. His ideological opposite, Robert Taft, had even endorsed him in 1946. On the one hand, having Joe McCarthy in the Senate added another stalwart conservative to the Republican team. One liberal rating group ranked him ninth from the bottom for his right-wing voting record—right next to Taft himself.[20] But by removing La Follette, Wisconsin voters also lost the seniority La Follette had enjoyed. McCarthy's committee assignments were not bad—the PSI, the Committee on Expenditures, and Banking and Currency—but they hardly promised to make him a particularly valuable or influential senator for his farm belt constituents.

Wisconsin's unions turned their back on McCarthy once they learned about his plans to support tough new antiunion laws.[21] The Wisconsin American Legion, which ought to have been one of his most vociferous boosters, also turned against him when he came out against compulsory military train-ing, a long-standing Legion cause. The *Badger Legionnaire* accused him of "definitely letting them down." Then halfway through his first term, when Re-publicans drew up their new committee assignments for 1949, McCarthy was taken off the Banking Committee and relegated to the obscure Commit-tee on the District of Columbia. McCarthy wrote a long, pleading letter to the leadership, asking for a more important assignment. "I am the only Republi-can singled out for no major committee," he complained, "which will be ex-tremely embarrassing to me in my state." No one, not even the elders in his own party, was willing to help. His political stock fell to a new low.[22]

He had also made important enemies. One who would plague through-out his career was the progressive editor of the *Madison Capital Times*, William Evjue, who never forgave McCarthy for beating La Follette. Crusty, humorless, and overbearing, Evjue treated his employees poorly and paid them next to nothing. Those who worked with him hated him as a person, but they had to admire his stubbornness on liberal and progressive causes. Once he bit on an issue, he never let go. And now he and his assistant, Miles McMillin, fastened onto McCarthy. They would continue to hound him until he was in his grave.

The first issue they seized on was the old question of whether Mc-Carthy could legally run for the Senate while still a judge. The *Capital Times* launched a campaign calling for McCarthy's immediate dis-barment.[23] When that failed, Evjue and McMillin revived the old Quaker Dairy case and spread stories that as a judge, McCarthy was fond of grant-ing "quickie divorces" for his influential friends (McCarthy's enemies would later pick up this story and circulate it as fact). Evjue also began asking embarrassing questions about McCarthy's handling of his 1944 campaign finances and took credit for prompting a state five-year audit into McCarthy's tax records, which ultimately resulted in McCarthy's receiving a refund.

Stung by these repeated attacks, McCarthy struck back hard. In November 1949 he issued a statement accusing the *Capital Times* of being nothing less than a "Communist mouthpiece" and its city editor, Cedric Parker, of being a member of the Communist Party—and that Evjue himself had said as much in an editorial in 1941. He called for a statewide boycott of the *Capital Times* and dared Evjue to sue him. "Mr. Evjue can select the time, the place, and the forum and I'll be happy to debate the number of times the *Capital Times* has followed the party line." The result was a firestorm of publicity, more in fact than McCarthy had ever received in Wisconsin since being elected. When Evjue denied he had ever said Parker was a Communist, McCarthy happily whipped out a photostat copy of the editorial and showed it to reporters.[24] McCarthy was learning how to use allegations of Communist influence for his own advantage. He gave his Wheeling speech less than four months later.

McCarthy also managed some positive accomplishments. He sponsored an important bill providing housing for disabled veterans. He became the guiding force on a joint committee on public housing and fought hard for what would become the Housing Act of 1948. He showed he could take a strong stand on principle, even clashing with fellow conservative Republicans, but could also compromise and do a deal with the best of them. But with his other legislative project, ending wartime sugar rationing, he misstepped badly. Decontrolling sugar was another solidly Republican issue, since it involved reducing government regulation and its interference in business and people's lives. But McCarthy's bill offended New England Republican senators, whose constituents liked the artificially low prices that rationing had brought them. Democrats were quick to charge that McCarthy was trying to snatch sugar from housewives and the mouths of children to dump it in the laps of corporations that needed large quantities of sugar, like the big soft drink companies. When it turned out McCarthy had also taken a personal $20,000 loan from a Pepsi bottling executive, the innuendo flew thick and fast, with Evjue's *Capital Times* taking the lead. A new nickname replaced "Tail Gunner Joe": the "Pepsi-Cola Kid."

The truth was, as usual, slightly different. McCarthy had acted in the interest not of the soft drink companies but Wisconsin sugar beet growers; the loan had saved him from personal bankruptcy (McCarthy's finances were always in a precarious state); the bottler in question, Russell Arundel, was actually opposed to sugar deregulation since rationing had helped to pad his costs.[25] McCarthy's dealings with Pepsi turned out to be perfectly legal and open, as was his deal with the Lustron Corporation, which paid him $10,000 for writing a short book on public housing, *A Dollars' Worth of Housing for Every Dollar Spent.* Certainly McCarthy's links to Washington big money were no worse, and rather a good deal better, than many of his Senate colleagues. Compared with the likes of Bob Kerr of Oklahoma, or even Lyndon Johnson, he was a relative innocent. Soon his notoriety as a red hunter would overshadow everything else. Yet the early rumors that he was just a corrupt hustler willing to sell his office (in Richard Rovere's words) to "the seediest lot in Washington" plagued him for the rest of his career.

Then came the Malmédy case. In 1949 a group of Waffen SS prisoners went on trial for the massacre of unarmed American prisoners of war during the battle of the Bulge near the French village of Malmédy. The German defendants charged that their captors had forced confessions out of them by beatings and torture. The accusations made headlines, as did the trial. As a senator from a state with large numbers of German-Americans, McCarthy decided to investigate the case for himself. By every objective standard, he managed to make a fool of himself. He somehow convinced himself that the Army was engaged in an elaborate cover-up of judicial wrongdoing and browbeat the Senate into holding public hearings.* He fumed, lost his temper with Army witnesses, interrupted fellow senators Lester Hunt and Estes Kefauver, and then one day angrily stormed out of the committee vowing never to come back. He publicly charged that the special subcommittee was "afraid of the facts" and the hearings "a shameful farce."

It was a strange and self-defeating performance. He managed to offend chairman Millard Tydings and members of one of the important committees in the Senate, Armed Services, who issued a statement repudiating McCarthy's "unusual, unfair, and utterly undeserved" charges. By taking up the prisoners' cause, and even casting doubt on some of the evidence relating to the Malmédy massacre, McCarthy became in the public's eye an apologist for Nazi war crimes. The *Capital Times* gleefully seized on the Malmédy matter, as did later critics, who liked to suggest that McCarthy was really a crypto-Nazi.[26] McCarthy believed, of course, that he was continuing the class of '46 tradition of fearlessly taking on sacred cows like the U.S. Army and insisting that the federal government be accountable for its actions. He was fond of saying, "These are American courts, [and] American prestige to a great extent

---

*At first McCarthy wanted PSI to carry out the investigation, since they had conducted a probe into the Army's conduct of its trial of Nazi camp commandant Ilse Koch. But Tydings's Armed Services Committee took over instead.

depends on the way we mete out justice. . . . Should we adopt Hitler's rules of evidence or follow our own?"

One also suspects McCarthy was copying the example of Robert Taft. Taft had earlier spoken out against the international Nürnberg tribunal's death sentences against Göring, Ribbentrop, and other Nazi leaders. However terrible Germany's crimes, Taft had said, the United States had no business imposing what amounted to ex post facto justice on its defeated leaders. His unpopular stand, which even members of his own party had denounced (Jacob Javits of New York called it "a disservice to all we fought for and to the cause of future peace"), simply added to the luster of the Ohio senator's growing reputation as a man of uncompromising principles. It even led John F. Kennedy to include a chapter on Taft in his *Profiles in Courage*.

But McCarthy was no Robert Taft. His handling of the Malmédy case revealed a side that even McCarthy's friends had not seen before he arrived in Washington. The flip side of his tremendous energy and drive turned out to be a corresponding impatience, even rage, at those who seemed to stand in his way or dared to question his judgment. The transformation could be sudden and unnerving. Once when Republican whip Kenneth Wherry came up behind McCarthy on the Senate floor to offer his help on an unimportant matter, Joe whirled on him and snarled, "I can take care of myself."[27] Wherry, like McCarthy's other colleagues, soon learned to leave him alone. They realized that the man who could be funny, genial, and spontaneously kind (Jack Anderson remembered McCarthy's once volunteering to watch a woman's two children while she went into a grocery store—there he was, "a United States senator, babysitting for people he had never met before") was also a loaded pistol.[28]

Eventually McCarthy became an isolated figure. Outside of a small, trusted group of colleagues, like Jenner, Malone, and later Herman Welker of Idaho and Barry Goldwater, the presence of his fellow senators seemed a constant irritant and provocation. Most learned to shrug off his moody behavior; several, including crusty old liberal Theodore Green of Rhode Island, who bitterly fought with McCarthy during the Tydings Committee hearings, even attended McCarthy's wedding. Their staffers often felt otherwise. Pat Holt, who worked for Green on the Foreign Relations Committee, would not even acknowledge McCarthy's presence when they passed in the corridor. Once he was sitting beside Senator Walter George in the Senate chamber as McCarthy subjected the elder statesman to a drumbeat of questions. When Holt leaned over to whisper in George's ear, McCarthy snapped, "I want the senator's answer, not yours." Forbidden to speak on the Senate floor, Holt instead turned to McCarthy and framed out with his lips, "You son of a bitch."[29]

By 1950, when he gave his Wheeling speech on Communists in government, McCarthy had largely lost the confidence of even his fellow party members. Republicans would rally around him less out of a sense of collegiality or personal loyalty than a conviction that he was fundamentally right.

Harry Truman called the Eightieth Congress the "do-nothing Congress" and the name has stuck. However, it was "do-nothing" only to the degree that it did things Truman didn't like, in accordance with a conservative philosophy of less government rules and regulation, and more of a free hand for businesses and the marketplace. It passed the country's first balanced budget since 1930. It reduced taxes by $4.8 billion (roughly the equivalent of $60 billion today), and took almost seven and a half million low-income people off the tax rolls. It blocked compulsory national health insurance and, over Truman's veto, passed the Taft-Hartley Act, which shrank the power of labor unions to impose closed shops on businesses and organize collective strikes. It trimmed wartime economic regulations, abolished the Office of Price Administration, and created the Hoover Commission to oversee government waste and abuse. It passed the National Security Act, which created the CIA and merged the Army and Navy into the Department of Defense, and the Marshall Plan (after some initial opposition from conservative Republicans).

The Republican Congress also lived up to its promise to investigate corruption in high places. McCarthy watched as Senator Owen Brewster and then Homer Ferguson of Michigan led the PSI into the murky world of defense contracts and military procurement. The background assumption was always the same: the executive branch under Roosevelt's New Deal had been run by "a small group of men" (Robert Taft's phrase) who ruthlessly used their power to advance themselves and their friends. Their rationale had been, according to Senator Ferguson, "that they know best what is good for the people, and that the people are to do what they are told."

Inevitably Republican probes into this liberal governing class included looking at how Communist influence had found its way into the Roosevelt and Truman administrations. In the wake of the *Amerasia* espionage case and Elizabeth Bentley's revelations, and in the face of what he perceived as White House indifference to news of Soviet infiltration, the FBI's J. Edgar Hoover decided to take his case to the Republican Congress. His testimony before the House Un-American Activities Committee in March 1947 was the opening salvo in an offensive against domestic communism. It soon turned Republican against Democrat in a bitter partisan struggle.

In reply to skeptics who pointed out that Communist Party of the United

States made up less than 1 percent of all registered American voters, Hoover explained to committee members Richard Nixon and Karl Mundt and chairman J. Parnell Thomas that that was still a larger percentage of Communists than had existed in Russia in 1917 on the eve of the Bolshevik revolution. He emphasized that it was not the size of the Communist Party that was decisive to its political success but its "ability to infiltrate." Communist propaganda had always been slanted, he said, to draw in liberal and progressive support: "I do fear for the liberal and progressive who has been hoodwinked and duped into joining hands with the Communists."[30]

The PSI was pursuing a parallel track under Homer Ferguson. On July 30, 1948, the committee, with Republican whip Kenneth Wherry sitting in, heard Elizabeth Bentley describe the Communist underground inside the U.S. government. She had begun her work as courier for underground Soviet agents in the government in July 1941 and had picked up secret political and military information from figures in the major departments of the executive branch. The senators listened open-mouthed as she described at least twenty government employees with whom she had clandestine contact, while knowing at least another twenty who were working for other Soviet espionage networks. She explained that one unnamed agent had worked to encourage the United States to support Soviet allies in China; another had secretly told the Soviets that American intelligence had broken their most important diplomatic codes; and another, whom she identified as William Remington of the Commerce Department, had been transferred to an agency in charge of regulating exports to the USSR and its satellites.*

They then heard from Louis Budenz, who had once been executive editor of the *Daily Worker.* He called the Communist Party of the United States "a fifth column" working for the Soviet Union, with its underground roots leading directly to Moscow. He refused to speculate how many secret Communists were now working in the government: perhaps hundreds, even thousands, he said, if one included low-grade employees. Budenz also warned the committee that anyone who took up the cause of exposing this Communist network would be automatically labeled a red baiter. But "how can a man help being a red baiter" if he truly wants to defend America from its enemies? "If he exposes any activity of the Communist Party instead of there being an honest rebuttal . . . they resort to these attacks," Budenz said.

*Despite skepticism in some liberal circles, virtually everything Bentley said would later turn out to be true. The Soviet agent working on China policy was Lauchlin Currie, who fled abroad after testifying before the Un-American Activities; Currie also told the Soviets about the American code breaking (the Venona project). See Haynes and Klehr, *Venona,* 47–49.

"The American people are beginning to understand that. If they don't, of course," he added, "America is lost."[31]

That was on Monday, August 2. The next day, Whittaker Chambers appeared before the House Un-American Activities Committee to tell what he knew about a former State Department employee named Alger Hiss.

As it happened, McCarthy missed the PSI's session with Elizabeth Bentley and Budenz. But he had managed to raise the domestic communism issue even earlier. During the debate on the Taft-Hartley bill, in May 1947, he offered an amendment allowing employers to fire anyone whom a union representative had identified as working for the Communists or promoting the Communist line. This was McCarthy's first venture onto this terrain. It frankly baffled the bill's sponsor, Robert Taft, who pronounced it "unnecessary." But once again, any questioning of McCarthy's position prompted him to dig in and argue more insistently. When Taft had tried to intercede, McCarthy turned on him. "Let me finish," he furiously blurted out. Finally, Democrat Millard Tydings of Maryland rose and with magnificent condescension urged McCarthy to reconsider his amendment. "When we get down to the determination of what someone says, as to whether a man is promoting the policies of the Communist party," Tydings chided his young colleague, "we often run into a twilight zone and the examination might turn into a witchhunt." Let the senator from Wisconsin simply allow employers to bar Communists outright, Tydings said, and leave out the question of persons following a "Communist line," which "quite often causes abuses which I know he does not have in mind." McCarthy refused to back down, and his amendment was unceremoniously defeated. Taft-Hartley moved quietly on.[32]

It was an ironic moment. These two men, McCarthy and Tydings, were soon to become bitter enemies over this issue of whether promoting a policy that overlapped with Communist policy constituted promoting communism per se and whether those who did so ought to be held accountable. Tydings's position was at least clear. He believed they could not: "There are many things in the Communist doctrine, not all of them, but there may be many in its printed doctrine, which are also American doctrine." McCarthy, like J. Edgar Hoover, would argue that it was precisely this similarity that made communism so dangerous. If the liberal fell for the trap that the Communist had set for him, by appealing to high-minded principles or emotions, then the liberal was as unfit to serve in the government as his Communist manipulator.

Republicans pointed out that New Deal Democracy, like socialism, was built on the notion of a planned economy, with a corresponding curtailment

THE CLASS OF '46

of freedom. The liberal Democrat, like the Marxist, liked to speak in terms of classes and group interests rather than individuals. Republicans worried that liberalism would inevitably slide into socialism, and from socialism into communism. "Those who accept the principle of socialism," Taft wrote, "of government direction, and of government bureaucracy have a hard time battling against the ideology of Communism."[33] In the harsher words of a Taft speechwriter, Forrest Davis, "The liberal has looked on the face of evil and pronounced it half-good."[34] Of course, liberals rejected that view, and attacked such worries as typical right-wing paranoia. But the historical record of liberalism and Soviet communism lent Republican critics at least a prima facie case.

Chapter 3

Fatal Attraction: Liberals and Communism

A ssistant Secretary of State Adolph Berle had unexpected two guests for dinner at his home overlooking Woodley Park in Washington, D.C. One was Isaac Don Levine, columnist for the *New York Journal-American*, who had just published a series of stories about Soviet espionage activities. The other was Whittaker Chambers, an editor at *Time*. It was September 2, 1939, and host and guests discussed the Nazi invasion of Poland the day before and its implications—especially for the Soviet Union, which was now an ally of the Nazis.

After dinner, sitting outside in the cooling evening, Chambers began to talk about the real reason for their visit. For the next two hours in a nervous, faltering voice, Chambers outlined his personal knowledge of Soviet espionage efforts within the government. He named nearly thirty secret agents active in the Departments of Treasury, Interior, and State, including Alger Hiss, assistant to the political adviser for the Far Eastern division of the State Department, and his brother, Donald, an aide to Dean Acheson (then an assistant secretary at State). Chambers and Levine wanted Berle, the State Department's special intelligence liaison, to understand what was happening under his nose and to alert other government officials. They had already tried to see the president but were unable to make an appointment.

When they left, Berle looked over his notes and wondered. Chambers knew about the espionage network because, he said, he had been a member himself and worked directly with its Soviet spymaster. Some of those he had named were known Communists; others, especially the Hiss brothers, were not. Berle was inclined to discount the whole story, but the more he thought about the possibility of people in significant administration posts secretly working for a foreign government, the more uneasy he became. He raised the issue with President Roosevelt a few days later, but the president told him in no uncertain terms he was not interested.[1] Berle then took his qualms about "the Hiss boys" to two men who knew them best. One was their law school professor and mentor, Supreme Court Justice Felix Frankfurter, the doyen of American liberalism. Frankfurter assured him that he could vouch for them absolutely. The other, Dean Acheson, dealt with Berle's question by ordering Donald Hiss into his office and asking point-blank if he was a Communist. When Hiss said no, Acheson told Berle to dismiss the matter from his mind. After a time, Berle did. In fact, five years later Berle invited the accused Soviet spy Alger Hiss to join his security staff.[2]

The Berle story is a kind of parable about New Deal attitudes toward communism. The basic assumption was that because Alger and Donald Hiss came from the right social class (both were graduates of Johns Hopkins and Harvard Law School) and worked for the right people (Felix Frankfurter and the Roosevelt administration), they could not possibly be "real" Communists, let alone dangerous subversives. If later on opponents accused McCarthy and others of blurring the distinction between liberalism and communism, it is worth remembering that many of the New Deal establishment had done the same thing. Rebecca West described the situation perfectly: "Everyone knew there were Communists, but very few people really believed it. . . . This knowledge seemed to them outside reality, like a dream, the recollection of a film seen long ago, a detective story read in childhood." And if there really were Communists, as Leslie Fiedler later put it, "they were, despite their shrillness and bad manners, fundamentally on the side of justice."[3]

In the minds of many American progressives, Communists were just "liberals in a hurry," much as Earl Browder of the Communist Party of the United States (CPUSA) and his subordinates claimed. Communist goals for the Soviet Union seemed to be pretty much the same as those of New Dealers for America. In the thirties the Soviet Union enjoyed the same sort of intellectual respectability that Mao's China would in the 1970s. The plain truth—that Stalin was a mass murderer who governed through compulsory labor, prison camps, and the systematic murder of his own supporters—was ignored, explained, or shrugged away.

Then, with the coming of the cold war, the Popular Front version of liberalism backfired. Cozy associations with Communists and communism came back to haunt its practitioners. It was no wonder liberals came to view congressional hearings and probes, and government loyalty boards, with dread. They knew that the danger was not that these investigations would spread false information about Communist links to the New Deal, but the truth—a truth that, when taken out the context of the tense and uncertain thirties, would make liberals look like quasi-traitors. Later, many of those who had joined the Communist Party in a moment of misplaced enthusiasm or signed on to various front organizations would lose their jobs and feel abused by their treatment. Other Americans felt they got off easy. If Popular Front liberals had not been guilty of actual disloyalty, at the very least they had shown intellectual irresponsibility in the face of genuine evil.

The first liberal-Communist links were forged before World War I when Louis Fraina joined the staff of the *New Review* with Max Eastman and Walter Lippmann.[4] An Italian socialist, Fraina had translated Lenin and Marx's works, would later become head of the Communist Party of America (CPA), and was a secret Comintern agent. The CPA's rival, the Communist Labor Party,* was led by John Reed, a young Harvard graduate who had gone to Russia in 1918 to witness the revolution that he and many others believed signaled the end of capitalism around the world. His *Ten Days That Shook The World* created a heroic vision of the Bolsheviks and their socialist program that would influence generations of Communists and liberals alike. He returned to America two years later armed with secret funds for organizing a revolutionary Communist Party at home. "Communism," its original manifesto stated, "does not propose to 'capture' the bourgeois state, but to conquer and destroy it."[5]

All of these plans ran afoul of the red scare of 1919–1920. The Wilson government had already flexed its muscles in silencing socialist opposition to America's entry to World War I by rounding up figures like Eugene Debs and Fraina. Then, on April 30, 1919, a postal clerk in New York City discovered twenty package bombs set for detonation on May Day. Two were not caught in time: one blew up in front of Attorney General Mitchell Palmer's house, killing the deliveryman and scattering parts of his body across the sidewalk; another exploded at the house of a U.S. senator, taking off the arm of his Negro maid. The Senate passed a resolution ordering the Justice Department to take immediate action against all radicals and aliens who advocated the overthrow by force and violence.

The result were the Palmer raids. Again, it is worth remembering that in the "McCarthy era" of the fifties, no one went to jail without a legal warrant,

*After much factional fighting, the CPA and the CLP (or its hybrid successor, the United Communist Party, or UCP) would merge into the American Communist Party at a convention held in Woodstock, New York, in May 1921. In 1929 it became the Communist Party of the United States, or CPUSA.

no one was convicted without a trial, or even had to appear before a congressional committee without legal representation. In 1920, by contrast, dealing with the red threat meant massive roundups and deportations (organized by Palmer's young assistant, J. Edgar Hoover). Angry mobs took the law into their own hands and attacked suspected Bolsheviks and "subversives" in the street. A socialist newspaper office in New York was burned and gutted, and the leader of a radical labor union brutally murdered in Centralia, Washington.

In May Felix Frankfurter and twenty other distinguished lawyers wrote a public protest against the officially sanctioned hysteria. They concluded that the real crisis was not the "vague and threatened menace" of communism but "a present assault upon the most sacred principles of our Constitutional liberty." The lawyers' report managed to stop the raids, released the majority of those in prison, and forced Palmer to resign. It also encapsulated a basic liberal assumption for the future: that all attacks on Communists or attempts to limit their activities were really attacks on civil liberties for all Americans.[6] Yet for all its brutality and unconstitutional proceedings, Palmer's raids did manage to break the American Communist movement. Membership fell off by 80 percent, leaving a hard core of underground radicals who had to wait for the right opportunity before reemerging into public view.[7]

That turned out to be the Sacco-Vanzetti case. Nicola Sacco and Bartolomeo Vanzetti were not Communists at all but anarchists who had been convicted of robbery and murder in 1921. The Communist International decided it could exploit their case to rebuild its political base in America; it launched a huge publicity campaign to reopen the Sacco-Vanzetti charges and argued that the two Italian immigrants were innocent victims of a class-biased judicial system. The appeal netted the Communists their first major catch of liberal supporters, including Felix Frankfurter (who published a long essay in the *Atlantic* in 1927 casting doubt on the evidence), Walter Lippmann, Heywood Broun, John Dewey, Robert La Follette, Sr., Max Eastman, John Dos Passos, James Rorty, Upton Sinclair, Maxwell Anderson, Katherine Anne Porter, and Jane Addams. They were drawn to Sacco and Vanzetti as symbolic underdogs and unquestioningly accepted Communist claims about the injustice of their conviction. Emotions ran high. The young novelist Howard Fast even compared Sacco and Vanzetti's convictions to the Crucifixion.[8] For a generation of American progressives, including the young Alger Hiss, the electrocution of Sacco and Vanzetti on August 23, 1927, triggered an awakening of social and political conscience, and a new sense of solidarity with the Communist Party.

But that awakening was built on a lie. Sacco and Vanzetti were not martyrs but murderers; they were not underdogs, but revolutionaries who were prepared to kill and maim for their beliefs. Subsequent ballistic tests conducted in the 1980s confirmed that it was they who had pulled the trigger.[9] However, American liberals and the left saw the pair not for what they were, but for what they symbolized: the oppression of the working class by the capitalist system. They wanted to believe Sacco and Vanzetti were innocent, and so they *became* innocent. The symbol became reality, which confirmed the truth of their own progressive views.

On the other hand, if Sacco and Vanzetti turned out to be guilty (or later Alger Hiss, or the Rosenbergs), then an entire version of reality—the progressive one—would have to be thrown out, leaving its believers without political bearings.[10] Sacco and Vanzetti forged an important bond between Communists and their liberal sympathizers. They now shared a single version of reality that, however much one might disagree on specific measures or remedies (such as whether to destroy the "bourgeois state"), no amount of corrective facts seemed to disturb.

Meanwhile, American liberalism in the twenties was mired in a crisis of confidence. It became disillusioned with Woodrow Wilson, the failure of the League of Nations, and the string of Republican electoral successes from Harding to Hoover. Its spokesmen grew tired of the inevitable ups and downs of democratic politics. "No more dashes into the political jungle," wrote Herbert Croly of the *New Republic*. "No more intervention with reservations . . . and without specific and intelligent political preparation."[11] But when it came to Soviet communism, many of his colleagues were prepared to throw caution to the winds.

On their obligatory visits to the Soviet Union, they displayed an amazing credulity. They were willing to believe literally anything that cast a favorable light on Soviet society and a bad light on their own. Long working days meant that the Russian people were committed to the success of the revolution. Grinding poverty meant that Russians were no longer interested in superficial capitalist affluence. Theodore Dreiser admitted that "in Moscow there is poverty. There are beggars in the streets. But," he added, "Lord how picturesque! The multi-colored and voluminous rags on them!" Progressive journalists praised the Soviets' strict censorship of the press, pacifists cheered their military parades, and churchmen their abolition of Christianity. The lavish banquets foreign visitors enjoyed at official functions proved that the Soviet economy was a success, and the lack of dissent demonstrated that people living under communism had nothing to complain about.

Everything in the Soviet Union seemed to exude a sense of revolutionary solidarity and purpose. The American pacifist Sherwood Eddy wrote that "Russia has achieved what has hitherto been known only at rare periods of history, the experience of almost an entire people living under a unified philosophy of life," resulting in "a flood of joyous and strenuous activity."[12] For disenchanted progressives, that vision proved irresistible. Lincoln Steffens returned from Russia with the famous observation, "I have been over into the future—and it works," implying that neither claim applied to the capitalism in his own country.

The Great Depression seemed to prove him right. Even liberals who were still dubious about "the great Soviet experiment" were shaken by it. Nearly a third of American workers were unemployed. The earning power of those who still had jobs plunged by two-thirds, and productivity fell by more than half. The year 1930 seemed to sound the death knell of laissez-faire capitalism. It seemed to many intellectuals that the United States was drifting without plan, guidance, or goal.[13] In their minds, salvation lay in two directions. The first was Roosevelt's New Deal, which revived interest in the Democratic Party as the rallying point for American progressives of all stripes. The other was Soviet communism. If the Soviets had not succeeded in generating industrialized affluence, observers believed, at least they had avoided depression (not noticing that what was economic collapse in America and Europe would have seemed like unimaginable prosperity to most Russians). The editors of the *Nation* stated in 1933 that poverty that accompanied progressive reforms, as in Soviet Russia, was preferable to poverty in the midst of plenty, as in America. Lenin and Stalin seemed to be pointing toward a new direction for America, which the New Deal might heed. As Eugene Lyons later put it, "In a time of head-splitting questions, the communists offered answers."[14] If a few worried about the possible consequences of adopting a Lenin-style dictatorship, others did not. As Stuart Chase, a former liberal economist and now a committed socialist, wrote nonchalantly, "A better economic order is worth a little bloodshed."[15]

The two leading voices of American liberal opinion, the *New Republic* and the *Nation*, latched onto the Soviet Union early in 1933 and never let go. They argued that New Deal liberalism and communism were not so different from each other after all. Both shared a belief in centralized planning and in social betterment. Further, they argued, Communists and liberals shared a "belief in the brotherhood and inherent value of man, a belief in equality, a belief in objective reason and science"—and while fascism tried to preserve capitalism and imperialism, communism pushed for world peace and the elimination of capitalism.[16] In 1934 George Soule's *The Coming American Revolution* directly equated Roosevelt's New Deal with Stalin's Five Year Plan. If critics like Robert Taft and Samuel Pettingill worried about where all this expansion of the federal government was heading and believed the New Deal was merely a "smokescreen" for a more vicious and insidious form of collectivism, leading liberal opinion was hinting at the same thing. The fellow-traveling academic

Frederick L. Schumann proclaimed enthusiastically in the pages of the *New Republic*, "Underneath their skin, communism and liberalism are blood brothers"—precisely what McCarthy and others would claim a decade later, albeit in a very different tone.[17]

By 1935 the way was clear for the Popular Front. Even as the Communist Party itself was still violently anti–New Deal, and attacked Roosevelt as little better than a fascist, progressive intellectuals were embracing the Soviet experiment and its advocates. The result was a strange situation. While old-style American socialists like Norman Thomas, A. J. Muste, and Sidney Hook were fiercely anti-Communist, many mainstream liberals were convinced that the Communists' professed humanitarian principles were genuine and were prepared to overlook certain "details"—including constant rumors about murderous purges, shootings, and mass starvation in the Soviet Union—in order to arrive at a common understanding.

However, Muste, Hook, and the socialists knew there was no common understanding possible. They had a far better grasp of what was actually happening in the Soviet Union and had learned from bitter experience that Communists were interested in nothing less than total control and the elimination of any rivals on the left. They had seen how Communists could infiltrate an organization or a labor union with their members by disguising their true identity, and then work to direct it for their purposes—and what they could not control, they were content to disrupt or destroy. It was a bitter lesson most liberals still had to learn.

The creation of the Popular Front in 1935 permanently altered the battle lines of the American left. It sprang up on the one hand as a response to the growing menace of fascism. On the other, it was Stalin's own tactical move to facilitate Communist infiltration of mainstream politics. It soon divided liberals into those who were willing to accept the principle of a united front of parties and factions on the left and the reality of Communist leadership—the so-called fellow travelers—and those who did not.

Fellow traveler was a term coined by Stalin himself to describe people who were not members of the Communist Party but sympathized with the revolution and were willing to contribute their efforts as intellectuals, artists, and writers to the cause.[18] Of course, the liberal fellow traveler's uncritical regard for the Soviet Union predated the Popular Front. But now under its auspices, the party reached out to another group of progressives: people who might dislike communism as a revolutionary ideology but were willing to work with its practitioners toward what seemed to be a common goal: the defeat of fascism and "reaction," symbolized by the rise of Hitler, Mussolini, and their imitators around the globe. Because of the Communists' efficient enthusiasm and organizational skills, their liberal allies were willing to sit back and allow them to set the agenda in labor matters, as well as cultural and political matters.

In the late 1930s Communists extended their influence into the American labor movement, particularly the CIO. Hollywood's Screen Writers Guild was for all intents and purposes Communist controlled, through organizers V. J. Jerome and John Howard Lawson, as was the Conference of Studio Unions.[19] Communists broke into mainstream politics through their domination of the American Labor Party in New York, and after having nearly destroyed the national Farmer-Labor Party in 1923, they were invited back by Governor Olson of Minnesota. In 1936 Earl Browder gave a speech at the National Press Club, which, if not exactly endorsing Roosevelt, urged defeat of his Republican opponent. By 1939 Communist Party membership had swelled to nearly seventy thousand.

Under the influence of the Popular Front, American progressives by the hundreds stepped up to show their solidarity with their Communist peers. Respectable academics like Philip Jessup, feminist judges like Dorothy Kenyon, and idealistic law students like Fred Fisher (all of whom would later run afoul of McCarthy) joined "front" organizations and signed petitions. They donated their money to Communist-led fund-raising drives and their names to open letters published in the *Daily Worker*. Hollywood fund raisers alone drew on average $50,000 per event. All these activities were ostensibly in support of good liberal causes, but were in fact designed to bolster Communist influence over political and cultural life. Liberals learned to ignore the nature or origin of the organization and responded to the professed ideals and intentions instead. As Eugene Lyons observed caustically, the Popular Front "was the perfect recipe for those Americans who wanted the thrill of revolutionary forms, but none of the substance in blood and death and sacrifice."[20]

One of the most successful front groups was the League for Peace and Democracy (LPD).* Born at the World Congress Against War in 1932 (another Stalinist front), it used the usual appeal to unexceptionable principles (who would oppose "peace" and "democracy"?) to manipulate its liberal allies into assenting to positions that edged increasingly closer to the Moscow line. At one time or another, LPD members included a governor of Minnesota, the mayor of Cleveland, four U.S. congressmen, and Harold Ickes, Roosevelt's secretary of the interior, as well as leading clergymen, writers, and public activists. Ickes wrote a letter of welcome to the league when it met in Washington for its fifth national gathering, stating: "The name of your organization

---

*Originally the American League Against War and Fascism, the organization changed its name in 1937.

must mean that you are committed to the policy of peace and the policy of democracy." Its chairman, Harry Ward, professor of Christian Ethics at Union Theological Seminary in New York City, even stated that the Soviet system was the fulfillment of the teachings of Jesus.[21] Claiming twenty thousand dues-paying members and more than seven million affiliate members, the LPD became an important Washington lobbying group, pushing various "progressive" causes, until it was swept away by the Nazi-Soviet Pact.[22]

Some fronts were "respectable" professional and civic organizations, such as the National Lawyers Guild, the American Newspaper Guild, the League of American Writers, the American Artists' Congress, and the American Youth Congress. Others were ad hoc, like the Hollywood Anti-Nazi League, Friends of Spanish Democracy, and the Theater Arts Committee, set up in 1937. But all had the same agenda: to disguise any direct Communist connotations and to give party members the upper hand in shaping policy and raising money. The Communist Party used them as a means of drawing in new recruits for the party. They also helped to provide useful cover for the other aspect of the Communist Party's activity: espionage.

Despite the pretense of unity and solidarity, the Popular Front did not involve the normal give-and-take of other political alliances. It involved Communists' taking, and liberals' giving up, control over both organizations and their agendas. The Popular Front became in effect a series of tests that every fellow traveler or Communist sympathizer had to undergo to prove his solidarity with his allies on the left, followed by unpleasant events or revelations he had to rationalize or explain away.

First of these were the purges of non-Stalinist Communists, such as followers of Trotsky and Jay Lovestone—the regenade Lithuanian-American labor organizer and party secretary who was purged from the Party in 1929—and his handful of followers; the so-called Lovestonites. Many other professed Marxist-Leninist intellectuals also found themselves in disgrace on one pretext or another. Although the Popular Front pretended to openness, in fact it permitted no criticism of the USSR, in either the past or the present. What counted was one's "political correctness," as the Party called it, meaning adherence to the current Stalinist position. Liberal editors and reviewers had to learn whose books were to be praised or damned, whose articles to be published and whose to be rejected, which organs of progressive opinion to be taken seriously and which to be ignored (such as the *New Leader* or *Partisan Review*). Even as Communist playwrights like Clifford Odets were submitting their works for political criticism to their Communist Party superiors, Popular Front liberals in effect did the same thing.[23] It was the Communist, not the liberal, point of view that mattered.

Then came the Moscow trials, when Stalin began arresting, trying, and shooting members of his own party on the grounds that they were spies for foreign powers. Stalin's political purpose in staging the show trials to get rid of inconvenient rivals seemed obvious. The "confessions" of defendants (usually extracted after beatings and promises that family members would be spared death, which were afterward revoked) were manifestly ludicrous and the circumstantial evidence more than suspect. However, since the Stalinist line was that the trials were genuine, that the long series of distinguished Bolsheviks being executed had always actually been traitors, Popular Fronters had to accept it as genuine also. Questions and doubts were quashed. Sympathetic observers who attended the trials like Roosevelt's own ambassador to the Soviet Union, Joseph Davies, came away impressed by its overall fairness and objectivity. "We see no reason," wrote editors of the *New Republic* in September 1936, "to take the trial at other than its face value."[24] One scholar by the name of Owen Lattimore called the purges the sort of "habitual rectification" that would encourage others to speak out and criticize other senior members of the party. "That sounds like democracy to me," he said.

The final test came with the Nazi-Soviet Pact of August 23, 1939. Mortal enemies became allies overnight; Stalin and Hitler decided to parcel out Poland and the Baltic republics between them. After spending the last six years excoriating Hitler as the enemy of humanity, Foreign Minister Molotov now remarked that fascism was a "matter of taste." German tanks struck across the Polish border a week later, on September 1, and the Russians followed suit on September 17.

The Nazi-Soviet Pact proved to be the moment of revelation for many Popular Front liberals, as they realized that they had been lied to and misled by their Communist allies. The *Nation's* Russia correspondent, Louis Fischer, called the pact a "crime" and said that Stalin and Hitler were now in effect partners: to support one was to support the other. In the *New Republic* another prominent fellow traveler, Vincent Sheean, renounced his earlier support for the purge trials and collectivization. Stalin was not building socialism, he said, but slavery. Others nevertheless remained committed to the Soviet cause, among them Harvard professor Harlow Shapley, Williams College's Frederic L. Schumann, the millionaire's son Corliss Lamont, and Anna Louise Strong, who insisted that Soviet Russia had invaded eastern Poland "for the sake of peace." But many of those who were disillusioned by the pact still insisted on the validity of their earlier support for the Soviet ideal. It is not we but Stalin who has changed, they claimed. The chief worry on the editorial boards of the *Nation* and *New Republic* was that the Nazi-Soviet Pact might lead to an anti-Communist backlash.[25]

A decade later, many liberals would face public embarrassment and even the loss of their jobs based on their past membership to this or that pro-

Communist organization during the Popular Front period. Nevertheless, we have to bear in mind that membership in such groups was proof at the very least of an intellectual fecklessness, if not actual intellectual dishonesty. Like those who deny or cast doubt on the reality of the Holocaust today, the fellow traveler denied the brutal reality of the Soviet Union. The scale of Stalin's atrocities in the 1930s might not have been as shockingly obvious as those of Hitler would be, although in terms of sheer numbers Stalin's put the Holocaust in the shade. Still, the evidence through eyewitness reports, objective observers, and simple common sense (as in the case of the Moscow trials) was there for anyone to see or hear. As Sidney Hook pointed out later, Khrushchev's "secret speech" of 1956, the Soviet Union's first public admission of Stalin's crimes, contained no information or revelations that had not been circulating for years, including during the Popular Front period.[26]

Of course, denying or covering up a staggering record of massacre and terror in a foreign country is not a crime, let alone treason. No red hunter, not even McCarthy, would ever make such a charge. But it did suggest that for the sake of an ideological vision, the Popular Front liberal had voluntarily given up the power of rational judgment. Later investigators and loyalty boards might be willing to forgive one front membership, but a pattern of joining such groups, or allowing one's name to be used on a petition or a public manifesto for Communist propaganda purposes was enough to set off alarm bells. To the conservative critic, American society required a firm rational and moral foundation. It demanded from its citizens a basic ability to distinguish right from wrong. This was something the habitual fellow traveler had shown he or she could not do.

Perhaps the best example was the notorious Open Letter of August 14, 1939. It was written in response to anti-Communist liberals and progressives on the Committee for Cultural Freedom who had called on condemnation of all forms of totalitarianism, whether in Nazi Germany and fascist Italy or the Soviet Union. Totalitarianism, argued Sidney Hook, John Dewey, Arthur Schlesinger, Jr., and others, "threatens to overwhelm nations where the democratic way of life, with its cultural liberty, is still dominant," including the United States. It implied "a hatred for the free mind" in which "intellectual and creative independence is suppressed and punished as a form of treason," with art, science, and education as forms of indoctrination. Intellectuals, they argued, had a direct stake in a democratic society, albeit a capitalist one, rather than in Hitler's Germany or Stalin's Russia.

The manifesto received a blistering reply under the auspices of the American Council on Soviet Affairs, another Communist front organization. The Open Letter dismissed the members of the Committee for Cultural Freedom as "fascists and allies of fascists" who were trying to prevent "a united anti-aggression front" with the Soviet Union. The Open Letter claimed more than four hundred sponsors, although only 165 signatories were listed. It included many of the most prominent names of Popular Front liberalism. Some were writers, like Langston Hughes, Donald Ogden Stewart, S. J. Perelman, William Carlos Williams, Louis Untermeyer, Clifford Odets, and George S. Kaufman. Some were journalists, like I. F. Stone, George Seldes of the *Chicago Tribune*, and Carey McWilliams of the *Nation*. Others were distinguished names from academia, civic life, and the Protestant clergy, including the ubiquitous Harry Ward of the League for Peace and Democracy.

This time they had put their names not just on a letter of solidarity with the Soviet Union, but on an agreed picture of the Soviet Union itself. They denied Stalinist Russia was a police state and asserted that the Russian people enjoyed complete freedom of speech, full emancipation of women, independent trade unions, full employment, and an enviably high standard of living. Stalin had eradicated racial prejudice and anti-Semitism, the Open Letter claimed, which insisted that his dictatorship was only a transitional phase toward participatory democracy. Above all, the Soviet Union was "a bulwark against war and aggression."

In fact, every one of these claims was false, and a conservative observer would have noted that those claims that were true—that the Soviets had collectivized agriculture and industry, imposed nationwide socialist planning, and abolished all forms of religion—were listed as desirable liberal goals. As for being a "bulwark against war and aggression," events were to give that the direct lie. Ironically, the letter appeared in the *Nation* the same day that it announced the Nazi-Soviet Pact.[27]

Chapter 4

The Forties: Democrats and Communists

Whatever embarrassment or second thoughts Popular Fronters might have experienced about their earlier enthusiasm for the Soviet Union were soon swept aside. Hitler invaded the Soviet Union on June 22, 1941, and declared war on the United States six months later. Once again it became safe to wax eloquent about "the Soviet people" and "Uncle Joe" Stalin, and to list the Soviet Union among the United Nations, as they were then called, who were fighting fascism.

The standard liberal version of World War II was of a two-sided struggle, pitting the Axis powers against the Allies, including the Soviet Union. What conservatives understood, and many liberals did not, was that World War II was in fact a *triangular* conflict.[1] On one side stood Hitler and the Axis powers; on the other, the United States and the democracies. And on the third side were Stalin and his Communist Party allies, many of whom were now active in labor unions and political organizations in democratic countries.

When war broke out in September 1939, the first stage of the struggle saw Hitler and Stalin as allies against the Western democracies. Having divided Poland between them, they then cooperated in rounding up political dissidents and Jews. Domestic Communist parties became in effect Hitler's own fifth column. Communist-led unions called dock strikes in Britain to hamper the war effort, and in New York they fought against Lend-Lease.[2] When Hitler invaded France in May 1940, Communist Party leader Maurice Thorez had made radio broadcasts from Moscow urging his fellow Frenchmen not to resist the German advance. Acting on Stalin's orders, the

Communist CPUSA organized the American Peace Mobilization, denounced the British, not Hitler, as the "greatest danger to Europe and all mankind," and even sent out feelers to mainstream anti-interventionist groups like America First. The party's leader, Earl Browder, was arrested and put in prison for using a false passport and for being in effect the ally of a potential American enemy, Nazi Germany.

The second stage of the war began with the German invasion of Russia. Overnight Stalin had become the ally of the democracies. The American Peace Mobilization had planned a "peace march" on the White House the next day, which had to be hastily canceled. Instead, its organizer, and *Amerasia* magazine's patron, Frederick Vanderbilt Field, carried off the picket signs reading "THE YANKS ARE NOT COMING!" and came back with new signs reading "OPEN THE SECOND FRONT!"[3]

Some Western politicians, such as Winston Churchill, understood that this was an alliance of mutual convenience. Without Western and American aid, Stalin could not survive. Without the Russians, Hitler's domination of Europe would be permanent. Once Hitler was destroyed, however, the old antagonism between democracy and totalitarianism would resume; the triangular conflict would revert to a bipolar one.

On the whole, however, liberals remained oblivious to this triangular struggle. Many leading figures in the Roosevelt administration, starting with the president himself, were determined to include Stalin's Soviet Union among the "democracies" fighting "fascism," a position that the Communists themselves encouraged. FDR released Earl Browder from prison and permitted the Communist Party to pick up where they had left off.[4] In terms of postwar policy, Roosevelt always assumed he could deal frankly and honestly with Stalin, and he showed no interest in what might happen to Eastern Europe once the Nazis had been defeated. He enjoyed speculating on the future of British India and Hong Kong with the Soviet dictator instead, and making jokes about the English impulse for empire (as if Stalin were immune from the same impulse himself). The disastrous decisions at Yalta were the natural result.[5]

The Yalta Conference of February 1945 marked the high tide of liberal self-confidence—one might say gullibility—in dealing with Stalin. Roosevelt and, to an even lesser degree, Churchill were anxious to display their goodwill toward the man who would soon be absolute master of most of Eastern Europe. In exchange for a promise to enter the war against Japan and to permit Soviet-occupied countries to choose their own forms of government (a promise that Stalin made and quickly forgot), Roosevelt handed Stalin large concessions in the Far East and in Poland. FDR stressed that "there would be no difficulty whatever" with giving the Russians Sakhalin and the Kuriles, which Japan now occupied, a lease on Port Arthur in Manchuria, and a commanding presence in northern China. Stalin was permitted to keep that portion of Poland he had stolen in the original Nazi-Soviet Pact and to have a significant voice in governing the Poland that remained. Long afterward, critics like Joe McCarthy would insist that Roosevelt's poor health at Yalta had lowered his guard and blame his various cup-bearers, particularly Alger Hiss, for the "betrayal at Yalta." In fact, no one was to blame except Roosevelt himself. He convinced himself that Stalin could be trusted. Literally millions of innocent human beings, from Manchuria to Soviet-occupied Berlin, would pay for his mistake.

Roosevelt's secretary of the interior, Harold Ickes, was another one of the New Deal inner circle who remained convinced that communism could be a useful and constructive ally in the effort to promote a progressive America. He, like Eleanor Roosevelt, confidently dismissed any suggestion that groups like the American Youth Congress were Communist controlled or dominated and spoke to their rallies and meetings. The real enemies of freedom, Ickes believed, were the Communists' opponents. As he stated in a radio broadcast, "I suspect either the motives or the intelligence of those who would have us marshal our forces against a barely imaginary danger of Communism while fascism thunders at the gates of our citadel of liberty."[6]

Wartime cooperation between the United States and Stalin also brought out the softer side of the head of the American intelligence service, the OSS, William Donovan. In civilian life, Donovan had been a top-notch Wall Street lawyer. But as his chief of staff, Duncan Lee, noted, Donovan was "fascinated" by the Soviet Union. "He considers Stalin the most intelligent person among all [those] heading today's governments. . . ." Throughout the war and afterward Donovan showed a cavalier indifference toward the ideological leanings of his OSS agents, and bristled at any suggestion that those with Communist backgrounds might have divided loyalties.

In 1943 Donovan flew to Moscow to raise the possibility of joint OSS-KGB operations against the Third Reich in Yugoslavia and Greece. He personally briefed Soviet intelligence officials on OSS tradecraft, offered to give them a tour of his agency's training facilities, and even proposed exchanging formal representatives, with an OSS office in Moscow and a KGB office in Washington. The plan, supported by FDR's ambassador Averell Harriman, went all the way to the White House, until J. Edgar Hoover nixed it, protesting that this only gave the KGB easier access to American government secrets. The plan fell through, but it didn't matter—because unbenownst to Hoover or Donovan, Duncan Lee, the OSS trusted chief of staff, was himself a KGB agent.[7]

The attitude of Roosevelt's chief adviser, Harry Hopkins, was even more peculiar. In the early 1970s, a young KGB recruit named Oleg Gordievsky attended a lecture on Soviet espionage in the United States, conducted by one of the grand old men of the Soviet underground service, Anatoly Akhmerov. Akhmerov began with biographies of some of their most valuable American assets in the past, men like Victor Perlo and Gregory Silvermaster and Alger Hiss, whom he mentioned only briefly. By far and away the most valuable asset the KGB had enjoyed during World War II, Akhmerov told his pupils, had been Harry Hopkins, special adviser to President Roosevelt himself.

As Akhmerov went on to describe Hopkins's activities on behalf of the Soviet Union, Gordievsky began to realize that Hopkins had not been a conscious agent for the KGB but rather an unconscious one.[8] Akhmerov and his colleagues had come to realize that Hopkins, who was in other ways shrewd and sophisticated, could be easily misled and naively believed in the sincerity of Stalin's profession of friendship and benevolence toward the United States. He also evidently believed in Akhmerov, with whom he had had several meetings during the course of the war. With very little effort, then, the Soviets managed to turn Hopkins into their willing accomplice and ruthlessly exploited his influence with Roosevelt to their advantage. Hopkins became the archetypal "Communist dupe"—the well-intentioned liberal who believes every lie the Marxists tell him, with disastrous results. In Hopkins's case at least, the stereotype reflected reality.

Hopkins dismissed Ambassador Harriman's warnings that Stalin was interpreting Roosevelt's conciliatory policies as a sign of weakness, and that a postwar Soviet Union "will become a world bully wherever its interests are involved." He permitted the Russians to receive military and industrial equipment under Lend-Lease that would be of use only *after* the war and rigorously tried to block Allied support for the Warsaw uprising against Hitler (which Stalin also wanted to prevent).[9] Contrary to later myth, it was Hopkins, far more than Alger Hiss, who encouraged Roosevelt to make major concessions to Soviet interests at Yalta.

Hopkins also kept close, comfortable relations with the men who would later be identified as Moscow's "agents of influence" in the government: Hiss, Harry Dexter White, and Lauchlin Currie. All this, plus the revelations from Soviet sources, has misled some scholars into concluding that Hopkins had to be a Soviet spy. This seems unlikely, but it is quite possible that Hopkins *knew these men were working for Soviet intelligence* and deliberately turned a blind eye. Soviet intelligence officers who secretly debriefed Hiss at Yalta, for example, simply could not believe that Hopkins and Roosevelt were unaware that Hiss was really working for them.[10] We also know Hopkins believed that the Soviet Foreign Office—the "Molotov clique," as he and others called them—kept Stalin from grasping the United States's sincere desire for friendship and understanding. Hopkins may have assumed that Communist agents like Hiss, White, and Currie could serve as a clandestine back channel to the dictator himself, so that the White House could send "the right message" whenever needed. Certainly such a notion would have appealed to Hopkins's own love of behind-the-scenes manipulation and Roosevelt's too. In any case, the notion that Stalin represented the "moderate" side of Soviet policy in contrast to the "hard line" Molotov, or that Hopkins could surreptitiously control a spy like White rather than the other way around, beggars belief.

Whether Hopkins knew how much influence Soviet agents were wielding in the White House may be irrelevant to the final result: that the Roosevelt team bent over backward to accommodate themselves to Soviet wishes and desires, to no good effect. But in Hopkins's defense, we must also remember that even those who knew better were not immune from the enthusiasm the joint U.S.-Soviet war effort had created. When the fighting ended in May 1945, George Kennan had watched a crowd of Soviet citizens slowly gathering outside the American embassy in Moscow. They started to cheer the Stars and Stripes hanging from the balcony. Soon the square was filled with tens of thousands of people. Kennan and the sergeant of the military mission stepped out to greet them, to a tremendous roar of approval. The crowd hoisted a Soviet soldier up onto the balcony, who "kissed and embraced the startled sergeant, pulled him relentlessly down to the waiting arms of the crowd . . . bobbing helplessly over a sea of hands." The cheering, singing, and celebrating went on well into evening: a moving sight, Kennan admitted. Yet even then he knew other events were casting a shadow on the hopes of any future cooperation.[11]

The first serious sign of trouble had come over Poland. When Warsaw rose up against the Nazis in late 1944, Stalin halted his armies' advance so that the Nazis could wipe out Polish resistance and save him future trouble. Even before Yalta, the sacrifice of Warsaw proved that the Soviet Union and the democracies existed in different moral universes, and would inevitably pursue different interests and aims at the war's end. Yet Roosevelt, Hopkins, and the chairman of the combined staff, General George Marshall, continued to push for closer cooperation. American troops halted their advance into Germany in order to allow Russians to take Prague and then Berlin— this latter decision at General Eisenhower's personal initiative.[12] By the time the atom bomb was dropped on Hiroshima in August 1945, other policymakers like Stimson, Acheson, and Secretary of State James Byrnes were uncomfortably aware that another conflict was looming ahead. The war was entering its third and final stage: Stalin against the democratic allies, with the United States at their head.

From the point of view of American liberals, World War II left a double legacy. Along with the New Deal, it confirmed the United States as a successful and progressive world power. Former Popular Fronters believed it no longer needed to emulate the Soviet Union or look to Soviet Union for the lead. Instead, they hoped that the United States and USSR would become the twin pillars of a new liberal, progressive international order, symbolized by the creation of the United Nations.

Referring to the Soviets in his fourth inaugural address, Roosevelt had said, "In order to make a friend one must be a friend." The new administration and its president, Harry Truman, at first reflected that view. Soviet judges presided at the Nuremberg trials alongside American, French, and British judges, and pronounced sentence on their former German allies for using slave labor and waging aggressive war (an anomaly Robert Taft did not hesitate to point out in his criticisms of the Nuremberg verdicts). The Russians, Truman wrote in his diary a few weeks after Roosevelt's death, "have always been our friends and I can't see any reason why they shouldn't always be."[13] Truman told Henry Wallace in October 1945, after returning from Potsdam, that "Stalin was a fine man who wanted to do the right thing." When Wallace argued that Churchill and the British were trying to promote a rift between the United States and the USSR, Truman agreed. "He returned to the fact that Stalin is an honest man who is easy to get along with—who arrives at sound decisions."[14]

In fact, Stalin was moving to exploit the weaknesses of postwar Europe for his own gains. He quickly consolidated Communist control in East Germany, Poland, Rumania, and Bulgaria, and later Hungary and Czechoslovakia. His secret police suppressed any prodemocratic political elements that the Nazis had not dealt with before. He laid plans for a new, more militant Communist Party abroad. He ordered the party leadership in Europe and elsewhere to move from the wartime attitude of accommodation to renewed confrontation with the capitalist West. He ousted Earl Browder as head of the CPUSA and replaced him with a pair of more reliable apparatchiks, William Z. Foster and Eugene Dennis.

At the same time, or even slightly earlier, Stalin transferred control over underground Communist networks from the Comintern (which he abolished in 1943) to the NKVD, the ministry in charge of Soviet security and spying, and GRU, or Soviet military intelligence. The Soviets had enjoyed considerable success in placing their agents in Germany before the war, as well as in Japan under master spy Victor Sorge. In Britain, Alexander Orlov's original Cambridge circle of spies—Guy Burgess, Donald Maclean, Anthony Blunt, and Kim Philby—now passed into the hands of the NKVD. In Canada, a similar network included the atom spy Allan Nunn May and Herbert Norman—who later became special assistant to Canadian prime minister Lester Pearson. Its American equivalent was the so-called Ware secret underground network and its offshoots, the Perlo and Silvermaster spy "cells," which operated at the very heart of the New Deal establishment.[15] Given this new Soviet aggressive mood in 1946 and 1947, excessive caution and suspicion would have seemed preferable to excessive trust.

Yet this was precisely the position of the great hope of the New Deal, former Vice President Henry Wallace. The progressive wing of the Democratic Party unanimously treated him as FDR's true heir. Raised a Republican and by conviction a Populist, Wallace had run the same Department of Agriculture that his father had run for Harding and Coolidge. He had made it a byword for innovation and new talent, including several outspoken Communists. Wallace had admired the USSR since the 1920s and commended its leaders for "building a new industrial system out of the wreck that the world war left." Like Lincoln Steffens, Wallace stood convinced that the Soviets had discovered "the future and it works."

He became the quintessential Popular Front liberal, if not a true fellow traveler. His positive view of the Soviets and Stalin mingled with a personal, rather muzzy Christian social democratic vision. *Democracy* was a key word for Wallace, and like other liberals, he found the Communists' constant evocation of the term irresistible. He found Republicans, particularly Robert Taft, far more frightening than Stalin. Wallace swallowed whole the notion that American conservatives were incipient fascists, and in his mind the world war had been an apocalyptic struggle between the forces of "democracy" and the "common man" (meaning liberals and the Soviet Union) and the forces of reaction and "militarism," meaning Hitler and the GOP.

Roosevelt trusted Wallace implicitly and in 1940 made him vice president over objections of old party bosses, who were as contemptuous of his erratic work habits (it was rumored that he fell asleep at cabinet meetings) as his leftward leanings. In the end, Roosevelt decided to replace him with the more conventional Harry Truman. When Roosevelt suddenly died in March 1945, it was Truman, not Henry Wallace, who was the clear heir to the throne of New Deal liberalism.

Harry Truman's own education on the Soviet question was slow and arduous. Contrary to left revisionist myth, Truman was not a cold warrior by instinct. When Winston Churchill gave his "Iron Curtain" speech at Fulton, Missouri, in March 1946, Truman was careful to distance himself from its anti-Soviet tenor. Today, most people recognize Churchill's words as prescient, a wake-up call to the United States about the threat of Stalinism. At the time, however, in the pro-Russian atmosphere of the immediate postwar period, it set off a huge controversy. The only figures in Congress who openly praised the speech were, in the words of two modern historians, "the extreme right wing." New Deal Democrats in Congress denounced the speech as "imperialist" and as a naked attempt to drive a wedge between America and her wartime Russian ally. The State Department's Dean Acheson, who was supposed to welcome Churchill at an official ceremony in New York after the Fulton speech, bowed out at the last minute. Truman himself avoided saying anything that might be taken as endorsing Churchill, and even offered Stalin a chance to come to Fulton at the United States's expense for "equal time" to respond (what Stalin thought of this offer, is unfortunately not recorded).[16]

However, Truman eventually learned that cooperation with the old dictator was impossible and that the only thing Stalin really understood was resolute, iron strength. Wallace was deeply distressed by Truman's hardening attitude. He believed that the way to deal with Stalin was by making concessions and that a tough line would only encourage Soviet militancy—when, in fact, the exact opposite was the case. Wallace pushed hard for the plan to share atomic secrets with the Soviets (a position shared by some other members of the administration, including Henry Stimson and Dean Acheson) and then for demilitarization of its use in the United States. In the end, Truman forced him out. But Wallace quickly found his footing as a spokesman for the old liberal ideals and became editor of the *New Republic*, the flagship journal of Popular Front sentiment. "I intend to carry on the fight for peace," he told a radio audience the night he was forced to resign. Wallace never gave up his view that Soviet system and New Deal America shared the same goals—that they "seem to tend toward the same end although they start from different points"—a point not lost on his conservative critics.

By 1947 Wallace came to believe that he had to oppose Truman personally in the presidential election. His campaign organization had already been prepared for him by the Progressive Citizens of America, a coalition of old Popular Fronters, fellow travelers, and active Communists.[17] In fact, Wallace's Progressive Party became a classic front organization, with active Communists and even espionage agents inserted at every level. Its chairman, C. B. Baldwin, was a secret Communist; his deputy, John Abt, was a member of the Ware spy cell. The platform committee reflected the same dual personality. Its chairman, Rex Tugwell, was one of the old Roosevelt Brain Trust; its recording secretary, Lee Pressman, was another secret Communist; Wallace's favorite speechwriter, Charles Kramer, was actually a NKVD agent.[18]

Together progressives, Communists, and various leftists shaped a platform that pushed New Deal liberalism firmly into the Marxist camp. "We hope for more political liberty and economic democracy throughout the world," it declared. "We believe that war between East and West will mean fascism and death for all." It endorsed Wallace's view that "there are no differences between the Soviet Union and the United States which cannot be reconciled without sacrificing a single American principle or a single American life." The sentence "we condemn the totalitarianism of the Left no less than the totalitarianism of the Right" was dropped. It dismissed anti-Russian sentiment as "a mask for monopoly, militarism and reaction," which now included the Truman administration.

It was the closest the Soviets ever came to choosing and nominating a candidate for the American presidency. On the campaign trail Wallace dutifully read the speeches Kramer prepared for him. He denounced J. Edgar Hoover as an "American Himmler" and accused him of conducting a Hitlerian campaign of terror against liberal government employees. If reporters asked about possible red influence on his campaign, he denied it. But when Hubert Humphrey asked him to control his more radical supporters in Minnesota, Wallace blithely suggested Humphrey talk to the Soviet embassy, since it had more influence over them than he did.[19]

The 1948 campaign, and the hopes it raised among Popular Fronters, proved a disaster. In the atmosphere of the Berlin airlift (which Wallace opposed), the fall of Czechoslovakia (which he blamed on the Americans), and the first revelations about Alger Hiss, the Progressive Party won fewer votes than Strom Thurmond's Dixiecrats. Mainstream liberal Democrats attacked both breakaway wings, but they also recognized that Wallace's Progressives posed the greater danger, to both the Democratic Party and the future of liberalism. They formed a liberal anti-Communist lobby within the party, headed by the Americans for Democratic Action (ADA). Men like Humphrey, Joseph Rauh, and Arthur Schlesinger ended up denouncing the man who had once been their ally and hero, as disappointed Wallace supporters enjoyed pointing out.[20]

The bitter truth was that liberalism's organizational anti-Communist roots were shallow and recent. The first active concern about the Communist threat had come not from within the New Deal establishment but from outside. Its prime mover had been Congressman Martin Dies of Texas and his legislative assistant, J. B. Matthews. In 1938 Dies sponsored a resolution to create what would become the House Committee on Un-American Activities (liberal House members preferred the term *Un-American* since this implied investigating fascist and pro-Nazi groups as well as Communist subversion). Dies and Matthews published a book on domestic totalitarian groups entitled *The Trojan Horse in America*. However, as soon as Dies opened hearings for what would become the Un-American Activities Committee (HUAC) in 1938, he became the object of ridicule and reproach.[21] A flamboyant and self-promoting Hill Country Democrat, Dies was a holdover from an earlier era of red hunting, when communism was associated with "aliens" and foreign immigrants. He vastly exaggerated the totalitarian threat (he once estimated the number of potential Nazi recruits in the United States at half a million), and he labored long and hard to prove that FDR's administration was riddled with Communists. Yet Dies also understood the larger issues at stake. "I regard Communism and Nazism and fascism as having one underlying principle," he said, "dictatorship—the theory that government should have the right to control the lives, the fortunes, the happiness, the beliefs . . . of the human being."[22]

In many ways, Martin Dies prefigured McCarthy's career. Liberals and others were able to rehearse the sort of attacks they would later direct at McCarthy. One hostile biographer called the Dies Committee a "front organization for reactionaries" that had "usurped the authority of the Congress, the executive, and the judiciary."[23] He was accused of punishing people for what they thought rather than did, and of using the whole anticommunism issue for his own political advancement. His assistant, J. B. Matthews, would become one of McCarthy's closest and most valuable advisers.

Whatever political advantage Dies may have sought as Congress's most aggressive red hunter proved elusive. In 1944, in poor health and facing a tough reelection fight, Dies retired. Yet like McCarthy, Dies's only real offense was taking Communists at their word. If they preached the overthrow of the capitalist system, including America, he assumed they meant it. If they saw the New Soviet Man as the future of humanity, shorn of religion and conventional morality, they meant it. If in doing so they found common cause with liberals, then that was the liberals' problem, not their opponents'.[24]

Conservatives like Dies also noticed that anti-Communist liberals like Walter Lippmann and Drew Pearson never seemed to express quite the same vehemence or antipathy toward Stalin and his admirers that they did toward Hitler and Mussolini. To Robert Taft or Joe McCarthy there was no appreciable difference. McCarthy called Nazism "an enterprise of gutter intellectuals to gain the power of a great state" in the guise of national socialism, just as communism "was a drive for power by a disciplined minority with welfare as its cloak."[25] Both systems were vicious, and both posed a similar threat to democratic societies. But liberals were willing to entertain the idea of joining forces, or at least entering a "dialogue," with extremists on the left, while raging about the same illiberal attitudes on the right.

The proof came with the liberals' treatment of extremist figures like right-wing broadcaster Gerald L. K. Smith, the anti-Semitic Father Coughlin, and William Pelley of the Silver Shirts, a self-professed American fascist. Although they were more successful in generating headlines than gaining public support, their presence convinced many liberals that American democracy was threatened by what Heinz Eulau of the *New Republic* called "a fascist-oriented fundamentalism." Sinclair Lewis wrote a novel, *It Can't Happen Here,* which predicted a fascist takeover of the United States; in the nonfiction category, Richard Rollins's *I Find Treason* warned of the threat of a fascist-Republican alliance. In 1936 Popular Front Hollywood offered up the film *Black Legion,* in which Humphrey Bogart portrayed an average American working guy falling in with a gang of jack-booted, black-hooded American storm troopers. Liberal public citizen groups like the Non-Sectarian Anti-Nazi League and the Friends of Democracy published long lists of "pro-Nazi and fascist" groups and their members. The Friends of Democracy launched negative publicity campaigns against selected right-wing targets like the anti-Semitic Smith that were so harsh and abusive their own founder described them as "pitiless." Yet Friends of Democracy had very little to say about the dangers of communism.

American entry into World War II raised fears of a pro-Nazi fifth column to extravagant heights. Hollywood produced a series of films (such as *The Confessions of a Nazi Spy, Across the Pacific,* and Alfred Hitchcock's *Sabotage*) suggesting that Hitler and Hirohito had found willing allies among America's prominent and powerful. Justice for right-wing extremists was swift and sure. The FBI kept Gerald Smith under constant surveillance, and the Justice Department indicted the leader of the anti-Semitic group Defenders of the Christian Faith, and arrested and eventually convicted William Pelley. The Smith Act of 1940, which banned all political groups that advocated the violent overthrow of the United States, was actually hailed by many liberals as useful legislation against the fascist right.[26]

Another significant fruit of that same fear would be the round-up and internment of Japanese-Americans on the Pacific coast. Probably the most massive violation of civil liberties of American citizens in this century, it offers a strange reversal of stereotypes. Opponents to internment included J. Edgar Hoover (who thought it unnecessary) and Robert Taft, the only member of Congress to oppose the internment bill in March 1942. Supporters included leading liberals such as Justices Felix Frankfurter and Hugo Black; the governor of California and future champion of civil rights Earl Warren; and Joseph Rauh of the American Civil Liberties Union (ACLU). A leading organizer of the internment program, Charles Fahy, would later win his reputation as a liberal judge on the Washington, D.C., Court of Appeals by regularly overturning loyalty board decision in the 1950s.[27]

If locking up innocent Japanese-Americans or pro-fascist right wingers made sense during World War II on the grounds that they constituted a "clear and present danger," it seemed the height of hypocrisy to attack similar calls for silencing similar leftist groups, such as the Communists, during the cold war. Yet this is precisely what many leading liberals and Democrats would do. George Seldes of the *Chicago Tribune* was an enthusiastic supporter of the Popular Front. Yet he wrote a series of articles warning about a coming "Axis America," and even wrote a book accusing the American Legion and *Reader's Digest* of being linked to a "Fascist International."[28] California congressman Jerry Voorhis pushed for an investigation of William Pelley's Silver Shirts as part of "an attempt to form a united fascist movement" in the United States, but later cried foul when Richard Nixon used Voorhis's links to Communist front organizations to label him as pro-red. Liberals, even the anti-Communist ones, seemed to believe that the most serious threat to American democracy came from their fellow countrymen on the political right rather than from the sworn agents of Stalin on the left.

Then the *Amerasia* case broke in the summer of 1945. Soon afterward Elizabeth Bentley and Louis Budenz confirmed J. B. Matthews's theory of an underground Communist network, which liberals had dismissed as a paranoid fantasy and which Whittaker Chambers reconfirmed. J. Edgar Hoover's appearance before HUAC on March 2, 1947, not only brought the domestic communism issue into public prominence. It was also a direct slap in the face of the Truman administration for its failure to do something about it.[29]

Yet the effort to take it seriously still hung fire. Under chairman J. Parnell Thomas, HUAC hearings were disorganized and soon degenerated into fishing expeditions. Its inquiries into Communist influence in Hollywood, for example, brought as much discredit to the committee as it did useful information. To the mainstream press, HUAC seemed an outrageous freak show. The Truman administration made plans to abolish the committee if Democrats took back the House in the 1948 elections. And indeed the election proved to be a stunning defeat for Republicans. Their presidential candidate, Thomas E. Dewey, had decided to play it safe. He did not emphasize the domestic communism issue, even though the Eightieth Congress had uncovered some explosive political material. He also steered away from endorsing its tax-cutting, deregulating, and antistatist record, much to the frustration of Joe Martin and Robert Taft, who had wanted to be the Republican nominee.[30]

Truman proceeded to confound the pundits and pollsters by beating Dewey 50 percent to 45 percent (Wallace's Progressives scored 2 percent), and the Democrats recaptured Congress. Truman made plans to take back the ground liberals had lost, including repealing the Taft-Hartley Act.

Chairman Thomas went to prison for pocketing public funds. Congressional investigations into Communist influence in the United States retreated to the back pages.

Yet in retrospect, the 1948 election proved to be the Communist Party's last hurrah. Wallace's embarrassing performance ended the party's bid for political influence; it sank in numbers and influence. It organized one final Popular Front–style international gathering of intellectuals, artists, and academics—the infamous Waldorf Conference on World Peace in New York in March 1949. Meanwhile, Walter Reuther of the United Auto Workers and the CIO's Philip Murray were driving Communist-dominated unions out of their organizations. By 1950 Communist influence over organized labor was virtually a dead letter.[31]

However, the cause it had served, Stalinism, was still on the march. By the end of 1948 Stalin's iron grip over Eastern Europe was secure. Then in January 1949, Communist forces entered Peking. A chastened State Department told the American public that there was no way to prevent Chiang Kai-shek's defeat, and in August it released on 800-page apologia, the China "White Paper," justifying its failure to support the Nationalists. When asked, a majority of Americans rejected the State Department's White Paper's claim that communism's success had been inevitable less out of faith that Chiang might still have won (almost half believed he could not) than out of frustration that the United States seemed so helpless to influence events.[32] A month later, on September 23, 1949, Truman announced that the Soviets had successfully tested their own atomic bomb—following months when Dean Acheson and others had argued that the Soviets could not develop such a weapon until mid-1950 or 1951.[33] The global balance of power was suddenly shifting, to the disadvantage of America and its allies. Confidence that America could contain the advance of communism around the world was replaced by a new fear that the Soviets were winning not because of their inherent strength but because of American weakness. Conservatives were no longer the only ones who worried that America might lose the cold war, not on the plains of Germany or in the mountains of Manchuria but directly in the corridors of power in Washington. Then, suddenly and catastrophically, came the Alger Hiss case.

Four months before Truman's reelection, on August 3, 1948, Whittaker Chambers told HUAC the same story he had told Adolph Berle almost a decade earlier: of how he had helped to run an extensive underground Communist network, organized by Harold Ware, that included figures in various New Deal agencies and departments. The most important, and most senior, of the Ware group had been State Department diplomat Alger Hiss.

Once again, the secret Ware network revealed the links between Communist plans and liberal Democratic aspirations. A committed Communist before 1932, Harold Ware had begun his government service in the Agricultural Adjustment Administration (AAA). Despite its lowly status, AAA had been the cutting edge of progressive young New Dealers for forging a new interventionist role for American government. Its ranks included Adlai Stevenson, Abe Fortas, Thurman Arnold, Telford Taylor, and Alger Hiss—as well as Communists such as Ware, John Abt, Lee Pressman, and Nathan Witt. Liberals like Stevenson were untroubled by the radical Marxist ideas of men like Abt and Witt. In fact, they discovered that they shared a common vision of government, in which an enlightened elite would take over state agencies and use them to intervene in workings of the marketplace for good.[34]

But Ware grew impatient with the New Deal's failure to go further in dismantling the capitalist system, so in 1934 he set up a secret underground network in Washington directly linked to the Soviet Union, with seven cells, each with its own leader. The original members included AAA colleagues Pressman, Abt, Alger Hiss, Witt, Charles Kramer, and Nathaniel Weyl; it soon expanded to include Henry Collins of the National Recovery Administration (NRA), and Victor Perlo, who during World War II moved to the Office of Price Administration. The entire network was connected to Soviet intelligence through CPUSA official J. Peters (whose real name was Jozsef Peter). Whittaker Chambers was Peters's man on the scene.

Peters directed the group to steal documents and memoranda with the help of another secret agent, John Herrmann. But Peters had bigger plans: he hoped to enable cell members to penetrate the State, Interior, Treasury, and War departments and, by rising to senior positions, to influence American policy directly. Like the stolen documents, this slow-motion penetration had to be done secretly. If some cell members like Witt and Abt were already known as Communists, then it was imperative to keep the true identity of others, such as Alger Hiss, hidden.

In 1935, Ware died in an auto accident, and the AAA group lost their jobs and dispersed to other agencies. Peters decided to split the network into two units: the original Ware cell and one headed by Victor Perlo. Eventually that cell included seven members, including one (Harold Glasser) in the Treasury and another in the wartime OSS, the forerunner of the CIA. A third network, headed by Nathan Silvermaster of the Farm Security Administration, also sprang up. Two agents linked to that cell—Solomon Adler and Lauchlin Currie—would have an important role in directing American policy in China and the defeat of Chiang Kai-shek.[35]

Now, more than a decade later, it was a frightening story Chambers had to tell. He detailed how Hiss, another State Department employee named

Julien Wadleigh, and the assistant secretary of the treasury, Harry Dexter White, had stolen government documents and passed them to him and Hermann. This had gone on for four years, until Chambers suddenly left the underground and went into hiding. Since then, Hiss had gone on from strength to strength. He left AAA in 1935 to become assistant counsel with the Senate Committee on the Munitions Industry. Then, with the help of powerful friends, Hiss moved to the Justice Department, before joining State in September 1936. He served as assistant to the department's political affairs officer and then joined its Far Eastern Division, where for the first time he had to confront rumors that he was in fact a Communist.[36] Hiss told the FBI they were lies and then pushed ahead, undeterred. He became deputy director and then director of the Office of Special Political Affairs. He proved invaluable to his seniors because of his easy access to key officials, including those in the White House. Hiss attended the Yalta Conference, and had access to virtually every important State Department document relating to the meeting (hence later accusations that he had engineered the "betrayal at Yalta"). He was executive secretary for the international conference that created the United Nations and served temporarily as its first secretary-general in San Francisco in April 1945. As director of special political affairs, Hiss had access to virtually every classified report coming in or going out of the State Department, as well as constant contact with ranking officers in the War and Navy departments (soon to be the Defense Department).* At forty-one, slim with chiseled features, Hiss stood at the brink of becoming America's premier career diplomat—and yet all the while he was also a secret Soviet agent. Indeed, if Henry Wallace rather than Harry Truman had become president when Roosevelt died in 1945, Hiss might well have become undersecretary of state—with another Soviet spy, Laurence Duggan, as secretary of state and a third, Harry Dexter White, as secretary of the treasury.[37]

Yet the FBI had known about both Alger and Donald Hiss (who also worked for the Ware cell) for years. They warned his superiors, questioned Alger Hiss several times, but although they kept him under constant surveillance for nearly a year, they could not prove their case. Hiss finally left the State Department to become president of the prestigious Carnegie Endowment for Peace in 1947. He had been working there, comfortable and well paid, when Chambers revealed the amazing story of Hiss's Soviet connections.

Alger Hiss angrily and categorically denied the charges. Chambers was

---

*In September 1945, Hiss even proposed attaching a special assistant for military affairs to his office, which would have given him access to information regarding atomic energy, arms procurement, and military intelligence.

"a self-confessed liar, spy, and traitor," Hiss said. Republicans on the committee were using him to launch a vicious partisan offensive against New Deal liberalism. Hiss claimed that the attack on him was actually aimed "to discredit recent great achievements of this country in which I was privileged to participate," including the founding of the United Nations. His superiors and protectors agreed. President Truman dismissed the whole Hiss case as a "red herring"—an unfortunate turn of phrase, as it happened, not just because of the choice of color (although it was a reporter who had used the term red herring in his question), but also because red herring had become a cliché phrase in the Communist *Daily Worker* for describing any attack on the cause of world socialism.

The Hiss case became an instant cause célèbre, with furious exchanges of accusations and denials. A white-faced Harry Dexter White appeared before HUAC to deny that he had ever been a Soviet agent and then went home, where he dropped dead of a heart attack.[38] The political establishment immediately rallied around Hiss. He secured depositions attesting to his excellent character from such eminent figures as Felix Frankfurter, Adlai Stevenson, the majority and minority leaders of the U.S. Senate, Supreme Court Justice Stanley Reed, three former secretaries of state, Eleanor Roosevelt, President Bowman of Johns Hopkins, and Columbia University professor and Carnegie trustee Philip Jessup. Dwight Eisenhower and John Foster Dulles, chairman of the Carnegie Endowment, offered Hiss their support. The mainstream media were skeptical of the charges, while Hiss's lawyers and the left-wing press (especially the *Daily Worker* and *New Masses*) insinuated that Chambers was mentally unstable and a closet homosexual.[39]

In the end, it was Richard Nixon's single-minded determination that Hiss not be allowed to escape that forced the case to its denouement. The confrontation between Nixon and Hiss also involved a cultural clash. Nixon, the son of a grocer from Whittier, California, found the Hopkins- and Harvard-educated Hiss arrogant, insolent, and self-righteous. As the committee's legal counsel later put it, "Nixon set his hat for Hiss." But Nixon was also convinced that Hiss was lying through his teeth. Finally, Chambers offered to the committee a series of documents he had stashed on his farm (the so-called Pumpkin Papers) that largely proved his case. After two wrenching trials, Hiss was convicted of perjury (incredibly, the statute of limitations on espionage had expired) and went to prison. The case for anti-Communist vigilance had been made, along with Congressman Nixon's career. In 1948 both Democrats *and* Republicans in his district nominated him for reelection. He was comfortably poised for a run at the Senate in 1950.

The Hiss case is worth summarizing at length because it served as an important model for McCarthy's later investigative efforts and a model of how he assumed they would come out. Hiss could never have risen as far, or stayed as long, without the willing help of powerful friends and patrons. Long afterward, declassified State Department memos would show that by the spring of 1946, the secretary of state and everyone in the department's security staff believed Hiss was working for the Communist underground, yet no one ordered him out.[40] In the face of official intransigence and denials, the FBI had been helpless to act. It was only when Congress stepped in and dragged the sordid story into the light of day that Hiss was finally brought to justice. It is not surprising that Hiss's most loyal defenders—Dean Acheson, Philip Jessup, and Adlai Stevenson—would be among McCarthy's favorite targets.

At first, the truth about Hiss had been greeted by howls of protest and derision. The press had vilified Hiss's accusers and made *their* credibility, not *his*, the central issue. Then Chambers had proved his case, the truth had prevailed, and Hiss was convicted of perjury. But instead of admitting that they had been wrong, liberals had simply redoubled their attacks or had fallen discreetly silent. In fact, skepticism as to whether Alger Hiss had *really* been a Soviet agent would linger for more than forty years, until evidence from the other side of the iron curtain finally laid the last doubts to rest.[41] As a red hunter, Joe McCarthy was unwilling to wait that long for vindication. His instinct was to press on, and the thicker and faster the assaults on his reputation flew, the more he became convinced he was on the right track.

The final lesson McCarthy learned from the Hiss case was that anyone who accused a member of the Democratic establishment of being a Communist or a Communist dupe sooner or later could make the accusation stick. The lesson other conservatives learned was more profound and disturbing. New Deal liberalism had proved vulnerable on the Communist issue at two levels. First, it was compromised by its associations and flirtations with communism in the thirties. Second, and more devastating, the New Deal establishment liberal, for all his professed anti-Soviet views, seemed unable to deal effectively with the kind of ideological challenge communism represented. Inevitably, he would buckle and give the Communist what he wanted, thanks to his seemingly fatal attraction to the goals and aims, if not necessarily the methods, of communism.

Or so it seemed to critics on the right. At first glance, it seemed to be an absurd and outrageous charge. After all, no one would seem to have more to lose in the face of a proletarian revolution than a wealthy, well-connected member of the Washington establishment, or the president of the Ford Foundation or a prestigious university, or a correspondent for a major newspaper such as the *New York Times*. Yet the historical record reflected again and again the same dismal result of liberals giving the benefit of a doubt to a monstrous political system, or even lying in order to protect it.

There was the *New York Times*'s chief Russian correspondent, Walter Duranty, who had repeatedly lied about the Great Famine in Stalin's Russia in exchange for official favors, and won a Pulitzer Prize. There were the other liberal pilgrims to the Soviet Union, who had seen tyranny unfolding before their eyes and pronounced it freedom.[42] There were reporters in China like Theodore White of *Time*, Brooks Atkinson of the *New York Times*, and Arch Steele of the *Herald Tribune*, who convinced themselves that Mao's Communist cadres were really "agrarian democrats" who could save China. Like the State Department's leading Far Eastern experts, they avoided discussing Mao's links to Soviet communism in order to create a more favorable view in the American public. "We were reluctant to paint them as real Communists," Arch Steele would recall many years later, "because we knew that that would go against the American grain."[43] By downplaying or even covering up Mao's Marxist-Leninist roots, they misled many into believing America could do a deal with the new Chinese regime, at a time when Mao viewed the United States as his prime adversary.[44]

Then there were the Rockefeller Foundation and the Carnegie Endowment, which had provided the seed money for the Institute for Pacific Relations, the Far Eastern policy group with numerous Communists and multiple links to the *Amerasia* espionage case. Harvard and Berkeley had numerous Communist professors on their faculties.[45] Later, liberals would complain bitterly when congressional committees began to ask about Communist infiltration of the universities, or leading foundations, or the press or Hollywood. For McCarthy and his ideological allies, something more important than liberal sensibilities was at stake. If the liberals were left to their own devices, as McCarthy put it in a speech in June 1951, "this nation, this civilization, will pass from the face of the earth as surely as did those other great empires of the past which were destroyed because of weak leadership which tolerated corruption, disloyalty, and dishonesty."[46]

In August 1951, critic Leslie Fiedler published a powerful essay on the cultural aftermath of Alger Hiss's conviction for perjury, entitled "The Age of Innocence." Fiedler had noticed something striking about another accused Soviet spy who had appeared at Hiss's trial, Julien Wadleigh. Like Hiss, Wadleigh was a State Department employee, a self-proclaimed progressive, and a certifiable member of the country's Anglophile establishment. And yet, with the evidence of his own treason laid out before him, Wadleigh "cannot, even in the dock, believe that a man of liberal persuasion is capable of wrong." Fiedler, who was himself a liberal, then oberved:

> It is was this belief that was the implicit dogma of American liberalism during the past decades, piling up a terrible burden of self-righteousness and

self-deceit to be paid for on the day when it would become impossible any longer to believe that the man of good will is identical with the righteous man, and that the liberal is, per se, the hero.

It was time, Fiedler concluded, for liberals to acknowledge that although they had done great good, "we have also done great evil."[47]

It was a crucial point. When American liberals regarded Stalinism and its supporters, they had assumed they were looking in a mirror and seeing themselves: the heroes of history. Joe McCarthy was about to offer up a new kind of hero, the people's tribune, who would save the republic by exposing that arrogance and the liberals' complicity with evil, and stop them in their tracks.

For conservatives the cold war had become the hinge on which the fate of civilization itself would turn. In his Wheeling speech, delivered just two weeks after Hiss was convicted, McCarthy proclaimed that the most important difference "between our western Christian world and the atheistic Communist world is not political, ladies and gentlemen, it is moral." The question in his mind, and in the minds of many other Americans, was which side the liberals were really on.

II

RISE

There is thus a profession of faith which is purely civil and of which it is the sovereign's function to determine the articles, not strictly as religious dogmas, but as sentiments of sociability, without which it is impossible to be either a good citizen or a loyal subject. Without being able to oblige anyone to believe these articles, the sovereign can banish from the state anyone who does not believe them; banish him not for impiety but as an anti-social being, as one unable sincerely to love law and justice, or to sacrifice, if need be, his life to his duty.

—Jean-Jacques Rousseau, *The Social Contract* (1762)

"I don't have much of a case."
"You don't have a choice. . . . Even now they're trying to destroy your credibility. Your only chance is to come up with a case. Something, anything—stir the shitstorm—set off a chain reaction. . . . Fundamentally, people are suckers for the truth. And the truth is on your side."

—*JFK* (movie, 1991)

Chapter 5

The Enemy Within

The alarms of the fall of 1949 extended into the winter. In November the Soviet Zone of occupied Germany established a Communist government, as thousands fled East Berlin for the West. In December the Chinese Nationalists fled to Formosa, while Mao established the People's Republic, which Soviets immediately recognized. By the new year, the issue of recognition of Communist China was inching toward public debate. Despite Secretary of State Acheson's public assurances that there were no such plans in place, no one believed him. In fact, declassified sources now reveal that Acheson had lied. Leaks suggesting that the State Department was planning to abandon Chiang and Formosa in the case of an invasion from the mainland were true. Acheson even entertained suggestions from his staff that the United States should encourage a Formosan nationalist movement, to overturn Chiang and thus get rid of a major obstacle to an accommodation with China. Had these musings become public, they would have fueled the uproar already building about the administration's seriousness in dealing with the Soviet threat.[1]

Robert Taft delivered a major foreign policy address on January 11, 1950, charging that "the State Department has been guided by a left-wing group who have wanted to get rid of Chiang, and were willing at least to turn China over to the Communists."[2] Two weeks later, Alger Hiss was convicted of perjury and sentenced to five years in prison. Testimony had exposed the Communist cells that had been operating in the heart of government and the government's long failure to react. That morning reporters asked Dean Acheson about his views on the conviction. Acheson called the Hiss case a "tragedy" and said, "I do not intend to turn my back on Alger Hiss." He explained his position by referring reporters to the Sermon on the Mount: "I was a stranger, and ye took me in: Naked, and ye clothed me: I was in prison, and ye came unto me."

Acheson believed he was being loyal to an old friend. Most Americans, however, were aghast at the spectacle of a secretary of state defending a man who was, at the very least, a Communist and very probably a Soviet spy. A firestorm broke over the Truman administration. Acheson and the president's office were deluged with hostile mail. Congressman Nixon termed the remarks "disgusting" and his HUAC colleague Karl Mundt called for an investigation of Hiss's continuing influence in State Department circles. McCarthy went to the Senate floor to ask if Acheson intended to protect the other Communists in the government. Nixon warned, "This is only a small part of the whole shocking story of Communist espionage in the United States."[3]

Taken together, the fall of China and the Hiss case were for Democrats a disaster waiting to happen. Now Joe McCarthy decided the time had come to shake up the State Department.

In the autumn of 1945 the Department of State merged with a pack of other executive agencies left over from the war. Almost thirteen thousand employees transferred wholesale to the State Department payroll, ostensibly in the interests of economy.[4] The merger was part of a major reshuffling of the old tradition-bound Foreign Service. Familiar figures like Joseph Grew, Adolph Berle, and Stanley Hornbeck were out; new men like Dean Acheson, John Carter Vincent, William Benton—and Alger Hiss—were in. Of the new employees, more than four thousand stayed on, although many had no security clearances or adequate background files. As evidence of Communist infiltration surfaced in other government agencies, the State Department had barely begun to clear its four thousand new employees, let alone its twenty thousand career employees, none of whom could be dismissed without a formal hearing.[5]

Meanwhile, members of the Democratic Seventy-ninth Congress began to ask questions and demand answers. On July 26, 1946, Secretary of State James Byrnes wrote to Congressman Adolph Sabath of Illinois. "Dear Adolph," he began. "Certain allegations [have been made] on the floor of the House" that thousands of State Department employees had had to be fired for their communistic leanings. This was not true, Byrnes said. Of the four thousand new employees, almost three thousand had been screened "in a preliminary examination," and only 284 were found to be unfit for permanent employment. Of that number, 79 had left. Twenty-six had gone because they were aliens and therefore by statute were unemployable; another 13 were disqualified for one reason or another. Forty had affiliations or connections or "past records, indicating a high degree of security risk." This last group almost certainly included persons with Communist backgrounds, although Byrnes did not feel able to provide any details.[6]

Byrnes felt that this disclosure should be enough to reassure everyone. It was not. That same month Congress had passed a provision to the State Department's appropriation bill (the so-called McCarran rider) permitting the secretary of state to fire any foreign service employee without a hearing if he believed that person to be a security or loyalty risk. In the six months after its passage, the secretary of state exercised that option exactly once.[7] Yet some one thousand new employees as well as all the old State employees remained to be screened.

When the new Republican Congress met in 1947, it faced a massive backlog of security investigations at State. Persons with divided loyalties or varying degrees of unfitness could be handling sensitive documents, assigning staff positions, and preparing reports, even while the proof of their unfitness was mired in red tape. Yet, as the White House was debating what constituted "reasonable grounds" for dismissing security risks from the government, the State Department under Marshall and Acheson was busily dismantling its own security staff. Its security board chairman, Robert Bannerman, and its security director, J. Anthony Panuch, were forced out and replaced by John Peurifoy. On one side, this was not surprising given Panuch's hostility toward his new superiors, which prompted him to make incredible and irresponsible charges against them to the FBI.[8] But on the other, it left State's ability to police its own security in disarray.

The Republicans watched with growing frustration and anger. The House Appropriations Committee looked at the files of 108 "past, present, and prospective" State Department employees still waiting to be processed, and discovered more than enough information to suggest that they were "poor risks." Although he did not recommend dismissing them outright, Congressman Karl Stefan of Nebraska did wonder aloud "why it is that these people are on the payroll when the people of the United States are to get behind the government to fight communism. . . . And here we find them employed in the State Department." The entire committee, Democrats and Republicans, endorsed the report condemning the State Department's negligence. A spokesman then informed Congress that of those 108, 42 had been dismissed.* No one was very reassured; it meant that at least 57 people

---

*That number seems suspiciously similar to Byrnes's claim about 40 being dismissed—more than a year earlier.

whom congressional investigators deemed "poor risks" were still circulating in the State Department at the beginning of 1948.

Some critics would later claim that "only" 108 security risks out of twenty-four thousand State Department employees hardly seems like a major problem. But the investigations had just begun; that number, like the 40 Byrnes had mentioned in his July 1946 letter, would certainly grow once the remaining twenty thousand or so were processed. The situation was murky at best, and it was made murkier still on March 13, 1948, when President Truman ordered all federal employee loyalty files sealed. This meant that when the revelations about Alger Hiss became public that summer, Congress had no way of assessing Hiss's case from any objective evidence. From that point on, anyone who wanted to learn more about possible Communist infiltration in the State Department or any other executive agency had to rely on the word of the sitting officials themselves—not a very trustworthy source, as the Hiss case had proved.

Discontent on the Hill with what was going on seethed for another year. At some point late in 1949, McCarthy learned the gruesome details. He sensed a cover-up and decided to pounce.

Journalists and historians ever since have tried to discover when and why McCarthy decided to launch his one-man anti-Communist crusade. The least credible accounts are McCarthy's own. In 1952 he claimed that shortly after arriving in Washington, he had had lunch with Secretary of the Navy James Forrestal, who told him about the seriousness of the internal Communist threat. Before that McCarthy had noted "that our wise long-time foreign policy was being scuttled," but, he added, "I frankly had no idea that traitors were responsible." Now, "day after day I came into contact with evidence of treason." Then, while visiting friends in Arizona and meeting the "real Americans who are part of the Arizona hills . . . who are the heart and soul and soil of America," McCarthy resolved that he would bring to account "the men who made those policies—the specific traitors or the dupes, well-meaning as they might be."[9] Yet McCarthy told a very different tale to Roy Cohn. Late one night before Thanksgiving in 1949, McCarthy said, he had been approached by a former Army intelligence officer who showed him an FBI report on Communist subversion in the government. McCarthy became an overnight convert to the cause. Nothing exists to corroborate any part of the story, however, and Cohn seems to have been the only person to hear it.[10]

Another frequently cited story has McCarthy eating dinner with Georgetown's Edmund Walsh, dean of the School of Foreign Service, and a group of friends in January 1950. McCarthy confesses he needs a campaign issue for his 1952 reelection bid. Father Walsh says, "How about Communism?" He sketches out the details, and McCarthy likes what he hears. When Walsh and the others warn him he must be scrupulous about his accusations and use of evidence, McCarthy quickly assures them he will and departs—without any intention of heeding them. The Georgetown "Colony dinner" story originally appeared in Drew Pearson's column (Pearson's lawyer was supposed to have been one of the dinner guests). Since the prominent figures at the dinner were all Roman Catholics, the image of Georgetown Jesuits' secretly directing Joe McCarthy's career gives the story a subtle but piquant anti-Catholic flavor. But it has no more basis in hard fact than McCarthy's own mysterious midnight visitor.[11]

For one thing, McCarthy had already begun his anti–State Department activities that previous November. He visited Kenosha on November 15, where he accused State Department of being "honey-combed and run by Communists" and named his first name: John Stewart Service from the *Amerasia* scandal.[12] Anticommunism and Communists in government were solid Republican issues, of course, and McCarthy as a solid Republican was committed to them. And here McCarthy's own account does contain one detail with the ring of authenticity: his conviction that the Democrats were perverting America's traditional role in the world, and the "small group of men" who controlled its foreign policy were not just fuzzy-minded liberal internationalists but front men for traitors. Expose the traitors, was the rationale, and the front men will collapse under their own weight.

McCarthy decided to start the ball rolling with a speech he was scheduled to give on Lincoln's Birthday, on February 9, 1950, in Wheeling, West Virginia. Lincoln's Birthday was a traditional speech-making day for Republican politicians—an opportunity to ruminate on the nature of the GOP and the American political tradition. Many in 1950 were using the occasion to talk about communism and the cold war. McCarthy, however, would put them all in the shade. His talk before the Ohio County Republican Women's Club is one of the most famous, and the least read, speeches in modern American history. It deserves a passing glance.

The speech was actually the product of two newspapermen at the *Washington Times-Herald*, Jim Waters and Ed Nellor. McCarthy had approached Waters first about composing a talk for his Lincoln Day engagement. Waters tried and got stuck, and called in Nellor to help. Nellor's regular beat was Capitol Hill. He had interviewed McCarthy back in 1948 and had found him to be "amusing" but clearly "a lightweight."

Nellor had also been one of the early reporters to latch on to the Hiss case. He accompanied Nixon and Robert Stripling on photo ops as they crossed Whittaker Chambers's farm to the site of the cache of documents dubbed the Pumpkin Papers, which had definitively proven Hiss's guilt in espionage. So it was Nellor, it seems, who first suggested doing a speech on Communists in government. Given Hiss's recent conviction and the speeches by Nixon and Karl Mundt, the issue was much on people's minds—and of course on McCarthy's.

But Nellor could also offer up something to give the issue some solidity. This was the list the House Appropriations Committee had prepared of the 108 security risks in the State Department, with 57 cases still pending. McCarthy's heart must have skipped a beat when he saw the list for the first time: Here was documentary proof that Communists and Communist sympathizers had made themselves at home in the State Department during the Democrats' watch. As Nellor said later, "he was like a kid opening a Christmas present."[13]

In 1946 McCarthy had told voters he intended to get the Communists off the government payroll. Now that promise became an imperative, thanks to the tense and uncertain cold war atmosphere. The fall of China, the Soviet atomic bomb, the conviction of Alger Hiss, and on February 3, the arrest of Klaus Fuchs for atomic espionage—the junior senator from Wisconsin, still struggling to make a name for himself, had finally found a live issue.

The version of this speech that McCarthy's office later issued as the official text is probably closest to his true intentions, although it may differ from what people heard on February 9 (the speech was broadcast, but no recording survives). McCarthy did not read speeches as written (his speech on General George Marshall in 1951 was a rare exception). He added and embellished, digressed and expanded, improvised and harangued. Before delivering the Wheeling speech, he also scribbled some changes on the page, changes that would turn out to be its most controversial part.

McCarthy's main points were familiar ones to anyone who paid attention to recent Republican rhetoric about the origins and nature of the cold war. McCarthy described how the end of World War II had left Americans with a feeling of goodwill and peace for the future and how that feeling had been betrayed. "For this is not a time of peace. This is a time of the 'cold war,'" he pointed out, with the world divided into two "increasingly hostile armed camps." He spoke of how America had emerged as the most powerful nation on earth, "a beacon in the desert of destruction," and "a shining living proof that civilization was not yet ready to destroy itself." And how in six short years, the communistic world had expanded from 180 million to 800 million people "under the absolute domination of Soviet Russia," while America sat helplessly by as Stalin devoured entire nations and societies in his path.

The reason for this helplessness, McCarthy said, had nothing to do with the strength of communism or the Soviet Union. It was the result "of the traitorous actions of those who have been so well treated by this Nation," who have had "the finest homes, the finest college education, and the finest jobs in Government we can give." America was being betrayed by "bright young men who are born with silver spoons in their mouths," and who have become the secret allies of the Soviet Union. Alger Hiss was only the most recent example: "He is representative of a group in the State Department" who were still selling out the nation to the Communists. He mentioned John Stewart Service and one or two others, and then he said something like this:

> While I cannot take the time to name all the men in the State Department who have been named as active members of the Communist Party and members of a spy ring, I have here in my hand a list of 205—a list of names that were made known to the Secretary of State as being members of the Communist Party and who nevertheless are still working for and shaping policy in the State Department.

That was news. McCarthy wrapped up by hoping that Dean Acheson's shameless defense of Alger Hiss would spark "a moral uprising" on the part of the American people and lead to "a new birth of national honesty and decency in government." Then he left the stage. The next morning he was flying to Salt Lake City, Denver, and Reno. On the way to the airport he glanced over the *Wheeling Intelligencer*'s excerpts from the speech, particularly about Communists still at work in the State Department.[14]

At first there was not much of a rumble. An Associated Press account of the speech was carried by only eighteen papers on February 10 and ten others on February 11. But when McCarthy arrived in Reno that Saturday, he was met with a telegram from the State Department's assistant secretary for administration, John Peurifoy, demanding the names of the 205 alleged Communists. The story began to get legs. "STATE DEPARTMENT HAS 205 COMMIES," blared the headline in the *Nashville Tennessean*, and United Press carried the story of the State Department's challenge to the rest of the country.[15]

There were two questions every journalist who covered the story wanted to ask. First, what was the list McCarthy was referring to? Second, where did the number 205 come from? The answer was that McCarthy was using the list of 108 "poor risks" that Nellor had acquired from former House staffer Robert Lee (known forever after as the Lee list), and reading it in the light of the Sabath letter that mentioned finding 284 security risks and dismissing 79. A little simple arithmetic left 205, of whom, McCarthy reckoned, at least 57 from the Lee list were at last report still working in the State Department. To the last, McCarthy always insisted that *he had never said he had a list of 205 names, whether Communists or non-Communists.* What he *had* were the names of 57 people identified as Communists and security risks in the State Department, and he would cling to that number, not 205, for the rest of his speaking tour.

Yet his version of what he said bristles with problems. For one thing, Mc-Carthy's speech had the number 205 written on the page—although in versions he gave the press, *205* was crossed out and *57* written in. Some people who listened to the speech would remember hearing him say 205, although no recording survived to check.* The confusion over numbers was important for two reasons. First, by later denying under oath that he had ever uttered the words "a list of 205," McCarthy laid himself open to perjury charges, which his opponents sought to prove on numerous occasions. Second, the claim that the State Department "knew" it had 205 disloyal employees bore far less relation to the truth than a claim about 57. Even that latter figure was more than two years old; there was no way McCarthy could tell how many of those had been dismissed in the interim. That, of course, was part of Mc-Carthy's point: *there was no way of telling.*[16] But the confusion McCarthy fostered over whether he was talking about 205 Communists, or 57, or 81 (that would came up a little later) gave birth to his reputation for recklessness, obfuscation, and untruth.

It also obscured the fact that McCarthy was making a good point badly. The Truman administration, he was saying, knew there were employees who were security risks working in its own State Department, and it had done little about it. People needed to ask how they got in there in the first place, and why it took so long to get them out—and how many more there might be. But behind those questions was McCarthy's most explosive charge. A critical but sympathetic observer might argue that the State Department's problems had been an avoidable accident and the result of bureaucratic inertia. McCarthy was saying they were deliberate and the result of treason.

To McCarthy's surprise and delight, reporters were starting to besiege him with questions the moment he stepped off the plane and to follow him to his hotel, just as they would follow him everywhere he went for the next five years. In Reno McCarthy told the press he had sent a telegram to the White House summarizing his charges. He warned President Truman that if he did not order Dean Acheson to release everything he knew about disloyal persons still working in the State Department and revoke the order sealing all loyalty

---

*The changes he made in the rest of the speech suggest that he had penciled in the number 205, then with the Lee list changed it to 57—as copies indicate. In the flow of the speech, he repeated 205 by mistake. Perhaps he caught himself and said 57. Perhaps not. No one knows now, and no one really knew then.

files, he would be labeling the Democratic Party "the bed-fellow of international Communism."* Truman angrily fired back the next day: "Your telegram is not only not true. . . . It shows conclusively that you are not even fit to have a hand in the operation of the Government of the United States."

Two reporters managed to catch McCarthy in George Malone's office in Reno, talking on the telephone to someone in Washington about the publicity his speeches had been getting. He was repeatedly tapping the receiver with a fountain pen and told the astonished reporters that this was to break up any wiretap.[17] He stopped, listened intently, and began writing down some names. "That's great, that's great," McCarthy said, "give me some more." The reporter looked over his shoulder and read the name "Howard Shipley." Later, when some other reporters asked him where he was getting his names, McCarthy grimly smiled. "I've got a sockful of shit," he said, "and I know how to use it."

He was, however, still changing his story. In Salt Lake City McCarthy spoke of "fifty-seven card-carrying Communists" in the State Department. When he spoke in Reno at the Mapes Hotel, they became "fifty-seven cases of individuals who would appear to be either card-carrying members or certainly loyal to the Communist Party," and "are working for the State Department" had changed to "are still helping to shape our foreign policy." He also rounded off the Sabath letter numbers to "300 security risks," of whom only "80" had been dismissed. McCarthy would discuss only 4, none of them exactly household names. None was on the Lee list either: John Stewart Service, Mary Jane Keeney, Gustavo Duran, and Harlow Shapley (obviously, the "Howard Shipley" he had written down earlier).

They were an ill-fitting mix. Service was an experienced political officer in the State Department's Far Eastern Division and a leading China expert. Both Mary Jane Keeney and Gustavo Duran, a Spanish émigré, had jobs at the United Nations, and Harlow Shapley was a professor of astronomy temporarily employed at UNESCO. After the speech and enthusiastic applause from four hundred Republican backers, reporters asked him if he was saying those four were traitors. "No," he admonished them, "and I didn't call them Communists, either." Under questioning, he admitted, "I should have had a line in there saying they were specific cases of people with Communist connections." The reporters, and the audience, were a little disappointed. The *Chicago Sun-Times* headline read, "SENATOR MCCARTHY NAMES 4 'REDS,' THEN BACKS DOWN."[18]

Meanwhile, the hostile editorials were beginning to appear. The *Wash-*

---

*He added: "Certainly this label is not deserved by hundreds of thousands of loyal Democrats throughout the nation and . . . in both the Senate and the House."

ington Post ran one called "Sewer Politics," which accused McCarthy of "political foul play" and evasion. "Rarely," it concluded with understandable exaggeration, "has a man in public life crawled and squirmed so abjectly." On February 13, as McCarthy arrived in Las Vegas, the State Department's Peurifoy held a news conference in which he flatly denied every one of McCarthy's assertions. He stated that if he learned of a single Communist working in his department, that person would be "fired before sundown." Since 1947, he said, 16,075 State Department employees had been investigated, and not a single one had been found to be disloyal or a Communist. Not one.[19]

Of the four people McCarthy had named, Peurifoy added, only John Service was still employed in the Department of State, and he and Gustavo Duran had been specifically cleared by the department's loyalty board. When Senate majority leader Scott Lucas heard this, he told the press that if he had made McCarthy's charges, "I would be ashamed of myself for the rest of my life." He was obviously implying that McCarthy did not have a leg to stand on and was making everything up as he went along.

Yet the White House was privately worried about where McCarthy was getting his information.[20] Underneath the confident denials, and the contemptuous dismissals from a sympathetic press, lay a gnawing doubt. What if McCarthy had somehow stumbled onto another Hiss case? Truman's approval ratings had slipped to 45 percent in January (by May they would be down to 37 percent). Could his presidency survive another spy scandal like the one unmasked by House Republicans in 1948? In many ways, the vehemence of the Democrats' attacks against McCarthy for the next several months stemmed from a mixture of frustration, after having been so badly fooled in the Hiss case, and fear. If Democrats couldn't undo the damage from that previous fiasco, they could at least direct all their anger at this ill-mannered political novice and prevent another.

So they would charge that he had manufactured his evidence, was ignorant of his own charges, and was willing to launch these reckless and fantastic charges simply to get headlines. However, there was one charge that not even his harshest liberal critics were willing to make: that he was exaggerating the secret Communist threat.

Conspiracy theories have been part of the American political tradition since before the Republic. In 1765 John Adams blamed the thirteen colonies' problems with the British crown on "a wicked confederacy" of corrupt Anglican clerics and aristocrats who were using their power to force the people into "a blind, implicit obedience of civil magistracy." The "paranoid style" extended in the nineteenth century to fears of conspiracies of Catholics; then Jacobins; then Freemasons. After the Civil War, it was Negro freedmen, or international Jewish finance, or, in the minds of radicals like Jack London and John Reed, wicked capitalists who pulled the strings on political events around the world. Then came the red scare. In the thirties, liberals like Jerry Voorhis pushed Martin Dies into investigating a supposed "unified fascist conspiracy" against the United States.

However, American communism achieved something unique. For the first time, it introduced an element of reality to this interplay of fear and fantasy. Like its Soviet counterpart, American communism was built and thrived on the power of conspiracy to achieve its objectives.

It is hard today to realize how much of the anti-Communist rhetoric about "red infiltration" and "subversion" reflected the underlying truth about the Communist movement itself. Anyone who has been raised to believe reflexively that talking about a Communist conspiracy constitutes McCarthyism lacks the fundamental tools for understanding exactly how much of what McCarthy said was in fact accurate and how much was not.

Secrecy had been essential to the survival of bolshevism in czarist Russia, and those habits and mentality carried over after the Revolution in 1917. Lenin wrote that "conspiracy is so essential a condition . . . that all other conditions [such as the number and selections of members and their functions] must be made to conform to it."[21] Clandestine organization and activities became the hallmark of the Communist International (Comintern) and of Communist parties in other countries. In 1930 Comintern official B. Vassiliev wrote to the CPUSA that "all legal Parties are now under the greatest responsibility in respect to the creation and strengthening of an illegal apparatus . . . [and] an illegal directing core." Breaking the law and lying posed no difficulties for the dedicated Communist; the rule of law and keeping one's word represented the sort of "false" bourgeois institutions a proletarian revolution would overthrow.

The CPUSA learned to work hand in glove with Soviet espionage efforts. Recently released documents from the Soviet Union show that the CPUSA's leading officials regularly recruited Americans to spy for Stalin and helped Communist agents penetrate the wartime OSS and the Manhattan Project.[22] The party also received large secret subventions from the USSR throughout its history, laundered by pro-Soviet businessmen like Armand Hammer. The party leadership always understood that its underground apparatus and its covert agents were as important as overt political activities or union organizing.[23]

The effort paid off. By the war's end there may have been as many as 350 secret Soviet agents working in the United States, in addition to the fifty-four thousand party members who were in effect their willing accomplices. Some spies were illegals, who had been smuggled in with false passports, like J. Peters of the Ware cell. But most were American born and bred. Covert penetration of the federal government was by no means limited to the Ware network. In the thirties, Communists secretly installed themselves in the National Labor Relations Board, the Senate Education and Labor Committee, the National Youth Administration, the Senate's Wheeler Committee investigating the railroad industry, the National Research Project of the Works Progress Administration, the Federal Theater Project, the Treasury—and the Department of State.[24] The war boosted the numbers even more, as temporary agencies like the Office of War Information, OPA, and the OSS provided new havens for eager and able bureaucrats who also happened to be Communists.

How many government secrets did they steal? How much damage did they really do? No one will ever really know. But Allan Weinstein and Alexander Vassiliev, two scholars who have had recent access to the KGB's own archives, compiled a list of the classified materials taken by its American sources and agents in the thirties and forties. It ran to over 150 single-spaced pages. And Weinstein and Vassiliev admit that this probably represents only a fraction of the total.[25]

However, anyone trying to track the Communist presence in government, business, or labor unions usually drew a blank because the party's strategy of deceit included party members' disguising their affiliation. Some of the most dangerous and highly placed covert agents, such as Alger Hiss and Britain's Kim Philby, were not identifiably Communist or even leftist; the men and women who actually ran the underground, of course, did not "exist" at all. But even people who were not actually agents were under strict orders to keep their membership in the party secret. Figures who were integral to the Communist Party's larger strategy, like Longshoreman's Union organizer Harry Bridges, or C. B. "Beanie" Baldwin of the Progressive Citizens of America, or Frederick Vanderbilt Field of *Amerasia* and the left-leaning Institute for Pacific Relations (IPR), a group with a shadowy history (see Chapter 8), could truthfully claim not to be formal Communists. Under oath others would deny or evade questions about party membership—hence the term "Fifth Amendment Communist." In short, the Communist Party itself erased the distinction between being a Communist (an open member of CPUSA) and "being a Communist" in the sense of secretly following orders and pursuing the same goals as the Soviets. One could protest to a congressional committee or a jury, "I am not a Communist," and be telling the truth in the first, strict sense, but lying and misleading in the second.

In the early days of the cold war, when fears about Soviet spies became a reality, the American public ran up against a classic problem familiar to all counterintelligence operatives: that the deepest and most dangerous agent is the one most difficult to detect. A lack of any Communist or leftist affiliations could simply be good cover for someone who was a spy. Because the party's inner workings were so secret, proving intent to commit espionage or even party membership to the satisfaction of an American court of law was extraordinarily difficult, often impossible.

What the public did not realize was how much the professionals already knew about the Soviet espionage problem. This was not just because of Whittaker Chambers's revelations or Elizabeth Bentley's. Since 1939 the government had been intercepting coded or encrypted Soviet diplomatic cables, and wondering what they said. By 1942 specialists had managed to crack Japan's diplomatic codes and the German Enigma system. So why not the Russian version (setting aside for the moment the fact the Russians were currently allies)? In February 1943 a decoding office secretly opened its doors in a former girls' school in northern Virginia. Insiders with Army intelligence would refer to the decoding operation by the name of the school, Arlington Hall. Others, including modern historians, use its official code name: Venona.

The Venona codebreakers found themselves looking at thousands of intercepted cables, with each secret message arranged in blocks of character sets or letters, for which only one key existed for messages that specific day (the so-called one-time pad). It was not until 1945 that American cryptographers managed to get their hands on a partly damaged one-time pad to help with some of the decryption; otherwise, they had to rely on their own hard work and intuition to try to crack the Soviet code.[26] It was not until the summer of 1946 that an Arlington Hall cryptographer named Meredith Gardner decoded the first set of secret KGB code sets, which referred to Soviet spying efforts in Latin America. On December 20, Gardner picked up another cable and managed to decipher enough character sets to get a sense of the cable. To his amazement, it was a list of atomic scientists working at the supersecret research center at Los Alamos. Army intelligence had found the first clue that the Soviets had successfully penetrated the American nuclear weapon effort. The next important cable disclosed that the Soviets also had a source on the War Department's general staff. The race to figure which government employees and public servants the KGB and GRU (Soviet army intelligence) might have recruited to spy for them had begun.

The problem with the Venona decrypts, as they were called, is that the information they disclosed was retrospective. A cable sent in 1942 or 1943 might not be decoded until four years later, long after any damage to national security had already been done. A good example was the cable relating to a Soviet agent code-named Liberal, who clearly had enjoyed access to classified secrets relating to the atomic bomb since 1944 and who became known to Army Intelligence (or G-2) only when the cables were decoded in 1947. Fortunately, one of the cables relating to Liberal's wife mentioned her directly by name: Ethel. It required a quick personnel check to confirm that Soviet agent Liberal was in fact Julius Rosenberg and that Ethel Rosenberg's brother, David Greenglass, was also a pivotal figure in the spy ring. Venona made it possible to catch the culprits, but not until after the fact. Taking preventive action against the Soviet effort was going to require more hands-on measures, such as secret surveillance, wiretaps, and the occasional discreet burglary, which demanded skills other than those at Arlington Hall.

By 1948, when G-2 brought the FBI in on the project, Venona was providing an incomplete but precious series of snapshots of Soviet underground activity throughout the forties. However, it also remained profoundly secret; even the White House was kept in the dark about the fact that Venona had turned up at least two hundred active Soviet agents operating in the United States (not to mention American agents run by Soviet military intelligence, or GRU, about which Venona as yet disclosed nothing), as well as hundreds of other sources or contacts. Some were low-level contacts, but at least fourteen were working inside the OSS, and no fewer than five others had direct access to the White House.[27] The Venona decrypts were crucial to shaping attitudes about Communist penetration of security officers like Hoover—attitudes that liberal critics, who were unaware of what was happening, dismissed as right-wing paranoia.

Then in 1949 the FBI learned that its own counterespionage efforts were themselves being betrayed by a Soviet agent in the Justice Department, named Judith Coplon. Agents caught her in the New York subway passing documents to her controller, Valentin Gubitchev. They also learned that when the Justice Department had hired her in 1944, it knew about her Communist associations but took her on anyway. The Coplon case was doubly frustrating because her conviction was overturned on appeal on technical grounds, even though the evidence was overwhelming that she was a Soviet spy.[28] Much the same had happened in the *Amerasia* case four years earlier. Hoover and other intelligence officials became quite cynical about their chances of prosecuting Soviet espionage cases in the courts, and about the support they could count on from government bureaucrats in getting Communists out of sensitive posts. Hoover would support McCarthy's efforts to ferret out Communists in government, at least at the beginning, partly because Hoover believed that whatever McCarthy's obvious shortcomings, he was willing to do something about the problem.

Anyone trying to assess the "Soviet threat," then, had to take into account between two hundred and four hundred active espionage agents; fifty-four thousand Communist full-time party members and, according to Hoover's own estimate, at least a half-million active sympathizers, who were protected constitutionally from surveillance or even close scrutiny—protected, as it happened, by the very laws that Communists wished to see destroyed in order to establish a foreign utopian dream. In this sense America faced a threat far out of proportion to the actual size of the Communist Party or its secret apparatus. The real danger was not that the Communists might take over the country or organize a coup or give away government secrets (although that is what they did in the Manhattan Project). Rather, through their agents and networks, Communists could set in motion a series of actions or bureaucratic decisions at crucial moments, or leak classified or background information, or set traps for the unwary that would undercut America's ability to deal effectively with Stalin's cold war maneuvers. The term *subversion* literally means "turning from underneath." It could take large dramatic forms—again, the theft of atomic secrets gives the ready example. But it could also take innumerable small forms—subversion could be almost imperceptible without a clear understanding of what was going on behind the scenes.*

Taken together, all this added up to a massive and intractable security problem. Hence the pressing need for security and loyalty screening programs. In July 1946 the House of Representatives urged setting up a commission to study how a single program could be created for the entire federal government and what criteria for hiring and firing should be applied. Truman dragged his feet until the 1946 election made it clear that the American electorate wanted some action on the anti-Communist front. Two weeks after

---

*A good example is how Soviet agents in the Treasury, including Harry Dexter White, Solomon Adler, Frank Coe, and Harold Glasser, managed to stall the Roosevelt administration's dispatch of $200 million in gold to the Chinese Nationalists to prop up their faltering currency. White and the others convinced Treasury Secretary Morgenthau that the gold was largely unnecessary or would be stolen, and urged caution in delivery. By July 1944, of $200 million promised, only $12 million had reached China. At the other end, Adler and Coe introduced a secret Communist agent, Chi Ch'ao-ting, into the Nationalist government as adviser on monetary policy. By the time shipments resumed under Truman in May 1945, it was too late. The Nationalist yen had collapsed, and rampant inflation and a worthless currency (all under Ting's direction) set the stage for Chiang Kai-shek's defeat in the coming civil war. Details are in Rusher, *Special Counsel*, pp. 100–102.

the Republican victory, Truman appointed the first temporary loyalty board, which became permanent in March 1947. Over the next six years the board would permit the FBI to look over some 4.7 million job applications of existing and prospective federal employees. Questions of loyalty or pro-Soviet leanings arose in 26,236 cases: 16,503 would be cleared, others would appeal, and almost 7,000 would leave the civil service voluntarily. Exactly 560 persons, out of more than 2 million employees, were dismissed or denied a federal job between November 1947 and the end of April 1953.[29]

By then even liberals understood something had to be done. The ADA endorsed the program, as did columnist James Wechsler of the *New York Post*. Sidney Hook explained that "the purpose of the security program is not punishment for acts committed but prevention of acts" by those who are either active agents or those *"whose behavior or habits make them dangerous risks."*[30] First, the program assumed that government employment was a privilege, not a right. Critics then and later would complain that denying people a job on the basis of their political beliefs violated civil liberties and free speech. Chief Justice Fred Vinson had the standard reply: "The First Amendment requires that one be permitted to believe what he will. It does not require that he be permitted to be the keeper of the arsenal."

Then one had to distinguish between "security risks"—people who were unfit because they were alcoholics or compulsively indiscreet or subject to blackmail for philandering or homosexuality—and "loyalty risks"—people who were unfit because their first priority was advancing the cause of communism and the Soviet Union. Then the review board members had to recognize that guilt by association might be unfair tactics in a courtroom but permissible for deciding whether someone should keep a federal job. A policeman whose best friends are drug dealers might not be engaged in criminal activity, but one can legitimately ask why he is allowed to remain on the police department payroll. One had to distinguish between rules of evidence in a legal sense and evidence that was, in Sidney Hook's words, "bearing on a person's qualifications for a position of trust."

Here, ironically, security officers benefited from the New Deal's openness to communism in the thirties and early forties. On the negative side, Communists and Communist sympathizers, including active sources and agents, had been able to get sensitive government jobs almost with impunity. On the other, that made it easy to identify them, thanks to their open membership in front organizations or other groups on the attorney general's continuing list of subversive organizations.[31] This sort of evidence was often useless for identifying the dangerous spy, who would avoid any political affiliation whatsoever. But it could expose someone whom Communists could manipulate through a basic ideological commitment or sympathy.

From this perspective, the four people McCarthy had named in Reno turned out not to be quite as clean and innocent as Peurifoy and the State Department claimed. Gustavo Duran, for example, turned out to be not only a Communist but a central figure in Stalin's cold-blooded purge of his Trotskyite and anarchist allies during the Spanish Civil War. Duran had been an officer in the notorious SIM, the Spanish Communist secret police that conducted many of the arrests and mass shootings. When Franco's forces took over Spain, Duran had fled to the United States, where Ernest Hemingway convinced the American ambassador of Cuba, Spruille Braden, to hire him as an assistant. Someone in Army intelligence told Braden about Duran's sordid past, but Braden brushed their warnings aside. Later he brought Duran back to the United States, where he found him a job at State. In October 1946 Duran left and took a management position at the United Nations.[32]

When McCarthy first brought up his charges, friends and associates rushed to Duran's defense. Duran himself protested his innocence and made a long, sensitive face when pressed on the evidence. Liberal intimates like Michael Straight of the *New Republic* indignantly dismissed it, including testimony from Spain's former Socialist prime minister and a photograph of Duran in SIM uniform, as right-wing Francoist propaganda. "The ordeal of Gustavo Duran" became famous in anti-McCarthy circles as proof of the insanity of the red scare. Of course, what Straight did not tell his readers was that he himself had been recruited as a Soviet agent while studying at Cambridge University and had been a co-conspirator along with Anthony Blunt, Kim Philby, Burgess, and Maclean. Straight became one of the most eloquent critics of the loyalty program and of Joe McCarthy.[33]

In the thirties, Philip and Mary Jane Keeney were librarians by profession and members of the Communist Party. Philip lost his job at the University of Montana because of his radical activities, but then found a position at the Library of Congress in 1940. He joined the OSS during the war, and Mary Jane ended up the Bureau of Economic Warfare (BEW)—but not before both of them had been recruited by Soviet military intelligence, the GRU.

Venona and other sources provide little direct information about what work the Keeneys did for their Soviet spymasters. Philip's position as OSS librarian, with access to hosts of sensitive and classified materials, must have made him a useful recruit. In any case, toward the end of the war (that is, between August 1944 and November 1945), they moved from GRU handlers to the KGB. By then Philip was working on MacArthur's staff in occupied Japan, and Mary Jane on the Allied Staff on Reparations in Germany and then Federal Economic Administration, which in 1946 became part of the State Department.

However, their espionage careers were about to be cut short. The FBI was beginning to catch on to what they were doing, in the aftermath of the Bentley-Gouzenko defections. Agents broke into Mary Jane's New York apartment and photographed her diary, which diligently listed all her meetings with her KGB handlers. What the Soviets would have thought if they had known about this sort of indiscretion is not difficult to guess. It did cost both the Keeneys their employment with the federal government, but only temporarily.[34] Mary Jane soon found a new slot for herself—with the United States delegation at the UN, where she established ties to the Soviet espionage networks operating there. In fact, the entire story of the Soviet spy ring in the United Nations is a classic example of how the federal government was missing what was happening under its nose in regard to Stalinist espionage.

In 1947 former State Department employees had warned that the United Nations was honeycombed with Communist agents, and so Secretary of State George Marshall appointed a citizens' commission to investigate. They returned with a confident dismissal of the allegations as "irresponsible" and damaging to the United Nations's public image. The *New York Times* chimed in with the hope that their finding would end "hysteria" about Red spies at the United Nations.[35]

How did this massive breach of security occur? In the early spring of 1946 the Office of Special Political Affairs decided to leave all security clearance decisions regarding Americans working at the United Nations to that body rather than to the State Department. It sent to the secretary general lists of names of former State jobholders to the United Nations's secretary-general for prospective hire. Forty-three became permanent employees. The head of special political affairs in 1946 was—Alger Hiss.

The story did not end there. The State Department had reversed its policy regarding United Nations employees in 1949 and ruled that there were to be no Communists on its payroll. At that time it knew Keeney had been considered an adverse risk, but it did nothing. It was not until *after* McCarthy brought up her name that the State Department began to pay attention to her file. It ordered her suspended on December 27, 1950, and she lost her job in the United Nations Documents Bureau at the end of March 1951. In the end, no one could prove beyond doubt that she was actually a Soviet courier at the United Nations or whether she was still working for the KGB. But the fact that the State Department took almost five years to sever its contacts with her did not exactly refute McCarthy's claim that its security program was a charade.

At first glance, the evidence against John Stewart Service seems overwhelming. He had been arrested in June 1945 along with *Amerasia*'s staffers, and many of the classified documents found on the premises had come from Service's files. But Service's role in the affair was both less, and more, than appearances made out. A missionary's son, Service had been born in China, in Szechwan province, and was one of the more gifted China hands in the State Department. He was a year younger than McCarthy, tall, lean, and darkly handsome—Gregory Peck to McCarthy's Broderick Crawford. In 1944 he had enthusiastically urged sending an American mission to the Communist base in Yenan, and Service became the first American civilian to meet Mao Tse-tung in an official capacity.

There he became a convert to Mao's cause. He began to refer to the guerrillas as "so-called Communists" and tell his superiors that they represented a movement for "agrarian reform, civil rights, and establishment of democratic institutions." His warmth toward the Maoists got him in trouble with the pro–Chiang Kai-shek faction in the embassy; they sent him home in 1945. There he met Philip Jaffee and Andrew Roth of *Amerasia*. He began leaking information to them in order to damage the Nationalists, whom he despised, even though he clearly knew Jaffee had secret Communist connections.

Service's guilt in the *Amerasia* affair remains unclear, and historians still debate whether he actually passed on highly classified material or once said in a bugged hotel room to Jaffee, "What I just said about military plans is very secret," as the FBI claimed.[36] Lauchlin Currie, the Soviets' man at the White House on China policy, pulled strings and managed to protect him from prosecution; he was even reinstated. But Service's real problem was his connections in China. As political officer in Chungking he had become friends with the Treasury Department's Solomon Adler, who was certainly a Soviet agent, and Chi Ch'ao Ting, the Chinese Communist mole in the Nationalist government. Service and his defenders argued, rightly, that associating with "radicals" and others who did not hew to the American line was part of his job. The question was whether the association went beyond the professional. At the very least, his arrest in the *Amerasia* case ought to have cast doubt on Service's judgment, if not his loyalty. But his superiors had decided to keep him on.

The case of Harlow Shapley was less dramatic than the other three. He was the typical fellow traveler. He had organized the Waldorf Conference and was famous for his unending credulity regarding anything the Soviets said. But Shapley, a Harvard professor of astronomy, also had the unusual distinction of being even more committed to the Stalinist cause *after* the Nazi-Soviet Pact. By the time McCarthy discovered him, Shapley had joined more than twenty-one front organizations, eight of them on the attorney general's baleful list. As with Keeney and Duran, the State Department tried to claim that Shapley was not one of their employees. But in fact, as a member of the UNESCO delegation, Shapley was paid through State Department funds (as were Keeney and Duran). And since he was a member of groups the attorney general had ruled subversive, keeping him on the payroll was a clear violation of the law.[37]

Four different individuals, four different relationships with the Soviet Union and communism. The alien with a hidden past, the underground courier, the aider and abettor of spies, the fellow traveler and dupe: each had been compromised in one respect or another. In 1950 the Truman loyalty board had been up and running for more than two years. Yet all four were considered fit to be on the State Department payroll.

Of course, nothing was quite that simple. How much history did one have to go over to detect a double life like Duran's? How many front organizations did someone have to join before one stopped being a misguided liberal and became a fellow traveler like Shapley? How did one distinguish secret Communists from those who merely sympathized and promoted their views, like Service? And how did one separate out the really dangerous spies—a Mary Jane Keeney or Judith Coplon, or Harry Dexter White—from all the rest? Loyalty boards and security officers had to learn to make decisions on what evidence was put in front of them. Often they made contradictory or poor ones.[38] But we should remember that they were struggling with a real problem, not a witch-hunter's fantasy.

The Wheeling speech was McCarthy's first venture into this dark, bloody, and confusing arena. Unlike others, he decided to lump where others took care to split, and to use his accusations to break the administration wide open.

Chapter 6

The Tydings Committee

I n the late afternoon of February 20 McCarthy went to the Senate floor to deliver a formal denunciation of the State Department's security program. In defiance of the critics and using the Lee list, he offered details on eighty-one State Department employees, including a White House speechwriter, David Demarest Lloyd, who were, he said, either known Communists or known security risk.

The speech took six hours. McCarthy was subjected to a constant battery of interruptions and insulting questions from Democratic senators (majority leader Scott Lucas interjected himself sixty-one times) while Republicans tried to bolster his claims. When the Senate finally adjourned fifteen minutes before midnight, the main issue boiled down to this: Had McCarthy's public airing of his charges of Communists in the State Department rendered the country a signal service (as Republicans contended), or was it unsubstantiated malicious gossip, none of which McCarthy had proved and which did a disservice to patriotic government employees "who are attempting to carry on in the great world crisis in which we find ourselves," as Senator Lucas put it?[1]

The furor over McCarthy's charges makes sense only when viewed against a larger political backdrop: the constant battle between Democrats and Republicans for control of government. On one side, Republicans were looking for an issue to break Democratic dominance, just as any other opposition party would. On the other, Democrats were deeply worried. For all their professed outrage at McCarthy's "star chamber methods" and "reckless"

113

charges (starting a litany that would shape McCarthy's public image from that point on), Democrats understood that McCarthy was raising an issue on which they had made themselves vulnerable: ignoring Communist influence in governing circles. Even if McCarthy's specific charges proved to be baseless, as Lucas and others believed, the loyalty issue would remain a dangerous thorn in their side in the 1950 elections. They believed their best strategy was to discredit McCarthy in the court of public opinion even before the substance of his charges could be heard.

That substance was simple and straightforward. The Truman administration had allowed, and continued to allow, various security risks, including known Communists, to be employed at the State Department. McCarthy had put together a speech very different from the one he had delivered in Wheeling two weeks earlier. There, McCarthy had been interested in grabbing headlines. Here he was acting like a district attorney summarizing evidence before a grand jury, "so that anyone who reads the record will have a good idea of the number of Communists in the State Department."[2] He ran through the eighty-one examples, listing them as Case No. 1, No. 2, and so on, pointing out which ones had been members of front organizations, which ones had signed sworn affidavits that he had been a member of the Communist Party, and so on. The totality of evidence pointed a finger of guilt—not so much at the employees themselves but at the Truman administration for allowing them to stay on in government service.

Like good defense attorneys, the Democratic senators took it on themselves to cast doubt on the charges or, failing that, at least to prevent them from being heard. Halfway through McCarthy's presentation, Lucas tried to get the Senate to adjourn. He lost. He and the other Democrats demanded to know the connection between this group of 81 State Department "loyalty risks," and the 205 McCarthy may or may not have mentioned in Wheeling, and the 57 he brought up afterward. McCarthy retorted that the 57 were all included in the cases he was now summarizing before the Senate. Beyond that he refused to be specific. After Wheeling and Reno, the numbers game was an issue McCarthy preferred to stay away from.

The Democrats also demanded that McCarthy present the entire case both for and against the individuals, not just quick (and, as it happened, often misleading) summaries, and identify the employees by name. "When the Senator gives the cases," said Withers of Kentucky, "the press and the country at large would like to know who they are." By naming names, they said, McCarthy could separate those State Department employees who were under suspicion from those who were not.[3]

In short, the Democrats were insisting that McCarthy not just summarize his findings but substantiate them on the spot. However, McCarthy would not be swayed from his purpose. He was not interested in indicting or even naming the eight-one employees. "I thought that would be improper," he told Brien McMahon of Connecticut, adding, "I do not have all the information about these individuals." Nor was he saying everyone was a Communist, let alone a spy. His one goal, he stated over and over again, was "to show that there is something radically wrong" in the State Department's loyalty investigation program.[4] After all, if so many doubtful cases were still circulating, what were the odds that still other security risks, even Communists, remained undetected?

Lucas and the other Democrats, however, knew their best tack was to keep the focus on McCarthy's original claim that he had found a cabal of Communists in the State Department. And here McCarthy found himself on very shaky ground. Although he tried to convey the impression that he had somehow obtained his information hot from secret sources at State, it was in fact two years old. He also exaggerated the content of the summaries, dashing indiscriminately from one case to the next as he tried to outrun the constant cries of "Will the senator yield?" A "suspected Communist" became a "Communist Party member," "a friend of someone believed to be a Communist" became "a close pal of a known Communist," and so on. In one or two cases, he may have acquired more hard information from his almost weekly meetings with J. Edgar Hoover. His mention of the David Lloyd case rested on a report from Drew Pearson's assistant Jack Anderson.[5] But the bald truth was that McCarthy did distort several of the list summaries in order to make his point. At one point he even said "I am not presenting anything except what is confirmed by the files," when he clearly was not.[6]

Critics then and now rightly blame McCarthy for this. Usually they offer it as proof of his blatant disregard for the truth. A more likely explanation is that he simply believed the bald summaries were not enough to generate maximum public impact, in the face of an administration and a Democratic Party wilfully determined to block any sort of investigation. But whatever the motives, the move became typical of McCarthy's subsequent performances. When cornered or challenged, he preferred to exaggerate—even lie—about what cards he actually had in his hand. During his short and meteoric career as the Senate's leading red baiter, McCarthy learned to bluff his way through, in hopes that subsequent research would confirm the bulk of it. While the public might forget the denials and details, he believed they would grasp what was the essential point: someone at the top was covering up.

And for all of McCarthy's crude mishandling of sensitive information, that was the essential point on February 20. The Lee list revealed that numerous untrustworthy characters had been employed in the State Department, including persons suspected of handing over documents to Soviet agents, and that no one had taken serious action on it. In fact, many were still there. (Later, it would turn out that in February 1950 forty-one of the fifty-seven were still on the payroll.) This was a far cry from McCarthy's more sensational claims in Wheeling and Reno, but no one could deny it made the administration look dangerously lax about security.

And here the Democrats made a mistake. When opponents wanted to know why he didn't alert the State Department or the White House to the existence of Communists in their midst before dragging his charges out in public, McCarthy's reply was devastating. They already knew, he said, and hadn't done anything about it. Herbert Lehman asked why he didn't send the information to Secretary of State Dean Acheson. "They are in the files of the Secretary of State," he roared back, "all the information I am giving on the floor of the Senate has been available for a long time." That was why he had decided to go public, he said: to let the American people know what going on behind their backs and encourage the Senate to take up an investigation—a suggestion Henry Cabot Lodge enthusiastically endorsed.[7]

This was the opening the Democrats had been waiting for. Lucas told the Senate there would indeed be an investigation, but that this was bad news, not good news, for McCarthy and his supporters. "Before the committee," Lucas intoned, "he will not be able to hide behind numbers. He will have to tell the facts and disclose the names of the persons within the State Department who are Communists." The next day, the Senate leadership planned their strategy. They decided not to hand the investigation over to the Permanent Subcommittee on Investigations, which Democrat Clyde Hoey now chaired, since McCarthy was a member. The Republicans proposed the Appropriations Committee; that was ruled out of hand. In the end, with Dean Acheson's approval, the leadership decided on the Foreign Relations Committee, with a special subcommittee to be chaired by Millard Tydings. Secretly Democrats were delighted. They believed that McCarthy would get "his head so thoroughly washed" by the committee, as columnist Stewart Alsop put it, that he would not put it up again. The Democrats knew from experience that "as the investigation proceeds the headlines get smaller" and, when the final report comes out, all but forgotten.[8] Their hope was that the Tydings subcommittee would silence the Republicans, and embarrassing questions about the administration's handling of domestic communism, forever.

On February 22 the Senate passed Lucas's Resolution 231 authorizing a special subcommittee to investigate McCarthy's charges regarding the State Department. As the debate unfolded, Republicans began to smell a rat.

As the Democrats described it, the hearings would be set up to prove or dis-prove the *guilt* of the persons McCarthy would name. Republicans knew that an investigative committee could at best only determine whether the label of "Communist" or "loyalty risk" had merit, and then leave any questions of guilt to the Justice Department. Liberals were in effect raising the bar of what would pass as proof of McCarthy's charges. Wayne Morse even demanded that the entire proceedings be conducted in public like a regular trial, which Republicans knew would make presentation of confidential sources or sensitive materials impossible. Bourke Hickenlooper tried to explain to his colleagues that deciding whether someone was a security or loyalty risk was not like determining whether someone was guilty of treason. "There are various grades of either guilt or suspicion which are involved" in a security matter like this, he said. "Sometimes it is in the public interest to make things public," as when McCarthy alerted America that its State Department was not doing its job. But sometimes "it is definitely in the public interest to refrain from making things public," especially if it endangers important witnesses.[9]

The Morse amendment was defeated, but the Democrats' other require-ment, that the committee not be allowed to subpoena State Department files, held. Republicans asked, not unreasonably, how the committee could deter-mine the truth or falsity of the charges without seeing the evidence them-selves. McCarthy himself asserted that without full subpoena power, the committee's proceedings would be a simple whitewash. "Unless we secure those files," he warned, "there is no use of even starting the investigation." But Resolution 231 passed without giving anyone full subpoena powers, and limiting the investigation only to those cases McCarthy had raised in his Sen-ate speech, rather than a full probe into the State Department's security pro-gram, as Republicans had urged. Senate Republicans voted for the resolution, but with a growing sense that it was their colleague McCarthy, not the State Department, who would be on the hot seat.[10]

In retrospect, it is not difficult to fault Lucas and the Senate leadership for proceeding precipitously, not to mention disingenuously. They failed to take time to consult with the White House on the scope of the inquiry and were so anxious to move ahead that they never considered what might hap-pen if some of McCarthy's cases had any substance. Even if the bulk of his list of eighty-one "risk cases" was two years old and supposedly out of date, the existence of *any* active loyalty risks or Communists would be bound to make McCarthy and the other Republicans look vindicated. Instead, the Democra-tic leadership believed the junior senator from Wisconsin was an easy mark and that they could dispatch him without difficulty.

The choice of members of the committee was a clue to what was coming. Brien McMahon of Connecticut, a typical progressive Democrat, had been among the vociferous hecklers of McCarthy's speech on February 20. The chairman, Millard Tydings of Maryland, was fifty-nine years old and chairman of the Armed Services Committee. He had opposed Roosevelt on conservative principles and fought a tough reelection campaign in 1938 when his own president had attacked him as "a betrayer of the New Deal." However, he was also a Senate establishmentarian and a good friend to President Truman. He took over the subcommittee assignment with a larger ambition in mind: by crushing McCarthy and beating back the GOP's anti-Communist offensive, he would win the gratitude of Truman and secure a place for himself in the cabinet, possibly even as vice president in 1952. A careful, objective look at the State Department's loyalty program, and McCarthy's charges, played no part in his plans.[11]

The same was true of Theodore Francis Green, a rich, aristocratic Wilsonian Democrat from Rhode Island. For men like Tydings, Green, and majority leader Scott Lucas, the baselessness of McCarthy's charges was a given. They belonged to an earlier generation of American politicians (Green had first entered public office in 1906) for whom the idea of Soviet spies on secret missions and fellow Americans working for the other side seemed very farfetched. They hankered after the prewar days when America's defense needs were small, and each armed service had its own self-contained budget—which also represented more opportunities for political patronage. Far more than Robert Taft and his allies, they were the true "isolationists" in the Senate. In fact, Tydings and McMahon were both advocates for nuclear disarmament at the very time the Soviet Union was busily readying its own atomic weapons program; and all three were inclined to dismiss any idea of an internal Communist threat.

Of the Republicans, only Bourke Hickenlooper of Iowa was likely to be a McCarthy ally. Henry Cabot Lodge of Massachusetts was a committed bipartisan, and Lucas and Tydings probably counted on him to support the Democrats. But in fact, Lodge proved a surprise. Although he loathed McCarthy as a person, he realized that his charges against the State Department probably had more basis in truth than did the furious denials being issued by the White House and the Democrats.

The key battle was going to be over what evidence the Tydings Committee would be allowed to see to evaluate the truth of McCarthy's claims. Here again, the Democrats acted in a way that raised, rather than dampened, suspicions of a cover-up. On February 23 Truman denounced McCarthy's Senate speech but refused to open any security files to scrutiny. Faced by White House intransigence, Tydings had no choice but to press on as if the information contained in the files were incidental rather than central to establishing the truth or falsehood of McCarthy's charges. However, the pressure would soon begin to mount to permit the committee to make its own evaluation, and determine for itself and the public whether the worries about a State Department vulnerable to subversion or even espionage were correct. In the end, the biggest obstacle to Tydings's agenda for the committee turned out to be not McCarthy but his own president.

The Tydings Committee met on March 8, 1950, in the Senate Office Building, under the glare of television lights, to hear McCarthy give the substance of his charges. McCarthy began with a careful disclaimer about knowing all the details about the State Department employees he was about to bring up before the committee. In his mind, he was just a witness presenting whatever evidence he had (most of which was admittedly rather stale) and to leave it to the committee to discover the rest. Tydings, and then the other Democrats, refused to accept those ground rules. The real target of their investigation, they made clear, was not the State Department but Joe McCarthy.

"You are in the position of being the man who occasioned this hearing," Tydings told him, "and so far as I am concerned you"—extending his finger at McCarthy—"are going to get one of the most complete investigations ever given in the history of the Republic."[12] Tydings had even dispatched investigators to Wheeling, to get a transcript or a recording of the Lincoln Day speech, in order to prove McCarthy had lied when he denied saying there were 205 Communists in the State Department.* Tydings also tried to get McCarthy's February 20 speech entered as testimony under oath, in order to catch him up on possible perjury charges—which McCarthy, taken aback by the idea of retroactively treating a Senate speech as a sworn statement, refused to do.

McMahon and Tydings also tried to make McCarthy accept full responsibility for holding public hearings. This was not in fact accurate; McCarthy had been maneuvered into it by Lucas and the leadership. He had specifically asked Tydings to hold the hearings in executive rather than public session, and Hickenlooper repeated that request before the committee. However, the Democrats had voted to make them open to the public and press.[13]

McCarthy began the day with that assumption, handing out copies of his testimony and previewing it with reporters. Now, even as McCarthy was uttering the name of the first person he would discuss—Dorothy Kenyon—Tydings asked him whether he wanted to adjourn to executive session. McCarthy realized it would now be pointless, and said no; he would proceed in public.[14]

*There was none.

This shrewd move by Tydings made McCarthy, not the committee, the villain; it helped to label McCarthy as a publicity hog, someone willing to drag "innocent names" through the mud for the sake of headlines.

As a means of establishing individual guilt or innocence, the public hearings proved a disaster. The press was overtly sympathetic toward the people McCarthy had named and toward the committee chairman. The old conservative segregationist suddenly became a hero to liberals and acquired a reputation for flinty integrity that he would never entirely lose. Tydings compelled McCarthy to present his cases one by one before an openly skeptical audience and punctuated by constant interruptions. The witnesses McCarthy brought in to support his charges were limited in numbers and in their time to testify, while full opportunity was given to the accused to refute the charges.

When Dorothy Kenyon appeared, she spoke indignantly about "guilt by association." She said that naming organizations such as groups she had belonged to in the past as subversive without a public trial "sounds to me like Mr. Hitler and Mr. Stalin." She did admit that she had belonged at one time or another to twelve different Communist front organizations, and also that her employers at the State Department had never bothered even to ask her about her past affiliations—all of which tended to confirm, rather than refute, McCarthy's main point: that the State Department had been lax in dealing with people who might be security or loyalty risks.[15]

That was precisely the issue Tydings wanted to avoid. Instead, he worked to force McCarthy to prove each and every point of his accusations himself. McCarthy was forced into an untenable position. Lacking access to any files or hard evidence and denied any resources for a systematic investigation of his cases, he was forced to turn to a scattershot approach, tossing out whatever evidence came to hand in hopes that something would give credibility to his original charges, which in turn encouraged the press to see him as "reckless" and engaged in "indictment by association and smear."

Squeezed by time and lack of resources, he fell back on the Owen Lattimore case. It is not clear how McCarthy first learned about him.[16] However, on March 22 in a special executive session, McCarthy suddenly named Owen Lattimore as "Moscow's top spy" and told the committee that files on Lattimore at the State Department and the FBI would back up his claim that Lattimore was "at the top of the whole ring of which Hiss was part." Although Lattimore was little known to the country at large, the accusation sent shock waves through foreign service and academic circles, and it stunned McCarthy's opponents. After three weeks of floundering in front of the Tydings Committee, McCarthy had reversed the controls and raised fears (and hopes) that he had discovered the equivalent of another Alger

Hiss. McCarthy himself told the press that he was willing to let his reputation "stand and fall" on the Lattimore case.

Who was Owen Lattimore? At the time he was director of the Walter Hines Page School of International Relations at Johns Hopkins University. An expert on Mongolia who had mastered obscure Asian languages with ease, Lattimore was one of the original "China hands," along with John Stewart Service. However, Lattimore was not a diplomat or career State Department employee: Acheson said that he had never even heard his name before McCarthy mentioned it.[17] Lattimore had served instead as an adviser and consultant while editor of *Pacific Affairs*, the magazine published by the Institute of Pacific Relations, a group McCarthy accused of being "riddled with Communists," since some of its members had been connected to the *Amerasia* espionage case. After serving as head of the Pacific division of the Office of War Information for two years, Lattimore had stayed on after the war as a minor consultant at State, which did not even issue him an office— hence the ridicule that greeted McCarthy's portentous claims about "Lattimore's desk" at the State Department.

But if Lattimore was hardly the architect of State Department policy that McCarthy charged, he was also not as insignificant as he tried to make himself appear. In 1941 he had served as FDR's personal adviser on China; in 1944 he had accompanied Henry Wallace to China and Russia, and helped to shape his views on American policy there (it was on that visit that Wallace convinced Chiang to allow a military mission to be sent to Mao's forces at Yenan). In those years Lattimore had been a close confidant of Lauchlin Currie, who also happened to be a Communist spy.[18]

Furthermore, Lattimore enjoyed an influence that went beyond any formal connection to the foreign service. His books and articles on China and Asia were treated with great intellectual authority, and were part of the normal talking shop among China hands and younger personnel at the Far Eastern desk at State. They had all absorbed and accepted his basic thesis: that the Chinese Communists were really more nationalist than pro-Soviet and that Mao would eventually break with Stalin and strike off on his own. Once this happened, a Communist victory in the civil war in China would prove to be a magnificent opportunity for American foreign policy, not a defeat.

In the long run, Lattimore turned out to be correct. In the short term, the belief he fostered that a Sino-Soviet alliance was unlikely proved to be a disaster. Lattimore's influence encouraged the State Department to see Mao as a more independent figure than he really was. By pulling the plug on Chiang Kai-shek, he and John Stewart Service had argued, America was only yielding to the inevitable—and would gain the favor of Chinese Communists after their victory. All these fond hopes would be cruelly dashed following Mao's takeover in February 1950, when he signed a direct alliance with the Soviet Union.

Even more ominous was Lattimore's view of the Soviet Union. Like other liberals in the thirties, he had treated Russia as a model "progressive" and "democratic" nation. His determination to follow the Stalinist line on the purge trials in the thirties—"that sounds like democracy to me"—did not escape the notice of critics or McCarthy. On his visit with Vice President Wallace to the Magadan labor camp in 1944, he had compared the Gulag outpost to the Tennessee Valley Authority and spoke warmly of their host's sense of civic responsibility. (One can imagine the uproar if someone had similar statements after a visit to Dachau or Buchenwald.) In fact, throughout his career Lattimore had maintained an eerie public adherence to the Soviet line. He had been an ardent anti-interventionist during the Nazi-Soviet Pact; when the Soviets were attacked in June 1941, Lattimore suddenly reversed his view. When the Soviets supported Chiang, Lattimore supported Chiang; when they reversed their position, so did he.

Lattimore the fellow traveler also played a curious double game as editor of *Pacific Affairs*, dressing up the pro-Soviet views of his contributors so that they appeared to be the sensible result of careful scholarly research. In private he was more candid. He wrote to the Institute of Pacific Relations's sister institution in Moscow to ask its members to send articles that would help to develop the magazine's approach to sensitive issues. He added, "If the Soviet group would show in their articles a general line—the struggle for peace—the other articles would naturally gravitate to that line." He also offered this advice to IPR's executive director: "For the USSR—back their international policy in general, but without using their slogans and above all without giving them or anybody else the impression of subservience."[19]

This meant that those who sought his advice often did not realize his motives for giving it. In 1948 Lattimore had attended a crucial meeting with Secretary of State Marshall and other State Department officials debating whether to curtail assistance for Chiang Kai-shek. Lattimore sketched out what he termed a "realistic" approach for future policy in Asia, arguing that support for Chiang and the Nationalists had done severe harm to the U.S. image. That is what the Soviets hoped the Americans would believe; Lattimore then also urged withdrawal from both Korea and Japan. He claimed, "Japan can keep herself alive by coming to terms with her neighbors in Asia, principally China"—or rather, a victorious Communist Party–controlled China. Marshall and the other State Department people probably assumed they were getting advice from a leading authority on China when in fact they were getting advice from a leading pro-Soviet ideologue.[20]

McCarthy's charges against Lattimore went beyond the issue of his pro-Soviet views, however. McCarthy also had the results from the FBI's investigation of Lattimore, which considered him "part and parcel" of the Communist Party. McCarthy had a reliable witness, Louis Budenz, who could name Lattimore as part of a ring of active Soviet agents (although the FBI had found no such evidence and did not consider Lattimore a full-fledged spy). If it were true that Lattimore really had substantially influenced the China policy leading to Mao's victory and collapse of Chiang, and at the same time had been a secret Communist, then McCarthy's charge that Lattimore was "one of the top Communist agents in the country" was not so far-fetched as it first appeared.

If it were true. What McCarthy faced in the Tydings Committee would not be a thorough investigation of the evidence against Lattimore but a closing of partisan ranks. McCarthy's offer to make Lattimore the acid test of his own credibility would haunt him for the rest of his career.

Meanwhile, the slim, bespectacled professor with his dapper David Niven mustache sprang into action. He flew to Washington to hear McCarthy's testimony against him and swiftly mobilized support from the influential and powerful. One was Drew Pearson, who was still smarting from McCarthy's unauthorized use of his gossip about David Lloyd. In a March 26 radio broadcast Pearson identified McCarthy's "top Russian spy" as Owen Lattimore, adding, "I happen to know Owen Lattimore personally—and I only wish this country had more patriots like him."[21] Senators Green and Tydings publicly dismissed McCarthy's charges as reckless and unfounded even before they had heard Lattimore's defense.

The next act of the drama began on April 6. Owen Lattimore appeared before the committee with a packed audience, flanked by friends, colleagues, his wife, and even his parents. Senators both supportive and hostile (including McCarthy himself) lined the chairs behind the committee members. The very picture of the shy, diffident college professor, Lattimore read an hour-and-forty-five-minute statement blasting McCarthy's charges. Lattimore denied being a spy or doing anything "which might conceivably have suggested this even to a perverted mind." McCarthy said nothing as Lattimore defended the Institute of Pacific Relations and his work there, denying that he had ever thought of associates like Philip Jaffee or Frederick Vanderbilt Field or Chi Chao-ting, his colleague from Johns Hopkins, as possible Communists. The whole thing was hallucinatory madness, Lattimore managed to imply; he was a scholar, not a spy.[22]

Four days later, McCarthy put his own witness forward. In his Communist days Louis Budenz had been editor of the *Daily Worker*. Now he was an FBI informant. Two years earlier, he had testified in front of the Permanent Subcommittee on Investigations on Communist infiltration of the federal government. Now, to a hushed and amazed audience, he testified that the Institute of Pacific Relations was indeed part of an active Soviet spy network. In 1944 leading CPUSA officials had told Budenz that Lattimore was doing secret and important work for the Communist Party and that the *Daily Worker* needed to help conceal his true loyalties. Officials had further told Budenz that Jaffee, Field, and Owen Lattimore were all part of the Communist network at IPR and that John Stewart Service—the same State Department employee and China hand arrested in the *Amerasia* case—was Lattimore's protégé.[23]

Budenz withstood a furious counterattack by Senator Greene and the Democratic counsel. He admitted that his evidence of Lattimore's activities was almost entirely secondhand, but he stood his ground. Lattimore demanded his chance to refute the shocking charges, pounding the table and calling Budenz a "smear artist" and his story "a pure, unvarnished lie." However, as Lattimore left the room, thoughtful listeners for the first time began to wonder if McCarthy might have something after all.

Lattimore's supporters were unmoved. As with McCarthy's original charges, they made the issue Budenz's credibility rather than Lattimore's. Here Lattimore showed that he was not above a little personal attack and character assassination himself. Budenz had put his own credibility on the line; opponents were quick to point that he had never mentioned Lattimore before McCarthy had brought up his charges.[24] Through his lawyer, Abe Fortas, Lattimore leaked a string of nasty gossip about the Fordham professor, which the newspapers picked up and McCarthy opponent Dennis Chavez, together with Tydings and Lucas, put into the record on the Senate floor. They alleged that Budenz had had children with three different women out of wedlock and been arrested twenty-one times. Chavez said that "as a Catholic" he found Budenz's bigamy reprehensible. "My ancestors brought the Cross to this hemisphere. Louis Budenz has used the Cross as a club."

Defenders pointed out that Budenz had been a labor activist before he joined the Communist Party and was bound to have spent some time in jail. They also pointed out that since the Communist Party had viewed marriage as a "bourgeois institution," it was not surprising that Budenz had had irregular relations with women in and out of the Party. In any case, what did this have to do with a man who had since converted to Catholicism and now taught at Fordham University? By attacking Budenz in this fashion, Chavez had certainly engaged in a smear and defamation of character as egregious as anything McCarthy had done or would do. The mainstream press said little or nothing about it or Lattimore's tactics in leaking the story. But as Robert Morris later pointed out, the incident effectively served notice that those who testified against Lattimore would be subject to the same sort of personal attack.[25]

On May 2, Lattimore returned to the Tydings Committee to launch a direct attack on McCarthy. The duty of the committee, he informed the senators, was not just "to clear the individuals who have been unjustly slandered by this man McCarthy." It was "to warn such character assassins they will not be permitted to run riot or publicly spread their venom." Those who use the techniques of "personal attack and character assassination," he said, undermined "the great American traditions of freedom, decency, and faith in one's fellow man." (Lattimore's own smear of Budenz was apparently an exception.) He read from a letter he had received from his very good friend, Professor Zachariah Chaffee of Harvard, which likened McCarthy and his supporters to "a barbarian invasion" that would destroy the civic fabric of America.

Warming to his task, Lattimore asserted that McCarthy "has been contemptuous of this Committee . . . has lied, distorted, and vilified . . . has disgraced his party and the people of his state and nation . . . and grievously prejudiced the interests of his country." As a final touch, he brought up McCarthy's involvement in the Malmédy hearings: "I hope with all my heart that Joe McCarthy will come to understand that the principles of justice and fairness which he loudly proclaimed on behalf of Nazi murderers are also the birthright of American citizens." The committee room exploded into applause.[26]

It was a masterful, if somewhat arrogant, performance, with the professor lecturing United States senators on their constitutional duty and diverting attention toward McCarthy and away from himself. To liberals and Democrats, Owen Lattimore was the hero of the hour. Like David against Goliath, he had confronted the whole effort to brand liberals as pro-Communist, an effort now symbolized by the unsavory person of Joe McCarthy. Herbert Elliston of the *Baltimore Sun*, Al Friendly of the *Washington Post*, Drew Pearson, I. F. Stone, Eric Sevareid, and Martin Agronsky all lined up in his support. The *New York Post* even declared that "all those who believe in freedom in this country are in the debt of Owen Lattimore." Swept along by this wave of approbation, Lattimore published his own account of the proceedings in a book entitled *Ordeal by Slander*, which won him further plaudits and praise.

Ordeal by Slander is important for three reasons. First, it made the term "McCarthyism" part of the vocabulary. "McCarthyism," Lattimore wrote, "insists constantly, emotionally, and menacingly that the man who thinks independently thinks dangerously and for an evil, disloyal purpose." This was a clever argument. It played on the instinct of many liberals to believe that any attack on Communists was really an attack on intelligent, open-minded people such as themselves. Anyone accused of being a Communist was by definition an innocent victim, and anyone who did the accusing was by implication a crypto-fascist or "McCarthyite." Lattimore compounded this by linking McCarthy and ex-Communists like Budenz to the "political underworld" of "pro-Fascists, American Firsters, anti-Semites, Coughlinites"—groups every good New Deal Democrat had learned to despise. "A tide of fear has swept Washington," he concluded, "undermining the freedom of the nation," and it was McCarthy's fault. And this was the third reason why Lattimore's book was so important: For the first time, it gave liberals and Democrats someone to blame for their discomfort on the Communist issue. McCarthy, "the junior senator from Wisconsin," a man steeped in lying, deceit, and chicanery, was now the personal embodiment of the red scare—and his faults, real or imagined, soon became its faults.[27]

In the end, however, Lattimore's own deceptions and evasions would be unmasked. Robert Morris had sat in the GOP's legal counsel's chair and watched the Tydings Committee with incomprehension and a growing sense of outrage. Two years later the chairman of the new Senate Internal Security Committee, Pat McCarran, hired Morris and asked him to take up the threads that McCarthy had exposed regarding Lattimore and the Institute of Pacific Relations. Unlike McCarthy, McCarran had no partisan ax to grind and managed to conduct the sort of investigation that Tydings had refused to do.

What they discovered was that McCarthy had been largely correct. An official from State told the Tydings committee that if the Stalinists had been trying to take over the Institute of Pacific Relations, the record showed that they had "failed completely."[28] In fact, IPR had sheltered no fewer than *eight* active espionage agents: Michael Greenberg, one of the Cambridge spy circle, who had been Lattimore's successor as editor of *Pacific Affairs;* Chi Chao-ting, a Communist Chinese agent who received IPR money and helped to create *Amerasia* magazine, and later worked for Lattimore at Johns Hopkins; Chen Han-shen, a former Comintern agent and member of Richard Sorge's Tokyo spy ring, who later helped Lattimore edit *Pacific Affairs* from 1936 to 1939; Agnes Smedley, another Sorge agent; Herbert Norman; GRU agents Thomas A. Bisson and Joseph Bernstein; and Guenther Stein, a German journalist with NKVD connections. They had been surrounded by a large circle of Communist Party members and sympathizers, including its first executive secretary, *Amerasia's* Philip Jaffee, and Frederick Vanderbilt Field, *Amerasia's* financial backer and a member of IPR's board.[29]

It also turned out the FBI had been keeping Lattimore under surveillance since 1949 and had tracked his close associations with many figures identified as Soviet agents, including figures at IPR. If Lattimore was not himself a spy, he did manage to surround himself with them. Lattimore's private correspondence with IPR's Moscow affiliate came to light, as did a series of revealing remarks regarding South Korea. In 1944 he had told a colleague that he thought the best solution for Korea would be a Soviet takeover (Lattimore vigorously denied ever saying this), and in 1949, shortly before the Communist invasion, he wrote that the best policy would be "to let South Korea fall—but not to let it look as though we pushed it."[30] The McCarran Committee concluded that Owen Lattimore had been since the thirties a "conscious, articulate instrument of the Soviet conspiracy." He was eventually indicted for perjury, although a judge threw out the bulk of the indictment on technical grounds.

Decades later, even more of the truth would come out. The first was Lattimore's close, even intimate association with Lauchlin Currie, whom the Venona decrypts definitively identified as a Soviet agent. It was Currie who sent Lattimore to China as FDR's representative and later as part of the Wallace mission. It was also Currie who instructed Lattimore to hire the Cambridge spy Michael Greenberg as his assistant at *Pacific Affairs*.

Then, in 1988, Chen Han-shen published *My Life During Four Ages*, his memoirs of serving as a Communist secret agent, first as a member of Comintern and the Sorge spy network, then as an operative of the Chinese Communist espionage service in the thirties and forties. Chen described how his superiors dispatched him to the United States in 1936 to serve as Lattimore's coeditor at *Pacific Affairs* at Lattimore's personal request. There Chen used his position to carry out espionage activities in New York, with the help of another agent, Rao Shu-shi. According to the memoirs (which had been heavily edited by Chinese authorities), Chen did *not* tell Lattimore he was working for Chinese intelligence or inform him of his own clandestine activities. On the other hand, Lattimore did put his request for a Chinese assistant through Comintern channels—so it is unlikely in the extreme that he was ignorant of what kind of assistant he was really getting or of what Chen Han-shen's real job would be (since at that date Comintern ran the Communist Party's underground apparatus).[31]

Who was Owen Lattimore? Historians Ronald Radosh and Harvey Klehr conclude that if "he was not actually a Communist, he was certainly an opportunist." The most recent revelations expose him as something more than that, something closer to the McCarran Committee's evaluation that he was a "conscious and articulate" instrument of Stalinism. Lattimore used his reputation as a scholar to disguise his real agenda and, when his game was exposed, to surround himself with trusting and gullible colleagues like Professor Zachariah Chaffee to protect him. It protects him to this day. Yet if Lattimore was no "top spy," he was no martyr to McCarthyism either.

If none of these later revelations did McCarthy's reputation any good, it was his own fault. If Lattimore had not been what he claimed, neither was he what McCarthy had claimed. Had McCarthy proceeded with the great care and diligence the case demanded, he could have emerged vindicated. But McCarthy did not, and by inflating the Lattimore case in order to salvage his position he had instead damaged it. He had also damaged his relationship with FBI director Hoover, who was privately furious with McCarthy's mishandling of the sensitive data he had supplied.[32]

In the end, McCarthy learned an important lesson: to be more careful in deciding who was a spy and who was merely a fellow traveler, Stalinist sympathizer, or a "loyalty risk." But the behavior of Lattimore and his supporters communicated another, less noticed lesson: while liberal opponents decried McCarthy's methods as smear, distortion, and misrepresentation, they were willing to do at least the same—and even worse—to discredit him.

The Tydings investigation was a frustrating experience for McCarthy. Although he had more information pouring in about Communist influence in government circles during the thirties and forties, and almost weekly meetings with J. Edgar Hoover, Tydings was still denying him a chance to air further charges. At the end of March McCarthy took to the Senate floor again to back up his charges against someone more central to policymaking, Philip Jessup.

Jessup was a former Columbia University professor, but no minor consultant or academic "egghead." He was a major player on Secretary of State Acheson's diplomatic team: Acheson had named him ambassador at large in February 1949. A leading expert on international law, Jessup had served at the United Nations before stepping in to handle sensitive dealings with Soviet UN ambassador Malik on lifting the Berlin blockade as well as various negotiations in the Far East. There he attracted the attention of pro-Chiang critics like Alfred Kohlberg, and hence the attention of Joe McCarthy. Jessup, it turned out, had edited the State Department's white paper justifying its role in the fall of China. He had also served on the board of the Institute of Pacific Relations and signed an affidavit testifying to the good character and patriotism of Alger Hiss.

The Jessup case came up not from McCarthy's initiative but the committee's. On the first day of testimony, McCarthy had casually dropped an aside regarding Ambassador Jessup's "unusual affinity for Communist causes." Although he promised to say more later, the committee never let him have the chance. Jessup flew in from a fact-finding mission in Pakistan to present his case.

Far more than Owen Lattimore, Philip Jessup was a member of the political establishment.[33] He made it clear that any attack on him was an attack on the foreign policy of the United States and "showed a shocking disregard for the interests of the country." "It is a question of the utmost gravity," he told the committee with just the slightest touch of self-importance, "when an official holding the rank of Ambassador at Large is held up before the eyes of the rest of the world as a liar and a traitor." Of course, McCarthy had not yet said any such thing, although he had mentioned that Jessup had been a member of Communist front organizations in the thirties. When Hickenlooper asked him about these, Jessup vehemently denied it and pointed out that he had even been subject to Soviet vilification on several occasions (although for his official role as United Nations ambassador, not for any particular actions on his part).

Jessup offered up two letters of support from Generals Dwight Eisenhower, the commander of the North Atlantic Treaty Organization (NATO), and George Marshall, denouncing the attacks against him and praising Jessup's "devotion to the principles of Americanism." Tydings carefully and slowly read the letters aloud into the committee record. As historian David Oshinsky later noted, "here, to be sure, was a classic case of *innocence* by association."[34] While McCarthy and Hickenlooper fumed, McMahon and Green insisted on shaking Jessup's hand and congratulated him on his sterling performance. When McCarthy asked for a chance to cross examine Jessup, Tydings refused—on the grounds that Jessup had not been present to cross-examine McCarthy when McCarthy first mentioned his name. Angry and frustrated, McCarthy took to Senate floor to outline what he knew about Jessup.

He pointed to Jessup's membership in a series of pro-Soviet front organizations in the thirties. This was in fact the weakest of his arguments against Jessup's fitness to serve.[35] More interesting was Jessup's role as vice chairman of the American Council of IPR and as research editor for IPR's official journal, *Far Eastern Survey*. But here again McCarthy overstated his case by claiming that Jessup had "pioneered" the journal's attacks on Chiang Kai-shek (which were, it later turned out, largely Communist inspired) and was the "originator" of the idea that Mao's Communists were really just democratic reformers. Jessup had certainly known what was being published in the journal associated with his name and who was doing it, but his connection had been too slight to sustain the sort of guiding role McCarthy was suggesting.

In the final analysis, McCarthy's case against Jessup rested on a single thesis: that Jessup was a well-intentioned liberal whom genuine Communists like Owen Lattimore found easy to manipulate and corrupt. In his March 22 speech, McCarthy called Jessup "a well-meaning dupe." This provoked howls of outrage from Jessup's supporters and colleagues, but it was certainly far from calling him a traitor. Instead, Jessup belonged to what a conservative would have called "the Yalta crowd"—diplomats who saw Stalin and the Soviet Union as a country that could be dealt with on even terms and whose word could be trusted. Like many of his colleagues, Jessup assumed that the cold war arose from misunderstandings rather from than a basic ideological conflict, misunderstandings that could be accommodated through normal diplomatic channels. He foreshadowed a view of the cold war that would later become popular among academics and intellectuals: that of a "moral equivalence" between the Soviet Union and the United States. Americans lived under one version of democracy and the Soviets another, he wrote. Just as Americans lived with a political division between Democrats and Republicans, he had written, so "the Soviet and American forms of government can co-exist in the world." "It is our task," he wrote in 1947, "to see to it that the weak shall be free to choose their own ways of life, be those ways American, or Russian, or something different from either."[36]

Conservatives would have choked on the notion that any people might freely choose to live under the "Russian way of life." But that belief had obviously affected his work with the pro-Communist members of the IPR board. Jessup learned to swallow whole the notion that Marxist guerrillas like Mao represented indigenous democratic movements. Jessup believed that communism "finds most fertile soil where there is already autocratic government and economic distress" and clearly included Chiang's Nationalists on his list of autocrats (a difficult case to fit Poland or Czechoslovakia or even Spain in the thirties). As one of Acheson's key advisers on China, he supported Lattimore and others in their calls for curtailing support for Chiang in 1948. When Mao took over the next year, Jessup warned Truman and Acheson against taking any provocative actions against the mainland and strongly urged official recognition of red China.[37]

None of this added up to a portrait of a man who was anti-American or disloyal, and McCarthy knew it. He was instead raising the issue whether a person who could not meaningfully distinguish between being a member of the Democratic Party and a member of the Communist Party ought to be in charge of sensitive negotiations with the Soviet Union.

At the core of the Jessup case was the clash between liberals and conservatives over how to conduct the cold war. Was a liberal like Jessup, who saw no evil and heard no evil at IPR and publicly defended its record of "objectivity," really too inclined to accept communism's premises to resist its conclusions? Philip Jessup might never blab or leak sensitive secrets to Communist agents, as John Stewart Service had; unlike Harry Hopkins, he actively disliked the Soviet Union. But since he was inclined to be receptive to advice from those who did have divided loyalties, such as Lattimore and Field, he could *with the best intentions* direct policy toward ends that actually promoted Communist rather than American interests. In terms of legal and moral guilt, the difference between a Hiss and a Jessup was enormous. In terms of their eventual impact on national security, there might almost be none.

Such an attack, and its sticky implications for those who shared Jessup's views, was not about to go unanswered. The publicity campaign against McCarthy redoubled, with a new thesis: that McCarthy was actually aiding and abetting Moscow with his attacks.[38] Former Secretary of War Henry L. Stimson, a mentor figure to both Jessup and Dean Acheson, wrote a long, dignified letter to the *New York Times* implying that McCarthy was seeking personal political advantage by damaging his country's interests. Truman called McCarthy the "greatest asset the Kremlin has" and compared his attempts to "sabotage the foreign policy of the United States" in a cold war to shooting American soldiers in the back in a hot war.[39] When Taft angrily said the president had slandered McCarthy, Truman expressed his personal belief that it was not possible to slander the junior senator from Wisconsin—not remarks that tended to support Truman's claim that it was Republicans who were undermining "bipartisanship" in foreign policy.

But despite the furious denials of McCarthy's charges, the damage had been done. Neither Truman's insults nor Tydings's tactics could shake McCarthy's determination to press on and gain public attention, if not exactly public sympathy, for his charges. Far from being exposed as groundless, McCarthy had managed to raise reasonable doubts about what was happening in the upper reaches of the administration where an Owen Lattimore served as a president's special assistant and a Philip Jessup as an ambassador at large. The *New York Times* noted that Democrats on the Hill believed that McCarthy's charges were wounding the administration and that "the answers so far have not caught up with the charges."[40] Given the exposure of one vulnerable figure after another and the exchange of charges and denials, the only way to clear it up was to bite the bullet and do what Republicans and McCarthy been demanding: open the State Department files. Tydings was determined to hold the line for Truman, but privately warned that if Truman could release some of the sealed materials, he could help defuse the case.

Truman had an ally in this refusal. FBI director Hoover wanted to prevent raw intelligence from the pawing attention of a committee of senators and their staffers. Hoover even appeared as a witness on March 27 to explain why the files should remain sealed. However, the real issue now was no longer one of security but of political credibility. Senator George, a Democrat, was quoted as saying that without the files, the committee investigation would seem a "whitewash," using McCarthy's word for the first time. On April 12 Tydings wrote to Truman that he had to release some of the files in order to help to "reestablish the White House and the Truman Administration as the foe of Communism."[41] At last on May 4, Truman relented.

On May 10 the files were stacked one by one on the committee table. Reading them was a daunting task; each contained page after page of raw data, which professional FBI men, not professional politicians, were trained to evaluate—yet the committee's chief counsels, Morgan and Morris, were specifically barred from looking at them. It took Tydings two entire days just to look through thirteen files. Lodge and Hickenlooper became disgusted; they concluded the whole exercise was a waste of time, and that in the end the committee Democrats would accept the evaluation the White House put on the files and do nothing more. And in the end, this is what they did.

McCarthy was more explicit and sensational. He told the press that he feared the files had been "skeletonized" before leaving the State Department, "raped" by clerks on order of their superiors. The FBI assured the committee that the files were intact, but McCarthy managed to turn up four affidavits from people who had helped remove derogatory materials from personnel files back in the fall of 1946. The State Department retorted that those had been the *personnel* records, not the security files, which were kept in a separate division. However, they did not explain how a probe of personnel files conducted after the loyalty board had been set up in 1947 could have proceeded if derogatory materials in those files had been destroyed. It would be another three years before McCarthy, as chairman of PSI, finally cleared up the confusion. In the meantime, it gave McCarthy a plausible excuse for dismissing the Tydings Committee's insistence that the files showed nothing to support his charges.

"How much deceit and dishonesty must we be subjected to before we can get some honest action," he asked a Republican audience in Chicago, "how much of this nonsense does the Administration think the American people will buy?" He blasted Dean Acheson as the heart of the problem. "Sugared phrases in a British accent are fine for Washington teas. But this is not a tea party." McCarthy urged Truman to call in Hoover, the head of the Secret Service, and the director of the CIA to review all the State Department's hiring decisions. "We can as a country no longer stand idle as the prancing mimics of the Moscow Party line sell us short."[42]

And while the delays and partisan wrangling slowed the committee to a crawl, events in the outside world raced ahead.

On June 25, 1950, North Korean troops launched their drive across the 38th parallel and smashed through South Korean lines. The outbreak of fighting between Soviet-trained and -equipped (and, it later turned out, Soviet-led) Communist troops and an American ally pushed the cold war to a new level of tension; the invasion of Korea seemed the curtain raiser for another world war. It also raised dangers of an internal Communist threat, of persons systematically undermining America's ability to deal effectively with aggressive Soviet actions, to a new urgency.

Having been accused of the moral equivalent of shooting American soldiers in the back, McCarthy got his revenge in a speech on July 6. He blamed the disaster in Korea on "highly placed Red counselors" in the State Department, whose advice was proving "far more deadly than Red machine gunners in Korea." Events had suddenly thrown his earlier remarks on America's blunders in China, and the role of men like Lattimore, Service, and IPR in shaping Asia policy, into sharp relief. Republican Homer Capehart introduced a Senate resolution that the *Amerasia* espionage case be the subject of a full and separate investigation. More than anything else, the Korean War gave McCarthy a new credibility with his colleagues and the American public. If America was losing the struggle against Stalinism, perhaps Joe McCarthy knew why.

The Democrats' attempt to make McCarthy, not the Truman administration, the issue had backfired. Yet the Tydings Committee stolidly proceeded as if nothing had happened. In every case it simply endorsed the State Department's earlier findings. It pretended that the security issues raised by the Lee list did not exist. It cleared Lattimore of all charges, concluding that McCarthy had engaged in "a distortion of the facts on a scale as to be truly alarming." On Jessup, it wrote, "His IPR connections do not in any way reflect unfavorably upon him when the true character of the organization is revealed." On John Stewart Service, that he had been "extremely indiscreet" in handing over documents to Philip Jaffee and *Amerasia* staffers but he was neither "disloyal, pro-Communist, or a security risk."

The Democrats on the committee were determined to permit nothing to distract from their main conclusion: that the whole thing had been a wild goose chase and that McCarthy's charges constituted "the most nefarious campaign of half-truths and untruth in the history of this Republic." For the first time, Tydings wrote, "we have seen the totalitarian technique of the 'big lie' employed on a sustained basis."

Senator Lodge wanted the report to show that not every issue McCarthy had raised had actually been cleared up. He insisted on including a list of nineteen questions he and others still wanted answered—for example:

- What officials were responsible for placing Hiss and [Julien] Wadleigh in the State Department?
- What are the procedures whereby Communists gained entry into the United States upon the basis of visas obtained through our consular service abroad?
- Who in the State Department was responsible for obtaining the services of Frederick Schuman and Owen Lattimore as speakers for the Department's indoctrination course for Foreign Service employees?
- Investigation has not been made of all these whom Mr. Lattimore is supposed to have brought into the Institute of Pacific Relations.

When the final report was published, Lodge discovered that the questions and thirty-five pages of other supporting material Lodge wanted on the record had been "mistakenly" cut out. Despite his outraged protest, the report stood as edited.[43]

Lodge had submitted his list of questions to the subcommittee on June 28. The day before, Communist troops had taken Seoul, the South Korean capital. On the 29th, Truman authorized American troops to stop the invasion as Douglas MacArthur arrived to take command. The impending crisis pushed McCarthy and Tydings off the headlines as the first American troops went into action, while tanks uneasily patrolled the border in Berlin and nuclear-armed bombers waited on airfields in North Dakota and Alaska. Where will the Soviets strike next? was the question on everyone's mind.

However, the Democrats still wanted their last measure of retribution against McCarthy. On a blazing hot July 20, the subcommittee issued its report. Tall, spare, with a grim clenched jaw, Millard Tydings strode to the Senate floor to finish the kill. An eyewitness, the reporter for the *New Republic*, said the Democrats in their seats were "positively growling for revenge. . . . You could actually hear a hoarse, angry mutter" rumble through the chamber. Afterward, veteran reporters agreed that it was one of the nastiest and most divisive sessions in the Senate they could remember.[44]

Tydings flew into a two-hour fury, tearing apart McCarthy's evidence, his character, his shifting story of the numbers of suspected Communists in the government, and the basic honesty and integrity of the Republican Party. Whenever a Republican senator rose to object, the Democratic hubbub built to an uproar and drowned him out. Tydings set up an enormous chart with quotations from newspaper accounts of the Wheeling speech, and waved a phonograph record that he implied contained the original speech (it did not;

Tydings was bluffing, or misleading the Senate, depending on one's point of view). He even did a mocking imitation of McCarthy, rolling his eyes and hitching his pants. Tydings launched a stinging side attack on Senator William Jenner who had denounced the subcommittee as "Whitewash, Inc." He made angry innuendos about Jenner's connection to an "isolationist press axis" and about his war record that were so unpleasant that the chair ordered him to sit down. However, the Democratic chorus instantly rose as a body to overrule the chair's ruling and allow Tydings to continue his diatribe.

At last, he reached the climax of his speech. "What is there here other than a fraud and a hoax," Tydings thundered, concluding that it was on the "conscience of the Senate" to decide what to do with the subcommittee's findings. When he finished, his shirt was soaked from his exertions as he and fellow Democrats triumphantly shook hands. On a 45-to-37 partisan vote, the Senate approved the report. The *Nation* had already urged that McCarthy be expelled from the Senate; Tydings believed he should be charged with perjury.

McCarthy listened without a word and left. Outside the chamber he spoke to reporters. "Today Tydings tried to notify the Communists in government that they are safe in their positions. However, I want to assure them that they are not safe. . . . We started with eighty-one," he said. Two were now gone: Alger Hiss and William Remington, the Commerce Department employee who had been indicted by a grand jury in June. "That means two down and seventy-nine to go. The others will be dug out, one by one."[45]

In fact, the same day that the Tydings Committee was writing its report blasting McCarthy and assuring the public that "the government is free of Communist infiltration," the FBI announced it had arrested Julius Rosenberg on charges of espionage.

135

III

FALL

Had it pleased heaven
To try me with affliction; had they rain'd
All kinds of sores and shames on my bare head,
Steeped in poverty to the very lips,
Given to captivity me and my utmost hopes,
I should have found in some place of my soul
A drop of patience: but, alas, to make me
A fixed figure for the time of scorn
To point his slow unmoving finger at!

—*Othello*, IV, ii, 47–55.

Chapter 7

Failure at the Top

Julius Rosenberg had worked not for the State Department but for the Army. But even if McCarthy had had to back down from his claims about fifty-seven card-carrying Communists in the State Department, he had been proved more right than wrong in terms of the larger picture.[1] Further revelations regarding the Rosenberg case and atomic espionage would reinforce McCarthy's main charge, which through vanity and bravado he had almost botched: that Democratic administrations had been unconscionably lax in dealing with an internal Communist threat. His charge also gained credibility as every day brought more evidence that Truman's people were floundering in their attempts to deal with the external threat on the cold war's global stage.

On the whole, McCarthy's confrontation with the Democrats on the Tydings Committee had done him far more good than harm. Joe McCarthy was now a national political figure. While reporters, columnists, and cartoonists like Herbert Block of the *Washington Post* reviled him for his "reckless smears" and denounced "McCarthyism," they also recognized he was good copy. Newsmen now eagerly awaited his reaction to a statement from President Truman or Senator Lucas, since they knew it would put the story on the front page. The Washington Gridiron Club gave him a celebrity spot during its annual dinner in June. Invitations to fund raisers and speaking forums began to flutter into his office from around the country. Eminent anti-Communists like Whittaker Chambers and J. B. Matthews were offering him advice and information, while ordinary people sent him checks or even cash to help him in his efforts to expose the Communist threat to America. The volume of mail reached twenty-five thousand letters a day. Donors would receive a certificate, designating them a "card-carrying anti-Communist," and while McCarthy used the money to finance his own investigations, he also used part of the tax-free largesse to settle his last remaining personal debts.[2]

McCarthy had now hired Ed Nellor to work for him full time as a speechwriter. Nellor soon learned, however, that his principal job was handling the thousands of leads on Communists in government that were pouring into McCarthy's office from every direction. The telephone would ring without respite; "people," Nellor recalled, "would stop you on the street and hand you documents." Nellor, McCarthy's Senate staff, Ray Kiermas, and other McCarthy friends spent their weekends in the office going through cardboard boxes of material. Ten- or twelve-hour days became normal. "It almost ruined my health," Nellor remembered. McCarthy, on the other hand, was unfazed. For a manic personality like his, this was the ultimate high, and while he pushed his office staff on until four or five o'clock in the morning, he remained as energetic and ebullient as ever.[3]

His personal life took a turn for the better. Jean Kerr had moved from the PSI to his Senate staff in 1949. The first time McCarthy saw her, he had told his secretary, "whoever she is, hire her." She and Joe began dating, although he was almost twenty years her senior and other staffers from PSI warned her not to (given McCarthy's reputation as a freewheeling bachelor).[4] Pretty, well bred, and smart, Kerr gave McCarthy's personal image a much-needed boost. He increasingly allowed her to decide what suits he should wear, how his office should be run, and even what targets he should pursue next. Her attitude toward him bordered on hero worship, which continued until the day she died.

McCarthy had also struck a rich vein of public support in the place where it really counted, in Wisconsin. In March Wisconsin Republicans in the House such as Glenn Davis and Frank Keefe began to speak in support of McCarthy. His political patron, Tom Coleman, did not forget that 1950 was an election year. He jubilantly predicted that McCarthy had found the sort of hot political issue that could finally rout New Deal Democrats. "Our party is finally on the attack," Coleman told a national Republican policy group, and added, "Best of all, we may get rid of many Communist sympathizers and queers who now control foreign policy."

On June 9 McCarthy gave the keynote address to the Republican state convention in Milwaukee. In front of a huge and enthusiastic crowd, he lashed out at Truman, Dean Acheson, and Philip Jessup, and distributed packets of mimeographed documents that reinforced his case. People flooded the rostrum to shake his hand and get his autograph. The crowd became so dense that McCarthy couldn't get out and had to leave by the back stairs. It took him nearly an hour to pass through the hotel lobby as strangers stopped him to express their admiration. A rapturous Republican convention passed a resolution praising McCarthy's "courage, patriotism, and loyalty," a sentiment millions around the country shared. For the upcoming election campaign, McCarthy had more than thirty speaking engagements in fifteen states.

To say that all this adulation turned his head would be a gross understatement. Somewhat later Tom Coleman began to complain to friends about McCarthy's "Christ-like complex." Certainly McCarthy was convinced that anticommunism had now become *his* issue, and that the GOP needed to rally around it—and him. Coleman pressed him to ease off now that war in Korea had started. "I think it would be well to make a complete recast of the situation before making any important moves," he said. McCarthy rejected the hint. He believed that as the war bogged down and the casualties began to mount, people would "realize that there was something rotten in the State Department." Then the McCarthy bandwagon would have just begun to roll.[5]

On the other hand, the effects of the Tydings hearings on his relations with Senate colleagues and fellow Republicans were more mixed. The Taftites had dutifully rallied around. When Tydings had denied McCarthy any resources for proving the charges McCarthy thought Tydings was going to investigate, conservative colleagues in the House and Senate provided what help they could.[6] Meanwhile, a group of moderate Republican senators had endorsed Margaret Chase Smith of Maine's "Declaration of Conscience" speech in June 1950. Later it became a benchmark for measuring high-minded disgust with McCarthy, asserting that "those who shout the loudest about Americanism . . . are all too frequently those who, by their words and acts, ignore some of the basic principles of Americanism: the right to criticize; the right to hold unpopular beliefs." But the Declaration also hit hard at the Truman administration, which had, it said, "greatly lost the confidence of the American people by its complacency to the threat of Communism here at home and the leak of vital secrets to Russia through key officials of the Democratic administration. There are enough proved cases to make this point without diluting our criticism with unproved charges." It concluded by adding, "A Republican victory is necessary to the security of this nation."[7]

The Declaration of Conscience accomplished nothing. Soon afterward Senator Ives repudiated his stand and admitted McCarthy might have a case after all.[8] Fundamentally, it expressed the usual moderate distaste for harsh partisan rhetoric, and a "plague on both your houses" approach to the whole anti-Communist issue. McCarthy himself could not have cared less. "The way to get to be a political leader," he told his friend Urban Van Susteren, "is to just lambast the hell out of the Democrats—in every way."[9] And the political warfare between a desperate if demoralized Democratic Party and an energized GOP was just beginning.

This time Republicans were realizing that they had a new, if unpredictable, weapon in that duel—someone who would willingly act as their lightning rod in the face of Democratic criticism. They had discovered McCarthy was totally undeterred by attacks or even refutation. On the contrary, it made him dig in deeper and hit back harder. This was less the result of a thick skin than of an utter conviction that he was right in the big things, if not always in the details. It heartened his allies and infuriated his opponents. But in 1950 it also summed up the public frustration with what was happening to their country in the face of an inexorable Soviet advance.

By the end of the summer, the North Koreans had pushed American and South Korean armies down to a tiny corner of the peninsula's southern tip. Generals began to tell their men to "stand or die." MacArthur was desperately calling for reinforcements, which the Joint Chiefs tried to fill with a severely limited budget. Since 1946 the United States had drastically cut its military outlays, from $81 billion in 1945 to $13 billion in 1947. Some of it was Republican cost cutting in the Eightieth Congress, but most of it was Truman and the Democrats. The Republicans had left money for a two-million-man army and a budget for a seventy-group Air Force. The new Eighty-first Congress had cut that to 1.4 million, and only forty-eight air groups.[10] Much of that went to shore up NATO forces in Western Europe rather than to Asia. To congressional observers, it was easy to foist the collapse in Korea on the same policymakers who had abandoned China.

Now a whole new Pandora's box had opened up: that of atomic espionage. The public knew only the barest outlines of the Rosenberg case, but it all pointed to a single inescapable conclusion. The Manhattan Project, the largest and most secret single undertaking by the U.S. government in history, equipped with America's best scientific minds, had also been a beehive of Soviet spies. In fact, we now know that thanks to Soviet espionage, Stalin found out about the atomic bomb before Harry Truman did. "They neatly stole just what we needed," Foreign Minister Molotov recalled years later.[11]

The Rosenberg case infuriated and horrified American public opinion more than any other domestic spy case. The United States had managed to survive two world wars without civilian casualties or deaths at home. Stalin now had a weapon that could reduce New York or Philadelphia or Washington to the ruins of Hiroshima in seconds—and it turned out he had acquired it through espionage.[12] If a top-secret program like the Manhattan Project contained more than its share of spies, how many more might be lurking in the other organs of government?

The atom spy story seemed like just one more in an unbroken string of

Soviet successes and American failures: the takeover of Eastern Europe, the division of Germany, the loss of China. Now there was the invasion of Korea, even as intelligence was reporting that a massive Red Chinese invasion fleet was assembling in the south, possibly for an attack on Formosa. What had gone wrong? All eyes turned, not unreasonably, to the men at the top.

O ne of the most persistent myths of the McCarthy era is that of the "Wise Men"—of how a handful of public-spirited men in the Truman administration carried the nation through the early days of the cold war and halted Stalinist aggression. The roll call is impressive. Dean Acheson, Robert Lovett, Averell Harriman, John J. McCloy, and James Forrestal. Clark Clifford, Charles Bohlen, George Kennan, and General George Marshall. And then, slightly later, Paul Nitze, Dean Rusk, and George Ball. The list of achievements is equally impressive. The Long Telegram, emergency aid to Greece and Turkey, the Berlin blockade, the Marshall Plan, NATO, the creation of the CIA and NSC-68—these stand as their historical monuments, and the official record asserts, their triumphs. Their brilliant and polished memoirs, particularly Dean Acheson's *Present at the Creation*, added to their granite-like luster. That luster sometimes obscured the fact that they were also men who held public trust at the behest of the voters. By 1950 their track record had eroded that trust to a dismal low.

Years later, leftist revisionist historians would assail them as cold-blooded architects of the cold war who instigated a confrontation with the Soviet Union in order to protect the capitalist order from socialism and Third World insurgence. It was true that the Wise Men did form a powerful old boy network, whose members had attended schools like Groton and St. Paul's, and then Harvard, Yale, and Princeton. Personal connections enabled them to shuttle back and forth between jobs at State, the White House, and the Pentagon with ease. Taken as a group, they were the wealthiest, most talented, and most socially distinguished group of men to wield direct political power in America since the Civil War.

They also took the Soviet threat seriously. Acheson's reputation for being somehow "pro-Russian" was undeserved and probably the most serious misconception of all Republican prejudices against the Truman team.[13] It was also true that they drew on a fund of personal talent and, in the case of Kennan and Bohlen, an acute knowledge of the Soviet Union. As a group, they enjoyed the virtues of their class: projecting an air of imperturbability in the midst of crisis, the leisure to be able to take the long view, and to weigh issues on their intrinsic merits rather than political advantage. And unlike other ruling classes past and present, they had a keen understanding of the nature of capitalism. They were determined to maintain America's leadership role economically as well as politically—just the thing for which critics of the left would later castigate them.[14]

They also understood that the cold war was a global struggle, involving many complex parts and elements, which the narrower perspective of Taft Republicans missed. But they saw the confrontation with the Soviet Union in more confident, even arrogant terms than their conservative critics. Kennan's "Long Telegram" set the standard and paradigm. In 1946 he pronounced: "Gauged against the Western world as a whole, the Soviets are still by far the weaker force." The strategy of containment, which Kennan proposed and the Truman administration embraced, assumed that the Soviet Union could not last long in isolation. Eventually it would have to come to terms with the industrialized West. In the end, they believed, economic reality would overcome ideology—just as Marxists did—except in this case, the Soviets would need Western markets, and even Western aid, in order to survive, and that from that economic leverage would come political leverage, and peace.

In the long term, they turned out to be correct. But seeing the collapse of the Soviet Empire in 1989–1990 as proof that containment worked ignores its major weaknesses, which critics on the right like Robert Taft had pointed out. One was that nothing guaranteed that the West would in fact stand firm over the long term. Kennan did recognize that Stalin might succeed in making the Soviet Union the dominant power in the world, and his degree of success "will really depend on the degree of cohesion, firmness, and vigor which the Western world can muster." But Kennan, like the rest, understood this cohesion and vigor in diplomatic, rather than ideological, terms. To the Wise Men, institutions like NATO were more important bulwarks against Soviet aggression than any strong anti-Communist sentiment.

In part this was because Kennan, Acheson, and the others understood America's conflict with Russia as geopolitical. They believed America had stepped into the role that Britain had played in the nineteenth century, as guarantor of the international economic order. Containment was only part of a strategy for using American money, diplomacy, and, if necessary, military force to maintain a stable world—in short, a *Pax Americana* to replace the vanished British one.

The questions of whether that was in fact possible and whether the Soviets might enjoy an additional advantage in the energy and discipline of communism as an ideology was given short shrift. Kennan, for one, believed that "at the bottom the Kremlin's neurotic view of world affairs" sprang from a traditional Russian sense of inferiority regarding the West.[15] In short, Stalin was a Russian who happened to be a Marxist, rather than vice versa, and, similarly, Mao and the Chinese Communists. Here Kennan and the Wise Men overlapped with Jessup, Service, and even Lattimore. It led them to underestimate the weight of the Soviet attack on that *Pax Americana* through espionage and subversion, even as it was taking place under their noses. If critics like Wherry, Jenner, and McCarthy lacked the knowledge and subtlety of a Kennan, Bohlen, or Harriman, they enjoyed the ice-cold clarity of their revulsion toward communism as a doctrine. They instinctively grasped that trying to deal with the Soviets as a conventional power, in conventional geopolitical terms, would be to lose the larger struggle.

One of the few Wise Men who understood that was Truman's secretary of defense, James Forrestal. Although he was as much a product of the Establishment mill as Acheson or Bohlen, Forrestal always remained an outsider. For one thing, he was Irish Catholic; his father had been active in Democratic politics in New York State and a close ally of FDR. A man of relentless energy and capacity for hard work, Forrestal had pushed his way through Princeton and then to the top of the investment banking house of Dillon, Read at age forty-six. As the first secretary of defense in 1947, Forrestal confronted the massive problems of getting America to face the global Soviet threat without ruining itself financially. He had been dismayed at what he saw as the lethargy and apathy in Congress and the country at large. He believed Americans had a tendency to "take for granted that other nations have the same objectives as ourselves," including Stalin's Soviet Union. But the aftermath of World War II had shown otherwise, and shown what a difficult challenge communism as an international movement could be.

Forrestal supported containment. But it also dawned on him that bombers and tanks, and even the atomic bomb, were no real safeguard against a Marxist ideology that defied international boundaries and was as much a system of faith, with its own standards of truth and reality, as a system of politics. He enlisted Edward Willett of Smith College to produce a paper on Marxist doctrine emphasizing the ideological challenge of communism. He sent copies to columnist Walter Lippmann and to *Time*'s Henry Luce, who was bowled over by it. Kennan received a copy and wrote a five-page, single-spaced rebuttal. The Russians only wanted Communist countries under their direct control, Kennan said. This was as true in Asia as it was in Eastern Europe. Even if Communists took over the United States, Kennan added, the Kremlin would probably term it fascism unless it was directed by their own underlings.[16] He didn't bother to speculate about what Americans themselves might say.

And this was the other problem with the Wise Men: their self-confident arrogance. Republicans who challenged them on NATO or Korea were not just wrong. They were "primitives" and "Neanderthals," rock-ribbed reactionaries engaged in a "shameful and nihilistic orgy" of recriminations.

Truman, who bore the brunt end of Taftite attacks, called Republicans "those animals." He told Acheson, "Privately I refer to McCarthy as a pathological liar and [Kenneth] Wherry as the block headed undertaker from Nebraska."[17] He was joined by a chorus of sympathetic journalists such as Stewart and Joseph Alsop, James Reston, and Walter Lippmann. They regularly distinguished between "good" Republicans, like the ex-isolationist Arthur Vandenberg who had seen the light and supported the Truman team, and "bad" ones, who acted out of partisanship and ignorance. If some Republican attacks seem shrill in retrospect (as when Ken Wherry said of Acheson that "the blood of our boys in Korea is on his shoulders, and no one else"), we must remember that the Truman team gave as good as they got.

And there was no opponent they despised more than Joe McCarthy. He was working class; they were varsity class. He was hairy, loud, and sweaty; they were cool, clean, and antiseptic. Acheson reviled him as "the gauleiter and leader of the mob." Truman told Owen Lattimore's sister that "McCarthy has no sense of decency or honor." The hatred and bitterness that a liberal establishment under siege in the winter of 1950–1951 felt toward McCarthy went beyond anything they would later feel toward Richard Nixon. Perhaps only George Wallace, another angry working-class tribune, evoked the same degree of acute physical revulsion. McCarthy's presence had a "unifying effect" in official Washington, Stewart Alsop remembered a decade later. "To sensible and self-respecting Washingtonians, McCarthy was the common enemy."[18]

The furor over McCarthy and McCarthyism obscured the fact that the Wise Men made more than their share of mistakes. One had been the Berlin crisis and blockade, which might have been avoided if the Truman administration had negotiated a clear right of way for Berlin traffic to the West at Potsdam. Another was China. A third would be the Korean War. It was not just the "primitives" who noticed this. Sidney Hook later described the Truman team as "men of integrity and patriotism but either of mediocre intelligence or the most extraordinary ignorance of the nature of the international Communist movement—an ignorance, sad to say, accentuated by stubbornness in refusing to admit that any errors have been made."[19]

Probably the most cogent and influential critics of containment was James Burnham. His books found many readers in Republican circles, including Robert Taft, and were a useful reminder that there were alternatives to what many saw as the Wise Men's strategy of inertia. Containment, Burnham claimed, was the "Eastern college graduate's version of the instinctive viewpoint of the man in the street."[20] Its adherents proclaimed they didn't mean harm to anyone, not even Stalin; they spoke of "international peace" and "collective security," and banished expressions like "preventive war" or

146

"taking the offensive." The containment architect substituted money for deeds. While spending more on defense and assuming a larger international military burden than at any other time in American history, he also avoided having ever to leave the starting gate.

Containment had promised to keep communism within Soviet borders. But "in a profound sense," Burnham wrote, "there is no Soviet border." Wherever Communist doctrines spread, Stalin would find active accomplices and be able to challenge the Western allies. Burnham argued for a policy of active liberation instead. This did *not* mean provoking a war with the USSR, as liberals sometimes liked to charge. It simply meant trying to keep Stalin off balance instead of "letting history do it." America should treat exile governments from Eastern Europe as it treated the Free French and the Free Poles during World War II, as genuine allies rather than diplomatic embarrassments. This included Chiang's Nationalists. Taftite Republicans would always insist that Formosa was not an obstacle to dealings with Red China but a useful ally and asset—an "unsinkable aircraft carrier" in the Pacific, as Douglas MacArthur put it—which should be promoted, supported, and embraced.

Asia was central to the conservative critique of containment. World War II had taught the crucial importance of the Pacific rim to American interests, as the first line of defense for an exposed Western Hemisphere. Asia Firsters never wanted to abandon Europe, but they did ask why Western Europeans could not carry more of the burden of NATO, and whether containment's Eurocentric focus didn't distort America's priorities. Burnham noted that four-fifths of U.S. international aid was flowing to Western Europe (as in the Marshall Plan) and none to Latin America, while most of that earmarked for Asia went to Japan.[21]

To critics, containment's most fatal flaw, however, was that it presented the balance of power between communism and the free world as a status quo. It left Soviet power unimpaired and untouched. "Fill your slave labor camps," Burnham paraphrased Kennan and Acheson as saying to Stalin, "perpetrate your genocides. Organize the industry and manpower of your great sphere into a colossal war-making machine" and liquidate the indigenous cultures of the peoples living in the empire: Ukrainians, Poles, Rumanians, Balts, Kazhaks, Chechens, and others.[22] This was as unacceptable to conservative critics as it was to Joe McCarthy's Polish- and Czech-American voters in Wisconsin. America was trapped in a struggle to the death with communism. It should play to win, just as the Communists were doing. "There is no substitute for victory," said MacArthur. That phrase would become a battle standard for conservative Republicans.

The other problem was not just how, but where or even when, to contain.

The status quo turned out to be constantly shifting, and whenever the United States drew its line in the sand, Stalin and his allies seemed to able to ignore it without penalty. China was a favorite case in point. At Yalta the United States had conceded to the Soviets a strategically commanding position in Manchuria. There the Soviets were able to arm and supply Mao's guerrillas, which eventually meant Communist control over all of Manchuria. Civil war followed, and by 1949 all of China belonged to the Soviet camp. Still, the Truman administration affirmed containment as its policy. Then when Mao threatened to invade Formosa, the administration's initial reaction was to abandon Chiang to his fate—all the while still affirming that containment was American policy.

As Robert Taft later remarked, "Power without foresight leads to disaster."[23] The death of James Forrestal in March 1949 removed the last figure from the Truman inner circle for whom containment was a minimal, not a sufficient, strategy for dealing with the Soviet threat. In January 1950 Secretary of State Acheson made a speech at the National Press Club defining America's defensive perimeter in Asia. In it, he neglected to include South Korea. Five months later Communist troops crossed the 38th parallel and headed for Seoul. Acheson later claimed that he was simply reflecting the considered views of the Joint Chiefs of Staff, even Douglas MacArthur himself, that the Korean peninsula was untenable from a military standpoint.[24] Be that as it may, formerly secret Russian sources now reveal that Acheson's words helped to tip Stalin's hand and convinced him that if his ally Kim Il Sung invaded the south, the Americans would in fact do nothing.[25] Then, overnight, to everyone's surprise (including Stalin and Mao), Acheson and the administration decided Korea was indeed of vital concern and American soldiers should be sent to—what else?—"contain" Soviet aggression.

The Acheson speech and the Korean debacle were all part of the picture of a foreign policy, and a Democratic administration, out of control. Acheson's approval rating plunged to 20 percent by the end of 1950 and Truman's to 39 percent. Charges that opponents were just "isolationists" and "reactionaries" were beginning to wear thin. A willingness to fight in Korea became a crucial test of resolve. Confidence had sunk so low that many people, even in the administration, were amazed that America was going to stand and fight.[26] But to what end? To critics like Taft and McCarthy, Truman's efforts to build resistance to Soviet aggression through joint resolutions in the United Nations, rather than in Congress, seemed daylight madness. Americans, and Americans alone, should decide where and when American soldiers would fight and die.

The one ray of sunlight in the Korean debacle, at least in conservative eyes, was Douglas MacArthur. On September 15, 1950, MacArthur made his surprise amphibious landing at Inchon. After Truman and the Joint Chiefs had dragged their feet and tried to hobble his efforts, MacArthur had at one stroke reversed the course of the war. North Korean resistance collapsed as American forces raced back up the peninsula. For the first time since 1917, communism was on the retreat.

A week later, on September 23, 1950, Republicans joined concerned Democrats in passing the Internal Security Act. Truman promptly vetoed it, and Congress decided to override. In a profound sense, the act was the fruit of McCarthy's revelations about official laxness regarding Communist subversion, and the Hiss case. Academic historians have generally shook their head over the McCarran Act, as it was called, and treated it as a full-out assault on civil liberties.[27] But to Senator Pat McCarran, his Democratic colleagues, and Republicans across the aisle, it brought a breath of fresh air and honesty to the question of Communist subversion.

The McCarran Act made it illegal to conspire with others to commit acts leading to "the establishment of a totalitarian dictatorship in the United States." It banned anyone belonging to a subversive organization from holding government employ. It left in place the Truman loyalty program but established a five-man, nonpartisan Subversive Activities Control Board to evaluate and add groups to the attorney general's list. That list had been steadily shrinking since the war; now Congress wanted it strengthened and expanded. The law also empowered the president to round up and detain "subversives," which in 1950 meant Communists, in the event of a national emergency.

Those provisions made civil libertarians shiver, both then and now. Yet even when Truman was busy reinstituting the draft and considering other stringent wartime measures, he never evoked the relevant clauses of the act; nor did Eisenhower. No one was ever arrested or detained under the Internal Security Act.[28] It was just what its sponsors said it was—a measure for extreme emergencies—passed at a time when confidence in establishment institutions to protect the United States stood at an all-time low.

It also reflected a basic position that conservatives and even some liberals embraced: that there was more at stake in defending the United States than just protecting the right of dissident groups to say or do whatever they liked. That would become an increasingly unpopular position as time went on; today, of course, it seems barely recognizable. Yet it was basic to cold war attitudes. One admirer of the McCarran Act, Willmoore Kendall of Yale, explained the situation this way:

> By the late 30's, that is, by the end of the second decade after the Communist Revolution, every free nation in the world, whether it realized it or not, faced

149

the following question: Are we or are we not going to permit the emergence, within our midst, of totalitarian movements? . . . We [the United States]—whatever other free nations may do or not do—are going to put certain major obstacles in the way of such movements. . . . we at least are not going to facilitate their emergence.[29]

That may seem a bleak, self-defeating doctrine in retrospect. But proponents viewed the alternative—that Americans cannot take steps to protect their freedoms against a totalitarian movement because, paradoxically, they are committed to protect their freedoms—the same way.

Meanwhile, on October 7 U.S. troops crossed the 38th parallel, and MacArthur pushed on to the Communist capital at Pyongyang. On October 15, less than three weeks before the 1950 midterm election, Truman arranged to meet MacArthur at Wake Island—ostensibly to confer on the course of the war, in reality in hopes that some of the general's success would rub off on Truman's sagging political reputation. It didn't. Instead, a Republican tidal wave hit Congress, and the Senate. In the California Senate race Richard Nixon swamped his liberal Popular Front opponent Helen Gahagan Douglas by 700,000 votes. Challenger Everett Dirksen toppled majority leader Scott Lucas in Illinois; James Duff replaced majority whip Francis Myers in Pennsylvania. Robert Taft was reelected with 57.5 percent of the vote.

The most sensational victory belonged to John M. Butler, Joe McCarthy's handpicked candidate to defeat Millard Tydings in Maryland. It was a stunning vindication for McCarthy's cause. Both Butler and Tydings ran campaigns that hinged on the question of Joe McCarthy and Communists in government. Butler won by the largest margin a Republican senatorial candidate ever secured in Maryland: nearly 40,000 votes. Tydings later cried foul, pointing to some scurrilous Butler pamphlets that used a composite picture (it was clearly labeled as such) of Tydings standing next to CPUSA's Earl Browder. Tydings and other critics would claim that McCarthy had set up this and other "dirty tricks" to defeat his former tormentor. Certainly McCarthy had devoted extra time and resources to the campaign; he assigned Jean Kerr to work full-time with Butler's people. He also believed that Tydings's position during the hearings had been indistinguishable from that of Browder and the *Daily Worker*. But he had disapproved of using the picture, calling it "wrong" (Kerr, on the other hand, thought it fine and proper).[30]

In fact, Tydings had been in trouble even before he collided with Butler or McCarthy. As the high-profile chairman of the Armed Service Committee, he had to bear some of the blame for America's lack of preparedness in Korea. In addition, a new kind of Maryland voter had sprung up after the war: the suburban middle-class commuter who drove to work in the District of Columbia or Baltimore, and then home to Silver Spring and Chevy Chase, or Reisterstown and Hyattsville. For these voters, many of whom worked for the government and were veterans like McCarthy, the Tydings Committee hearings were in effect local news. They had heard the charges and counter-charges all that spring and summer, and made up their own minds. Further-more, two other groups of Maryland voters turned Republican that year: working-class Catholics and African-Americans. Black Marylanders were fed up with Tydings's support for Jim Crow; in one precinct in Baltimore, they voted for Butler by 85 percent.[31] As for Maryland's Catholics, McCarthy and anticommunism certainly played a part to steering them in Butler's direc-tion. But it was Maryland's changing political environment, more than Joe McCarthy, that ultimately toppled Millard Tydings.

The press, however, preferred to give the Wisconsin senator the credit for his rival's defeat—which McCarthy did nothing to discourage. Stories that he had laid out a trail of dirty tricks, even that his operatives had con-ducted "a reign of terror" across the state in order to destroy Millard Tydings, stuck fast.[32] McCarthy was now branded not just as a reckless smearer and pathological liar, but a sleazy political operative willing to use faked pho-tographs and false evidence to destroy anyone who stood in his way.

None of this could detract from the larger meaning of the 1950 election. As in '46 but not '48, Republicans ran hard on the anti-Communist issue, which was now inextricably McCarthy's issue. Democrats were still the fa-vored party on domestic and economic policy. They managed to retain con-trol of both the Senate and the House, although they continued to lose support in important suburban districts. Yet American voters were finding that Republican attacks on the Truman administration as the "party of be-trayal" contained a germ of truth. Democrats were proving incapable of deal-ing with a growing Soviet menace abroad, just as they had earlier allowed it to fester at home. Voters might not be ready to conflate the two, as McCarthy did when he referred to the Democrats as "Commie-crats" in a Maryland speech that fall.[33] But they were in no mood to reinforce failure. A huge polit-ical opportunity now loomed ahead for conservative Republicans, a chance to capture the terms of the debate and steer American foreign policy in a new direction.

The new year brought a deepening gloom, a sense of crisis and collapse at the center. In late November, Red Chinese armies had swept into Korea, and American intelligence had failed to detect than until it was too late. Soon the Communists were once again besieging Seoul. Bipartisan Republicans had long since defected from the Truman camp; now Democrats Pat McCarran and James Eastland called on Acheson to resign.[34] Under severe political pressure, Truman agreed to appoint a blue-ribbon commission headed by re-tired Admiral Nimitz to take another look at his loyalty program's system of vet-ting. The Nimitz Commission would find that the system had been too lax, much as McCarthy had originally charged, and recommended a much tougher policy regarding possible loyalty lapses. Reluctantly Truman agreed.[35]

McCarthy himself played only a small part in the next congressional clash with Truman—the so-called Great Debate of January 1951 over the power of the executive to make war and foreign policy without Congress. The Wherry Resolution tried to stop Truman from sending troops to Europe or anywhere else without prior congressional authorization. Truman argued that as commander in chief he was free to take whatever steps he considered necessary to do the job. Senator Karl Mundt put the issue at stake bluntly: "If we blindly surrender our authority to the Chief Executive . . . we shall be surrendering the constitutional authority which we have as Senators of the United States." A watered-down Democrat version of the resolution, admon-ishing but not requiring the president to be in touch before making any pre-cipitate moves, managed to pass. The Truman-Acheson position on the power of the chief executive to make war as he saw fit had held, but just barely: 45 to 41.

But the Truman administration's difficulties were just beginning. Even as its relationship with the Hill seemed to be returning to an even keel in the early spring of 1951, the White House ran aground on MacArthur.

Douglas MacArthur is the sort of figure people either revere or revile. As with Joe McCarthy, the middle ground tends to disappear. In 1951, MacArthur was America's most distinguished, and at seventy-one its oldest, commanding general. He could claim credit for the successful Pacific island-hopping campaign in World War II that had dismantled Japan's empire with a minimum of American casualties (although enemies never forgot his aban-donment of the Philippines). Then, to the amazement of critics, MacArthur installed a democratic, even progressive regime in postwar Japan and healed relations with that country. In July 1950 he had stepped into the breach and salvaged the war in Korea, turning it from a last-ditch defense to a stunning victory.

Liberals, and many fellow officers, viewed him as a pretentious wind-bag, with more ego than talent. Conservatives saw him as the one highly placed official after Forrestal's death who understood the real nature of the conflict with Soviet communism. He was their hero—in McCarthy's words, "the one man who, above all others, has stood in the way of Communist domination of all of Asia and the lands of the Pacific."[36] MacArthur had turned Korea into the sort of war of liberation Taft, Burnham, and others had been arguing for. As his troops took the Communist capital of Pyongyang in late October 1950, he and his staff toured the North Korean leadership's abandoned offices, where pictures of Stalin and Kim Il Sung still hung on the walls. On November 24 MacArthur told reporters he would "have the boys home by Christmas."

The very next day, 300,000 Chinese infantry suddenly attacked when Allied forces moved too close to the Yalu River border. MacArthur and the administration found themselves in "an entirely new war." The stakes were huge. All-out war with China would bring America to the brink of war with the Soviet Union, which meant possible use of nuclear weapons. All through the winter, as American forces fell back to the south, the White House could never be sure if the Chinese intervention in Korea was the main event or merely a feint for a Soviet thrust into Europe.

Almost half a century later, sources from both China and the former Soviet Union have helped to clear up the mystery. They reveal that Mao had intended to intervene in Korea from the very beginning, convinced that the United States's military deployment in both South Korea and the Taiwanese straits was a prelude to a strike at him (when in fact Americans were reacting to Mao's own threat to invade Taiwan). The only hesitations in his mind were whether the Soviets would back him up with air support (they would, with Russian pilots flying planes with Chinese and North Korean markings) and when his armies should strike. Claims by the Wise Men then, and historians later, that MacArthur's rash advance on the Yalu forced a reluctant China to intervene, have proved false. Mao's military men had encouraged him to delay only in order to draw the Americans deeper into North Korea. "To hook a big fish," Mao's top general told him, "you must let the fish taste your bait."[37]

If the Americans were unsure of what the Soviets and Chinese were up to (later MacArthur would even accuse Truman of concealing from him the evidence he did have via the Indian ambassador of Peking's intentions), their antagonists had no such problem. Thanks to two highly placed British spies, Guy Burgess and Donald Maclean, they were able to keep track of every move. From his post in the United Nations's Far East Commission, Burgess saw virtually every document that passed between the two allies: from military intelligence reports from MacArthur's headquarters to Anglo-American assessments of North Korean and Chinese troop strengths.[38] Maclean, meanwhile, served as head of chancery in the British embassy in Washington, and so was able to pass on even more valuable secrets, including British Prime Minister Clement Atlee's private meeting with Truman in December, when the president mentioned using the atom bomb to halt the Chinese advance.*[39]

At the same time, however, Truman and the Wise Men vetoed MacArthur's plan to bring Chiang and the Nationalist armies onto the battlefield. They believed, with reason, that any precipitate response to the Chinese attack might trigger an all-out war, which would also bring in the Russians. They forbade MacArthur to cut the Chinese lines of supply into Korea, then allowed him to hit the critical bridges across the Yalu River only so long as the bombs fell on the Korean, not the Chinese, riverbank.[40] For the first time, the U.S. Army learned what fighting a limited war meant: civilian bureaucrats in Washington dictating bombing targets, the enemy retreating to sanctuaries across the border, and United Nations resolutions controlling the rhythm of battle and its ultimate objectives. MacArthur fumed about a civilian interference in his command "without precedent in history" and leaked his dissatisfaction to the press.

Nonetheless, MacArthur and his new field commander, Matthew Ridgway, managed to turn the tide again. On March 14, 1951, United Nations forces retook Seoul. On March 19 Acheson, Secretary of Defense Marshall, and President Truman prepared to issue an appeal to the Chinese Communists for a negotiated settlement. MacArthur showed what he thought of that idea by delivering a direct ultimatum to the Chinese, ordering them off the peninsula or threatening to widen the war. Hopes of tempting the Chinese to the bargaining table collapsed.[41]

Truman's advisers were outraged. With a trembling voice, Assistant Secretary of Defense Robert Lovett accused MacArthur of usurping the president's authority to decide the nation's foreign policy. Acheson called it "a major act of sabotage against a Government operation." Truman had already decided to remove MacArthur when the general sent a letter to Republican House leader Joe Martin, which Martin released to the press. MacArthur complained that "it was strangely difficult" for some in the administration to understand that "here in Asia is where the Communist conspirators have elected to make their play for global conquest." He warned, "If we lose this

---

*Not until Maclean's defection to the Soviet Union in 1951 did American and British secret services realize what Maclean had been up to and gauge how much damage he and Burgess had done during their years in Washington. The Venona decrypt project, for instance, had revealed that someone in the British embassy had been leaking sensitive data about the Los Alamos project to the Soviets since 1944. Now everyone realized it had been Maclean. If anything proved that underestimating the reach of Soviet espionage and subversion could have very serious consequences, it was the Donald Maclean case.

war to Communism in Asia the fall of Europe is inevitable. . . . There is," he concluded, "no substitute for victory."[42]

On March 30 Julius and Ethel Rosenberg were found guilty of espionage. In sentencing them to death on April 5, Judge Irving R. Kaufman made it clear that he, and millions of other Americans, held them in some degree responsible for the Korean debacle. A nuclear-armed Russia had become a wild card in the international deck. Its allies had invaded Korea; they had pushed China into the war, and hamstrung America's ability to respond in the United Nations. It was all too easy, in the wake of the Hiss case and McCarthy's revelations, to believe that Soviet agents were secretly hampering General MacArthur's efforts to win the war as well.

In this tense atmosphere, Truman's dismissal of MacArthur on April 11, 1951, struck like a thunderbolt. Almost 100,000 telegrams deluged the White House, almost all of them attacking the decision. One wondered aloud if there wasn't "another Alger Hiss at Blair House." On April 14, the Republican Congressional Committee reported that the mail its members were receiving was running one thousand to one against Truman.[43] Both the Texas and Wisconsin state legislatures passed resolutions supporting MacArthur and inviting him to speak. The International Longshoreman's Union held a two-hour work stoppage to protest his dismissal. A Gallup poll showed 66 percent of the public disapproving of Truman's decision.[44]

Conservative Republicans, including McCarthy, poured onto the Senate floor to express their displeasure. William Jenner called for Truman's impeachment and warned that "this country today is in the hands of the secret inner coterie which is directed by agents of the Soviet Union." McCarthy made one of his harshest attacks on Truman and his advisers, charging that they had dreamed up MacArthur's dismissal during a "midnight Bourbon-and-Benedictine session" (a phrase that would become notorious). He called it "a great Communist victory" that "may well have condemned thousands of American boys to death, and may well have condemned Western civilization."

The new senator from California, Richard Nixon, was calmer. But like McCarthy and Jenner, he worried that the dismissal of MacArthur "means the pro-Lattimore-Jessup bloc in the State Department has prevailed." It seemed one more step in the fatal betrayal of America's interests in Asia, that began with its failed China policy. Under the influence of men like Owen Lattimore and John Stewart Service, the Truman administration had delivered China to the Communists. Now it seemed ready to deliver Korea over to the same fate.

Nixon turned to a Democratic senator who had said Asia was not the place to defeat communism in a war. "Maybe," Nixon said, "but Asia is the place where we can lose to Communism without a war." Then Kenneth Wherry strode in to ask if his colleagues had seen the last report on the Senate news ticker: Eugene Dennis, head of the Communist Party, was applauding the MacArthur dismissal, which Communist organs like the *Daily Worker* had been demanding for weeks. Perhaps now, he thundered, the Democrats would admit that the firing of General MacArthur was a victory for communism, and no one else.[45]

Republicans arranged for MacArthur to address a joint session of Congress, and southern Democrats such as Richard Russell cleared the way for congressional hearings on his dismissal. The same day that MacArthur's plane touched down at San Francisco International Airport, Senator Arthur Vandenberg, Truman's closest ally in the Republican ranks, died after months of battling cancer. Bipartisanship was not only over; it was swinging the other way. Joe McCarthy told Democrats they had "a glorious opportunity" to stand up "and let themselves be counted as being against treason." If they didn't, "they will forever, and rightly, have labeled their party as the party of betrayal."[46]

Douglas MacArthur's arrival in San Francisco on April 18 looked more like an ancient Roman triumph than a cashiered general returning home. Five hundred thousand people greeted him along his route from the airport to the city, where he rode in a massive tickertape parade the next morning. That afternoon MacArthur flew to Washington, where he gave an electrifying address to both houses of Congress. He repeated his call for victory, not stalemate, in Korea, and concluded with his famous "Old soldiers never die; they just fade away" farewell.

Nine days later Robert Taft delivered a blistering attack on the Truman administration. When Democrats claimed that MacArthur had to be dismissed in order to prevent an all-out war with China, Taft retorted we were already there.[47] When they claimed that MacArthur had usurped constitutional authority by his actions, Taft said that Truman had been doing that for months, by excluding Congress from any role in authorizing troops or declaring war, as the Constitution required. It was the president's judgment, not MacArthur's, that had to stand up to scrutiny. "The President started the Korean war," Taft asserted. "It is *his* war." Truman had intervened to prevent Communist aggression; yet now he and his advisers were willing to permit Chinese aggression by opting for stalemate rather than victory. "In short, under the present policy of the administration, they have abandoned every ideal that was asserted as a justification for the Korean War."

William Jenner joined Taft at the podium to say that Acheson's supposed blindness to the ideological threat of communism, along with MacArthur's dismissal, proved that "this nation and its foreign policy are still in the hands of the men who betrayed it in the past." In other words, there was no way to resolve the problem of a failed policy without asking whether its failures were accidental or deliberate.

Taftite Republicans had called for an investigation of MacArthur's dismissal in the context of the administration's East Asia policy. They wanted to focus on the role that men like Lattimore, Service, Lauchlin Currie, and Alger Hiss had played in shaping it. Senate Democrats narrowly managed to prevent public hearings, 41 to 37, but not the investigation itself.[48] Senators from the Armed Services and Foreign Affairs committees listened as General MacArthur described the dire situation in Korea.

> Our losses already, the battle casualties, are approaching 65,000. This conflict in Korea has already lasted almost as long as General Eisenhower's decisive campaign which brought the European war to an end. And yet the only program that I have been able to hear is that we shall indecisively go on resisting aggression. . . . If you do, you are going to have thousands and thousands and thousands of American lives that will fall. . . . Where does the responsibility for that blood rest?

Of course, MacArthur was wrong. Korea did not turn into the American bloodbath he and other conservatives had bleakly imagined (or, it should be added, that Mao and Stalin had hoped). But at the time the scale of the Chinese effort was not easy to gauge. During the first fifty days of the Chinese offensive, Mao's armies took more than 85,000 casualties, and still they kept coming.[49] Although the battle lines were hardening along the 38th parallel, China still seemed determined to overrun all of Korea, and America was certainly in a major shooting war. MacArthur rhetorically asked: "What is the policy in Korea?" Some were now arguing that the problem was not that there was no policy or a failed one, but that the administration's policy was proving to be all too successful: of allowing the Communists to consolidate their gains in Asia and to give the Soviet juggernaut yet one more success. For McCarthy and his supporters, the problem America faced was not so much failure at the top as betrayal.

Chapter 8

Supporters' Club

Why did people support Joe McCarthy? One way to answer that question is to listen to Robert Taft, the Republican Party's leading conservative, explaining to an audience of Ohio businessmen how New Deal liberalism and socialism promoted class conflict rather than individual freedom. "They are based," he explained, "on the theory that only government will protect the interests of different classes and control of all activity must be concentrated in a great central government. That principle the people of America rejected in 1950, and will reject in 1952 if we do a proper job of publicity and organization."

It is classic Taft: clear, logical, straightforward—and very dull. By contrast, when Joe McCarthy showed up at the Kansas Day Republican banquet on January 29, 1951, he told the story of an American boy named Bob Smith, from Middleburg, Pennsylvania, who was sitting on a hilltop in a Marine position near the Yalu River when Chinese troops attacked. "Before the red dawn broke over the mountains of Manchuria on November 30," McCarthy said, "much western blood and eastern blood had mixed in the Yalu River. As that cold red dawn broke Bob Smith was lying in a gutter near the Changjin Reservoir. Three cold bloody dawns he saw break, as his bullet-riddled body lay in the gutter covered only by a raincoat." McCarthy described to his spellbound audience how the Chinese Communists, those so-called agrarian reformers, entered the trench and, thinking Bob Smith dead, stripped his body. After three more days lying exposed to the elements, Smith finally crawled to safety and was rescued during a Marine counterattack. "Bob Smith is home today," McCarthy went on, "but his hands and legs are still in the hills beyond the Yalu River."

Private Bob Smith, McCarthy explained, was the victim of a failed foreign policy, of men who were leading America down "a road strewn with Bob Smiths . . . and watered with the tears of American wives and mothers." Acheson, Jessup, and the other Wise Men had ignored the threat of communism until it was too late, and which was now wreaking havoc and death in Korea. "Here the treason of Yalta was brought to full bloom." He came back to the young GI in his thunderous peroration:

> Bob Smith has no hands for us to shake today. He has no feet on which to walk . . . but some day he will have artificial limbs and when he does he should walk straight to the headquarters of the United Nations. He should walk to the office of the secretary of state. He should say to him: "Mr. Secretary, as I fought up the slopes of the Changjin Reservoir I was met by Communists firing rockets from horseback—a reincarnation of the horsemen of Genghis Khan. Mr. Secretary, do you still think they are agrarian reformers? . . ."
>
> Bob Smith is the symbol of the courage we need. He is the symbol of the honesty we do not have. He is the symbol of the honesty which we must regain if our civilization is to survive.[1]

Why did people support McCarthy? One theory holds that his core supporters were "a coalition of the aggrieved," men and women who had never come to terms with the world created by the New Deal or World War II and wanted out. Richard Rovere dismissed them as low-class, low-intelligence "zanies and zombies and compulsive haters" who had followed earlier demagogues such as Huey Long and Father Coughlin.[2] Social scientists of the time worried that McCarthy was unleashing the forces of a radical, xenophobic populism, a "plebeian insurrection" that would lead to the sorts of movements that Hitler and Mussolini had spawned in Europe in the twenties.[3] One scholar, Martin Trow, studied McCarthy supporters in a Vermont small town and found they disliked big business as much as big government or big labor, while their anticommunism was overshadowed by their commitment to rugged individualism and agrarian moral virtues. McCarthyites were really nineteenth-century populists, not twentieth-century conservatives, Trow decided—and social scientists like Daniel Bell and Seymour Martin Lipset tended to agree.[4]

Alas, this ingenious theory does not hold up very well. Michael Paul Rogin has shown in careful detail that McCarthy found his biggest fans among typical Republican voters and that his appeal reflected, in Rogin's words, "the traditional constituency and traditional attitudes of the Republican right wing." McCarthyism, Rogin concluded, "was not a mass protest; it flourished within the normal workings of American politics, not radically outside them." But even this does not tell the entire story. Rogin showed that while Republicans tended to like what McCarthy was doing and Democrats did not, McCarthy "also received considerable backing in the polls from traditional Democratic ethnic and social groups." This included Roman Catholics and unskilled laborers and small business people. It did not include unionized labor, and it did not include American Jews, who were overwhelmingly anti-McCarthy.[5]

McCarthy's political base was both narrower, and broader, than his opponents imagined. At its center were Wisconsin's German, Polish, and Czech rural voters, who remained loyal to him almost to the end.[6] Beyond that, by 1954 McCarthy had won a dedicated following among roughly one-third of the American public, who backed him in the polls through thick and thin. Although detractors pointed out that McCarthy's supporters tended to be among the less educated, a look at the Gallup polls in those years shows that this was not absolutely true: people who never finished grade school, for instance, were among his strongest opponents. In general, people at the top of the social ladder, including professional and academic types, people in government and big business, and people at the bottom disliked McCarthy. It was those in the middle—people who might have gone to high school but not to college, who had to earn a living on their own without the benefit of a union or a professional degree, who were informed if not particularly well versed about what was happening in the world and in Korea—who were willing to give McCarthy a benefit of a doubt and believed that he had found an issue, domestic communism, of genuine concern to them.

In the 1950s there were large numbers of these people—in Wisconsin, in parts of the rural Midwest, the South (Texas was a major pro-McCarthy state), and in ethnic neighborhoods in northeastern cities—forming the geographic contours of McCarthy country. Far from being aggrieved or resentful, as the social scientists believed, they had found fresh opportunities and prosperity in postwar America. They were also anxious about whether those opportunities could continue and what America's future would be if Communists and their sympathizers were allowed to dominate the world outside.

Such were McCarthy's supporters—if, that is, they had heard of him. Millions of Americans had not. Almost one-third (30 percent) of respondents to a Gallup poll in July 1951 could not identify McCarthy by name; of those who did, the majority were not favorably disposed toward him (Republicans were almost evenly split). In another poll taken at the end of March 1953, almost two-thirds of those interviewed had no opinion at all about McCarthy.[7] It was not until early 1954, just before the televised Army-McCarthy hearings, that

McCarthy acquired anything like true national celebrity and a strong follow-ing (46 percent favorable rating). Even then, chances that Americans would follow him blindly anywhere he wanted to lead them, even to the White House, were remote. In December 1953 Gallup asked what would happen if Dwight Eisenhower and Joe McCarthy squared off for the Republican nomi-nation in 1956. Almost 80 percent of respondents said they would prefer Eisenhower. The prospect of a McCarthyite third party, the sort of radical pop-ulist specter many of his critics feared, garnered exactly 5 percent support.[8]

This seems a little surprising given the worries, even hysteria, that Mc-Carthyism generated among Washington insiders, journalists, and other es-tablishment figures. Yet it was precisely this hysteria that convinced others that McCarthy must be onto something and that, despite his excesses and often strange behavior, he was probably more right than wrong. As one sym-pathetic editorial put it at the time, "There is such a thing as a man gaining strength by the enemies he makes." It was as the liberals' whipping boy, not as anti-Communist crusader, that he attracted his most thoughtful defenders.

This was particularly true of the group we can call the professional anti-Communists—people who made a living pursuing and exposing Commu-nist penetration of American society. As a group it included J. Edgar Hoover and his FBI. It also included full-time investigators for congressional com-mittees or private firms, most of whom were lawyers or ex–FBI men; journal-ists who devoted their columns to exposing Communist targets and their liberal allies; and former Communists who wrote books and articles on the party, its front organizations, and its underground apparatus and regularly testified in front of Senate committees or HUAC. The expert testimony of a Whittaker Chambers or a Freda Utley before an investigating committee; the careful, patient collecting of documents, affidavits, and witnesses by a Robert Morris or a Jay Sourwine; an article exposing Communists in the unions by Willard Edwards in the *Chicago Tribune* and the scathing commentary of George Sokolsky in the *New York Journal-American* or Westbrook Pegler in the *Chicago Tribune*—all formed the larger backdrop for McCarthy's own ef-forts, and McCarthy quickly became part of their tightly woven network.

Then and later these figures were dismissed as paranoid red baiters and reactionaries.[9] However, as in the case of Whittaker Chambers's charges against Alger Hiss, and Bella Dodd's campaign against Communist teacher unions in New York, later revelations have tended to bear them out.[10] What they found in Joe McCarthy at least initially was a Washington politician who spoke out publicly on an issue they been pressing for years and was willing to go where the others feared to tread. "Joe McCarthy just puts it on the line," columnist George Sokolsky told his ABC radio audience in April 1950, although he admitted McCarthy's message of the real threat Communist subversion posed "may be too strong" for some.

Sokolsky was a Russian Jew who had spent his adolescence on the streets of New York and his young adulthood as a reporter in China. He was impressed by McCarthy's masculine proletarian appeal. When he stopped by McCarthy's office in April 1950 at the height of the Tydings hearings, they ate lunch on paper plates ("we actually used forks, but forgot the napkins"). Sokolsky swallowed whole McCarthy's mendacious account of his war service. But Sokolsky recognized in him a man like himself—someone who had received his education in the real world, "without the benefit of Groton and Harvard." Sokolsky believed, along with McCarthy, that Stalinist subversion held a dagger at America's throat even as it was struggling to win the cold war. Now "he has blown off the lid" on Communists in government, Sokolsky said, "and it will stay off."[11]

This was what the anti-Communists appreciated more than anything else: McCarthy's relentless determination to keep before the public eye the issue that they understood best: the threat of domestic subversion. It was Joe McCarthy who showed that Alger Hiss's treachery had not been a one-time fluke. It was McCarthy who challenged flimsy administration excuses for failing to deal with Hiss and other personnel with similar suspect backgrounds. It was McCarthy who first revealed to the public that Communist-run organizations like the Institute of Pacific Relations had had a direct adverse impact on American policymaking as well as serving as conduits for Soviet spying. In terms of alerting and summoning public opinion to their side, McCarthy proved indispensable to the anti-Communist cause. Very few imagined him to be an angel, but they recognized his usefulness, to both them and the country at large, and they were willing to help by keeping him informed on the true nature of the Communist threat.

The most famous of all, Whittaker Chambers, met with McCarthy and Jean Kerr several times at his Maryland farm, to instruct them on how the Communist underground functioned and how it garnered aboveground support. George Sokolsky became a trusted counselor; he would put McCarthy in touch for the first time with Roy Cohn. Hearst journalist Ed Nellor of the *Washington Times-Herald* wrote speeches for McCarthy (including, as we saw, the Wheeling speech), and Willard Edwards of the *Chicago Tribune* regularly helped him sniff out leads for future investigations.

McCarthy's connections with J. B. Matthews were typical. In the early fifties Matthews was working as a consultant on Communist matters for the Hearst newspaper syndicate (both George Sokolsky and Louis Budenz were among his protégés). Matthews was supposed to preside over a legendary collection of files called Appendix 9, which contained the names of 100,000 individuals with Communist affiliations along with an elaborate cross-index.[12] J.B., as friends called him, regularly advised McCarthy on where and how to find targets for his anti-Communist campaigns. McCarthy in turn would ask for help with leads and references and would arrange for Matthews to testify during committee hearings. Eventually he even put him in charge of his PSI staff.

Matthews had been Martin Dies's right-hand man, and the old resentments about the way he and Dies had been treated by New Deal liberals never really faded. He encouraged McCarthy to see New Dealers as the willing accomplices of Communist subversion; he explained the intricacies of the Ware spy cell and even introduced him to the esoterica of Communist conspiracy theories, such as the Bulwinkle committee and the dinner party of the infamous Dr. Wirt.* If any one person is responsible for McCarthy's rhetoric about a "conspiracy so immense," and seeing its hidden influence retrospectively in specific historical events, it was J. B. Matthews. At one point he even composed for McCarthy a speech showing how Harry Dexter White, the Soviet agent, had used his influence in the Treasury Department to provoke the Japanese attack at Pearl Harbor.[†]

Matthews, along with Sokolsky, James Burnham, and Freda Utley, also supplied a steady stream of articles in magazines like The *freeman* and *American Mercury* defending McCarthy in the teeth of liberal criticism and media hostility. They pointed out that the standard claim that McCarthy had never exposed a real Communist in the government was demonstrably false: that Gustavo Duran, Mary Jane Keeney, and Edward Posniak, not to mention Owen Lattimore and John Carter Vincent, were all either active Communists or had been so named. (Keeney's true identity as a KGB agent was still not known to the public.) They answered charges that McCarthy misused his senatorial immunity in order to smear innocent people, or that the Wheeling speech had made a mountain out of a molehill. Another defender pointed out in an *American Mercury* article in May 1954, every one of the security or loyalty risks McCarthy had brought forward in his February 20, 1950, Senate speech was now out of the State Department, by either resignation or dismissal.[13] In short,

---

*Dr. William Wirt had attended a dinner party in October 1933 at the home of a prominent New Dealer. Later he claimed that over dinner the assembled administration officials discussed their plan for a Communist takeover of the United States. (Wirt claimed a representative of Tass, the Soviet news agency, was also present.) Wirt presented his story to a special investigating committee headed by Senator Alfred Bulwinkle, who spent his time poking holes in it, which of course redoubled suspicions of a massive cover-up of Communist penetration of the Roosevelt administration. †As far as we know, McCarthy never gave it.

they provided a balance within the public sphere to the vituperation and attack that McCarthy normally faced.

The professional investigators and special legal counsel who worked for various congressional committees offered McCarthy similar support. Robert Morris began his career with McCarthy on the Tydings Committee, then joined the Internal Security Subcommittee under McCarran and Jenner, until he left in 1957. A careful and meticulous researcher himself, Morris did not find McCarthy's methods excessive or outrageous. On the contrary, Morris admired his courage and his thick skin. He, like the other professionals, realized McCarthy's limitations. "Hoover knew that Joe wasn't the best guy in the world to be doing this," Morris recalled. "We all did. But his attitude was, 'Thank God somebody's doing it.'"[14]

In 1956 a young lawyer named William Rusher came to Washington to work for Morris and the Internal Security committee. To Rusher, McCarthy, despite his Senate censure, remained a hero and a model of the tenacious anti-Communist investigator. Although Rusher admitted that McCarthy could not show any "achievements of the first rank" like HUAC's exposure of Alger Hiss, he believed his investigations could not be dismissed as the ravings of a paranoiac or an unscrupulous opportunist. "These fantastic caricatures," Rusher would remember years later, "were the products of men who either had good reason to hate McCarthy (e.g., the Communists), or who sincerely believed they had, and accordingly saw him only through the haze of their own animosities and fears."[15]

Later, McCarthy's disgrace would cast a permanent pall over the work of professional anti-Communist investigators and their reputations—a classic example of guilt by association. This is particularly true of Hoover and the FBI, whose anti-Communist investigations have given it the reputation of being a kind of American Gestapo. In reality, feelings at the FBI regarding McCarthy tended to be ambivalent. There has been much sensational speculation about how close the relationship between Hoover and McCarthy really was. There have even been suggestions that he was really just Hoover's stooge—not unlike what McCarthy imagined was the relationship between Acheson and Truman. Historian David Oshinsky has shown that in the early days of the Tydings investigations, Hoover kept McCarthy well informed at weekly meetings in his office. It was Hoover who had advised McCarthy to hire Don Surine, an ex–FBI man, as his top investigator, and Hoover who enabled McCarthy to expose Edward Posniak's Communist connections, which the State Department's own loyalty file had failed to show—although Hoover was careful to avoid letting the FBI be identified as the source.

However, McCarthy's gross misstep in the Lattimore case soured their relationship. Declassified records show that the FBI had had Lattimore under surveillance for years and was very much aware of his underground contacts. By dragging Lattimore into the limelight, McCarthy had endangered the entire operation. McCarthy's compulsion for making public what Hoover believed should be kept under wraps led to a growing distrust and distance between the two men. FBI agent Robert Lamphere, who oversaw the original Venona decryption program, noted that Hoover believed McCarthy to be a hopeless amateur, and Lamphere had to concur.[16]

Yet Hoover was willing to defend McCarthy publicly when the occasion arose. "Whenever you attack subversives," he told a reporter from the *San Diego Evening Tribune*, "you are going to be the victim of the most extremely vicious criticism that can be made." Hoover said he viewed McCarthy as a friend, "and I believe he so views me. Certainly he's a controversial figure. He's an ex-Marine. He was once an amateur boxer. He's Irish. Combine these qualities and you're going to have an individual who is not going to be pushed around."

Professionals like Hoover and Robert Morris took their anti-Communist investigatory work seriously. Slowly and reluctantly, they began to suspect that McCarthy was less dedicated to finding the truth than making headlines. When Frank McNamara of *Counterattack*, later an investigator for HUAC, heard on the radio that McCarthy had named Lattimore as "Moscow's top spy," he laughed out loud.[17] Those who knew McCarthy were constantly discovering to their astonishment how little McCarthy knew about the theory or practice of communism itself. No one doubted his sincerity. But his manic temperament clashed with the patient and painstaking style of the investigators who surrounded him. The details and paperwork of research bored him; he couldn't sit still long enough to check out a story thoroughly. McCarthy was interested in results, and if that required squeezing the material a bit, he was prepared to do so. Hoover, like the rest, learned to avoid being too closely tied to McCarthy's personal agenda. Even the faithful Robert Morris had to hesitate when McCarthy became chair of PSI in 1953 and asked him to leave the Internal Security Committee to become his chief counsel. Despite the pressure put on him to join, Morris decided to stay where he was.[18]

That same year Whittaker Chambers lost respect for McCarthy because of an incident involving McCarthy's love of publicity and press hype. On the eve of confirmation hearings for Charles Bohlen to be the next ambassador to Moscow, Joe paid a visit to Chambers's farm. Monday morning the front door bell rang. It was a reporter from the *Baltimore Sun*. What secret dirt on Bohlen was Chambers passing along to McCarthy? he wanted to know. Suddenly Chambers realized that McCarthy had leaked the story of his visit in order to generate the impression that the man who had publicly exposed Alger Hiss and Harry Dexter White was about to do the same to Chip Bohlen.

Chambers was appalled.[19] He announced in a press conference that he had absolutely no derogatory information about Bohlen, in effect rebuking McCarthy's efforts to rope him in. To his friend Ralph de Toledano, he admitted that his wife, Esther, urged him to say nothing, because it would only do damage to McCarthy, but he told her that the real issue was moral, not political, and that he had no choice but to speak out.[20]

Because of McCarthy's antics and his unreliability, Chambers eventually turned against him.[21] Others, like Toledano and Matthews and Sokolsky, did not. They believed that for all his faults, McCarthy had a firmer grip on the Communist menace than his opponents did. They also perceived, correctly, that many of the attacks on him were really oblique attacks on them. More was at stake than just the credibility or career of a senator from Wisconsin. Exposing McCarthy's mistakes, whether justified or not, would simply validate liberal claims that worrying about "subversive activities" and "exposing communism" was a waste of time, even an assault on civil liberties. In that, they were correct. His censure also became a judgment on them. As William Rusher noted years later, to their opponents on the left, "All that mattered was that *the United States Senate had voted to condemn McCarthy*. . . . The lights could be turned off; the show, at long last, was over."[22]

Anti-Communist investigators faced a dilemma. For good or ill, McCarthy had made anticommunism his issue, and the nation's issue. Their livelihoods and their fates depended on it; to that degree they were fated to sail with him toward whatever shores he chose.

Another controversial group that rallied early to the McCarthy banner was the so-called China Lobby. Again, the term is a misnomer. It was in fact invented by the New York Communist Party in 1949 in order to convey the impression that Americans who supported the Chinese Nationalist cause were paid agents of the Kuomintang. Owen Lattimore used the term to smear McCarthy and those who encouraged him. By April 1950 even the *New York Times* was beginning to ask, "Is there a China Lobby?" and wondered whether pro-Chiang lobbyists were feeding McCarthy negative information on the IPR and the Foreign Service's China hands.

In truth, however, public relations consultant William Goodwin was the only major figure in the China Lobby who ever actually took money for his services to Chiang's government.[23] Most were independent but politically astute businessmen who had had ties to China before the war, like silk importer Alfred Kohlberg and publisher Henry Luce, who had been born in Tengchow in eastern Shantung province in 1898. Others were military figures who had served in Asia, like Claire Chennault of the Flying Tigers and General Patrick Hurley, or former missionaries and teachers who had spent a large part of their lives in China like Walter Judd and Helen Loomis. They were in fact a disparate group, with divergent interests and perspectives. However, they agreed on two basic points. The first was that Chiang Kai-shek was America's best ally in Asia. The other was that a Communist victory in China would be a tragedy for both the United States and the Chinese people.

The China Lobby fell on hard times in the 1960s. Credulous intellectuals had discovered the virtues of Mao's Cultural Revolution, while President Nixon visited the mainland in 1973 to shake Mao's hand. It became exceedingly bad form to talk about "red China" or to praise the Nationalist regime and "the generalissimo." Men like Kohlberg were blamed for America's "lost opportunities" in Asia, including the debacle in Vietnam.[24] However, what had originally stirred Kohlberg and others to political action was not anticommunism, but Japanese atrocities in China during the thirties, like the rape of Nanking. The China Lobby had also fought to end discriminatory legislation against Chinese immigrants at a time when most Americans viewed them as a "yellow peril." Years before Pearl Harbor, they issued warnings about Japanese imperial ambitions while most of Capitol Hill remained ignorant of and indifferent to what was happening in Asia.

Proponents needed a symbol to galvanize American support for Chinese resistance against Japan, and found it in Chiang Kai-shek. Henry Luce, publisher of *Time* and *Life,* had started his infatuation with Chiang Kai-shek back in 1927. In 1941 Luce called him "the greatest ruler Asia has seen since Emperor Kang Hsi, 250 years ago." By 1945, the generalissimo had appeared on the cover of *Time* six times—more than any other mortal.[25] Chiang's Western-educated wife encouraged Luce and the group he headed, United China Relief, to believe that the Nationalists could erase China's decadent imperial past and make it a modern democratic nation. After Pearl Harbor, the China lobbyists imagined that a permanent American-Chiang partnership would take root and blossom. But policy planners in the State Department and the White House had other ideas, and the battle was on.

The problem was a confusion over policy aims during World War II. Why was the United States supporting Chiang's war against Japan? Was it to (1) defeat Japan or (2) restore China to stability after decades of revolution or (3) make Nationalist China a permanent ally and one of the Big Four? By 1945 the debate was raging at every level of government. The State Department's Old Guard, led by Stanley Hornbeck and Joseph Grew, pushed for option 3. But the Young Turks in the Far Eastern division, like John Paton Davies, John Stewart Service, Ray Ludden, and John Carter Vincent, argued that although Chiang might be useful for option 1, he was hopeless for achieving the most important goal of all: option 2. They wanted a "united, democratically progressive" China, just as the China Lobby did. But Service and Vincent saw Mao's Communist guerrillas as the means to do it, preferably in some sort of condominium with Chiang's more tradition-minded forces.

By contrast, men like Kohlberg and Congressman Walter Judd of Minnesota saw Mao as the puppet of yet another foreign invader following on the heels of the defeated Japanese: the Soviet Union. The China hands' relative success in trimming support for Chiang infuriated them. In December 1945 George Marshall went to China to try to arrange a truce between the warring factions and to propose a coalition government. Chiang refused, and despaired of Marshall's and the American government's naiveté in dealing with the Communists.[26] The result was an American aid embargo to force Chiang's hand, which lasted until April 1948—while Mao's Communists were receiving constant supplies and training from Stalin. When the Truman administration finally lifted the embargo and authorized an aid package of $400 million, it delayed delivery until November. By then the Communists had secured control of Manchuria and were poised for their victorious campaign for the rest of China.

This is not the place to rehash the issue of who, if anyone, "lost" China. Sinister figures like Lauchlin Currie flit in and out of the story, and journalists like Theodore H. White, and FE officials like Service and Vincent worked hard to undermine official and public support for the Nationalists. One of the critical factors in Chiang's collapse, a rampant inflation and a worthless currency, was certainly engineered by Soviet agents in the Kuomintang and American Treasury Department (see Chapter 5). Still, scholars now seem to agree that Chiang's defeat in the civil war was unavoidable. By 1948 he had lost the one essential political base, the peasantry, who identified him with the old landholding system no one wanted to resurrect. But when all is said and done, if Chiang would have been an inadequate leader for the Chinese people, Mao was a disastrous one. If Chiang was willing to countenance corruption and incompetence, Mao was prepared to commit mass murder: perhaps as many as fifty million Chinese would die between 1949 and 1969, thanks to Mao's policies.

The China hands had convinced Acheson that permitting a victory by the "so-called Communists" would permit the United States to drive a wedge between China and the Soviet Union. Mao would inevitably turn to the Americans for material and economic support, they argued, while antagonizing him would, in Dean Acheson's words, "deflect from the Russians to ourselves the righteous anger . . . of the Chinese people which must develop."[27] That policy turned out to be too clever by half. It completely ignored the degree to which Mao saw himself as Stalin's protégé and ally as early as the 1930s and was willing to subordinate Chinese interests to those of the Soviet Union.[28] In the short term, it meant that China became the pawn of Stalin's ambitions in Asia and then Korea. It also led to a timidity about publicly supporting Chiang in exile in Taiwan, which further upset his American supporters.

They became consumed with discovering who had dreamed up this scheme for casting Chiang into the darkness. When in 1941 Alfred Kohlberg began to hear stories about Kuomintang incompetence, corruption, and a lack of a will to win, he went to China himself to check them out. He toured five Nationalist provinces without official approval or permission and found nothing to substantiate the rumors. He concluded that most had come from publications sponsored by the IPR. A quick comparison of Communist publications and articles in the IPR journal *Pacific Affairs* confirmed his suspicions. He wrote to IPR officials to warn them that "your employees have been putting over on you a not-too-well-camouflaged Communist line."[29] Kohlberg quit the IPR board and began a one-man campaign to undermine its influence in the State Department and Congress. In 1946 he helped to found the American China Foreign Policy Association, to serve as the ideological counterweight to the institute.

Kohlberg later became a heavyweight villain in standard left-leaning accounts of cold war Asia policy, a right-wing ogre second only to Joe McCarthy himself. He was in fact an enterprising San Francisco businessman who had fallen in love with the colorful Chinese silks he had seen at the Panama Pacific Exposition back in 1915. From that point on, he devoted himself to importing Chinese textiles from his headquarters in New York (on 37th Street, "just off Fifth Avenue," as his letterhead said), and then producing low-cost domestic knockoffs when the supply dried up. It was true that a Communist takeover of the mainland dealt his import business a severe financial blow— but if it was the desire for profits that moved him on China policy, then advocating ostracization of the Communist regime and a trade embargo was a strange way to do it. It was also true that Kohlberg, a Jew, was a lifelong Republican; but his "Manchuria Manifesto" of 1946, which protested the Yalta agreements regarding China, included left-of-center signers such as Sidney Hook, Max Eastman, Felix Morley, and Norman Thomas. In fact, Kohlberg's worries about what was happening in Asia were not as eccentric or as extremist as defenders of the China hands later liked to claim, and it was his frustration with what he saw as American fecklessness in the Chinese civil war that led him to the anti-Communist cause rather than vice versa.

Kohlberg poured his own money into the effort. He sponsored an anti-red magazine called *Plain Talk*, edited by ex–Communist activist Isaac Don Levine, who had brought Whittaker Chambers to the attention of Adolf Berle. He provided discount space in one of his Manhattan office buildings to a trio of ex–FBI men who founded American Business Consultants, which offered their services to businessmen wondering if their employees' unions might be Communist tainted. He became a key benefactor of the American Jewish Anti-Communist Committee. However, his chief anger was directed at the State Department. By 1949, the principal villains in the China "sellout" were obvious: Service, Vincent, Davies, and Jessup in the front rank, with Owen Lattimore, Raymond Ludden, and a circle of lesser foreign service officers and IPR-linked publicists following up in the rear. Their superiors, particularly Acheson and Marshall, were blamed for permitting them to operate with impunity. Kohlberg and his congressional allies had been circulating the notion that America's interests in Asia had been betrayed from within for more than a year before McCarthy fastened on to it.[30]

In 1949 Kohlberg wrote an angry letter to the chairman of New York's Republican Committee turning down an invitation to attend a Waldorf-Astoria fund raiser, because of his frustration with the Dewey-dominated party's refusal to open up the "who lost China" issue. He was, he said, "ashamed" of the Republicans' failure to protest the sellout of Eastern Europe and now of Asia.[31] McCarthy's willingness to take on the administration directly came as a welcome breath of fresh air. They first met in late March 1950, after the Tydings Committee hearings had begun. McCarthy told him he wanted the full story of the "China sellout" over dinner and he got it, with Jean Kerr quickly scribbling notes as Kohlberg poured on the details. McCarthy's March 30 speech on the Senate floor denouncing Lattimore and Jessup was the result.

Kohlberg would remain a McCarthy supporter down to the end, even after his censure and disgrace. At the same time, McCarthy refused donations to his campaign because he didn't want to look beholden to Kohlberg or the other China Lobby figures.[32] He never became linked to the pro-Chiang group as a whole, even though he served as a principal spokesman for the "China betrayed" thesis. In the summer of 1951 McCarthy resumed his attack on the Foreign Service officers still employed by the State Department, particularly John Paton Davies and John Carter Vincent, saying (correctly) that Vincent had been named under oath as a member of the Communist Party. He accused them of following the Communist Party line and "torpedoing Chiang Kai-shek."

Was there anything to all this? In retrospect, it is very difficult to say. The China hands' supporters have generally had the upper hand since McCarthy's fall, and they adamantly defend their integrity and judgment against all critics. Most scholars today view them as hapless scapegoats, who lost their jobs for telling the truth, and martyrs to McCarthyism.[33] Yet much of their rehabilitation has rested on shaky premises: the belief that they had been correct about Mao's not being a real Communist or a Stalinist (now thoroughly demolished), and that their accusers were right-wing reactionaries who concocted the theory that the Democrats had "lost" China for their own purposes. Now we know better. No hard evidence exists linking any of the China hands to actual Soviet espionage efforts: their White House liaison Lauchlin Currie and intellectual mentor Owen Lattimore are a different matter. But they were sold a bill of goods on the Maoist cause a little too easily. They yielded to what historian Mao Chun-yu calls the "Yenan mystique" of heroic rebels making a new society in their mountain fastness. And they spread a profoundly distorted view of what a Communists victory might mean (regardless of whether they ever actually called the Chinese Communists "agrarian reformers"). Service and John Paton Davis became conduits for false reports about Communist guerrillas waging aggressive campaigns against the Japanese (in fact, Mao's forces were lying low, biding their time for the real struggle for China *after* the war), which encouraged the United States to rethink their support for Chiang's military. It is hard not to conclude that for all their expertise and knowledge, the China hands deluded themselves as to what was actually happening in China—although they had plenty of company, both then and later.

The climax of McCarthy's campaign against those who had "lost" China was his attack on General Marshall on June 1951. This too reflected Kohlberg's view: he had launched a furious attack on Marshall back in December, detailing his decisions to deprive the Nationalists of arms and ammunition, and concluding: "If [two] Soviet agents had replaced . . . Mr. Acheson and General Marshall, what policy could they have followed that would have more greatly benefited the Soviet Empire, and more damaged us?"[34] Yet McCarthy's assault on that most awesome pillar of the Washington establishment tipped the balance for the most important of the China Lobbyists. Harry Luce had followed McCarthy's initial accusations against Lattimore and Service with some interest and sympathy. Then one day in the spring of 1950 he wrote a memo to the editorial staff of *Life* stating that "communism has become too much . . . the scapegoat of everything that's wrong with us. The fact is, communism is no longer a real issue, even indirectly, in America." It was, he concluded, "time to hit [McCarthyism] hard."[35] About a year later, a guest at the Luces' heard Harry say he was tired of hearing about communism as a political issue. The guest thought to himself, That's the end of Joe McCarthy.

He was right, as least as far as Luce was concerned. In October 1951, four months after the attack on Marshall, *Time* published a cover article entitled "Demagogue McCarthy." It called his record of rooting out Communists "miserable," and complained that "his antics foul up the necessary examination of the past mistakes of the Truman-Acheson foreign policy." *Time* also played up his lower-class origins, his crude and uncouth behavior. It described his stay in Appleton with his friends the Van Susterens this way:

> He went into the kitchen, dumped some baking soda into his hand, threw it into his mouth, and washed it down with cold water. Margery Van Susteren winced. Next, he took off his coat and tie and shoes, dropping them where he happened to be. Joe has no interest in clothes. After every road trip, hotels send on clothing he has forgotten.

The article admitted that while McCarthy was a slob, he had a "sweat-stained, shirt-sleeved earnestness" and considerable charm, like a "tramp dog," and one observer was quoted as saying, "He comes up to you with tail wagging and all the appeal of a tramp dog—and just about as trustworthy." *Time* concluded that "no regard for fair play, no scruple for exact truth hampers Joe's political course." It finally suggested that McCarthy "must be dealt with" before any real discussion of America's foreign policy failures could begin, particularly with regard to China.[36]

Here Luce was wrong. McCarthy's fall presaged the fall of the China Lobby and all it stood for. Yet his career forms only one small chapter in its history. Wisconsin's junior senator found his most active and vocal supporters elsewhere.

One such place was among the ranks of America's leading conservative intellectuals and politicians. Figures like John Chamberlain, Suzanne La Follette, Frank Chodorov, Willmoore Kendall, John T. Flynn, Willi Schlamm, Frank Meyer, Max Lerner, Henry Regnery, and James Burnham all rallied at one time or another to the McCarthy banner as the liberal attacks began to mount. They did so for their own reasons and to varying degrees, but as a whole conservative intellectuals proved to be better defenders and apologists for McCarthy than the senator himself was. The classic summary of their view was Buckley and Brent Bozell's *McCarthy and His Enemies*, which remains to this day the most detailed and carefully documented account of McCarthy's activities up to the Army-McCarthy hearings. After weighing the evidence and criticizing McCarthy for his more obvious sins, including his attack on Marshall, its arch conclusion was not meant to assuage liberal feelings: "As long as McCarthyism fixes its goal with its present precision, it is a movement around which men of good will and stern morality can close ranks."[37]

Like Republican heartland politicians Kenneth Wherry, Bourke Hickenlooper, and Robert Taft himself, conservative intellectuals perceived in the McCarthy flap something more than just an argument over Communists in government. They expected, even welcomed, a confrontation with liberals on the larger question of what, if anything, America stood for, if it was not pre-pared to ostracize those who were prepared to serve a foreign enemy—*as well as those who were willing to protect them.* As Willmoore Kendall phrased it, "Is the United States entitled to strike at a body of opinion which consti-tutes a clear and present danger?" Conservatives answered in the affirmative. The fundamental question in their minds was not just whether communism constituted such a threat; it was whether liberalism itself did, for its own in-ability to act to protect the national interest or, rather, its ability to act in one direction but not in another. Older conservatives also saw McCarthy's fierce attacks on liberal Democrats for being soft on communism as just recom-pense for the attacks and smears they had endured at the hands of New Deal-ers. For the so-called Brown Scare of the later thirties had not just targeted far right groups like the Silver Shirts or the anti-Semite Gerald L. K. Smith. It had reached out to anti-internationalists and conservatives of the old right, particularly members of the America First Committee, which FDR and his acolytes had believed were part of a pro-Nazi conspiracy.

Roosevelt himself regularly branded America Firsters "unwitting aides of the agents of Nazism," and the liberal group Friends of Democracy de-nounced them as "a Nazi front." Secretary of Interior Harold Ickes attacked isolationists as appeasers and anti-Semites. Walter Winchell used to read long lists of right-wingers over the air, referring to them as "Americans we can do without." An outrageous "exposé" called *Under Cover* purported to show that figures like Congressman Hamilton Fish, Burton K. Wheeler, and Robert Taft were part of a pro-fascist conspiracy to keep America out of the war in Europe and allow Hitler to win.[38]

Even more infuriating, Stalinists and fellow travelers chimed in. George Seldes attacked both the American Legion and the *Reader's Digest* as proto-fascist. Heywood Broun of the *New Republic* blew up when civil libertarians suggested that smearing conservatives as fascists was no different from call-ing liberals Communists; instead of advocating "a policy of fair play," he fumed, civil libertarians should concentrate on defending the "underdog"— which meant the Communist left. Robert Taft came under a particularly nasty attack during the 1944 campaign when his Democratic opponent de-nounced him as a "reactionary" and the CIO in Ohio sponsored a pamphlet accusing him of being a friend to Hitler and Hirohito. It nearly cost him the election.[39]

The New Deal attacks went beyond name calling to official harassment. When Father James Gillis's Paulist radio station in Chicago dared to criticize Roosevelt's decision to pack the Supreme Court, the Federal Communica-tions Commission yanked its license.[40] In 1935 FDR ordered the FBI to launch a full-scale probe into a wide range of far right groups, a major step toward politicization of the bureau. He also ordered secret probes into America Firsters like Hamilton Fish, Joseph Kennedy, and Senator Gerald Nye, hoping to find evidence they were receiving money from the Nazis. When Hoover told the president he had found nothing, FDR ordered his attorney general, Francis Biddle, to try to get a grand jury indictment anyway. At cabinet meetings Roosevelt would grumble at Biddle, "When are you going to indict the seditionists?"

Roosevelt's obsession with proving that opposition to his policies sprang from subversive, if not treasonous, motives was given full rein with the coming of war. Various figures were arrested and indicted under the Espionage Act of 1917—not just real fascists like the German-American Bund, but also a group called the Friends of Progress, whose chief offense was that they had staged a public mock impeachment of FDR. Others, like Gerald L. K. Smith and Father Coughlin, were dragooned into silence. William Pelley of the Silver Shirts ended up in prison.

Attorney General Biddle's special assistant on right-wing subversive groups, William Maloney, did all the things people would later accuse McCarthy of doing. He publicized unsubstantiated charges against political opponents; he leaked grand jury testimony to the press; he indicted Hamilton Fish's legislative aide in hopes that he would implicate his boss as a German agent; and he ceaselessly charged that there was an active conspiracy between conservatives and far right groups like the Silver Shirts.[41]

It was not just traditional conservatives who grew bitter over this treatment. Burton K. Wheeler was an old-line western Progressive and an early New Dealer. Then he turned against FDR during the Court-packing case. Suddenly, he found himself the target of scurrilous public attacks, which stepped up when he came out against aid to Britain. Roosevelt's acolytes called Wheeler a Nazi, an anti-Semite, and a craven appeaser. Furious, Wheeler confided in 1943 to fellow isolationist John T. Flynn (an ex-liberal who suffered similar assaults), "The more internationalists try to smear people now, the more it is going to react against them when this war is over."[42] Wheeler turned out to be correct—and McCarthy was in many ways the instrument of sweet revenge.

John T. Flynn had been a fierce anti-internationalist, albeit a progressive on the domestic scene. Then he joined America First and was fired from his job as financial editor at the *New Republic*. Like Wheeler, he was subjected to attacks as a Nazi appeaser and anti-Semite. When he showed up to give a speech at the University of Illinois in 1944, student protesters tried to get him thrown off campus. In 1945 he wrote *As We Go Marching*, which warned that

World War II would lead to the creation of a permanent American military state alongside the permanent welfare state of the New Deal. Flynn carried the assumptions of thirties anti-internationalism directly into the cold war conservative camp. He would become an equally fierce McCarthy partisan and wrote a pamphlet entitled *McCarthy: His War on American Reds*. It praised McCarthy and lambasted his opponents for the "dark and cruel method of war" that they had waged first against Martin Dies, then Parnell Thomas of HUAC, and "now with greater malignance" against the junior senator from Wisconsin.

In fact, few conservatives saw anything new or unprecedented in McCarthy's efforts or in the hostile reaction it provoked. John Chamberlain pointed out that in the thirties, any author who attacked communism could count on a similar smear treatment. "By their oblique control of writing in the thirties and the early forties," he wrote, "the Communists managed to poison the intellectual life of a whole nation—and the poison has lingered on."[43] For Flynn, Chamberlain, and many others, the struggle over McCarthy was part of a much older, longer struggle: the survival of a traditional conservatism in the face of a dominant liberal orthodoxy that seemed to find more to admire in Stalin's Russia than in its own country's traditions. "Two generations of American liberalism," wrote one conservative critic, "have called honorable men 'merchants of death' and Stalin a protagonist of human liberation; and for either misjudgment they had far less evidence than McCarthy did for his."[44]

How much all this past bad blood meant to McCarthy himself is hard to gauge. Just as no one should confuse McCarthyism with conservatism, so we should not make the mistake of equating Joe McCarthy—the former Democrat and four-time Roosevelt voter, who fought for subsidized housing for veterans as a freshman senator—with the traditional conservatives who became his strongest defenders.

Nor was it true that all conservatives were pro-McCarthy. Historian George Nash has detailed how some, like Russell Kirk, saw in McCarthy the classic demagogue and in his supporters the mindless revolt of the masses, much as their liberal counterparts did. They indignantly denied McCarthy the label "conservative." Still, if Kirk disliked McCarthy and what he represented, he was equally dismissive of left-wing attempts to suggest that McCarthyism represented a serious menace to liberty and law. Those who had cheered congressional investigations like the Nye Committee in the 1930s, he said, had no business complaining now about senatorial inquisitions and witch-hunts. New Deal liberalism also had to take some of the blame for the popularity of a figure like McCarthy. "I suspect," he wrote, "that these are the

175

consequences . . . of a growing realization that many persons endowed by the public with high responsibilities had lost all idea of what is loyalty to a nation's traditions."[45]

However, there was one group of supporters with whom McCarthy had no problems identifying himself: American Catholics.

To what extent was Joe McCarthy a national Catholic hero in the 1950s? Certainly members of the Catholic hierarchy, of civic and patriotic organizations, and Irish-American groups like the Hibernian Society considered him one of their own. On April 3, 1951, McCarthy gave a speech at the Queens County Chapter of the Catholic War Veterans of America in Elmhurst, New York. The group had been founded in 1935 to combat the "the menace of Communism, in philosophy and tactics" and to promote principles of Americanism. The Elmhurst chapter was heavily Irish and Italian in origin, as the names on the organizing committee indicate: Ferrari, Milligan, Mulvaney, Murphy, Kavanagh, and O'Doherty. The ceremonies that day began with a trooping of the colors and the American flag, followed by an invocation by Father Joseph Grogan. But then there were speeches by Rabbi Benjamin Schultz and by Alfred Kohlberg, as national chairman of the American Jewish League Against Communism. McCarthy's own speech, the pièce de résistance, came last—after a long display of patriotism, piety, military pride (including an organ performance of "Halls of Montezuma"), and vows of solidarity with a group calling itself the Defenders of the Constitution, who stood against world government and for "God and Country."

This was the true heart of McCarthyism—or so it seemed to many observers. The Catholic War Veterans, the Knights of Columbus, the Holy Name Society of the New York City Police Department, and figures like Cardinal Francis Spellman, Father John Cronin, Edmund Walsh of Georgetown University, Patrick Scanlon of the *Brooklyn Tablet*, and Richard Ginder, whose pro-McCarthy column, "The Priest," appeared in *Our Sunday Visitor*—here was a Catholic anti-Communist crusade that had fastened on to Joe McCarthy as their Savonarola, "a scourge of God" to cleanse America of its secular heresies as well as its civil liberties. Certainly Miles McMillin of the *Capitol Times* believed that; so did Dr. John MacKay, moderator of the Presbyterian Church USA, who warned that McCarthy's investigations were an "American version of the Sixteenth Century Spanish Inquisition." As with the Colony dinner story, McCarthy's associations sometimes triggered old anti-Catholic prejudices. Robert McCracken, pastor of the fashionable Riverside Episcopal Church in Manhattan, solemnly told his congregation in February 1954 that McCarthy was a member of a church that "has never disavowed the Inquisition" and "makes a policy of conformity."[46]

It was true that American Catholics were more inclined to support Mc-Carthy than any other religious group. Gallup polls from 1951 to 1954 show that a majority of Catholics (56 percent) took a positive view of McCarthy's activities, while Protestants were more evenly split (45–36 percent), and Jews were overwhelmingly negative (83 percent).[47] But the Catholic factor in Mc-Carthy's public support was exaggerated and misunderstood. It was anticommunism, not the man himself, that drew Catholics to his camp. Here they reflected the attitude of most Americans across the country, regardless of religious or ethnic affiliation. At the top, Catholic intellectuals and public figures divided on McCarthy along conservative and liberal lines; at the bottom, ethnic loyalties, especially among working-class Irish, were more decisive than religious faith. If Protestants sometimes saw Catholic support of McCarthy as monolithic, American Catholics can be forgiven for wondering how much of the abuse and antipathy heaped on the senator from Wisconsin was also obliquely directed at them. McCarthy himself, of course, was a strictly observant Catholic who rarely missed mass. Friends would remember him breaking off fishing trips or speaking tours on Sundays in order to find a nearby church for services. But just as McCarthy was not an ostentatious Catholic (not a candle-lighting Catholic, he liked to say), so he also did not play it for political advantage. For example, he played no part in the campaign to free Joseph Cardinal Mindszenty in 1949 and 1950, although it was a major cause célèbre in the Hearst papers and in the Roman Catholic press.[48] Nor was his lead issue—Communists in government—designed to attract much attention from Catholics. Edmund Walsh, supposedly McCarthy's mentor on the anticommunism issue, barely mentioned it in his manifesto on the threat of communism, *Total Power* (1951). McCarthy's interest in communism was political in the broadest sense of the term: he wanted to use it to force liberals and Democrats from power and to shatter their morale forever. It could only have hurt, not helped, to translate it into a religious crusade or a sectarian cause.

On the other hand, many Catholics did feel that anticommunism was *their* issue. Polish and Czech Catholic voters in Wisconsin knew about the torture and persecution of their co-religionists in Communist countries firsthand. McCarthy's appeal for a reversal of "twenty years of treason" in American foreign policy and a purge of communistic elements in American public life hit a deeply resonant chord with these people, as well as with other Roman Catholics. As Father Edmund Walsh explained, the struggle against communism was one "between two moral opposites" that cannot be resolved by politics alone: "The Soviet creed must be met and answered by chapter and verse of an integrated philosophy of life," a "renaissance of spiritual power" that religion, and particularly the Catholic church, could offer the free world.[49]

What worried figures like Walsh was not the strength of communism but the frailty of the free world's chosen champion, modern liberalism. Could liberals really be trusted to protect the West from its most insidious enemy? Father Richard Ginder did not think so. "A Catholic is naturally suspicious of them, viewed over the wreckage of the past twenty years." He added, "They were wrong, horribly wrong on the crucial issue of our generation," and "now liberals would like to bury their past mistakes."[50]

McCarthy also had his share of liberal Catholic opponents. Most important was the journal *Commonweal*, edited by John Cogley and James O'Gara. But there was also the Jesuit periodical *America*, the *Catholic Worker*, the Association of Catholic Trade Unionists, and distinguished individuals like Bishop Bernard Sheil, Truman's Secretary of Labor Maurice Tobin, and George Schuster, the president of Hunter College. In 1954 *America* ran an editorial so harshly anti-McCarthy (it accused him of trying to engineer a "peaceful" but "piecemeal" overthrow of the presidency and the rule of law) that the superior of the New York Jesuits had to order them to stop in order to placate the storm of protest. "The same Irish voices kept calling," someone later recalled. *Commonweal* took pride in being ferociously anti-Communist as well anti-McCarthy. But its plan for fighting communism was not more investigations but "an expansion of social programs designed to end hunger, disease, deficient housing, and the other . . . ills that drove men into the hands of the Marxists."[51]

Like their Protestant counterparts, conservative Catholics saw in the faces of McCarthy's liberal opponents a hatred born of a guilty conscience. Liberals claimed to opposed McCarthy in order to protect the idea of a free society, but their definition of a free society flew in the face of the definition conservatives embraced, whether Protestants or Catholics. Conservatives believed that a free society must also be a *moral* society, with a clear sense of its own priority of values. Liberals not only insisted on protecting individuals and groups who challenged those values and "the American proposition."[52] They also wanted to banish religion, the bedrock of any moral consensus, to the outer fringes. Conservatives and Catholics believed that religion was central to American culture. They read the doctrine of separation of church and state in a very different light than did their liberal opponents. Far from diminishing the role of the sacred and the scriptural in "the public square," it allowed its expansion as individuals and groups, not the government, saw fit. Implicitly, it should also protect that role from the prying, skeptical eyes of atheists, agnostics, and other "eggheads."

In their eyes, the cold war was at bottom a moral conflict. Interestingly, McCarthy himself touched on this in his Wheeling speech. He had argued in 1950 that the real bone of contention between the Communist world and

the free world was not over economic systems, or democracy, or even Soviet expansionism. These were differences that could be reconciled, and
"the East and the West could most certainly still live in peace." The "real,
basic difference" was what McCarthy called communism's "religion of im-
moralism"—its complete rejection of concepts of God, justice, and moral
absolutes, which "will more deeply wound and damage mankind than any
conceivable economic or political system." Fulton J. Sheen (who never
mentioned McCarthy's name or took a position on any political issues)
framed it slightly differently when he wrote that "the basic struggle today is
not between individualism and collectivism, free enterprise and socialism,"
but a moral and spiritual struggle over whether "man shall exist for the
state, or the state for man, and whether freedom is of the spirit or a conces-
sion of materialized society."[53]

In other words, behind the Protestant-Catholic split over McCarthy lay
another deeper conflict, between two contrasting visions of what made
America a "free society." It was the same conflict that would eventually
spawn the abortion controversy. Certainly it is no accident that the same
Catholic communities in rural Wisconsin and the same working-class neighborhoods in Chicago and Boston that supported McCarthy would also become strongholds of the pro-life movement. Since McCarthy became
something of a personal hero to many Irish, Italian, and German Catholics, it
was easy to overestimate his influence on them at the ballot box. In his reelection campaign in 1952 he got fewer, not more, Catholic votes than in 1946.
When he campaigned against William Benton in Connecticut and Harley Kilgore in West Virginia, states with large concentrations of Roman Catholic
voters, Democrats quailed. When they studied the returns, however, both
Benton and Kilgore turned out to have done *better* than, or at least as well as,
in Catholic districts than in non-Catholic ones.[54] The truth was that American
Catholics were voting more and more like their Protestant neighbors, along
ideological and political rather than religious or ethnic lines. Some stood
foursquare against him; others saw in McCarthy the kind of fighting spirit
they admired. As Cardinal Francis Spellman expressed it, "He is against
Communism and he has done and is doing something about it."[55]

The worry was that American liberals failed to see this because they
were infected with the same materialistic, secularist virus—hence the
strange affinity between the Communist and the New Dealer, between the
progressive and the totalitarian visions of the maximalist state. What else had
made communism so attractive to the Best and the Brightest, that class of
young men like Alger Hiss or his friend Noel Field or Harry Dexter White,
bred to power, intellect, and influence in the freest society on earth? That
question often crossed Whittaker Chambers's mind, as well as McCarthy's

179

when he had spoken of subversives "born with silver spoons in their mouths." Another figure remembered hosting a picnic on his Washington estate in the early thirties that was attended by the "bright young things" of the New Deal, including Alger and Donald Hiss, Noel Field, Henry Collins, and Laurence Duggan:

> They all came from Harvard or Princeton or Yale, and highly respected families, a group of young aristocrats, polished, athletic, vigorous looking, lively and full of interests. You could see in a moment that they were real gentlemen. At the time, they all seemed to be young liberals, just good pacifists with the courage to speak out against what was wrong and with nothing to hide.

Yet all five became part of the Soviet espionage apparatus.[56]

Whittaker Chambers, who knew them as well, decided that answering that problem required a theory of history. The modern age's degradation of humanity and spiritual values had come in a devastating one-two punch, with liberalism taking the lead, then communism in the follow-through. Even those who found that view too simplistic, and who were less pessimistic about the future, worried that in trying to excuse the abysmal political judgments of a Hiss or a Paul Robeson or a Dorothy Kenyon, anti-anti-Communists had abandoned "the very principle of Western civilization—the axiomatic tenet that man is entirely responsible for the intellectual choices he has made in an exercise of his free will." Joe McCarthy, insisted Willi Schlamm, at least "takes man seriously" for the choices he makes; his opponents "insist that man is morally a vegetable and intellectually an eternal child." Liberals "stipulate a brand-new inalienable right of man—the right to sell his soul."[57]

All this may have meant little to the average McCarthy backer, Catholic or not (although it probably mattered more than McCarthy detractors assumed). To him, McCarthy appeared as a typical all-American sort of guy, the "fighting Marine" who dealt two-fisted forthrightly with enemies at home as well as abroad. In confronting the Soviet threat some were up to the task and the sacrifice, and others were not. McCarthy, MacArthur, J. Edgar Hoover, Bill Jenner—these men were ready to do the job, and to interfere or stand in their way seemed absurd or disgraceful, even treasonous.

At certain moments, McCarthy's ability to connect with that public feeling could be overwhelming. In midsummer 1951 the *New York Times* reported that the Truman administration was planning an all-out offensive against McCarthy, targeting veterans' organizations as well as Catholics. Truman himself spoke at the dedication for the new American Legion headquarters in Washington, decrying the "wave of uncertainty and fear" that was gripping the nation on the communism issue. He called on his listeners to put "a stop to this terrible business . . . take the lead against the hysteria that threatens the government from within." Then Maurice Tobin, Truman's Catholic secretary of labor, spoke to the Veterans of Foreign Wars convention in New York. He avoided mentioning McCarthy by name, but when he spoke out against "slanderers" in the Senate who were undermining people's confidence in their government, the VFW delegates knew whom he meant. One of the chairmen on the podium grabbed the microphone from Tobin and suggested that the VFW invite McCarthy himself to speak and to hear *his* side of the story. Cheers and applause drowned out the hapless labor secretary, as the convention resoundingly approved the invitation. McCarthy was on a speaking tour in Idaho when he heard the offer. Delighted, he immediately accepted and flew to New York the next day—just the sort of spontaneous grandstanding stunt he loved.

When he came straight from the airport to the convention hall, the VFW delegates were on their feet, chanting, "Give 'em hell, Joe" and even "McCarthy for President." When they finally settled down, he told the delegates that Tobin was "a fine young gentleman who was ordered to do the job he did." For the next hour and a quarter, before his appreciative audience, McCarthy proceeded to rip into Dean Acheson, Philip Jessup, Gustavo Duran, John Stewart Service, and Harry Truman. He offered to submit the evidence he had of their perfidious conduct to a trial by jury, with McCarthy acting as special prosecutor. If he couldn't get a jury of ordinary Americans to convict, he would agree to quit public life; if they did convict, then Acheson, Truman, and "the whole motley crew" would have to agree to resign, beginning with Acheson himself. The delegates whistled and stamped their approval. Two hours earlier they had passed a resolution calling on Acheson to resign. The Democrats learned their lesson, and Tobin's lecture tour of veterans' groups came to a halt.[58]

In fact, that summer had not been a particularly good time for McCarthy. He was in trouble with his Senate colleagues, and his Marshall speech had seriously damaged his already shaky reputation. However, the Democrats were self-destructing even faster. By the end of the year, three out of four Americans were giving Truman a failing grade as president. McCarthy was telling reporters that he welcomed Truman's challenge to fight on the communism issue and that in the upcoming 1952 election, citizens would have the chance to choose "between Americanism and a combination of Trumanism and Communism."

In the final analysis, the key to McCarthy's success was that he was a single-issue candidate. That issue was communism. That, and the Korean War, sustained him through all his mistakes and missteps, all his lies and distortions. In June 1952 the National Opinion Center discovered that some 60 percent of the American electorate approved the ongoing committees investigating Communist subversion, while less than 20 percent approved of McCarthy himself. Two years later, the Stouffer poll asked Americans whom they thought was the person best able to handle the threat of domestic communism: J. Edgar Hoover, Dwight Eisenhower, or Joe McCarthy. Of those who answered McCarthy, 58 percent said it was because they agreed with his view on the seriousness of the Communist threat, while only 31 percent named him because they trusted him as a person. In the case of Eisenhower and Hoover, the numbers were almost exactly reversed.[59]

Late in his career, after his censure, McCarthy was asked by Roy Cohn what issues he now intended to run on in the next election. McCarthy instantly replied, "My issue. Communism in government. There's nothing else as big." A substantial section of the American public agreed with him. It was the political class in Washington that felt otherwise.

Chapter 9

McCarthy Rampant

As members of the Eighty-second Congress took their seats in January 1951, McCarthy was warning everyone that he was planning a new offensive on Communists in government. He was now the ranking Republican on the PSI, and he planned to shine his investigative flashlight on both the Commerce and Agriculture departments. He was bringing on board the new senator from California and Alger Hiss sleuth Richard Nixon.* Nixon and McCarthy promised to be the dynamic duo of PSI, dedicated to hunting down what McCarthy termed "the Communists and crooks" lurking in the executive branch.

Like most unprejudiced observers, Nixon found McCarthy likable, energetic, and audacious. But he also found him "irresponsibly impulsive."[1] Nixon had carefully researched his probe into the Hiss case and spent time thinking about the nature of America's confrontation with communism. His own anticommunism reflected an introspective and cautious nature. He found McCarthy's by-the-seat-of-the-pants approach bracing, to say the least. Nixon also recognized that as a senator, he needed to have other political irons in the fire. While Nixon would play a prominent part in exposing IRS influence peddling and other Truman administration scandals, McCarthy was bored by them. Nothing else mattered to him except fighting communism and its liberal friends.

McCarthy was now America's most powerful first-term senator, accord-

---

*He had arranged this by bumping his old antagonist Margaret Chase Smith.

ing to the *New York Times*. The twin defeats of Tydings and Lucas had not been lost on his colleagues on either side of the aisle. *Newsweek* proclaimed "Democrats Fume at McCarthy, But He Has Them Terrorized." "McCarthyism," the *Times* wrote, "is simply today a very considerable force in the Congress of the United States. And it seems here to stay." The *Christian Century*, no friend to McCarthy, proclaimed that "whether we like it or not . . . the Wisconsin senator has become an influential factor in American life."[2]

Yet McCarthy had less political clout than his enemies feared. As historian Richard M. Fried (no admirer of McCarthy) points out, "McCarthy's power was as remarkable for its limitations as for its destructiveness."[3] He had pretty much used up his repertoire of cases of Communists in the State Department; with the sensational exception of General George Marshall, the people he would publicly "expose" that summer and fall were increasingly minor figures or ones he had named before.[4] The new Senate Internal Security subcommittee under Pat McCarran was seriously pursuing the leads McCarthy had provided on Lattimore and the Institute of Pacific Relations, but McCarthy was not even a member. Republican elders still refused to trust him with any serious power and worked to keep him confined to his PSI satrapy.

In addition, Gallup polls showed that his approval rating had been steadily dropping since the Tydings hearings, which was turning out to be his high-tide marker. McCarthy was being overshadowed by the Korean War and the MacArthur dismissal and a Democratic administration in an extended state of collapse (in November 1951 Truman's approval ratings dropped to 23 percent). Fewer people, not more, knew who Joe McCarthy was and what he was fighting for. All the same, everyone on the Hill recognized he was a dangerous man to cross, not because of his clout with the inner circle, but because of his influence with voters.

That influence was largely misunderstood. For example, the major voices of public opinion were against him. Later, commentators would celebrate the willingness of this or that public figure to attack McCarthy as a display of political "courage." But the truth was that such attacks almost always won widespread praise. The man or woman who accused McCarthy of being a reckless villain or a threat to American democracy could count on accolades from the *New York Times* and *New York Herald-Tribune;* from religious publications like *Christian Century* or *Commonweal;* news magazines like *Newsweek* and *Time;* and columnists running the political gamut from I. F. Stone to James Reston. University presidents and deans, liberal-minded public interest groups like the ADA and the Committee for Cultural Freedom, not to mention various government spokesmen, would offer their solidarity and support.

Joe McCarthy, 1930. At age twenty-one, McCarthy entered Little Wolf High School in Manawa. Working by day and studying at night, he managed to complete four years of education in nine months. Impressed by his prodigious energy and ability, his fellow students even elected him president of their sophomore class. (*State Historical Society of Wisconsin*)

A different image of McCarthy from the more familiar anti-McCarthy cartoons by Herblock. This 1946 cartoon from the *Washington Star* shows McCarthy in his Marine uniform as he replaces an older generation of Washington politicians, represented here by Bob La Follette, Junior. As a member of the reform-minded "class of '46," which included both John F. Kennedy and Richard Nixon, "Tail Gunner Joe" McCarthy seemed to embody all the virtues of Americans who had served in World War II and who would now remake America—and Washington—in a new, more vigorous image. (*From the U.S. Senate Collection, Center for Legislative Archives, National Archives and Records Administration*)

Shots of McCarthy with Wisconsin constituents and relaxing in the Senate pool, taken as part of a *Saturday Evening Post* article on McCarthy in the wake of the public storm following his Wheeling speech, 1950. (*Oliver Atkins Collection, George Mason University Libraries*)

McCarthy shows *Saturday Evening Post* readers the recording device he had installed on his office phone after his Wheeling speech, in order to foil attempts to tap his phone. McCarthy's fears were not mere paranoia. The FBI would later discover illegal wiretaps on the phones of two of his staffers. (*Oliver Atkins Collection, George Mason University Libraries*)

Owen Lattimore leaves the hearing room after testifying before the Tydings Committee, March 1950— at the side of an evidently buoyant Joe McCarthy. McCarthy had accused Lattimore, a leading scholar at Johns Hopkins University and mentor to the State Department's China hands, of being "Moscow's top spy." Although McCarthy later had to retract that claim, subsequent disclosures would show that Lattimore was not as innocent as many liberals and McCarthy opponents believed. (*AP/Wide World Photos*)

Robert Taft speaking to a meeting of constituents, 1952. Taft was the chief ideological spokesman for the conservative wing of the Republican Party and inspiration for GOP members of the class of '46, including McCarthy. Taft would later draw fire for his refusal to rein in McCarthy's wilder accusations against members of the Democratic administration. "You are mistaken when you suggest I have influence on McCarthy," Taft admitted to a friend. McCarthy, he acknowledged, was "a hard man to work with." (*Oliver Atkins Collection, George Mason University Libraries*)

Left to right: Dean Acheson, Philip Jessup, and Dean Rusk. Secretary of State Acheson and his Special Ambassador, Jessup, were favorite targets of Republicans during the darkest days of the cold war, not least for their links to accused Soviet spy Alger Hiss. In public, McCarthy called Acheson "the heart of the octopus" that controlled American foreign policy from Moscow. In private, he called the secretary of state "that striped-pants asshole." What happened when McCarthy and Acheson met accidentally in a Senate elevator became part of Washington legend. (*AP/Wide World Photos*)

General George Marshall, former chief of staff of the United States Army, secretary of state under President Truman, and later secretary of defense. Republicans assailed Marshall for having "lost China" when, as Truman's special envoy to China during the civil war between Nationalists and Communists in 1946, he succeeded in terminating American aid to Chiang Kai-shek, ensuring a Communist victory. However, McCarthy went further, and on the Senate floor accused the austere and revered Marshall of being linked to a Communist conspiracy "on a scale so immense as to dwarf any previous such venture in the history of man." The June 1951 speech embarrassed McCarthy's supporters and seriously hurt his credibility with the public. (*Oliver Atkins Collection, George Mason University Libraries*)

Eisenhower and Nixon celebrate victory on election night, 1952. Ike's election as president signaled the rise of "modern" Republicanism and the eclipse of the Robert Taft wing of the Republican Party. Eisenhower would soon cross swords with McCarthy and, with Nixon's help, would engineer McCarthy's downfall. (*Oliver Atkins Collection, George Mason University Libraries*)

The glare of publicity: television lights and cameras dominate the hearing room as the Army-McCarthy hearings begin, April 1954. Contrary to myth, it was Joe McCarthy, not the United States Army, who was under investigation during the hearings. Seated at the table: (l. to r.) the committee's Chief Counsel, Ray Jenkins, Senator Everett Dirksen, Chairman Karl Mundt (after McCarthy had been forced to resign), and Democratic Senators Stuart Symington and John McClellan. "Someone had to rein Joe in," McClellan told a committee staffer. "He was getting out of hand." (*Oliver Atkins Collection, George Mason University Libraries*)

At the witness table: (l. to r.) Roy Cohn, McCarthy, and Francis Carr. Staffers Cohn and Carr were at the center of the charges that McCarthy had tried to blackmail the Army into giving special treatment to another staffer, David Schine (not pictured), after he had been drafted. At Cohn's recommendation, McCarthy and Carr declined to take legal counsel and decided to represent themselves. It was a fatal blunder. (*Oliver Atkins Collection, George Mason University Libraries*)

The opposition: representing the Eisenhower administration and the Army are (r. to l.) Counsel Joseph Welch, Secretary of the Army Robert Stevens, and Assistant Counsel James St. Clair. A skillful lawyer with a keen sense of the visual impact of television, Welch would turn out to be the star of the hearings. His famous riposte to McCarthy's attack on one of Welch's employees, Fred Fisher—"Sir, have you no sense of decency left?"—became immortal. However, almost no one who watched their dramatic confrontation knew the real story behind those remarks. (*Oliver Atkins Collection, George Mason University Libraries*)

Recess: McCarthy leaves the commitee room with wife Jean Kerr (shown here on crutches) and other spectators. (*Oliver Atkins Collection, George Mason University Libraries*)

A revealing scene at the committee table: (l. to r.) Counsel Ray Jenkins exchanges whispers with Senator McClellan behind the back of Chairman Karl Mundt; Democratic counsel Robert Kennedy broods in the background. A vigorous anti-Communist, Kennedy was an admirer of McCarthy and had briefly served as assistant counsel for McCarthy's committee on investigations. However, his determination to settle scores with Roy Cohn would lead directly to McCarthy's disgrace. (*Oliver Atkins Collection, George Mason University Libraries*)

McCarthy listens and makes a note during testimony by a witness. Physically and mentally drained, McCarthy believed he was mounting an effective defense against the Army's charges. Friends and intimates, however, understood that he was destroying himself. (*Oliver Atkins Collection, George Mason University Libraries*)

Joe McCarthy enters the Senate chamber to face his final censure vote, December 9, 1954. The vote of censure, 66–22, did not remove McCarthy from his chairmanship or committee posts. However, the condemnation by his colleagues, many of whom he had once treated with disdain, broke his spirit. In less than three years he would be dead, at the age of forty-seven. (*U.S. News & World Report*)

This *Washington Star* cartoon expresses the view of many supporters of McCarthy's performance in the Army-McCarthy hearings. (*From the U.S. Senate Collection, Center for Legislative Archives, National Archives and Records Administration*)

The only place where the anti-McCarthy consensus did not extend was among the voters at large. His ability to sway them won him the reputation of being a demagogue, but that ability had less to do with McCarthy than with McCarthyism. American voters were his final court of appeal because they were willing to support him on the issue he found all-consuming: how a liberal establishment had permitted America's enemies to direct its foreign policy.

McCarthy gave a speech in Cudahy, Wisconsin, on April 23, 1951, describing how he had heard Douglas MacArthur, "one of the greatest Americans ever born," speak to the joint session of Congress. "He wasn't there as a Democrat, he wasn't there as a Republican," McCarthy said. "He was there as an American." McCarthy explained that the "hue and cry" for MacArthur's scalp had begun on the editorial pages of the *Daily Worker;* it had ended in the Oval Office among Truman's most trusted advisers. McCarthy declared (one can imagine him pounding the podium, as he often did) that the Democrats seemed unaware that America was at war with communism—not just in Korea but around the world. "This is a war not of our choosing. We didn't start it. The Communists did. We cannot stop it except by victory," as MacArthur had warned, "there is no substitute for victory" over the international Communist conspiracy.

Truman believed he could fight a limited war against this formidable and cunning opponent. This was not Truman's fault, McCarthy confessed; after all, he was just an average guy who meant well, like most other Americans. But Dean Acheson and his advisers exerted "a tremendous, almost hypnotic influence over him." Truman had chosen between MacArthur and "the Hiss-Acheson-Lattimore-Jessup crowd," and Americans would have to live with the tragic result: the slaughter of American boys in Korea and the continued growth of the "sinister, many-headed and many-tentacled monster," the Communist conspiracy within the government, "one which was conceived in Moscow and given birth to by Dean Gooderham Acheson." Acheson, McCarthy declared to his audience, was "the very heart of the octopus."[5]

McCarthy always had many favorite targets for abuse—Lattimore, Jessup, Truman himself—but he reserved a special distaste for Dean Acheson, and it is not difficult to see why. Acheson represented everything McCarthy was not: the product of Groton and Yale, the protégé of Felix Frankfurter and Louis Brandeis, the Washington insider lawyer whose aristocratic eastern locution sounded to ordinary people like a fake British accent. When McCarthy uttered Acheson's name, William White of the *New York Times* observed, he made it sound like an expletive. McCarthy called him "Dean Gooderham Acheson," as if the "Gooderham" somehow made Acheson seem more decadent and pusillanimous. Acheson's demeanor also offended McCarthy's sense of masculinity. To friends like Urban Van Susteren, McCarthy called the secretary of state "that striped pants asshole." He saw him as the protector of Jessup and the other "cookie pushers" of the State Department, whose "silk handkerchief approach" and "prancing" was useless against the Soviets. He even hinted that Acheson had his own reasons for shielding the homosexuals and other "moral perverts" McCarthy believed to be circulating in the State Department. When Acheson made the fashion magazines' list of ten best dressed men, McCarthy began calling him the Red Dean of Fashion.

People were horrified by this assault, just as today we can be horrified by his and Kenneth Wherry's efforts to drive homosexuals out of sensitive government jobs. Yet it is difficult to know how much of this name calling McCarthy really meant, and how much of it was a mocking, needling teasing that he enjoyed dishing out to opponents, colleagues, and friends. Many people have remarked on McCarthy's dark, sardonic sense of humor and his predictably earthy language. Asses constantly appeared in his conversation; "stop assing around" was a favorite expression of his. Nothing suggests he ever held a malign and bitter resentment against even his worst enemies. Joe Kennedy, Sr., and other close friends never remembered him being vindictive or personally bitter: "If somebody was against him, he never tried to cut his heart out. He never said anyone was a stinker." The Kennedy attitude, needless to say, tended to run in the opposite direction.[6]

It was also an era when politicians were beginning to discover the importance of sound bites. McCarthy was the master of the memorable phrase and formula, like the "Bourbon and Benedictine" remark and "twenty years of treason." But then organized labor had routinely called the Taft-Hartley bill a "slave labor law," and Harry Truman (back in 1948) accused the Republicans of being both "under the control of special privilege" and "unwittingly the ally of the Communists in this country." Bitter partisanship raged on all sides, not just among McCarthyites. David Demarest Lloyd (himself a victim of the era's hard edge) was sitting in the president's office one day during the 1948 campaign, listening to a recording of one of Truman's speeches. After listening to a particularly nasty and mean-spirited line come out of his own mouth, Truman exclaimed, "Did I say that?" Then he smiled to Lloyd, "Demagoguery—that's part of the game."[7]

McCarthy professed to find this verbal banter amusing. People got the joke or they didn't. Acheson certainly didn't. Once he and McCarthy encountered each other on an elevator. Without hesitation McCarthy stuck out his hand and sang out, "Hi, Dean." Acheson trembled with rage and stalked off the elevator without even acknowledging McCarthy's existence. McCarthy turned to everyone in bewilderment: "What was the matter with him?" The bewilderment was probably genuine. Teasing, psychologists tell us, is a form of aggression. McCarthy's sense of fun defies the stereotype of Joe McCarthy as a rampaging, ranting fanatic, but it does not disguise the fact that he also meant to wound—as with his notorious "Alger—I mean Adlai" slip during the 1952 campaign.

Meanwhile, McCarthy continued to take potshots at Acheson's State Department. He got hold of some recent minutes (February 13 and 14, 1951) of the Civil Service Loyalty Review Board, which oversaw the State Department's loyalty program, and leaked them to the press. They revealed that the oversight board itself considered State's screening program a disaster. "The State Department, as you know," it quoted the Review Board's chairman as saying, "has the worst record of any department in the action of its Loyalty Board." One of his colleagues complained: "I don't understand their attitude at all." The executive secretary said, "They're taking the attitude that they're there to clear the employee and not to protect the government. We've been arguing with them since the program started [in March 1947]." Another added that he too had been "disturbed about the State Department" and wondered whether they shouldn't tell President Truman "that the program simply does not work in that Department and let him worry about it."[8]

If this was not embarrassing enough, the loyalty board chairman, General Conrad Snow, had to appear before McCarthy and other members of the Senate Appropriations Committee to explain what the board was doing and his own vociferous attacks on McCarthy on the lecture circuit.[9] Snow revealed himself hopelessly ignorant of his own department and its history of security lapses; his attitude toward the Hiss case had been that "one swallow does not make a summer," as he expressed it, and if there was no compelling evidence that someone was a Communist or a subversive, then there was no need for a hearing, let alone a dismissal. It also turned out that the State Department board had never separated anyone as a loyalty risk, even though fifty-four people had been allowed to resign as disloyalty cases and another three had been found disloyal but were still in the department pending appeal.[10] Truman's review board's view of State, and incidentally McCarthy's, retrospectively turned out to be correct: since 1947 the State Department had bent over backward to avoid dismissing anyone for Communist associations or pro-Communist views, and was willing to allow people of doubtful loyalty, as it was then defined, to remain rather than have to get rid of them.

Snow also had to explain what he meant by saying that McCarthy spent his time making "baseless accusations." Give us a specific example, McCarthy wanted to know. Snow demurred, and then brought up a name: Haldore Hanson. Before joining the State Department Haldore Hanson had been a reporter in China for Associated Press in the thirties. He had written a book on Mao's Communist guerrillas called *Humane Endeavor*, which spoke glowingly of their "democratic revolution" in Yenan and of Mao as "the most selfless man I ever met" and "a genius fifty years ahead of his time." He had also written for Owen Lattimore's *Pacific Affairs*, along with other pro-Communist journalists. Finally, Louis Budenz had named him as a member of the Communist Party in front of the Tydings Committee. As Snow looked over a summary of McCarthy's charges against Hanson (the case was now pending before Snow's own board), he had to admit that they were not in fact "baseless." He could not come up with any other examples of McCarthy's unfounded smearing of individuals.

McCarthy generously summed up Snow's predicament for the Appropriations Committee this way: "I think he feels that he is in effect trying criminal cases; that he must give everyone the benefit of a doubt. . . . It is the kindly thing to do, but makes him completely incompetent to act as head of that board." He turned to Snow. "I do not accuse you of being an evil man, Mr. Snow, but watching the results that come from your board, I am trying to figure out what prompts you." Perhaps, McCarthy concluded, "you are a kindly individual who just dislikes seeing a man lose his job."[11]

McCarthy, in the face of the State Department's intransigence, had no such qualms. In May 1951 he brought to the Senate floor the cases of Esther and Stephen Brunauer, another husband and wife whose pro-Communist associations made them unfit for government service. (Brunauer had been a close friend of Noel Field, the Soviet spy who disappeared in 1949.) Stephen Brunauer was suspended by the Navy and allowed to resign from its explosives research division before the Navy loyalty board acted on his case. Esther Brunauer was fired from the State Department as a "security risk" on June 16, 1952, almost two years after McCarthy first brought her name up before the Tydings Committee.[12] In June he turned to the case of Edmund Clubb, another controversial China hand. Clubb was suspended on June 27, briefly reinstated by Dean Acheson's direct order (on February 11, 1952), and then finally resigned. By March 1952, 2,726 of 9,300 State Department employees who had been cleared under General Snow were being "reevaluated," largely because of McCarthy's public pressure.[13]

In the fall McCarthy settled another old score. He managed to block the nomination of Philip Jessup for ambassador to the United Nations. Later historians would attribute the adverse vote on Jessup to McCarthy's intimidation of his Senate colleagues.[14] However, McCarthy also had unexpected help: from Harold Stassen, then president of the University of Pennsylvania. Stassen testified that he had seen Jessup's poor judgment displayed in the State Department's Policy Conference in October 1949, when Jessup and other members had enthusiastically pushed for recognition of red China and that the Chinese Communists should be allowed to occupy both Formosa and

Hong Kong, "if they insisted." Like McCarthy, Stassen believed that Jessup had helped to inspire "a pattern of action" that led to the fall of China. The Senate subcommittee overseeing the nomination voted 3 to 2 against it. McCarthy's long campaign against Jessup now finally seemed vindicated.

By now McCarthy was convinced that Jessup really was a Communist, virtually indistinguishable from a Hiss.[15] However, he believed it was no longer enough to get the Communists out; he needed to expose those higher up who had protected them—which was why McCarthy decided to turn the heat on General George Catlett Marshall.

McCarthy's attack on Marshall was an isolated event in McCarthy's career but not in that of George Marshall. Robert Taft had voted against Marshall as secretary of defense in September 1950, on the grounds that Marshall's mistakes in China had led to the situation in Korea.[16] Then William Jenner had given a hair-raising speech in the Senate, calling Marshall "a front man for traitors" and a "living lie," which provoked a minor outcry. Now Marshall's role in MacArthur's dismissal guaranteed that the issue was not going away. Walter Trohan published a devastating piece on Marshall in the *American Mercury* in April 1951. Another right-wing anti-Communist journal, the *Freeman*, brought up Marshall's name in connection with the Foreign Service officers who had abandoned China to the Communists and "lost the United States some 400 million Oriental allies."[17] That appeared on June 4. Meanwhile, Taft speechwriter Forrest Davis was putting together a book on American foreign policy under FDR, which revealed that Marshall's bungling in China had been only one of a series of missteps and gullible support of the "Communist line." He met McCarthy at a cocktail party and told him what he was doing. McCarthy eagerly asked to see it, and handed it over to Jean Kerr and his staff, who hammered it into a long, rambling speech called "America's Retreat from Victory."

On June 14 McCarthy went to the Senate and read it aloud—or, rather, about three hours of it, before handing over the rest for the record. By then everyone had left, as much out of boredom as shock and outrage. The speech was, as Ben Bradlee might have said, a room emptier. Filled with long quotations from original documents and studded with references to learned diplomatic historians, it was as far from a typical McCarthy performance as one could get. Yet even as severe an anti-McCarthy critic as Richard Rovere had to concede that most of it was true, albeit "tendentiously chosen" and "meanly slanted."[18]

McCarthy purported to show that Marshall's entire career since World War I had been characterized by incompetence, negligence, self-promotion, and unforgivably faulty judgment—not to mention servile adherence to the interests of the Soviet Union. Marshall's role in the Pearl Harbor disaster; his

eagerness to open "a second front" during World War II; his support for concessions to Stalin at Yalta; his failure as secretary of state to investigate spies
in the United Nations; his willingness to offer the Marshall Plan to Russia
and its satellites; his instrumental role in cutting off aid to Chiang Kai-shek:
all revealed a sinister pattern, McCarthy was arguing, "a pattern which finds
his decisions, maintained with great stubbornness and skill, always and invariably serving the world policy of the Kremlin." Together with Dean Acheson, Marshall "propounded a foreign policy in the Far East of craven
appeasement" and turned the Korean War "into a pointless slaughter." Their
goal had been to "diminish the United States in world affairs, to weaken us
militarily . . . and to impair our will to resist evil." McCarthy concluded
harshly:

> If Marshall were merely stupid, the laws of probability would have dictated
> that at least some of his decisions would have served this country's interest.
> . . . We have declined so precipitously in relation to the Soviet Union in the
> last six years, how much swifter may be our fall into disaster with Marshall's
> policies continuing to guide us? Where will this all stop?[19]

The press and McCarthy's colleagues were aghast. The *Milwaukee Journal* dismissed the speech as "garbage." Senator Leverett Saltonstall called it
"sickening, simply disgusting," and Margaret Chase Smith took a grim satisfaction in claiming it reinforced her earlier view of McCarthy.[20] Evjue's *Capital Times* dubbed the speech a "a smear marathon," while *Collier's* magazine
ran a full-page editorial declaring that McCarthy had "set a new high for irresponsibility" and urging the Republican leadership to disassociate themselves from his "senseless and vicious charges."[21] What counted in the press,
however, was less what McCarthy had said than what he was supposed to
have said. Critics bandied it about that McCarthy had called Marshall a traitor (he had not), a secret Communist (he had not), and even a coward (Drew
Pearson liked to repeat that particular claim). However, the real gist of Mc-
Carthy's speech was to point out the consistent willingness of a leading administration official to give the benefit of a doubt to Communist leaders and
policies, and to ask why.

What does the modern historian make of all this? Probably that George
Catlett Marshall in China in 1946 was the wrong man in the wrong place at
the wrong time. His attitude toward Chiang Kai-shek, like that of his predecessor and protégé, Joseph Stilwell, was contemptuous and censorious, as if
Chiang and the KMT were directly responsible for the vast problems of a
once-mighty empire now in dissolution and decay. Marshall's attitude toward
Mao and the Communists was far more charitable, even admiring: the weight
of pro-Communist opinion among the China hands lay heavy on him, as it had

on Stilwell. When they told him Mao and the Communists were liberals will-
ing to cooperate with the United States, he believed them. When they told him
Chiang, not Mao, was the source of friction in negotiations for the future of
China, he believed them.

At one point a seasoned OSS officer, Colonel Ivan Yeaton, could stand it
no longer and caught Marshall in his quarters as he was dressing for dinner.
Yeaton told him that, contrary to what Service, Davies, and other China
hands had been saying, the communism in Yenan was "pure Marx, Lenin,
and Mao," and the Chinese Communist Party's only hope of winning any
struggle for control of China was by obtaining captured Japanese military
equipment, which would require Soviet help (which is exactly what in fact
happened). Marshall showed no interest in anything Yeaton was saying, and
finished dressing; as Marshall completed tying his bow tie, he turned to
Yeaton and said, "Thank you." That was all. As Yeaton noted in his memoirs,
"The only person he listened to was Chou [Zhou En-lai]."

Indeed, Marshall's trust in Zhou En-lai, Mao's clever, charming, and
brilliantly manipulative lieutenant, knew no bounds. An anecdote demon-
strates the degree of Marshall's naiveté in dealing with this master deceiver,
who had fooled an entire coterie of China experts and reporters into accept-
ing the Communist line on China. In June 1946, Zhou En-lai was on a flight
on Marshall's plane on his way back to Yenan. By a rare oversight, Zhou left
a notebook on the plane which contained the names of and crucial information about leading Chinese Communist spies in the KMT, including one
Xiong Xiang-hui, one of Mao's key operatives in Chiang Kai-shek's high
command. Potential disaster, not to mention the end of Zhou En-lai. But
when one of the flight crew gave the notebook to Marshall, he immediately
ordered that the notes be returned—unread—to the Chinese Communist
leader.

In short, Marshall's sense of Olympian detachment, which won him admirers among the Wise Men and State Department figures like Dean Rusk,
became a serious shortcoming in dealing with the Chinese situation. As noted
by historian Mao Chun-yu, "When George Marshall was in China, Communist intelligence penetration into American agencies ran rampant," including
the passing of forged documents regarding Chinese Communist operations
to the China hands and then on to the White House. Marshall remained blind
to it all. The Truman administration's decision to cut off aid to the Nationalists, and thus guarantee Mao's victory in the civil war, was largely Marshall's.
If any single person can be said to have "lost China" (and perhaps none can),
it was George Catlett Marshall.[22]

Who was to blame for this? In an article significantly titled "The Treason
of Liberalism," Forrest Davis had written, "events since last June [1950, i.e.,

the invasion of Korea] have, in truth, dwarfed the chief men of the administration":

> Should not the debilitating malaise which gives to life in Washington its
> sense of negation, empty of honor and dignity, be diagnosed as a failure of
> the "liberal" spirit? Is not the prevailing political "liberalism" of the mid-cen-
> tury, that potpourri of indiscriminate do-goodism trending into statism and
> Marxism and blending so indistinguishably with treason, that is the deepest
> enemy of the traditional America and the West?[23]

McCarthy did not stop there. Marshall's mistakes had to be the result of
something other than the liberals' characteristic wishful thinking and failure
of nerve, or even identification with Marxism's final objectives. And here Mc-
Carthy began to wade out further into the murky waters of Communist conspiracy theories than his supporters were usually willing to venture. He
declared that Marshall's actions "must be part of a great conspiracy" that
brought Communists *and* liberals together to ruin America, "a conspiracy on
a scale so immense as to dwarf any previous such venture in the history of
man"—words that critics have mocked ever since.

But Joe McCarthy, like many others of his generation, was still struggling to come to grips with the sheer magnitude of America's ascent to global
power and the momentous stakes that hung in the balance if it lost its grip.
"How," he asked in his June 14 speech, "how can we account for our present
situation unless we believe that men high in this Government are concerting
to deliver us to disaster?"[24] A man who had fashioned himself from nothing
into a national political figure was impatient with explanations for failure
that rested on impersonal or abstract historical forces or even tragic fate. To
McCarthy, it smacked of making excuses—and he was not alone. As he explained to a sympathetic audience, "History does not just happen. It is made
by men—men with names and faces, and the only way the course of history
can be changed is by getting rid of the specific individuals who we find are
bad for America."[25]

McCarthy had spent the last year and a half pointing out those persons:
Acheson, Jessup, John Carter Vincent, and now George Marshall. Mc-
Carthy was accusing them of being guilty of more than just being suscepti-
ble to the blandishments of a Hiss at Yalta or a John Stewart Service at
Yenan, or a Zhou En-lai. To some degree they *must* have desired the disastrous outcome of their polices. His view can be stated as a theorem: If policy a aims at outcome x and results instead in outcome y, then the actual
object of policy a must have been x rather than y. The theorem is fallacious,
of course: no one can discern intentions simply from the results of an action, no matter how unfortunate or calamitous. Yet this is what McCarthy

purported to do: to argue that Yalta, Potsdam, Yenan, and Korea were all part of a deliberate unfolding of a single plan embraced by Communists and liberals alike, to weaken American resolve and "our will to resist evil" so that the United States will "finally fall victim to Soviet intrigue from within and Russian military might from without."

This was going too far, even for regular McCarthy supporters. It was one thing to suggest that Democrats and liberals were sympathetic to communism, and so played a losing hand from the beginning. It was something else to say that they were consciously gauging their actions in order to facilitate Communist success: that Soviet expansion and Stalin's successes were "brought about, step by step, by will and intention." The conservative press avoided coming to his defense when the liberal attacks started. In private Robert Taft treated the speech as "bunk" and in public told reporters: "I don't think one who overstates his case helps his own case. . . . [McCarthy's] extreme attack against General Marshall is one of the things on which I cannot agree." Even McCarthy eventually had to back off and trim some of his criticisms of Marshall in his own defense in his *McCarthyism: The Fight for America.*

Yet McCarthy in his own unreasonable way had raised a reasonable issue. To what extent had a floundering New Deal establishment, including men like Marshall, helped the Soviet Union become a superpower by their own poorly considered actions? Wasn't that record of failure more than sufficient reason for removing them from office?

Figures like Robert Taft understood this. Biographers and critics have wondered why Taft supported or at least sanctioned McCarthy for so long. As usual, they have the question backward. The issue is not why Taft would have put up with him, but what compelling reasons he had for trying to stop him. Like many others, Taft believed the Democrats had seriously underestimated the Communist threat. He knew *bipartisanship* was only a code word for silencing criticisms of the Truman foreign policy team and that the forces that assaulted McCarthy were also his enemies. He also understood that in the fight against an entrenched political party that had dominated the nation's governing institutions for two decades, it takes considerable effort to pry them loose. As he explained to friends, "The only way to beat the Democrats is to go after them for their mistakes."[26] Taft's notorious advice to McCarthy—"if one case doesn't work, get another"—earned him opprobrium from the liberals. In fact, he was merely recognizing that McCarthy had a genuine issue that, if used correctly, might finally oust the Democrats from power.

Nonetheless, much about McCarthy disturbed him. He conceded that McCarthy often got his facts wrong, and was stubborn and headstrong. His friend Tom Coleman warned him that McCarthy was "up in the clouds and expect[ed] . . . complete support of himself on all things. . . . I cannot feel that any sense of loyalty to any of us or to anyone at all has any part in the picture."[27] Taft had to agree. "You are mistaken when you suggest that I have influence on McCarthy," he wrote to a friend at the end of August. From the beginning of the storm over the State Department, Taft said, he and his fellow Republicans had tried to rein him in "but found it was impossible." It made McCarthy, he complained to another, "a hard man to work with." The Marshall speech confirmed all these doubts. When Jenner and Wherry asked whether McCarthy ought to be given a slot on the Senate Republican Policy Committee, Taft and Chairman Milliken forcefully said no.[28]

The Marshall speech was a turning point in McCarthy's career. It appeared in book form as *America's Retreat from Victory*, which predictably won praise from right-wing reviewers and damnation from left-wing ones. It is a strange monument to a strange era, when virtually everything a public figure in Washington did became the subject of a vicious battle of charge and counter-charge, when, as an observer wrote of another time and context, "anything, however preposterous, could be said and believed, and any public attitude, however grotesque, struck, without anyone finding it particularly odd."[29]

Columnist Marquis Childs had called McCarthy's speech "nasty political mudslinging." Yet it soon transpired that McCarthy's opponents could dish it out better than they could take it.

Chapter 10

McCarthy Triumphant

But having cleared himself of every suspicion, and proved his entire innocence, he now at once came forward to ask for the tribuneship; in which, though he was universally opposed by all persons of distinction, yet there came such infinite numbers of people from all parts of Italy to vote for Caius, that lodgings for them could not be supplied by the city; and the Field being not large enough to contain the assembly, there were numbers who climbed upon the roofs and the tilings of the houses to use their voices in his favour.

—Plutarch, *Life of Caius Gracchus*

At first glance, William Benton, Democratic senator from Connecticut, was McCarthy's antithesis. A Yale–Phi Beta Kappa–Rhodes scholar liberal, he had made a fortune as a Madison Avenue advertising executive. Charming, energetic, and cultivated, he was the sort of character Cary Grant might play in a movie. He was good friends with the University of Chicago's Robert M. Hutchins, and had served as the university's vice president before doing a stint in the State Department. Like his business partner Chester Bowles, he was a rich man dabbling in public service. He was also a tireless defender of Truman administration policy, including the dismissal of General MacArthur.

But he and McCarthy were more alike than was at first obvious. For one thing, Benton was also a Senate outsider. Appointed to the chamber in 1949,

Benton was as ignorant of procedure and process as McCarthy ever was. Like McCarthy, he radiated energy and a voluble zeal, to a point that often made other people uncomfortable. Slave-driving hard work was natural to him. "Bill, you'll never get an ulcer," someone once told him, "but you sure are a carrier."[1] A trained observer would probably describe him as hypomanic, prone to frenzies of furious activity that wore out enemies and supporters alike—not unlike McCarthy himself. As with Joe, resistance from others made him touchy and irritable; Benton's one-man campaign to oust McCarthy might have gone better if he hadn't managed to annoy his colleagues almost as much as McCarthy did.

Benton also understood by profession what McCarthy understood by instinct: how much modern politics involved manipulation of the mass media. The Benton and Bowles agency had transformed advertising on radio through singing commercials and product surveys. Benton's close attention to consumer needs had made him, according to one source, "the world's greatest authority on the sanitary napkin."[2] Unlike earlier McCarthy opponents, like Millard Tydings, Benton realized that defeating McCarthy required the full and active participation of the press. If McCarthy was good at securing headlines and well-attended press conferences, even when he had little to say or reveal, Benton proved to be at least as good. In the eyes of journalists, Benton became the undaunted David challenging Goliath.

Benton was drawn into combat by McCarthy's sustained attacks on his beloved State Department, where he had been in charge of its overseas information service. In February 1951 he pitched in with Senators Kilgore and Humphrey in a triangular attack on McCarthy's appointment to the Appropriations Subcommittee dealing with the State Department's budget. Given McCarthy's record as a "ruthless propagandist," they thought it was an outrageous selection. "The junior senator from Wisconsin," Benton railed, "is to be the judge, jury and prosecutor of the State Department. By this appointment he becomes his own kangaroo court." Republicans replied that McCarthy deserved the seat as a matter of seniority; from their perspective, McCarthy's record would make him an asset rather than a liability. Kenneth Wherry retorted to the critics, "I think he has done more to establish confidence in the hearts of Americans than any man I know. . . . When the record is written, when his service is done, he will go down in a blaze of glory."[3]

Benton's next opportunity came when Guy Gillette's Subcommittee on Privileges and Elections released its report on the Maryland election. A prevaricating document, drawn up by Democrat partisans and Republican moderates, it sternly surveyed the facts of McCarthy's involvement in the race and condemned what it called "back street" campaign methods "which are destroying the very foundations of our government." But the committee also admitted the evidence didn't add up to very much actual wrongdoing. The committee didn't believe Butler should lose his seat, nor did it recommend sanctions or penalties against McCarthy, although it did condemn his meddling in severe terms.[4]

Benton found the report compelling and worried it would be buried and forgotten. So on August 6, 1951, he offered a Senate resolution that the report should serve as the basis for hearings to expel McCarthy from the Senate. In reply, McCarthy told reporters that Benton was now "the hero of every Communist and crook in and out of government." He coined the phrase "mental midget" to describe the senator from Connecticut, and added, "I call the attention of all honest Democrats to how men of little minds are destroying a once great party."

As Benton was sounding the advance and waving the troops forward, he soon discovered that no one was interested to joining the charge. The members of the Privileges and Elections Subcommittee were less than pleased. Republican Margaret Chase Smith called the Benton resolution "unfortunate"; Alex Smith of New Jersey thought it "undignified"; Democrat Willis Smith told Benton "he was making a mistake because there was no chance whatever" of getting a two-thirds vote to expel. William Fulbright of Arkansas felt the resolution would set a "dangerous precedent," which really got to the heart of the matter. In dealing with their wayward colleague from Wisconsin, most senators confronted what political economists call the Punishment Dilemma: they were unwilling to invoke sanctions for bad behavior that might be used against one of them some day. No senator wanted to be denied the opportunity to be eccentric, or indiscreet, or cantankerous toward colleagues or even cruelly vindictive if it suited him or her. This predisposition to self-protection, far more than any ideological terror or "politics of fear," would always be the main obstacle to collective Senate action against McCarthy.[5]

Benton, however, was no more put off by the lack of collegial support than McCarthy would have been. After getting in touch with the Democratic National Committee and the attorney general's office, he pieced together a fifty-nine-page attack on McCarthy, then presented it to Gillette's committee and the press with great fanfare on September 28. He claimed in it that McCarthy had deliberately lied to the Senate on six separate occasions. These included his denial that he had said "205 Communists" in his Wheeling speech, his insistence that he had been forced to name names publicly by the Tydings Committee, and the accusations in his Marshall speech. Benton also charged that McCarthy had promoted "deliberate falsehoods" in the Maryland campaign against Tydings, and if that were not enough, that the $10,000 McCarthy had received from the Lustron Corporation in 1948 constituted a form of bribery that "set him apart from the rest of the Senate." He called Mc-Carthy "amoral," denouncing him as a man who "used the lie as an instrument of policy" and followed "a pattern of dictatorship and deceit." Benton concluded by arguing that if McCarthy really believed what he said about General Marshall, then the Senate should also think about expelling him as being "of unsound mind."

Benton's own lawyer called it the most libelous statement he had ever read. But Benton knew he was protected by senatorial immunity, and the Privileges and Elections Subcommittee reluctantly agreed to take up the report and investigate. When it asked McCarthy to appear, he wrote to the chairman, Guy Gillette of Iowa, "Frankly, Guy, I have not and do not intend to even read, much less answer, Benton's smear attack." It was, he said, the sort of trash that appeared daily in the *Daily Worker*. He would not waste time and effort appearing before a committee that was engaged in an exercise of pure partisanship.

The "Dear Guy" letter and another he wrote to the subcommittee in November would land McCarthy in considerable trouble. By taking committee Democrats to task on dubious grounds (suggesting, for example, that since one of Senator Hennings's former law partners was defending a prominent Communist Party member in a court case, Hennings should disqualify himself), he provoked men whose first inclination was to leave him alone. He didn't realize that left to himself, the brash and pushy Benton would undo himself even faster than he was undoing McCarthy—and now McCarthy was engaged in the same self-sabotage. In fact, the prospect of both men destroying each other lifted their colleagues' spirits; one senator called it "an ideal double murder."[6]

What Benton did manage to do was to turn up the heat in the media. The *New York Post* offered readers a seventeen-part series, "Smear Inc., The One-Man Mob of Joe McCarthy." *Life* ran a critical piece on McCarthy, calling on Taft and other Republicans to repudiate him. "The cumulative debasement of United States politics," it said, "has gone far enough." In October *Time* ran its "Demagogue McCarthy" piece, and Benton seized on a sensational news story that a McCarthy operative—one of his "private gestapo," as the *Capital Times* put it—had been convicted in Switzerland for espionage.

This was Charles Davis, a twenty-three-year-old African-American, who told Swiss authorities that McCarthy had hired him to spy on John Carter Vincent, then a minister in Bern, and to forge a telegram implicating Vincent as a Communist in exchange for money. Benton gleefully took the story to the Senate floor and quoted from documents describing Charles Davis as a homosexual and former Communist. "Here we have an admitted homosexual ex-Communist convicted as a spy on Senator McCarthy's payroll," he thundered, and passed the story on to the Gillette subcommittee. The problem was that Davis was lying. McCarthy actually had received letters from Davis offering to dig up dirt on Vincent, and paid some of his expenses when Davis met with one of McCarthy's contacts in Paris. But McCarthy soon lost interest in Davis when he turned out to have nothing to reveal, and he never requested any faked telegram. When the *Syracuse Post-Standard* ran a story saying he did, McCarthy sued and forced a retraction.[7]

The whole proceedings of the Gillette-Hennings subcommittee, with changes of chairmen, members resigning in disgust, the defection of one of its staffers to the McCarthy camp, all punctuated by McCarthy's own nasty and sarcastic letters, was a farce. No one emerges with very much credit. At one crucial point in the proceedings, its new chairman, Thomas Hennings, who was an alcoholic and a binge drinker, vanished for a week.[8] Deliberations moved at a glacial pace, since members recognized that there was no way to secure action on Benton's flimsy charges, but also no way to stop. They were goaded on by a liberal press, which suggested they lacked intestinal fortitude, and by McCarthy's taunting behavior.

Eventually, in January 1952, the subcommittee produced an inconclusive preliminary report and then fell silent. In early April McCarthy launched his own counter-resolution against Benton, charging him with sheltering Communists, engaging in his shady financial deals, and even peddling obscene books. He brought a $2 million libel suit against Benton, an action he knew he had no chance of winning. But he told friends that he wanted Benton to wake up every morning with the awful possibility that one day he might have to pay Joe McCarthy $2 million. "He'll sweat," McCarthy would chortle.[9]

This less than edifying spectacle dragged on through the rest of the year. Finally McCarthy's most vociferous enemies on the committee put together a document dredging up every piece of unfavorable information or gossip they could find. Their final report implied that McCarthy had solicited the $10,000 from the Lustron Corporation as a bribe, when he had not. It hashed over his political finances, including gifts from people who sent him money to help his "war against the Reds," but could not find no evidence of anything illegal, although it had tried. It touched on his Pepsi dealings, his supposed links to the China Lobby, and other matters without any conclusive evidence of wrongdoing. The report was a smear, pure and simple.[10] With the help of columnist Drew Pearson, its authors locked the hapless Hennings in his house so he couldn't have recourse to a drink, and compelled him to sign it. By contrast, the ranking Republican, the timid Robert Hendrickson of New

Jersey, required several drinks before he could be convinced to put his own name to it. The report was released January 2, 1953, just before the new Congress was to take its seat.

Ironically, the people who seized on it were precisely those were usually most outraged at McCarthy's unfair distortions or misrepresentations of evidence. The Americans for Democratic Action, the *New Republic*, the *New York Post*, and the Wisconsin *Progressive* all published large portions of the report; distinguished academics applauded it as a "damning document," and senators like William Fulbright, Ralph Flanders, and Wayne Morse would all rely on the Hennings report for ammunition in their various hit-and-run maneuvers against McCarthy.

Benton in particular felt vindicated. "It is manifest," he declared, "that the Senate will be compelled to unseat Senator McCarthy." But on January 3, it was William Benton, not Joe McCarthy, who was being unseated. Once again, incredibly, the voters had come through and defeated another McCarthy opponent, while sending McCarthy and the Republicans to an unprecedented triumph.

Early in 1952, as he was gearing up for his senatorial reelection campaign, McCarthy published *McCarthyism and the Fight for America*. It was written by Jean Kerr, in collaboration with J. B. Matthews and Ruth Matthews.[11] They wrote it in the form of a running interview, with questions ("Will you explain your use of the number 205 and 57 in your Wheeling speech?" and "Why do you condemn people like Acheson, Jessup, Lattimore, Service, Vincent, and others who have never been convicted of any crime?") and answers reflecting the standard charges that opponents were making in speeches and in the press. The book particularly went after those who claimed that they approved of McCarthy's aims (getting Communists out of government) but not his methods. "It makes me ill," it had McCarthy saying, "when I hear cowardly politicians and self-proclaimed liberals . . . parrot over and over this Communist Party line. They deceive good, loyal Americans into believing that there is some easy, delicate way of exposing Communists without at the same time exposing all of their traitorous, sordid acts." That was the book's main point: you could not have real anticommunism without McCarthyism, meaning exposing individual wrongdoers. "We are losing," he added, "either because of stumbling, fumbling idiocy on the part of those allegedly leading the fight against Communism, or because, like Hiss, they are planning it that way." Either way Acheson and the rest had to go.[12]

McCarthy read sections of the book and occasionally jotted notes in the margin, but he was largely uninvolved. Nevertheless, the book did capture his growing sense of being on the defensive and his capacity for self-dramatization—what Tom Coleman called his "Christ complex."

"The louder the screams of the left-wing elements of press and radio," the book had him saying, "the more damage I know I am doing to the Communist party." He was now regularly being attacked as a Hitlerite and fascist. The *Capital Times* said he was a "real threat to minority groups—especially Jews." The president of the Wisconsin AFL called McCarthy "a liar, cheat and fraud who even goes against his God."[13] One reader of an issue of the *New Republic* found the words "McCarthy" and "McCarthyism" appearing forty times in four separate articles. *McCarthyism: The Fight for America* had his last word on critics, in a quotation from Abraham Lincoln: "If the end brings me out all right, what is said against me won't amount to anything. If the end brings me out wrong, then ten angels swearing I was right would make no difference."

McCarthy's political battles were also taking a physical toll. In July he entered the hospital for a painful sinus operation. It failed, and sinus problems and migraine headaches would plague him for the rest of his life. Then he had to undergo an operation for a herniated diaphragm, which required doctors to make a twenty-four-inch incision and remove a rib. He was supposed to take two months to recover. Instead, McCarthy gave his first interview in less than twenty days, and soon was back on the lecture tour in Seattle, speaking to the Pro America Republican Women. However, pain from the wound would drive him to aspirin and the bottle.

McCarthy's drinking, which had been heavy before 1952, now began to spiral out of control. He started carrying a bottle in his briefcase and gulping down a tumbler of bourbon before speaking engagements. He became regularly drunk during his visits to the Van Susterens in Appleton. One reporter caught him in a hotel bedroom at seven in the morning with a pitcher of martinis; another saw him drink a glass of bourbon at breakfast topped off with a teaspoon of orange juice. When his stomach rebelled, McCarthy alternated drinks with handfuls of antacid tablets. On the eve of the election in November, an Appleton doctor warned him he was on the brink of physical collapse and ordered him to go to bed and avoid visitors. McCarthy ignored the advice and invited everyone up to his hotel room for a preelection celebration while he swilled drinks, shook hands, and stoically endured the agony of strangers slapping him on his injured back.[14]

For the high-flying McCarthy, heavy drinking became one outlet. Another was gambling. This, too, was nothing new. As a teen-age chicken farmer he had lost his truck in a poker game. Life at Marquette had centered on cards as well as beer parties; so did his time in the Marines. "He would bet on anything," friend Urban Van Susteren recalled.

But now the stakes were larger and the compulsion more serious. McCarthy had discovered the stock market during the war, and used the tidy sum he made on a hot tip to finance his first Senate campaign. Playing the market became a central part of the gambling mix, along with the green baize table and the racetrack. (One day McCarthy needed some money and asked Ed Nellor to cash some old unredeemed betting tickets. They were worth nearly $4,000.) Of course, all Washington politicians, then and now, profited from stock tips and insider investment schemes offered up by constituents and lobbyists. McCarthy eagerly did so. His $10,000 fee from Lustron in 1948 had come providentially at a financial low point. But instead of using it to pay off a series of outstanding loans, he had thrown it into the stock market—where he had another round of good luck and made a tidy bundle.[15] Later, his rich Texas oil friends, like Clint Murchison and H. L. Hunt, kept him abreast of hot deals, as did a Chicago commodities broker named Rice (who later became a big contributor to Joe's 1952 campaign).

However, McCarthy increasingly allowed this financial wheeling and dealing to run his finances and his life. Things started running in just two directions, either boom or bust. When things were booming, the bounty flowed out as gifts and presents to friends, employees, and even casual acquaintances: the world smiled on Joe McCarthy and he could do no wrong. When things went bust was the only time that friends could remember seeing him upset or emotionally shaken. Often he had to rely on loans from friends to keep himself going. The sums he lost were substantial. Once he told Van Susteren about a bad stock tip that had cost him $80,000. As Van expressed amazement, McCarthy just shook his head and repeated, "eighty thousand dollars." Another time McCarthy rang up his old friend to urge him to go in a scheme involving the grain market (presumably suggested by his commodities broker supporter). Joe kept yelling into the phone, "Mortgage the house and buy rye!" Van Susteren decided to keep his house. No such voice of prudence worked on McCarthy.[16]

And it was not just money or the stock market that brought out this reckless streak. It is not difficult to see the whole history of his anti-Communist forays in the same light. An adrenaline rush, a personal high that fed a soaring ego with feelings of grandeur and power. No wonder friends like Tom Coleman talked behind McCarthy's back about a "Christ complex." In his own mind, it was Joe McCarthy against the world, playing a sudden-death, high-stakes game against a Communist conspiracy that, in more expansive moments, seemed to include the entire Democratic administration and Washington establishment. In short, McCarthy's "obsession" with communism was not the product of paranoia, but a manic compulsion, like his gambling—while the fate of America, even of civilization itself, seemed more and more to hinge on whether McCarthy beat the odds.

The battle over Joe McCarthy was also evolving into a struggle over what political order would succeed to a moribund New Deal establishment. As McCarthy put it, "Stupidity and eagerness to keep a corrupt party at the public trough can destroy a nation as effectively and as quickly as treason— especially when traitors can use men of little minds who put party about country."[17] Ostensibly the issue was communism in government; in reality, it was a struggle for governance. For the first time in two decades, Republicans sensed that they were the party of the future and that power was within their grasp.

The Republican National Convention opened in Chicago on July 4, 1952, in the Chicago Amphitheater, the same place where Democrats would hold their national convention, and for the same reason: it was the perfect setting for television cameras.[18] Eighteen million television owners and their families across the nation could watch Republicans parading traditional American values and contrasting Republican promise with Democrat failure. They could see and hear Douglas MacArthur give the keynote address, attacking "those reckless men who, yielding to international intrigue, set the stage for Soviet ascendancy as a world power and our own relative decline." MacArthur was followed by Herbert Hoover, Senator Styles Bridges, and General Patrick Hurley—the last two being key figures from the China Lobby.

On July 9, the convention chairman introduced McCarthy to a tumultuous reception. "We will not turn our backs at any time," he shouted, "on that fighting Irish Marine, the honorable Joe McCarthy." The band struck up "The Halls of Montezuma" as a grinning McCarthy ascended to the platform. Wisconsin delegates carried their state banner to the center aisle and began a snake dance through the auditorium as placards appeared with the names "Hiss," "Lattimore," and "Acheson" emblazoned in red.

The speech was, as Jean Kerr might have said, a honey. McCarthy let the Republican delegates know that the free world was losing on average 100 million people a year to communism, and those responsible were still running Washington. "The loyal Democrats of this nation no longer have a party," he declared. In Korea the Acheson crowd had "squandered the blood of 110,631 sons of American mothers." He spoke of the Russians' political prisoners and of a brave American businessman unfairly charged with espionage who had just been released from Hungarian prison. By a prearranged signal, the television cameras swiveled to a corner of the audience, where businessman Robert Voegler and wife stood up as a spotlight hit them. The crowd roared their approval.

Liberals would later dismiss this little *coup de théatre*, but McCarthy was saving the best for last. He reminded the audience that American prisoners of war were being tortured and brainwashed in Chinese and North Korean prisons (and, it would later turn out, in the Soviet Union). He paused as a hush fell over the amphitheater:

> Mr. Truman, your telephone is ringing tonight. Five thousand Americans are calling, calling from prison cells inside Russia and her satellite nations. They are homesick, Mr. Truman. They are lonely and maybe a little afraid. Answer your telephone, Mr. Truman. It will be interesting to hear what you have to say.

Then came four ringing sentences, each punctuated with thunderous applause from below:

> *I say one Communist in a defense plant is one Communist too many.*
> *One Communist on the faculty of one university is one Communist too many.*
> *One Communist among the American advisors at Yalta was one Communist too many.*
> *And even if there were only one Communist in the State Department, that would still be one Communist too many.*

The speech stirred liberal critics to fury, especially the part about universities. Yet when all was said and done, the whole episode, melodramatic effects and all, barely raised McCarthy's national visibility.[19]

If the public at large was not very exercised about McCarthy one way or another, political Washington was in a flurry. Attacks in the press continued to mount. The *New York Post's* anti-McCarthy series dredged up the moldy stories about Quaker Dairy and the "quickie divorces" and even accused him (falsely) of having a homosexual on his staff in 1947. Drew Pearson's assistant Jack Anderson cowrote a scurrilous little book, *McCarthy: The Man, the Senator, the "Ism,"* and interviewed neighbors from Grand Chute to scrape together evidence that McCarthy had been a bully and a liar even as a child.

Democrats and Washington insiders hoped that all this might stir some anti-McCarthy resistance in the Wisconsin primary. They were sorely disappointed. Joe won the GOP nomination by 100,000 more votes than all his other opponents put together. Constituents spoke admiringly of their "fighting Marine" in the Senate. One told a reporter, "Joe's fighting a barroom brawl against a crowd that sure has messed things up for this country." McCarthy's primary victory was, the *New York Times* opined, "as overwhelming as it is depressing."[20]

After the convention, the press shifted its attention to the uneasy relationship between McCarthy and the Republican presidential candidate, Dwight Eisenhower. They speculated about how shameful it would be if Eisenhower campaigned on behalf of a man who had smeared his old patron, General Marshall. They greeted with satisfaction news that Eisenhower would insert a paragraph defending Marshall into a speech he planned to give in Appleton, on McCarthy's home turf, and then sighed when they learned he would not. In Appleton McCarthy smiled and spoke warmly of his party's nominee, and Eisenhower uttered some phrases about how Communists had pierced the highest reaches of the government under the Democrats. *Times* publisher Arthur Sulzberger telegrammed Eisenhower adviser Sherman Adams, "Do I need to tell you that I am sick at heart?" Herblock ran a cartoon in the *Post* with a leering ape-like McCarthy standing in a pool of filth with the sign "ANYTHING TO WIN" while Eisenhower apologized to a bystander, "Our differences have nothing to do with the end result we are seeking." Democratic candidate Adlai Stevenson crowed about Eisenhower's "capitulation" to the McCarthy vote and accused Eisenhower of mortgaging "every principle he ever held." According to columnist Joe Alsop, Eisenhower staffers referred to the Appleton visit as "that terrible day."[21]

Perhaps. But McCarthy's support helped, not hurt, Eisenhower's campaign. McCarthy's reputation as a fearless Commie basher inspired Republicans votes in traditionally Democratic working-class neighborhoods, particularly in the Northeast. In German, Irish, and Italian Catholic districts, from Boston to Staten Island and Queens, from New Jersey and Pennsylvania, the total share of Republican votes jumped.[22] In New York, middle-class suburban Catholics voted almost three to one for Eisenhower. In Massachusetts, McCarthy did not actually campaign for John Kennedy, but at Joseph Sr.'s urging, he declined to campaign for his fellow Republican, Henry Cabot Lodge, who lost. Together Eisenhower and McCarthy broke the loyalty of children of ethnic working-class immigrants who had been voting for the Democratic Party since 1928.

McCarthy's appeal was bipartisan, but not in the sense that liberal Democrats liked to use the term. He explained to his audiences that the Democratic Party of old—the party of the New Deal that had fought for ordinary Americans and made them feel protected and secure—had been sold out by its elite leadership. McCarthy launched several attacks on Stevenson during the campaign that prompted angry rebuttals even before they appeared, since the Democratic National Committee knew he would focus on the issue on which they were most vulnerable: that Stevenson stood for a bankrupt past. James Burnham, the anticontainment critic, wrote in the October issue of the *American Mercury* that Adlai Stevenson belonged to that class of New Deal liberals who "have provided the ideological cultural material in which pro-Communist points of view and individual Communist agents have flourished." He asserted, "A vote for Stevenson will be a vote of approval; a vote for Eisenhower will be a vote of protest."[23]

Eisenhower was the first Republican many Americans had ever voted for. They were tired of Truman and his administration's constant scandals. They were tired of his vacillations on the communism issue. They were tired of the war in Korea. Eisenhower beat Stevenson 55 percent to 44 percent, and Republicans recaptured both houses of Congress, although by very narrow margins. Scholars argue over whether McCarthy's support secured the Republican victory, but Eisenhower's victory was in any case part of a greater seachange in American politics: of a middle-class tide that was beginning to roll away from the Democratic Party. Eisenhower's gains in traditional Democratic areas in 1956, after McCarthy's fall, would be even greater.

McCarthy's own victory in Wisconsin showed the limits of his hard-core appeal. His final vote total was lower than in 1946. Labor union districts in Milwaukee, which had supported him against La Follette, reverted to the Democrats in 1952. McCarthy had strenuously campaigned for fellow Class of '46ers Harry Cain in Washington, who lost to Henry Jackson, and James Kem in Missouri, who lost to Democrat Stuart Symington. Analysts looking at the final numbers discovered that McCarthy had actually hurt congressional candidates he campaigned for by an average margin of 5 percent. This hardly suggested that McCarthy was on the verge of becoming an irresistible national demagogue, as some liberals feared. Certainly McCarthy never took final victory for granted. When he heard the final returns and realized he really had been reelected by the people of Wisconsin, Joe astonished friends by bursting into tears.[24]

Meanwhile, the liberal counterattack had collapsed of its own weight and lack of substance. William Benton went down to humiliating defeat in Connecticut. Although Benton pooh-poohed suggestions that McCarthy's three appearances there might have cost him the election, he did plant some of the blame on a young and militantly conservative Yale graduate named William F. Buckley, Jr., who had published a newsletter attacking Benton's record as pro-Communist. "A potentially dangerous young man," Benton warned Millard Tydings, as they shared electoral defeat woes.[25] In Arizona Barry Goldwater toppled another anti-McCarthy stalwart, Democrat majority leader Scott McFarland.

On January 3, 1953, the new Congress was sworn in. The Hennings report had appeared the day before. As he entered the Senate chamber, McCarthy delightedly clapped its chief author, Carl Hayden of Arizona, on the back, and stepped up to take the oath for a second term. Two weeks earlier, John Carter Vincent had been dismissed from the foreign service.

Sadly watching these events, Jack Anderson shook his head. "We had used up almost our entire bag of tricks against McCarthy, without marked effect," he wrote years later. "Three years had passed since Wheeling and he was still coming on strong."[26]

Yet McCarthy's hour of glory was almost over.

Chapter 11

Republicans Ascendant

O n January 20, 1953, Dwight Eisenhower stood on the windswept podium of the Capitol to be sworn in as president and deliver his inaugural address. "The world and we have passed the midway point of a century of challenge," he began. "The forces of good and evil are massed and armed and opposed as rarely before in history. . . . Freedom is pitted against slavery; lightness against the dark."

After that dramatic opening, Eisenhower was careful to avoid suggesting that "the forces of evil" included the defeated Democrats. He had no desire to dwell on the ambiguous legacy of twenty years of Democratic rule (prosperity and big government at home, weakness in the aftermath of victory abroad) or on the shortcomings of the Truman administration (although he detested Truman personally).[1] Instead, Ike spoke of the dangers of nuclear confrontation and the necessity of NATO and the United Nations. He said nothing about the welfare state's becoming the police state or about cutting taxes and nothing about the threat of domestic communism. In fact, beyond a reference to communism's "tutoring men in treason" and a call for "moral stamina," Ike's first speech as president was, according to the Democrats' new minority leader, Lyndon Johnson, "a very good statement of Democratic programs of the last twenty years."[2]

Most Republicans did not notice or care. The mere sight of a Republican taking the presidential oath of office was, as someone put it, "like walking into bright sunshine after being in darkness for a long time." If anyone should have been disturbed, it was Robert Taft. He was now majority leader, but the position he really wanted was Eisenhower's. He had had the support of the party's old regulars at Chicago for the presidential nomination, but Eisenhower's men had found a way around them—and him. Taft's disappointment had been bitter and profound, and he had serious doubts about many of the people in Eisenhower's administration. But he was unwilling to raise that issue in the flush of Republican victory.

For one thing, that victory had been razor thin. There had been a huge turnout for the 1952 election, more than any other election in American history. Although Stevenson and the Democrats had lost in every region of the country, they had hardly been buried in a landslide. Republicans controlled the House by only seven votes, the Senate by one. Eisenhower had decided that the key to electoral success was to stick firmly in the middle of the road, and that would be his policy as president as well. Hopes that a tough conservative agenda would come out of the White House or the Hill began to fade.

Taft himself was determined to remain on close terms with the new president in order to keep him and his advisers on the straight and narrow. He and Ike regularly played golf together. Then one day in April, after a few rounds, Taft felt unusually tired and out of breath. In less than three months, the hero of the conservative Republican right was dead of cancer. He left behind an empty throne and a power vacuum in the Republican Party. Kenneth Wherry was also gone, having died in the fall of 1951. The most prominent Republican in the Senate was now, improbably enough, Joe McCarthy.

"For once," wrote seasoned McCarthy watcher William White of the *New York Times*, "in the case of Senator McCarthy, the legend does not overreach, or even quite reach, the man." He spoke of McCarthy's "strange, half-hidden power, in the Senate, in the country and in the world," which "is not now diminishing, as many thought it might after Dwight D. Eisenhower took office. . . . It is still growing."[3] Not that McCarthy had higher ambitions in any formal sense. He left those to William Knowland, Taft's replacement as majority leader. McCarthy was content with becoming chairman of the Government Operations Affairs Committee and, with it, after six long years of waiting, of the Permanent Subcommittee on Investigations. He was busily putting together a staff that would turn PSI into the sort of aggressive and far-ranging anti-Communist investigative unit he had dreamed of. In 1953, *diversity* was an unfamiliar term for talking about ethnicity in America, but that was in effect what McCarthy achieved with his new team. Later he took pride in the fact that the PSI staff "represents all shades of religious, political and racial viewpoints," with Irish Catholics, Jews, Greeks, Italians, women, and Protestant white males all jostled together. Yet the result was not happy harmony but discord.

McCarthy had wanted Robert Morris, his old ally from the Tydings days, as chief counsel, but Morris had turned him down. Jean Kerr called Morris as he was vacationing in Nassau to urge him to accept. "You have to do it," she said. "You just have to do it. The pressures are enormous."[4] The pressure in this case was from Joseph Kennedy, Sr., who wanted his boy Bobby to be McCarthy's right-hand assistant. Joe's admiration for McCarthy was unbounded, as was his son's. While at the University of Virginia Law School, Bobby had invited McCarthy to come to speak and now was eager to prove himself on McCarthy's committee.[5] However, even after Morris finally, definitively turned McCarthy down ("I've made my commitment to the leadership and I'm going to stick by it," he later recalled telling McCarthy), Kennedy was crestfallen to learn he would be only assistant counsel. The top slot was going to another eager and aggressive youngster, Roy Cohn.

Given the fateful role Cohn would play in McCarthy's career, speculation has always been rife about how they originally met. The consensus now is that Cohn's own version, that they met in December 1952 through journalist George Sokolsky, is true. "My God, I'm glad to meet you," McCarthy is supposed to have said as they shook hands, "I just want to find out what's public relations and what's real"—a tag that might have applied just as well to McCarthy himself as to the twenty-six-year-old Cohn.[6] Brilliant and precocious, the son of a New Deal Democrat judge, Cohn had graduated from law school at age nineteen and went on to a prominent position in the U.S. attorney's office in New York. Witnesses he interviewed sometimes assumed they were victims of a practical joke: the slope-shouldered, sleepy-eyed boy sitting in front of them couldn't possibly be the feared assistant district attorney Roy Cohn.[7] But despite his evident youth, Cohn was already a veteran of high-profile antisubversion trials. He had helped convict William Remington for perjury and the Rosenbergs for espionage, and had helped to prepare the case against Owen Lattimore for lying to McCarran's Internal Security Subcommittee.

Roy Cohn had an unenviable skill for making enemies as well as friends. Many called him an opportunist on the anti-Communist issue. A more charitable interpretation would be that the young Cohn's approach was utilitarian rather than ideological. He had grown up in New York City, the epicenter of the American Communist movement. There Communist activists were not semimythical bogeymen but a powerful daily presence, especially in Jewish and ethnic neighborhoods. Fighting their influence in unions, city politics (they had played a decisive role in the mayoral election of 1945), and the public schools required a tough, combative stance, a willingness to hit hard and mercilessly whenever an opportunity presented itself—just as the Communists themselves did. Like Sokolsky, Cohn also saw himself as a living rebuttal to the popular perception that all Jews were Communist sympathizers. By the same token, Joe McCarthy wanted to protect himself from any hint that his anticommunism was really anti-Semitism in disguise, especially after the Anna Rosenberg debacle.[8]

So Cohn was not as strange a choice for chief counsel as it might first appear. Smart, savvy, and surefooted on the Washington scene, he enjoyed good relations with J. Edgar Hoover and was able to get access to confidential files and sources that might otherwise have been closed.[9] Five foot eight, slender with slicked back black hair, Cohn's innocent schoolboy appearance was belied by a conspicuous scar that ran down the length of his nose and dark, hooded eyes that could narrow and flash with fury when he lost his temper—which was often. Colleagues and subordinates he treated with equal measures of condescension and contempt. A confidential report prepared for Army lawyers described him this way: "The impression gained is of an unquestionably bright, alert, aggressive, vain individual who has been extended many personal favors and privileges . . . and who assumes that special privileges are a matter of right to him." But, the report pointed out, sometimes he moves "so rapidly in short-cutting procedures to his advantage that he overlooks some significant details."[10]

Cohn was twenty-six, Robert Kennedy twenty-seven. The third new member of the team, David Schine, reinforced the new PSI image of youth and aggressive vitality. At twenty-five, the son of a millionaire hotel chain and restaurant owner, David Schine was tall, blond, and slender and blessed with the dreamy-eyed good looks that, in Richard Rovere's immortal phrase, "one associated with male orchestra singers." Beyond the looks and a certain prep school charm, however, there was little to recommend him. Schine's one formal qualification was authoring an eight-page pamphlet, *Definition of Communism*, that the elder Schine had ordered placed in every guest room of his hotels. The real reason he was at PSI as chief consultant was that he was good friends with Roy Cohn, who prodded McCarthy to bring Schine on until McCarthy finally relented—but only so long as Schine signed on as an unpaid consultant and did not take up space on McCarthy's budget. It never occurred to McCarthy to ask why Cohn wanted Schine so badly, nor did he realize that by taking both of them under his wing, he was sealing his own doom.

Behind this youthful trio stood a phalanx of professionals: staff director Tom Flanagan, chief clerk Ruth Watt, investigators Tom La Venia and George Anastos, as well as McCarthy's own staff, led by Jean Kerr, now his fiancée. They included his personal secretary Margaret Driscoll and former FBI agent Don Surine (who had lost the bureau's favor when he became involved with a prostitute while investigating a white slavery ring). Other later additions, such as James Juliana and moonfaced Frank Carr, also came from the FBI or had FBI connections.

At the same time, however, that door to the FBI was about to close. Up until the 1952 election, Hoover had been more than just a McCarthy cheerleader. According to historians Athan Theoharis and John Stuart Cox, Hoover's assistance to McCarthy had been "manifold, including making supportive speeches, monitoring McCarthy's critics, and offering direct assistance"—including, it seems, altering documents he released to McCarthy in order to prevent them from being traced back to the Bureau.[11] However, unbeknownst to McCarthy and his staffers, Hoover had decided to end their relationship. In part this was due to McCarthy's increasingly erratic behavior. But it was also the result of the election. In 1950, Hoover had turned to McCarthy out of desperation, convinced that no one in the Truman administration took the internal Communist threat seriously. (This was one reason he had refused to tell them about the existence of Venona.) Now that Eisenhower and his people seemed ready to do the job, Hoover could afford to drop the McCarthy connection. From 1953 on Hoover would act as the ally of the White House, not of the junior senator from Wisconsin.

Meanwhile, having assembled this merry band, McCarthy was ready to roll. In front of him lay a tempting range of targets: Don Surine told HUAC investigators McCarthy was even prepared to subpoena former President Truman if he had to.[12] Certainly he planned to have another close look at the State Department, perhaps also the Federal Communications Commission and Voice of America, as well as the Treasury Department. None of the other senators on PSI was in a position to challenge his lead. John McClellan of Arkansas, the ranking Democrat, was a true believer in the anti-Communist cause. He was one of two men in the Senate for whom McCarthy had a sincere and unstinting regard; the other had been Robert Taft. According to Ruth Watt, McClellan viewed McCarthy's work on the committee with the same nonpartisan respect.[13] The other Democrats, Stuart Symington and Henry "Scoop" Jackson, were green freshmen. The two senior Republicans were McCarthy allies (Everett Dirksen of Illinois and Karl Mundt of South Dakota), and the junior member from Michigan, earnest and eager-to-please Charles Potter, was hardly in a position to make trouble for McCarthy—or so it seemed.

McCarthy explained on the CBS program *Chronoscope* that getting to the truth about Communist subversion in government circles would be far easier under the new administration. "When you have a committee, if you have the power of subpoena, you can get the records. If you have a Republican president we'd be able to get those records, I'm sure."[14] What he did not realize was that that prospect was a disconcerting one not just to Democrats but to the new White House.

One word defined the outlook of the Eisenhower team: *moderate*. They had defeated the conservative Taft forces in the Chicago convention by a combination of stealth and strong-arm tactics, and they saw keeping the Republican right at bay as a matter of political self-preservation.[15] Eisenhower's chief political advisers came from the party's northeastern liberal edge: his campaign manager Henry Cabot Lodge, chief of staff Sherman Adams, press secretary James Hagerty, and Herbert Brownell, an old Tom Dewey intimate who was now attorney general. Behind them stood speechwriter Emmett John Hughes, whom Eisenhower had borrowed from the anti-Taft (and now anti-McCarthy) Luce empire, and C. D. Jackson, also from *Time*, with whom Whittaker Chambers had sparred many times in vain to make Jackson's reporting from postwar Europe more consistently anti-Soviet.[16] It was a group savvy in dealing with the press and far more sophisticated than McCarthy in playing the Washington media game.

The unspoken assumption among the men in the Eisenhower White House was that the nation's business could not get done unless it rested on a solid bipartisan compromise. In their minds, the job of the nation's two major political parties was to act as filters for the various interest groups and constituencies under their umbrella and then bring those interests to the bargaining table. If Democrats brought on board the intelligentsia, the unions, and urban voters, the Republicans were assumed to supply prosperous farmers, business, and Wall Street types. The concerns of Taftites and other Heartland "reactionaries," as the Eisenhower people called them, or of the ethnic urban voters who steadfastly backed McCarthy and other anti-Communist activists, played no serious part in their political calculations.

The exception to this rule was *not* John Foster Dulles. For all his fearsome reputation as the coldest of cold warriors and for all his rhetoric about "liberating" Soviet satellites, Dulles dutifully upheld the Republican end of this bipartisanship. No other word mattered more to Dulles, in fact: in the case of the cold war, his desire to avoid tensions with his Democratic establishment predecessors was made easier by two key events: the death of Josef Stalin in March 1953 and the signing of an armistice in Korea in July. As East-West tensions gradually eased, Eisenhower and Dulles found no compelling reason for rethinking containment. The Marxist dictator of Yugoslavia, Tito, not the Free Poles, became the symbol of "rollback." When East Berlin dissolved into riots at news of Stalin's demise and Hungary rose up in defiance of Soviet rule in 1956, Dulles made sympathetic noises but did nothing as the Soviets brutally reestablished order.

Dulles, the ex–Wall Street lawyer, was also appalled by the crude and plebeian McCarthy. He pronounced him "sincere but misguided" and avoided any direct support (or criticism) of the charges McCarthy made against the Acheson State Department. Privately he called the Hiss case a "human tragedy" and since both he and Eisenhower had written letters of support for Hiss, they had no compelling interest in reopening those old wounds.[17] Dulles did hire a new loyalty board chairman, Scott McLeod, who bore the stamp of McCarthy approval, and he dismissed two of the people who figured in McCarthy's accusations and were now albatrosses around the department's neck: China hands John Paton Davies and John Carter Vincent. (Vincent quit; Davies was fired.) He also moved out Russia experts Bohlen and Kennan, and installed his own people. The Dulles years brought a sense of exile for people like Acheson, Kennan, Robert Lovett, and the other Wise Men, but Dulles never seriously challenged their consensus on containment or the assumptions that underlay it.

The decisive figure in shaping the administration's bipartisan attitude and the decisive figure in mobilizing its behind-the-scenes campaign against McCarthy was Eisenhower himself. Certainly no one can blame Eisenhower for being offended by McCarthy's attacks on his old patron George Marshall, or Bill Jenner's. But his distaste for them, and the entire Republican right, went beyond the matter of personal honor. As he told an aide, "We just can't work with fellows like McCarthy, Bricker, Jenner, and that bunch."[18] In the final analysis he agreed with Dulles, and Acheson, and Benton, and Tydings, and even Harry Luce: McCarthy was not "one of us," a part of America's political, corporate, and intellectual establishment. Eisenhower, we need to remember, was. He had originally been courted as a Democratic presidential candidate, in 1948. He had served as president of Columbia University and trustee at the Carnegie Endowment. His brother Milton was president of Johns Hopkins University, and another brother, Arthur, was a loud and pungent McCarthy critic.

Eisenhower was no stranger to "highbrow culture," to use an expression then much in vogue: he had certainly read more Karl Marx than Joe McCarthy ever had. Above all, he was no Douglas MacArthur. He represented the "good" side of the military to liberals, as Marshall had done and Colin Powell was to do. Here, after all, was a military man who shrank defense budgets. In a controversial decision, the mouthpiece for high-grade American liberalism, the *New York Times*, had decided to endorse Eisenhower rather than Stevenson for president in 1952, as did Walter Lippmann. Ike regularly won praise from liberals such as Elmer Davis and James Wechsler. Stevenson Democrats and later historians liked to portray Ike as a figure from the past. In fact, he was a figure from the future—or rather the short-term future, when Republicans had to learn to quit talking about dismantling the New Deal or winning the cold war, and respect liberal sensibilities on issues like civil rights. Eisenhower was struggling to secure the support of what was still a largely Democratic electorate. On the eve of the election, political scientist Samuel Lubell had published a profoundly influential book, *The Future of American Politics*, in which he argued that the rise of a new middle class in America would make it harder than ever before for either political party to command a clear majority. The New Deal coalition was disintegrating, and the gap between the two parties had narrowed. Lubell explained that in order to gain power, Republicans had to learn to accept the Roosevelt revolution. Lubell saw McCarthy as the voice of prewar isolationism whose basis was "ethnic and emotional" and whose power at the polls was steadily shrinking. Lubell asked, "Can the Republicans come to grips with the problems of our times? Or by ignoring them, will they restore the vigor and unity of the Democratic majority?"[19]

The result was the vogue in the GOP for "modern" Republicans. The modern Republican's catchwords were *consensus* and *convergence*. As Arthur Larson explained in modern Republicanism's manifesto, *A Republican Looks at His Party*, the important split in American politics was no longer between Democrat and Republican, or conservative and liberal. It was between the center and the opposition, whether emanating from the left (meaning socialists and Communists) or the right (meaning Taftites and McCarthy). The center was where the action was, was the implication, and Ike and his troops were determined to occupy it.

Eisenhower's vice president, Richard Nixon, served as front man to the Republican right,[20] but with Taft gone, they were too disorganized to form any serious opposition. Their one brief moment of rebellion came with the debate over the Bricker amendment, which would have required congressional approval for all future international agreements and treaties such as Yalta and Potsdam. But Eisenhower and Dulles fought it down, and Democrats and moderate Republicans alike celebrated as it passed into oblivion.*

If anyone was the antithesis of convergence and compromise, it was Joe

---

*The rationale for the Bricker amendment was that it would prevent "sellouts" of American interests during international summits like those at Potsdam and Yalta. It was fashionable for commentators then, and historians now, to sneer at the amendment and its backers; see, for example, Duane Tananbaum, *The Bricker Amendment Controversy: A Test of Eisenhower's Political Leadership* (Ithaca, NY: Cornell University Press, 1988). However, passage would undoubtedly have helped to head off the growth of the "imperial presidency" and the executive branch's abuse of its plenipotentiary powers over foreign policy.

McCarthy. Under Eisenhower, a strong anti-McCarthy faction began to take shape within the Republican Party; it wanted to end the partisan bickering over the cold war and restore the bipartisan consensus that Lodge, Vandenberg, and the Democrats had stitched together before the Hiss case had left it in tatters. Yet during the campaign, McCarthy had refused to leave the case alone and even brought it to bear directly on Hiss's old workmate, Adlai Stevenson.

A month before the election, without consulting the Eisenhower people, he offered to produce "ninety pounds of documents" emanating from his anti-Communist investigations that bore on the Democratic candidate and to review publicly the evidence against him. The Stevenson people were so terrified that they issued a denial in advance: whatever McCarthy had dredged up, they declared, was ipso facto untrue. In front of a Chicago audience, with 55 television and 525 radio stations watching and listening, McCarthy recited what his investigator had found. It was not much: how Stevenson had worked side by side with Hiss at the AAA and at the United Nations, how he had been recommended by Hiss and Frank Coe (another AAA employee turned Soviet spy) as a delegate to an IPR conference, and how his coterie of advisers included such supposedly unreliable types like Arthur Schlesinger, Jr., and Archibald MacLeish.[21] The crowning blow was his "Alger—I mean Adlai" slip, which made McCarthy and his audience snicker and liberals across the country shudder.

The Chicago speech was McCarthy's attempt to raise the political stakes, implying that it was not just Communists but Democrats who were "un-American" and had moved beyond the political pale. If communism's character was defined as "a drive for power by a disciplined minority with welfare as its cloak," McCarthy was saying, the same could be said for the liberal establishment with whom the new administration wanted to deal.[22] This was as disconcerting an accusation to moderate Republicans as it was to everyone else involved. McCarthy must be stopped, they began to whisper among themselves. Who knew when they might be next?

The common view was that Eisenhower was cowed, even intimidated, by McCarthy, but recently released documents and sources from the period reveal that this was untrue. The man who had grappled with Patton and Monty and beaten Rommel in Normandy was not about to be frightened by Joe McCarthy. But Eisenhower did worry that any direct attack on him would rupture Republican ranks. McCarthy was a "pimple on the face of progress," as Ike privately put it, but Eisenhower was convinced the best way to handle him was to "just ignore him." Eventually McCarthy would go too far and come a cropper, Eisenhower believed. Until then the best policy was not to contribute to his publicity-seeking campaigns by commenting on them. "I won't go down into the gutter with that guy," was the way he liked to put it to his staff.

The White House got an early dose of what was ahead when McCarthy learned that a State Department employee who talked to PSI investigators about loyalty program files was suddenly and unaccountably transferred. At the same time, a directive advised employees that they were not required to talk to any investigators if a senator was not actually present. "This committee is not going to be hamstrung by the State Department," McCarthy promised, and summoned Undersecretary of State Walter Bedell Smith for a talk. At a press conference, McCarthy and Smith announced that State would now appoint a special liaison officer to work with PSI. The transferred employee was reinstated.[23]

The press was stunned. The New York Times could not remember any executive branch department folding so quickly under pressure from a congressional committee. "With a few cracks of the whip," opined the Nation, "McCarthy brought John Foster Dulles, Walter Bedell Smith, and Donald Lurie [assistant secretary of state for administration] into line." Many close to Eisenhower became convinced that McCarthy had to have some larger agenda, even presidential ambitions, behind his grandstanding and defiance of executive authority. They were wrong, but it made things easier for them to boil the ideological issues down to a single, political one. To protect the president, they had to eliminate McCarthy as a possible rival. All they needed was an opening.

Roy Cohn's boyhood friend Anthony Lewis could never understand why Cohn took the job with McCarthy. "His family was a standard machine-Democratic family," Lewis later recalled. "When he became this Communist hunter, I just was surprised." This is not exactly true. Roy's father, a Bronx political operative, came from the Tammany Hall ring of the Democratic Party, which has resolutely anti-Communist—as well as pro-Catholic. But even if Cohn had never showed any precocious interest in communism or political philosophies, he had shown an interest in power—how to get it and how to hold on to it—and in 1953 Joe McCarthy represented power. A friend asked Cohn what the jurisdiction of his new job would be. Roy pulled out an organizational chart of the federal government and pounded it with his fist: "That's my jurisdiction!"[24]

Roy Cohn's basic attitude toward life can be summed up by the proposition: "Why should I have to—" and then filling in the blank. Why should I read this deposition? Why should I accept that judge's ruling? Why should I wait for what I want? "Roy was a boy who when he wanted it, he wanted it," his aunt recalled. "And it didn't matter what anyone else said."[25] The moment he arrived at PSI, the fireworks began: "never a dull moment," as Ruth Watt later put it. He and Schine insisted on moving out of PSI's rather cramped offices into their own private suite in another building. Frip Flanagan and Ruth Watt became alarmed when requisitions for expensive furnishings started arriving in the mail. Rumor had it the boys had even installed a bar.[26] They then launched a campaign to get a key to the senatorial bathhouse and sent a request to William Jenner of the Rules Committee. Jenner blew up and went to see his old friend Joe to tell him the request was impossible, that the other senators would have a fit if they found out. McCarthy said he knew that and he would break the news to his two youthful investigators.[27]

The relationship between McCarthy and Cohn baffled even insiders. Cohn was a master at manipulating McCarthy, not just on staff matters but also in pushing him onto possible targets for investigation. He became Joe's most important adviser after Jean Kerr, and was the only other person Mc-Carthy was unwilling to argue with or disappoint. By the same token, no one could figure out why Cohn put up with David Schine. He was hardly Cohn's intellectual equal, yet the normally abrasive Cohn allowed Schine to tease and even humiliate him in public without saying a word. Schine treated him with a familiarity bordering on contempt; a reporter wrote in a private memo, "He is most outspoken in his criticism of Cohn's mannerisms and acts generally as if Cohn were his inferior." Yet they were inseparable.

Friends and family believed that Schine brought Roy out of himself by taking him to parties and showing him the high life. Now we know that Cohn's link to Schine went beyond that. Cohn was a classic closet homosexual, who trolled Washington's gay bars by night while castigating "sexual perverts" in the State Department by day. It is not even clear whether he ever thought of himself as being a homosexual; in the parlance of the time, he was no "pansy," just someone who preferred to expend his sexual energies on men, not women. That included David Schine. There is no evidence that the young men were ever lovers or that Schine was anything but heterosexual. But without a doubt Schine's physical presence triggered a deep response in Cohn which, as time went on, bordered on obsession.

Perhaps, without knowing it, Cohn elicited a similar response in Mc-Carthy himself. Between the burly, ferociously masculine senator and the slender, dark "mama's boy" a powerful emotional bond took shape that both men could hardly acknowledge, although Cohn with his quick uptake was probably more aware of it than McCarthy was. McCarthy had a strong aversion to homosexuality. Once the subject came up in a conversation with his old friend Urban Van Susteren. Van Susteren asked, "What do you care if a man sucks someone else's cock?" McCarthy just growled in disgust.[28] In any case, McCarthy became convinced that criticism of Cohn (which was quite endemic, even at PSI) was really criticism of him, and as Cohn left a growing trail of disorder and outrage, McCarthy spent his time picking up after him like an overly protective father, if not a lover. When Senator Mike Monroney of Oklahoma one day referred to Cohn and Schine as a pair of "keystone cops," McCarthy angrily rushed to the Senate floor to defend publicly his chief counsel (Schine he could care less about). He thundered that Monroney was good at calling people names but relied on others, like fellow Cohn basher Herbert Lehman of New York, to provide the specifics. Apparently, McCarthy said, Monroney "did not have the guts to do it" himself (when Monroney asked McCarthy to repeat that last charge, McCarthy refused). McCarthy called Cohn "one of the most brilliant young men with whom I have ever worked" and deplored the "smear attack" on a "young man who had been active in almost every important Communist prosecution in the United States over the past 3 or 4 years." It was easy, McCarthy said, to deplore communism in general; "every fellow traveler does that." The hard part was unearthing and exposing actual Communists. That was what *he* was doing, and what Roy Cohn was doing as well. For good measure, McCarthy read into the record a letter that Herbert Lehmann had written to Alger Hiss expressing sympathy with his plight and confidence in his loyalty.[29]

It was a nasty, hysterical performance, but typical of McCarthy where Cohn was concerned. Later rumors flew that there was indeed something "unnatural" in their dealings. Such rumors were almost certainly untrue, but the strange emotional triangle—McCarthy-Cohn-Schine—would permanently link the lives and fortunes of all three. McCarthy become in effect a hostage to his leading staffer. Cohn's poor political judgment, combined with McCarthy's, would become a recipe for calamity.

Meanwhile, PSI was proceeding with a whirlwind of activity. In February 1953 it began holding hearings on that old McCarthy bugaboo, the State Department personnel files. They heard from Helen Balog, the supervisor of the foreign service file room, about how hundreds of people had easy access to supposedly confidential personnel files, how derogatory information was routinely removed from a file before being sent a promotion panel, and how John Stewart Service had spent a large part of 1949 working late at night among the confidential files, including those on himself and other China hands.[30] Then came hearings on the Voice of America—on whether Communist infiltration might be hindering its task of broadcasting pro-American propaganda across the iron curtain. That led to the investigation the State Department's information centers in embassies abroad and its teacher exchange programs in June 1953. Later that summer, McCarthy's committee was also looking into the Government Printing Office. By September it branched out into the Army and the United Nations. In October it heard evidence about the role that Harry Dexter White may have played in passing the plates for printing occupation currency in postwar Germany to the Soviets.

These hearings and investigations would be the basis of McCarthy's fearsome reputation as the red scare's grand inquisitor. Like the HUAC hearings, they have served as an archetype of political tyranny in America.[31] Hapless witnesses are summoned out of the blue and hauled before a panel of grim, impassive congressmen or senators, to answer a bewildering array of questions and identify a series of obscure names. Denied the opportunity to confront his accusers, the witness is then ordered to name names or otherwise abase himself before his interrogators, while the enraged chairman bangs his gavel at each inappropriate response and threatens the witness with a citation of contempt, or imprisonment, or worse. This is the stereotype of what Lillian Hellmann called the "scoundrel time" and Dalton Trumbo (another blacklisted Communist Hollywood writer) "the time of the toads." How much reality lies behind the stereotyped image is a different matter.

Consider the investigative committee itself. The truth was that liberals and progressives of various stripes had applauded most, if not all, of the very same inquisitorial procedures McCarthy and HUAC would employ when they had been aimed at suitable targets in the 1930s or later against organized crime or, still later, the Nixon administration during Watergate. The Pecora Committee of 1932 had investigated the machinations of Wall Street bankers and brought J. P. Morgan, Jr., up before it to answer embarrassing and hostile questions, much to the applause of the popular press. If critics accused McCarthy and HUAC of promoting a "carnival atmosphere" in their proceedings, the Pecora Committee had set the standard when gleeful reporters convinced a baffled and bemused Morgan to be photographed with a circus midget sitting on his lap.

Similarly, the Nye Committee won liberal plaudits in 1934 and 1935 when it probed the munitions industry and the so-called merchants of death who, it was widely believed, had pushed America into World War I. Its legal counsel had been Alger Hiss.[32] In 1936, Robert La Follette, Jr., steered his Senate Subcommittee on Civil Liberties onto the issue of big business intimidation of union organizers, which won more sympathetic liberal attention. Several of his staffers, including chief legal counsel Charles Kramer, had also been secret Communists.[33]

All these committees had employed what would come to be known as "McCarthyite" methods, and more. No congressman, or ambitious counsel for that matter, passed up a chance to use his hearings to secure favorable publicity for himself, as Alger Hiss had done when he badgered Bernard Baruch and Du Pont Company officials during the Nye proceedings. In 1941 a House committee had even seen fit to launch a probe into Hollywood and the motion picture industry for its alleged pro-British, pro-war stance: an early version of the Hollywood hearing HUAC launched later in the decade.[34] Senator Estes Kefauver had demonstrated the political advantage to be gained by exposing skullduggery in front of television cameras when he probed organized crime in 1951. Subpoenaing and needling hostile witnesses, rehearsing in public revelations that were already known to law enforcement or bureaucratic officials such as the FBI, concealing confidential sources, and giving vent to breast-beating speeches were all standard practice before McCarthy arrived on the scene, as was the carefully cultivated atmosphere of self-righteous indignation.[35]

Those who find themselves the target of this sort of public inquiry are rarely made happy by it, whether they are corporations, mafiosi, White House officials, or former fellow travelers. People would complain that an appearance before HUAC or McCarthy's committee ruined their reputation and that investigators had publicly aired accusations without clearing them up, in contrast to charges brought into a court of law. In fact, the purpose of any congressional investigation is not to decide guilt or innocence, but to hear evidence in order to make recommendations for drawing up legislation. The fortunes of the specific individuals brought before them are never their primary concern.

But witnesses brought before PSI did enjoy certain privileges they would be denied before a court, let alone a grand jury. They were allowed to have an attorney with them at all times, in both closed and open session, and could get advice before answering each and every question. Executive sessions, which opponents represented as McCarthy's secret "star chamber" proceedings, also helped to protect witnesses by preserving their anonymity. Later, Roy Cohn could point to literally hundreds of subpoenaed witnesses who in executive session were allowed to look at the evidence against them, and if they able to refute it, were dismissed. In short, those who did appear in public hearings were a fraction of those actually summoned—and if they were treated with no particular sympathy, it was because, as Ruth Watt noted, staff and senators had seen the confidential FBI reports on each.[36]

Looking at the official record of McCarthy's committee proceedings, it is important to remember that committee members, like McCarthy, were free to correct the record, punch up their own remarks, and even delete outbursts or statements by witnesses they considered irrelevant or would prefer not appear. Even so, certain impressions immediately come to mind.

The first is how infuriating it must have been dealing with witnesses who could or would not give a straight answer to simple questions, beginning with their membership in the Communist Party. Some would deny it outright; most preferred to evade it by pleading the Fifth Amendment on grounds that, in the considered legal opinion of the time, were spurious, to say the least.

When committee members like McClellan or Symington or Charles Potter tried to engage hostile witnesses on an ideological level, they would veer off on irrelevancies. Almost every one tried to enter a speech into the record, condemning the committee as "unconstitutional" or "a lynching." Some were overtly hostile, like Philip Foner and the novelist Howard Fast, who refused to tell the committee not only whether he was a member of the Communist Party (he was) but whether he would fight if he were drafted to go to Korea. Some were ignorant, like Herbert Aptheker, when he tried to confront McCarthy on the implications of pleading the Fifth when he asked if was a member of the Communist Party. McCarthy's answer was a classic statement of the orthodox view on using the Fifth Amendment:

> Refusal to answer this question in a criminal court could not be used against to infer you are guilty. When you are asked a question as to whether or not you are a member of the Communist Party, and you say, "I honestly feel if I told you the truth it might incriminate me," that means to the average person, it means to me, that if you were not a member of the party, you, of course, could say, 'I am not a member of the Communist Party'. . . . I think we should have it very clear here that there is a difference between inference of guilt in a criminal case which could be used to send you to jail, and the inference which the reasonable man draws from your answer.[37]

Some were simply dim, like James Adams, the author of a pro-Soviet book that circulated in State Department Information Centers called *World Monopoly and Peace*, and who, when asked whether communism was evil, answered it could not be since "it is a system of society that has been adopted by more than one-third of the population of the world." Others were unpleasant. During the Voice of America hearings, an engineer named Ray Kaplan had committed suicide rather than testify as to his possible Communist background. He left an ambiguously phrased suicide note for his wife and child— "I have not done anything in my job which I did not think was in the best interests of my country. . . . I can say no more now"—and immediately became a martyr to the American Left.[38] Some days later a VOA employee named William Mandel took the oath before the committee, with this result:

> COHN: Mr. Mandel, would you please give us your full name, please?
> MANDEL: My name is William Mandel, and to save you the trouble of bringing out any possible pseudonym . . . I would like to make it clear that I am a Jew.

COHN: That you are a what?

MANDEL: That I am a Jew.

COHN: So am I, I don't see that that is an issue here.

MANDEL: A Jew who works for McCarthy is thought of very ill by most of the Jewish people in this country.

Mandel shouted at McCarthy: "You murdered Ray Kaplan." Under these circumstances, it is hard to see how the hot-tempered chairman could *not* have lost his self-control. However, he surprised his detractors, treating even the worst witnesses with a magisterial calm—with a single fateful exception.[39] Observing McCarthy at work in the spring of 1953, Alistair Cooke, a harsh former critic, noted "a developing discrepancy between 'McCarthyism' and McCarthy." Cooke and others realized that McCarthy was proceeding "with careful planning and masterly discretion. He is patient with witnesses whose FBI file would give innocent citizens the creeps. He has consistently protected the anonymity of highly suspect witnesses." This judicious and discreet McCarthy was "a new turn which," Cooke added, "liberals are loathe to acknowledge."[40]

Liberals were also loathe to admit that despite its wide-ranging schedule, conducting almost twenty-five full-scale hearings in little more than a year, McCarthy's committee did do some useful work. In March he opened hearings on American allies doing trade with Communist China. This was an issue that directly affected ordinary Americans. They were still fighting a war against the Chinese in Korea and were horrified to learn that their European allies were supplying Mao with war matériel and that two British-flagged ships had even helped to transport Chinese infantry.

McCarthy's decision to expose the often illegal trade with China and the Soviet bloc drew praise from the Washington establishment, even inveterate McCarthy hater Drew Pearson. [41] Robert Kennedy threw himself into the investigation, summoning witnesses and relentlessly digging up the facts. Kennedy released a report documenting "an absolute minimum" of 162 foreign cargo ships putting into Chinese ports in the first three and a half months of 1953, flying the flags of Greece, Norway, Italy, France, Japan, and many other supposedly "Allied" powers. Western Allied trade with China and other Communist regimes exceeded $2 billion. It included not just nonstrategic supplies, like raw cotton, chemicals, and fertilizers, but materials essential to war production, such as oil from Greek-owned tanker fleets.

While the administration frowned over these revelations and dragged its feet (the Defense Department wanted all trade with China stopped; the State Department did not), McCarthy acted. He called shipowners Stavros Niarchos and Aristotle Onassis and wrung from them a promise to halt all trade

with Communist nations. McCarthy announced the deal at a press conference on March 28, with Kennedy at his side, and confidently predicted it
would hasten final victory in Korea. When reporters asked why he had acted
unilaterally, he said, "I didn't want any interference by anyone." The White
House had a fit. Harold Stassen, mutual security director, denounced Mc-
Carthy as a dangerous meddler. Most Americans, including the press, disagreed. Drew Pearson and Marquis Childs applauded Kennedy's final report,
which appeared on July 1, while Arthur Krock of the *Times* called it "an example of congressional investigation at its highest level."[42]

Unfortunately, as the investigations swelled, the confusion and disorder
among the staff became intolerable. McCarthy finally decided to ask his old
friend J. B. Matthews, former Dies Committee staffer, to come on board to
straighten out the mess. On March 10 he wrote to Matthews's boss Richard
Berlin at the Hearst Corporation, asking him to give J.B. a leave of absence:
Cohn would remain chief counsel, and Matthews would act as staff director.
Matthews turned out to be an excellent administrator, according to Ruth
Watt. He managed to establish clear procedures and act as mediator between
Cohn and Kennedy, each of whom had discovered in the other his worst
enemy. But almost as soon as Matthews arrived, he left under a cloud. It was
a crucial turning point in McCarthy's fortunes and career.

At issue was an article Matthews had written for the July 1953 issue of
the *American Mercury* on communism and Christianity, which began with
the startling sentence: "The largest group supporting the Communist apparatus in the United States today is composed of Protestant clergymen." The rest
of the article pointed out that only a tiny minority of American clerics cooperated with known Communists and spouted the Moscow line. It pointed out
that most clergymen recognized that communism's dialectical materialism
was incompatible with a faith in God. But that damning first sentence ended
up on the front page of newspapers around the country.[43] It set off a firestorm
of outrage. The implication was clear: the Irish Catholic McCarthy and his
staff director were impugning the loyalty of America's Protestants, starting
with their clergy (ignoring for the moment the fact that Matthews himself
was an ordained Methodist minister).

Those stalwart champions of American Protestantism, the Senate's
southern Democrats, took it upon themselves to rebuke Matthews. Harry
Byrd of Virginia called him a "cheap demagogue," and Robert Kerr and
William Fulbright called on him to resign. Meanwhile, the PSI rose up in revolt against its chairman. Charles Potter, John McClellan, and the other Democrats threatened to resign if Matthews did not quit. When Matthews asked
for a hearing to establish his innocence, they refused. McCarthy realized he

had to let his friend go, but insisted on asserting his right to hire and fire sub-committee staffers as he saw fit.

That did it. The Democratic senators quit the subcommittee as a group and wrote a blistering letter to McCarthy saying they would return only if they could retain a Democratic counsel to match that of the majority counsel. On July 15 McCarthy pleaded with McClellan to return. "It has been my constant endeavor to maintain a fair and impartial attitude and . . . to make certain that no bigotry, prejudice, bias or partisanship should ever exist in the Committee." He pointed out that when Republicans had asked for a minority counsel, Democratic chairman Hoey had turned them down. He pointed out that he was no tyrant, that many other committee chairmen had the exclusive power to employ and discharge employees. "I sincerely hope," McCarthy concluded, "you will not permit such differences of opinion among us on de-tails of housekeeping to cause you not to continue the service which you have been rendering the country."[44]

But this was not a difference over detail. Matthews suddenly exposed a sharp sectarian division in fifties America in which Protestants were convinced that "what McCarthy had done, the Catholic Church had done" or at least sanctioned.[45] If liberal Catholic voices rushed to condemn the article (which few actually read beyond the first sentence), some conservative ones, like the *Brooklyn Tablet* and the *Los Angeles Tidings*, agreed with its general tenor, which offended Protestants even further. By an unforseen misstep, Mc-Carthy had exposed himself to a major scandal. The growing circle of liberal political consultants, publicists, and congressional staffers who called them-selves the Clearing House helped to organize a wave of "spontaneous out-rage" at Matthews's remarks.[46] Newspapers from the *New York Times* on down took a swipe. It was not just liberals who reacted. The Eisenhower White House also realized McCarthy's vulnerability and pounced.

Emmet Hughes, James Hagerty, and William Rogers phoned various dis-tinguished clergymen of the National Conference of Christians and Jews with an idea. The clerics agreed to send a telegram to the White House urging Presi-dent Eisenhower to condemn Matthews's article and "the damage to our na-tion" it did. At the same time, Hughes and Hagerty drafted a response to the telegram for Eisenhower to deliver to the press—a reply to a telegram that still had not been sent. After some delays and snafus (the telegram briefly landed on the desk of someone not privy to the stratagem), they told Ike what they had done, and he grinningly approved. He strode to the press room, read the telegram to reporters, and intoned, "Generalized and irresponsible attacks that sweepingly condemn the whole of any group of citizens are alien to America."

That same day McCarthy decided that Matthews had to go. He was on his way to the Senate Chamber to make the announcement when the White House learned what was up and frantically ordered him stopped. Rogers and Vice President Nixon managed to catch him in the hall and delayed him long enough for the president's statement to get out. After a few minutes, McCarthy said, "Gotta rush now," but it was too late.[47]

McCarthy, as usual, never realized what had happened behind his back. In his mind, the storm over J. B. Matthews was just one more assault by liberals and pro-Communist sympathizers, which the Eisenhower White House had unaccountably condoned. Meanwhile, anarchy was spreading among his staff. Cohn insisted on treating Kennedy "like a rich bitch kid," someone remembered long afterward, "a gofer," and one day ordered him to fetch the coffee once too often. Kennedy wrote a letter to McCarthy, announcing his resignation. It concluded: "I have enjoyed my work and association on the subcommittee. . . . Please accept my sincere thanks for the many courtesies and kindnesses you have extended to me during these past seven months."[48] Although he did not know it, McCarthy had just lost his one link to the next generation of Washington insiders, as well as the one subordinate who might have had the foresight to save him from destruction—and from himself.

Outwardly, McCarthy's position seemed as strong as ever. His wedding was the biggest social event in Washington since the inauguration. Held at St. Matthew's Church, the guest list included an intriguing mix of friends and foes: Bill Jenner, Bourke Hickenlooper, the chairman of HUAC Congressman Velde, Harold Stassen, Richard and Pat Nixon, Allen Dulles, Sherman Adams, Senators Green and Chavez from the Tydings imbroglio, Barry Goldwater, Jack Dempsey, Robert Kennedy, and John Kennedy, who had married Jacqueline Bouvier the week before. Roy Cohn served as an usher, Eunice Kennedy as bridesmaid. A jubilant crowd of four thousand gathered outside during the ceremony, and when McCarthy led out his bride they shouted, "Kiss her, Joe!" Admiring Texas businessmen bought him a Cadillac as a wedding present. Later that summer he received another unexpected present: Attorney General Brownell dropped all charges relating to the Hennings report. On August 3 McCarthy was guest of honor at the VFW's national convention. On September 25 he was scheduled to receive the American Legion's Bill of Rights Gold Medal for his "outstanding Americanism" that "has provided exceptional protection to our way of life."

But in fact things were unraveling. Even before the Matthews mess, he had had a long spell of choosing poor targets for his public anti-Communist campaigns, each of which served only to antagonize the White House and even fellow Republicans. The first was the nomination of James B. Conant as high commissioner of Germany in February 1953. McCarthy decided that Harvard's president was unfit to serve: Conant was just the sort of liberal establishment "egghead" McCarthy and others believed contributed to Communist successes in subversion.[49] The administration pressed on. McCarthy wrote a letter to Eisenhower detailing his reasons for opposing Conant. Eisenhower ignored it, and when McCarthy later publicly voiced his objections, Ike called them "wild charges" and pledged his support to Conant. After intense questioning about the presence of Communists and "pinks" at Harvard (including the ubiquitous fellow traveler Harlow Shapley), the Foreign Relations Committee approved the nomination. Since McCarthy had promised not to oppose Conant on the Senate floor, Conant breezed through two days later.

Then came Charles Bohlen's nomination for ambassador to Moscow. Bohlen had been at Yalta; he was a Marshall and Acheson protégé, and McCarthy had obtained an FBI file summary that mentioned rumors about Bohlen's possible homosexuality. (They were untrue.) McCarthy made it clear he intended to stop Bohlen at whatever cost; the White House and Dulles made it clear they would stand by their man. Then McCarthy overplayed his hand. He made a big scene about visiting Whittaker Chambers at his Maryland farm to question him about Bohlen, creating the impression that the man who had exposed Alger Hiss knew similar secrets about Bohlen. Chambers had nothing for him: Bohlen's anticommunism was beyond dispute, and everyone who knew his record believed him to be the ideal choice for ambassador. But Chambers was furious when he learned McCarthy had leaked the story of his visit to the *Baltimore Sun* and other papers and broke off all relations with him. The normally pro-McCarthy Hearst and Scripps-Howard papers refused to support him on this one, and Robert Taft read the same FBI summary McCarthy had and privately called McCarthy's charges "a joke." McCarthy and a few other right-wing senators made speeches against Bohlen, but the Senate confirmed him 74 to 13. It was a resounding defeat for McCarthy, and made Eisenhower more determined than ever to find a way to neutralize him. "McCarthy has the bug to run for the presidency in 1956," Ike suddenly announced to his staff. He angrily slapped his knee and added, "The only reason I would consider running again would be to run against him."[50]

McCarthy then decided he would make the CIA a target for his committee. It was a breathtaking choice: the notion of Joe McCarthy pawing through the intelligence agency's files and personnel records made not just administration officials but many senators blanch. Yet targeting the CIA for a probe of Communist subversion was not as reckless or as unprecedented as it appeared. Its wartime predecessor, OSS, had been riddled with high-level Communist agents, and director "Wild Bill" Donovan had been notoriously indifferent to his agents' political affiliations.[51] On October 13, 1952, the CIA's own director, Walter Bedell Smith, had told HUAC, "I believe there are Communists in my own organization," adding, "I believe that they are so adroit that they have infiltrated practically every security organization of Government."[52] Who could be surprised that McCarthy would treat this as an open invitation from the CIA director himself?

A carefully organized investigation and some congressional oversight might have done the agency, and the country, some good—and possibly forestalled some of the disasters of the future. But McCarthy once again picked the wrong target: William Bundy, the liaison between the CIA and National Security Council and son-in-law of Dean Acheson. It was easy for critics to dismiss McCarthy's inquiry as part of a vendetta against the former Red Dean of Fashion. Director Allen Dulles angrily refused to allow any of his employees to testify before any committee, and when the White House told McCarthy in no uncertain terms to lay off, he reluctantly agreed to back down. William Evjue, ever in the wings, crowed, "For the first time, McCarthy is on the defensive."

By early July 1953, McCarthy had a serious publicity problem on his hands even before the Matthews story broke: Roy Cohn and David Schine's investigation into the State Department's Information Service in Europe. The idea sprang out of the investigation into whether Communists and pro-Communists were undermining the effectiveness of Voice of America. Its basic premise was sound by the cold war standards of the time. Why should embassy information service libraries, whose sole purpose was to promote America's best image abroad, stock books that reflected pro-Soviet or anti-American themes and authors? If Londoners or Parisians wanted to read books by Communist authors like Dashiell Hammett or Howard Fast, or books that praised Russia as a model of democracy and attacked the United States as a cesspool of racism and oppression of the poor, let them go to Soviet information centers. This was the reasoning, and it did not belong to McCarthy alone; Eisenhower himself endorsed the basic principle.[53]

Roy Cohn convinced McCarthy that the best way to find out whether disloyalty was being promoted in State Department libraries overseas would be to send himself and David Schine on a personal tour—which also happened to include major cities like London, Paris, Berlin, Vienna, and Frankfurt with their world-class hotels and restaurants. McCarthy agreed and the boys set out, as accounts about what they were about to do spread through the State Department and the diplomatic service.

From the moment their plane touched down at Orly Airport on April 4, the tour was a disaster. It took them to nine cities in eighteen days, starting in Paris. The French and German press decided their real target was America's presence in Europe and NATO. Europeans tended to view McCarthy in terms of their own recent experience with the radical right and firmly believed Americans lived in daily fear of him. The distinguished English philosopher Bertrand Russell had published an hysterical piece in the *Manchester*

Guardian in 1951 asserting that the United States was as much a "police state" as Hitler's Germany. "If by some misfortune," Russell asserted, "you were to quote with approval by Jefferson you would probably lose your job and perhaps find yourself behind bars."[54] There were deep anxieties underlying absurdities such as this, however. Europeans worried that McCarthy would trigger a revival of the American isolationism of the thirties. They castigated Schine and Cohn as witch-hunters and "book burners." The media followed them everywhere, asking embarrassing questions, studying their bills at the Hotel Crillon, and questioning their chambermaids.

Their next unhappy stop was Bonn. The director of public affairs was openly hostile and dismissed them as "junketeering gumshoes." Cohn later got his revenge by exposing the director's own pink past (he had been a member of a front organization called the New Theater League) and rumors about the acting commissioner Samuel Reber's homosexual liaisons at Harvard. Both men had to resign (as Cohn's biographer puts it, "A misstep in a knife fight with Roy Cohn, and your career was over").[55] At the time, however, as the adverse publicity continued to mount, Cohn considered cutting the trip short and coming home. McCarthy, however, urged him to persevere.[56]

By the time they reached London, the British press was insinuating that Schine and Cohn—"the quiz kids," as they called them—were coming to investigate the BBC. Questions were even asked in Parliament, and when the government denied that it had any knowledge or given any permission to the pair's visit, headlines read "MCCARTHY'S BOYS 'PUT OFF' BBC PROBE" and "WITCH-HUNT BOYS GET COLD FEET."[57] They stayed in London only six hours before flying back to the United States, where Drew Pearson and other journalists picked up on the theme of "book burners" who had lavishly lived it up in posh hotels at the taxpayers' expense.

McCarthy's foes were delighted. The whole episode reinforced the widespread view of McCarthy as a heavy-handed enemy of free speech who was trying to dictate what people should read and think. The image of book burner stuck (it was true that Cohn and Schine had prompted some books to be removed from Information Center shelves, but none were actually burned). So did the reputation for grandstanding and rank amateurism, especially when a German reporter told a story about seeing David Schine chase Cohn down a hotel corridor with a rolled-up newspaper.

After all this and the Matthews debacle, McCarthy's political stock had fallen to a new low. McCarthy needed something to clear the air. In early August, he believed he had found it, when he began to hint to reporters that he had evidence of Communist penetration of the U.S. Army. His Army investigations would bring him his biggest headlines. They would also make him an object of national public scrutiny.

Chapter 12

McCarthy Against the Press

James Stewart: *"Why don't you guys print the truth?"*
Reporters: *"The truth? What's the truth?"*

—*Mr. Smith Goes to Washington* (movie, 1939)

A lot of ink has been spilled on the subject of Joe McCarthy's relationship with the press. We can cut through all the debate and controversy by pointing out one simple truth: that the American media used McCarthy for its own purposes, in both the short term and for its own greater glory in the long haul. As a headline maker, McCarthy generated public attention and sold newspapers. As a television performer, in both the Army-McCarthy hearings and Edward R. Murrow's *See It Now* broadcasts in 1954, he inadvertently helped to establish television's new civic role as American democracy's great magnifying lens, surveying and exposing otherwise hidden contours and flaws in the political landscape. To this day, the modern media's exalted self-image is tied up inextricably with the McCarthy myth.

It used to be claimed that the press fell down on the job in dealing with McCarthy. Even journalists castigated themselves for not exposing the "flimsiness" of McCarthy's charges earlier and allowing him to run amok or, alternately, for failing to question the assumptions of the red scare—that is, not being sufficiently anti-anti-Communist.[1] Then in 1981, Edwin Bayley of the *Milwaukee Journal* took a careful look at the press treatment of McCarthy, not only in the wire services and major press organs like the *New York Times* and *San Francisco Courier* but in local newspapers across the country. He found that McCarthy's supposed immunity from press criticism was grossly exaggerated. If newspapers did carry McCarthy's initial charges at Wheeling without analyzing them, it was not because they were gullible or complicit but simply because the evidence hadn't caught up with events. As time passed, the major organs of the media gave extensive coverage to McCarthy's critics and did their best to cast him in a dubious light. The *New York Times*, the *New York Herald Tribune*, the *Washington Post*, the *Christian Science Monitor*, the *St. Louis Post-Dispatch*, and many others stood foursquare against him from the start. Other papers, particularly local ones, did not see in McCarthyism an issue worth taking sides on. Even in 1952, fewer than half of Wisconsin's papers took any position regarding McCarthy's reelection, either for or against.[2]

In the end, what decided whether a paper criticized as well as covered Joe McCarthy was not a matter of love of truth or decency but of ideology. The one truth everyone recognized was that McCarthy was excellent copy. Unlike most other politicians, he said what he thought, and editors usually put it on the front page. He consistently obliged reporters who wanted to file a quotable quote. A *Washington Post* reporter remembered that "Milt Kelly [AP] or Warren Duffee [UPI] would come and say, 'I must have a story,' and McCarthy would go through his files until he found something."[3] And what he did say also could be counted on to draw a stinging rebuke from every Democrat from President Truman on down, also for the front page.

Even when McCarthy said nothing, it became a story. David Schine once described what it was like when McCarthy met reporters in the corridor after a morning's hearings. They would swarm toward him: "Who were you interviewing?" McCarthy would grin and reply, "Can't tell you, fellas." Then: "We just saw So-and-So come out. Was he a witness?" McCarthy would say again, "I can't say," but that afternoon the news would be that So-and-So had appeared at executive session of PSI, and when asked if So-and-So had testified, McCarthy had refused to comment.[4]

McCarthy had a reputation as a brilliant, almost uncanny manipulator of the press, particularly of the wire services. In the words of George Reedy, "His IQ was goddamn high. He could think through to fundamental principles. And, boy, he really had the press figured out."[5] But whatever media skills McCarthy acquired were as much a matter of self-protection as self-projection. He did have media supporters, and in the 1950s they enjoyed a wide audience: Hearst syndicate papers such as the *New York Journal-American*, the Scripps-Howard papers, Colonel Robert McCormick's *Chicago Tribune*, and Cissy Patterson's *Washington Times-Herald*, along with columnists like

George Sokolsky, Westbrook Pegler, and Walter Winchell.[6] But opponents out-weighed the supporters, in prestige if not in circulation. When in March 1954 the *Washington Post* took over the *Times-Herald* and brought it into the liberal camp, McCarthy lost the one morning paper in the capital that had consistently backed him. It was, insiders noted, a crucial setback.[7]

In Wisconsin, he could count on the loyal support of John Riedl's newspaper chain, including the *Appleton Post-Crescent* and *Green Bay Press-Gazette* (Milwaukee's *Sentinel* was a Hearst paper and therefore dependably pro-McCarthy).[8] On the other hand, McCarthy faced a formidable array of press opposition in his home state, starting with Evjue's *Capitol Times*, the *Milwaukee Journal*, the *Sheboygan Press*, and the *Chicago Sun-Times*. Reporters on the *Capitol Times* and the *Journal* also spent time funneling derogatory information to the loose association of anti-McCarthy journalists and public relations officials known as the Project,* as well as to the central figure for mobilizing attacks on McCarthy in the Washington press corps, Drew Pearson.

Pearson is hard to understand in terms of today's Washington media. A strong and fervent liberal, he was political commentator, investigative journalist, gossip columnist, and political blackmailer rolled into one. No other single person, neither journalist or politician, looms as large in the effort to derail McCarthy—not even William Evjue. Virtually every scandal that opponents used to besmirch McCarthy's reputation and brand him a shameless demagogue, from his "reckless smears" of Owen Lattimore to lying about his war record to his financial shenanigans with Lustron, can be traced to a Drew Pearson column. Pearson supplied William Benton with the inflammatory material in his speech offering to expel McCarthy from the Senate; Pearson helped to write the Hennings report and blackmailed Hennings into signing it by threatening to expose his drinking problem to the public. It was Pearson who accused McCarthy of anti-Semitism in the Rosenberg case, and who would turn David Schine into a household name and a national scandal. McCarthy was not his first cold war victim. Earlier, Pearson had made an example of James Forrestal, Truman's first secretary of defense. Pearson hounded him as a Nazi sympathizer, accused him of helping to arm Hitler while a partner at Dillon, Read, and blasted his cold war views. When Forre-

*Like the Clearing House, the nature of the Project lent a distinctly conspiratorial air to anti-McCarthy opposition. At one point, a letter from *Journal* reporter Robert Fleming to one of Senator Benton's assistants fell into McCarthy's hands, who leaked it to a Hearst reporter. It not only made reference to the Project and its secret doings, but included instructions to burn after reading (Bayley, 135). At another point Fleming spoke to Phil Graham of the *Post* and an editor of the *St. Louis Post-Dispatch* about hiring a private investigator to tail McCarthy. Nothing came of it; how far these men were prepared to go is described later in this chapter.

stal's mental health was failing, and burglars broke into his house, Pearson published a column implying that Forrestal had fled the scene leaving his wife alone to face the thieves. It was a lie and Pearson knew it. But the column certainly contributed to Forrestal's depression and suicide, as Pearson's former aide, Jack Anderson, acknowledges.[9]

Washington insiders generally disliked and distrusted Pearson. But when his national radio broadcasts and his "Washington Merry-Go-Round" columns gave them ammunition to use on McCarthy, they helped themselves. Pearson himself was, as his assistant Jack Anderson later realized, the archetype modern liberal, with a high-minded belief in "the rights of the weak" and "social justice." Pearson saw journalism as a weapon in a just war, with "truth as their only acknowledged restriction." And truth for Drew Pearson, Anderson realized, "was often a subjective matter."[10] When forced to choose between publishing a story that was accurate and one that damaged Joe Mc-Carthy, Pearson did not hesitate.

McCarthy expressed his own view of Pearson when they both showed up as guests at a charity dinner at the Sulgrave Club in December 1950. Pearson had raked McCarthy over the coals in more than fifty columns that year, including a story about a "sex pervert" working on McCarthy's staff.[11] With a mischievousness bordering on recklessness, their hostess seated them next to each other. They exchanged insults most of the evening; then as they were leaving they met alone in the cloakroom. Flushed with bourbon and rage, McCarthy attacked the older and smaller man, kneeing him in the groin. At that point, another guest, Richard Nixon, came in and pulled McCarthy away, but not before McCarthy slapped Pearson "harder," Nixon told a friend later, "than I've ever seen anyone slapped." "That one was for you, Dick," McCarthy growled and left.[12] Pearson sued, of course, and under oath McCarthy admitted to the slap but not the knee. If some were horrified and disgusted with what McCarthy had done, many were not. Briefly McCarthy became something of a hero. Senator Watkins came up to him with a grin and said he had heard rumors McCarthy had punched Pearson in two places, and he hoped both were true. Watkins was not the only person to congratulate him personally. A few days later McCarthy received an inscribed watch in the mail from an anonymous donor. Since the package came from Missouri, Joe and his pal Ray Kiermas guessed it had come from a certain ex-president who had crossed swords with Pearson many times. Joe wore the watch proudly for a long time afterward.[13]

McCarthy came roaring back three days later with a speech on the Senate floor. He lambasted Pearson's record as a purveyor of political sleaze and zeroed in on a member of Pearson's staff, David Karr, accusing him of being Pearson's "KGB controller" and calling Pearson a "Moscow-directed character assassin." Pearson and Karr dismissed the charges as another example of McCarthy impugning the loyalty of his critics. It now seems McCarthy was correct about Karr himself.[14] However, Drew Pearson himself did not need any former *Daily Worker* hack to feed himself his anti-McCarthy obsession, any more than Captain Ahab needed Starbuck. Again, it was liberalism, not communism, that conceived the greatest hatred and loathing of Joe McCarthy.

McCarthy, with his usual obtuseness regarding other people's motives, never understood this. The fact that liberal columnists like James Wechsler or Marquis Childs could mercilessly castigate his every move and seem more outraged by his activities than they were by dirty deeds in the Kremlin or its secret agents in the State Department baffled and then infuriated him. An editorial branding McCarthy a reckless demagogue and fascist would appear in the *Daily Worker;* the next day editorials would sprout up in the *Milwaukee Journal* and the *New York Post* repeating substantially the same thing. How can you explain this unless the liberals and the Communists really *are* in cahoots, McCarthy would ask himself as well as audiences on speaking tours, as he held up copies of the offending papers. He once blurted to an interviewer he had evidence that some four hundred Communists were working in the mainstream American media and influencing its views. An infuriated press asked how dare McCarthy suggest that, since some of them had a radical past, they were all a bunch of Communist dupes? "Senator, let's face it," the *New York Post*'s James Wechsler said when he appeared in front of McCarthy's committee on April 24, 1953. "You are saying that an ex-Communist who is for McCarthy is a good one and an ex-Communist who is against McCarthy is suspect."

"I feel you have not broken with your Communist ideal," McCarthy replied. "I feel you are serving them very, very actively. Whether you are doing it knowingly or not, that is in your mind."[15]

It was a dialogue of the deaf. In the end, it was a battle between two incompatible views of what the press's role in a free society should be. On the one hand, it should be free to criticize and expose any behavior by public officials it deemed irresponsible, especially if that behavior damages civil liberties, which includes freedom of the press. On the other, it should not do so in a way that gives aid and comfort to the nation's enemies, for whom the notion of civil liberties and freedom of the press are dead letters anyway.

Not every journalist who opposed McCarthy did so out of high-minded reasons. I. F. Stone, a consistent anti-McCarthy columnist in the socialist paper the *Daily Compass*, was, it now seems, closer to the Moscow line than even McCarthy imagined. The Venona decrypts reveal that in 1945 the KGB was actively recruiting American journalists for clandestine work on the Soviet side. One of the journalists they approached was Stone. Stone (code-named BLINTZ) at first avoided any direct contact, but then arranged a meeting with the Soviet agent. He confessed no ideological or ethical problems with working secretly for the Soviets; he also made it clear (according to his Soviet contact) that he was open to monetary inducements. His chief worry was that he might get caught. The contact broke off at that point, and Venona reveals nothing about any further meetings.[16] Stone defenders might claim that he merely led the KGB on, in hopes of learning more about Soviet espionage. But Stone's position, like that of the rest of the leftist press, was that there was *no Soviet espionage at all*, and that the whole thing was a fiction invented by the reactionary right to thwart modern progressivism. That became, in fact, I. F. Stone's stubborn claim throughout the entire cold war and that made him a journalistic hero: that McCarthy was running a political witch-hunt—even as he remained discreetly silent about his own secret contacts with one of the witches.

At the other end of the spectrum, the Alsop brothers, Joseph and Stewart, were vociferous McCarthy critics who blasted him from the standpoint of the anti-Communist Washington establishment. McCarthy, Stewart Alsop confessed later, "was the only politician or major public figure I ever actually hated." But their hatred was not just politically motivated; they also worried that McCarthy's crusade against homosexuals and "perverts" in Washington might eventually come to light on Joe Alsop himself.

McCarthy never caught on. But in 1957 Soviet agents managed to ensnare Joe Alsop in a "honey trap," catching him in flagrante with a young man in a Moscow hotel room in order to blackmail him. Alsop was forced to give a lengthy signed statement for the CIA, admitting to his homosexuality, which finally ended up in his FBI file. Ironically, it was not Joe McCarthy but the Eisenhower White House (in fact, according to biographer Merry, McCarthy foe James Hagerty) that tried to use this secret to silence his criticisms of *them*.[17]

Nor were liberal journalists afraid of stooping to "McCarthyite" methods themselves. Hank Greenspun, publisher of the *Las Vegas Sun*, tried to ruin McCarthy by running stories about his alleged homosexual affairs (his original source was, not surprisingly, Drew Pearson). "The persons in Nevada who listened to McCarthy's radio talk," Greenspun wrote, "thought he had the queerest laugh. He does. He is."[18] Two years later the *Sun* ran an article, "The Secret Lives of Joe McCarthy," insinuating that McCarthy was leading the fight against homosexuals in government in order to divert suspicion from himself. It mentioned that he had been seen kissing a Wisconsin Young Republican full on the mouth, had hired "tall, handsome, dreamy-eyed" David Schine, and had sent Jean Kerr off on an extended vacation to Hawaii in order to spend time alone with his homosexual lovers.

It even speculated on his need to "satisfy his perverse lust to physically scare and hurt women."[19]

In another case, reporters discovered an "N. B. Keck" who had donated money to McCarthy's campaign in 1952. They tried to prove that this was actually Howard B. Keck, a Texas oil-and-gas magnate, in order to show that McCarthy was in the pocket of the Texas energy industry. When they couldn't, they ran the story anyway.[20] But perhaps the strangest example of the media's lust for derogatory information regarding McCarthy is the story of Paul Hughes.

Hughes was a skilled, if slightly deranged, amateur confidence man, who convinced the publisher of the *Washington Post*, as well as key figures in the ADA, the Democratic National Committee, and the National Committee for an Effective Congress, that he was a secret operative for Joe McCarthy. In January 1954, he plopped himself down in the law offices of Joseph Rauh and detailed how McCarthy engaged him in numerous illegal activities, including fabricating evidence and blackmailing witnesses. He offered documents (which he had forged) to prove it. Delighted, Rauh passed him on to Philip Graham, owner and publisher of the *Post* (and husband of current owner Katharine Graham). He, Rauh, and managing editor Russell Wiggins listened with bated breath to Hughes's bizarre stories: of McCarthy's ring of secret paid informants in the government, of his clandestine links to the Eisenhower White House, of his marital problems—even how the cooking editor of the *New York Post* was actually a McCarthy operative.

Graham and Wiggins were convinced they had the story that would finally destroy McCarthy, but they wanted more hard evidence of prosecutable crimes before going to press. "When you strike at a king, you had to kill him," Rauh remembered Wiggins as saying.[21] Hughes promised to give them that too, but he also needed money in order to stay on McCarthy's staff as the *Post*'s secret informant. A bit reluctantly, they agreed.

Meanwhile, Hughes had found another eager and gullible mark: Clayton Fritchey, deputy chairman of the Democratic National Committee. He too was willing to believe the worst and pored over Hughes's forged documents with the Democratic Party's research director and with the DNC's legal counsel Clark Clifford. Fritchey paid Hughes (now code-named "Junius") $2,300 in cash for expenses. Hughes was able to hit up Rauh for more than $8,000.

For nine months Hughes kept his twin audiences enthralled. One day he showed up with the climax of his story: McCarthy and Cohn had secretly cached machine guns, Lugers, and an arsenal of other weapons in the basement of the Senate Office Building. The implication was clear: McCarthy was planning some sort of coup against the federal government.[22] Finally, in

October the *Post* prepared a twelve-part series on McCarthy based on the sensational Hughes "revelations." For the first time, Graham and his editors decided to do some background checking and soon discovered that every one of Hughes's "documented" cases was false. At the last minute, they killed the series. Rauh and Fritchey dropped Hughes like a stone. They do not seem to have asked for their money back.

McCarthy's opponents liked to claim that what made McCarthy reek in the nostrils of American democracy was not what McCarthy was doing but how he did it: the public airing of unsubstantiated charges, the use of smear and innuendo, and "confidential informants, dossiers, political spies," as Joseph Rauh himself had written in May 1950. "No one can guess where this process of informing will end." The Hughes case proves that some of them were willing to do at least the same to him. When the chips were down, they were prepared to do whatever was necessary to defeat what they perceived as a dire threat to American liberty—just what McCarthy himself claimed to be doing.

High-minded liberals like Tom Wicker called covering McCarthy "the sewer beat." Establishment columnists like the Alsops, Walter Lippmann, and Arthur Krock despised him. But many other reporters liked McCarthy. "There was," recalled one *New York Times* reporter years later, "some fascination for all of us in covering Joe, because while his kind has appeared frequently on the stage of politics, he was the top banana for his kind of act in his time, and while it was a burden and a trial for some of us, it was a joyous thing for Joe at all times." He enjoyed dropping by a reporter's home unannounced with a bag of groceries, then "shooing the woman out of the kitchen" and cooking up a batch of his famous fried chicken.[23] The contempt McCarthy felt for their editors never extended to the reporters themselves. "I know your bosses are sons-of-bitches," he would say, then add, "I know because *I'm* a son-of-a-bitch." With his disordered office piled high with files and papers, his jacket discarded on a chair, his rumpled shirt and rolled-up sleeves, shouting into the phone—McCarthy might have been Frank Capra's image of the fighting editor of a small-town paper.

Above all, they understood that McCarthy was utterly fearless. He was willing to take on anyone, regardless of the consequences, and fight any battle he thought worth fighting—and winning. Now, in the fall of 1953, that fearlessness, to the point of foolhardiness, was about to be tested. McCarthy was about to take on the U.S. Army, the White House, and his own political party.

Chapter 13

McCarthy Against the Army

ort Monmouth, New Jersey, had been set up in 1917 to house the Army Signal Corps's radio and technical research laboratories. In 1954 it was a series of drab barracks and Quonset huts where almost eight thousand civilian scientists, engineers, and other employees worked on developing guided missile systems and radar networks. In terms of national security, Fort Monmouth was, as Willard Edwards of the *Chicago Tribune* put it, more important than Los Alamos.

During World War II, the Army had allowed their Soviet allies to work at Fort Monmouth and to examine classified material. A regular visitor to the base was Julius Rosenberg; another was his contact Martin Sobell, who worked for an electrical company that did contract work there. When Rosenberg was arrested, two other former army engineers, Joel Barr and Alfred Sarant, fled to the Soviet Union. They too had been employed at Fort Monmouth in the forties.[1] Meanwhile, an East German defector claimed to have seen more recent material originating from Fort Monmouth and said that his Soviet contacts had boasted about how easy it was to get it.

In January 1952, three Army officers and seven civilian security personnel filed a formal request for an investigation of the lax security and "Communist talk" on the base. They asserted that certain important documents were missing from the base and had probably been stolen. The Army looked into it and said, no, just as the Air Force questioned the East German defector and decided he was lying. More than a year later these stories about Fort Monmouth's leaky security reached the ears of Roy Cohn. He saw the FBI reports on thirty-four civilian employees who had connections to persons in the Rosenberg-Sobell spy ring, at least half of whom were still employed at the base.[2] Cohn was so impressed that he interrupted Joe's honeymoon in West Palm Beach by ham radio and virtually ordered him to return to Washington.

Cohn convinced McCarthy they had stumbled on a spy ring rivaling the one that had given the Soviets the atom bomb.[3] It looked like a replay of the State Department fiasco that had launched McCarthy's career: the same slipshod security program; the same history of allowing persons with divided loyalties to handle sensitive material; even a list of names, originating from the FBI, that belied glib assurances that all was well. The difference was that this time McCarthy could count on cooperation from top administration officials (or so he thought). Since the Democrats on his committee were still boycotting his proceedings, he was free to do as he pleased. Within two days of returning to Washington, he began holding hearings in New York. Some he held by himself, with no other senators present. PSI had become a one-man operation as McCarthy dispensed subpoenas and grilled witnesses with the help of the inseparable duo Cohn and Schine.

On the first day Cohn introduced a deposition from Julius Rosenberg's fellow spy, David Greenglass, who detailed espionage efforts inside the Signal Corps, which, as far as he knew, "could very possibly be continuing to this day." Fort Monmouth's commander, General Kirk Lawton, proved to be a pleasant surprise. He seemed to be as disturbed by news about subversives and possible spies operating at Fort Monmouth as McCarthy was, and he personally led his security team on a hunt through the base for missing or mislaid classified materials. He suspended five employees with suspect backgrounds on October 6. On October 15 the number of suspensions had risen to ten; on October 26th it was twenty-seven people. Cohn told a national radio audience, "It is because what the FBI found was ignored that we have to have our investigation today."[4]

McCarthy and Cohn took a tour of the base with Lawton and the Secretary of the Army Robert Stevens. "An extremely bad and dangerous situation has existed here over the years," McCarthy told reporters, but he admitted he was "impressed and surprised" by Lawton's cooperative attitude. Stevens concurred, and praised McCarthy's work as an example of the new teamwork that now existed between the executive branch and the Army's commander in chief and the legislative branch.

Underneath the pleasantries, however, was a foreboding tension. Privately Lawton told McCarthy that by cooperating with him in the investigation, he had just thrown any chance of future promotion "out the window," as he put it.[5] During their tour of the Evans Signal Laboratory, McCarthy was joined by Stevens and Lawton on a special tour of a highly classified section of the base. Security officers explained to Roy Cohn and the others that staff members were not cleared for the tour but offered to show them a less classified display that had been prepared for visitors. Cohn, for whom special privileges were a matter of right, not permission, was furious. He told the base's director of countermeasures, J. J. Slattery, that "this was a declaration of war" and that he was not going to forget it.[6] The incident made Cohn even more determined to drag out whatever dirt he could find about the Army's "coddling" of Communists and subversives.

Later, some would insist that the Monmouth investigation never uncovered any evidence of espionage, and that since so many of those accused happened to be Jews, it was fueled by anti-Semitism.[7] This diverts attention from the fact that from the point of view of security, Fort Monmouth leaked like a sieve. Witnesses said it was everyday practice to take classified documents home. One employee, who also happened to be a friend of both Rosenberg and Sobell, had been discovered with more than forty but faced no disciplinary action. The FBI could never assemble convincing proof that the Soviets had established an espionage ring at Fort Monmouth, although Secretary Stevens did state that they had found evidence of attempted espionage during the war.[8] But clearly there was nothing to stop the Russians if they had tried.

If the Army thought that facing up to these embarrassing revelations would placate McCarthy, they were mistaken. They only convinced him he needed to investigate further and bring those responsible to account.

At first glance, McCarthy's campaign against the Army for "coddling Communists" seems baffling. Our standard image of the cold war military is of a phalanx of rigid anti-Communists and of the Pentagon as a bulwark of reactionary Republicanism. But this was far from the case in the fifties. For more than a generation, the American military had seen itself as above petty politics, including questions of ideology. From Joe Stilwell's dealings with the China hands to George Marshall's relations with Zhou En-lai (see Chapter 9), Army brass had shown themselves to be at times almost wilfully naive when it came to assessing security threats within their own circles.

The other notorious example was General Leslie Groves, director of the Manhattan Project, and his handling of the Oppenheimer case. Robert Oppenheimer was a brilliant scientist, of course, and superb manager of the most top secret government project in the nation's history, but both his brother Frank and wife were members of the Communist Party. Kitty Oppenheimer was a lifelong friend of Steve Nelson, a former Spanish Civil War volunteer who was a key figure in the Communist Party's underground apparatus.[9] Everyone knew that "Oppy" was unhappy with the plans to keep the atomic bomb secret from America's Soviet ally, just as he himself was aware that there were people secretly working for Soviets in the Los Alamos facilities (there were in fact three). It is not necessary to accept the claims of former KGB officers that Oppenheimer was a conscious Soviet asset to see that he might be tempted, for personal or ideological reasons, to let certain information fall into the hands of those who could do something with it. Despite being conscious of the Soviet threat, Groves adamantly refused to consider Oppenheimer himself a security risk, although one of his Army counterintelligence officers, Peer de Silva, did. Groves, like millions of other Americans both in and out of uniform, was unwilling to believe that people he knew and trusted could possibly be Communists or hostile to American interests—in the Manhattan Project case, the failure was systematic. As two recent historians note, "All three known spies at Los Alamos had been members of the Communist Party or offshoots of it, yet the CIC [Counter Intelligence Corps.] wasn't aware of their connections."10

There were other reasons Taftite Republicans did not love the military. They, like McCarthy, saw the Pentagon for what it was: another branch of the federal government, subject to the same inefficiencies and corruptions, and requiring the same budgetary discipline. For generations Americans had been taught that a large military establishment or standing armies were tools of tyranny. "A standing force can be for nothing but [Royal] Prerogative, by whom it hath its idle living and subsistence."11 The cold war added a new level of concern: that the globalization of American interests and power would lead its armed forces to forget their primary objective, the defense of the United States. Men were not immune from the corruptions of empire just because they wore a uniform.

Conservatives worried not that the cold war military was becoming too politicized, but that it was not politicized enough. Its leading officers seemed unwilling to interject themselves into the larger debate on cold war policy and blindly accepted the orders of statesmen and policymakers, no matter how unfeasible or unrealistic. Douglas MacArthur had been the exception that proved the rule. He alone of officers of his caliber and class had been willing to appeal to public opinion and Congress to reverse a Korea policy he considered disastrous. That daring experiment had cost him his job, while Marshall and the Joint Chiefs did nothing. If the MacArthur incident seemed to liberals to confirm their belief that in politics generals must be seen and not heard, it convinced conservatives that the military's top brass, left to themselves, would protect their own interests instead of the national interest.

McCarthy had established to everyone's satisfaction that something had to be done about the Army's security program. The fight would be, at least at first, over who should handle it. McCarthy and his fellow Republicans saw

Congress as the proper tool. In some regards McCarthy followed in the footsteps of his distinguished predecessor, Senator Harry Truman, and his probes into military procurement and corruption in the early forties. Truman and his fellow senators considered the military's general approach, in the words of their modern chronicler, "rigid, shortsighted, and ignorant." Like McCarthy, they had seen their investigations as "an instrument for helping to shake the military loose from hidebound ways of doing things," however much its defenders might howl.[12] The crucial difference was that Truman had labored to maintain a steady bipartisan consensus. True to form, McCarthy was venturing more and more out on his own. Yet everything he did sprang from Congress's traditional oversight powers.

On the other side, the White House believed that the job of cleaning up belonged to the commander in chief and his deputies, including the secretary of the army, Robert Stevens. Although he was a product of the same background as the Wise Men (graduate of Andover and Yale), Stevens was no Robert Lovett or Jack McCloy. He had no stomach for the sort of political game he was about to play; dealing with McCarthy was a task beyond his powers. His first instinct was to cooperate and try to placate the senator and his minions, especially the aggressive Roy Cohn. Then he began to feel pressure from the opposite side—first from his Army generals but also from the Eisenhower team not to be *too* cooperative. Stevens became a deeply unhappy man. Pinned between an irresistible force and an immoveable object, he would earn the scorn of both.*

It was McCarthy against the Pentagon and, by implication, the White House. He convinced himself that if he yielded, he would be abetting a coverup, just as the White House believed that if they yielded, they were abetting the political fortunes of a potential rival. However, even larger issues were stirring underneath. The battle between the junior senator from Wisconsin and Eisenhower became a struggle between the power of the chief executive, as it emerged from two decades of the New Deal and global war, and traditional legislative oversight. The worries that had prompted the Bricker amendment would reemerge in the McCarthy battle in the form of the question of whether, as one senator put it, "the Army is supreme over Congress, other agencies, and the American people, and can enjoy special dictatorial immunity in covering up its own wrongdoing"—only to be swallowed up in the clash of personalities and swirl of headlines.[13]

The White House moved first. Suddenly, in late October 1953, it decided

---

*Cf. James Hagerty's diary for March 6, 1954: "Sat next to Bob Stevens at head table [of White House correspondents dinner]. Is he jittery. And is he talking. . . . Very unstable and excited. Says, 'he's all alone in this fight.'" *Diary*, p. 26.

to lower the temperature from warm to icy. Eisenhower began by telling reporters that he hoped domestic communism would no longer be a political issue in 1954, by which he meant that any trace of internal subversion would be definitively snuffed out. McCarthy and his allies, however, thought he meant that communism itself should no longer be an issue and responded firmly. Then the Pentagon refused to allow McCarthy's committee any opportunity to interview loyalty board members or see confidential files. Defense Secretary Wilson agreed with Stevens that General Lawton was proving to be too zealous and that he needed to be relieved of his post. McCarthy was caught off guard by Lawton's sudden transfer out of Fort Monmouth, and then his discharge from the Army on grounds of disability, although Lawton himself believed that he had been removed for cooperating with McCarthy.[14]

Then came another disappointment: David Schine received a draft notice, ordering him to report for duty on November 3, 1953. Roy Cohn immediately guessed that Schine's induction into the Army was politically motivated, and in one respect it was. Drew Pearson had learned that Schine had originally been classified 1-A by the California draft board but then underwent a second examination at Governor's Island in New York that earned him a deferment as a 4-F, revealing two herniated discs and "a schizoid personality." The fact that this was the same place where Roy Cohn had earned his own 4-B draft deferment made the whole thing rather suspicious.[15] Pearson proceeded to hound the board until it consented to review Schine's case. A new Army medical exam on June 30, 1953, discovered that Schine's back problems were not imaginary but that they had considerably improved. The doctor found no trace of schizoid personality either and certified that although Schine was hardly in perfect physical condition, he was "capable of certain military duties" and suitable for induction. Schine's draft notice went out three and half months later.[16]

A distressed Cohn made a spate of telephone calls to Secretary Stevens among others, trying to arrange for his friend to be spared the humiliations of ordinary induction. He even got McCarthy to write a letter on Schine's behalf, all to no avail. On November 10 a glum Private David Schine appeared at Fort Dix, New Jersey, to report for duty. However, Cohn was not yet finished with Schine—or the Army.

At about the same time, Eisenhower's attorney general made a startling public revelation that seemed to confirm, rather than weaken, McCarthy's cause. Herbert Brownell announced that the Justice Department had definitive proof that Harry Dexter White had been a Soviet spy and—even more damning—that President Truman had known since the end of 1945 and had done nothing about it. Indeed, after learning that White was a spy, Truman had recommended him as head of the International Monetary Fund. We now know that it was the Venona decrypts that allowed Brownell to be so certain of these facts. But the announcement was a serious blow to liberals who had tried to claim that the red scare was all "hysteria" and pure partisan politics, as well as being an unexpected vindication of McCarthy and his efforts. Truman furiously denied the story—although both former Secretary of State James Byrnes (delighted to see his old boss on the hot seat) and FBI director Hoover contradicted him. Even the *New Republic* had to conclude that the evidence against White—and Truman—was "convincing."[17]

But now, since Truman had mentioned McCarthy by name in his angry public denial, he had to get into the act. He demanded free air time from the major networks to issue a triumphant reply from New York on November 24. He got J. B. Matthews to help him draft the speech, which would be broadcast on both television and radio. An air of celebration surrounded the event. McCarthy, Cohn, and counsel Frank Carr were joined by Assistant Secretary of the Army John G. Adams, whom Cohn treated to lunch at the Stork Club, where they had chicken hamburgers ("à la Walter Winchell," Adams noted in his diary) and a bottle of champagne. Adams arrived at the studio later that evening just as the broadcast was getting under way, and then joined the party when McCarthy and the others adjourned for more drinks at the Stork Club. Although Adams must have heard the bulk of the address, he may not have realized what a political turning point it was.

McCarthy and Matthews had decided to award to Joe the role of spokesman for his party and the anti-Communist cause. In doing so, they did not hesitate to pass judgment on the Eisenhower administration for being insufficiently motivated in trying to retrieve American POWs and missing in action in Korea and for condoning the illegal trade with Communist China. In his broadcast McCarthy told viewers and listeners of "the failure of my party to liquidate the foulest bankruptcy of the Democratic administration" by permitting the China trade to continue, and promised that "this trading in blood-money will cease." He added, "We must regain our national honor regardless of what it costs."

That night, C. D. Jackson was home listening to the speech on the radio and at once assumed, as he told columnist James Reston the next day, that it was a "declaration of war" against the White House. It was in fact quite mild by McCarthy standards: he even explained how "infinitely better" the situation was now compared to when the Democrats were in charge. But the speech set off a furor in the Eisenhower back room. On November 30, staffers met and laid their cards on the table. A few still thought it would be a serious mistake to go after McCarthy directly, that it might hurt relations on the Hill and with Catholic voters. But Jackson, James Hagerty, and the rest believed that unless Ike took some forceful action, he would injure his presidential image. The next day they met with him in the Oval Office. Jack Martin, a former Taft aide, warned Eisenhower "that a vacuum existed in this country, and it was a political vacuum, and unless the President filled it somebody else would."[18] Eisenhower squirmed but realized he had to act.

David Schine had reported for duty at Fort Dix, New Jersey, on November 10, a Tuesday. Cohn immediately phoned the fort's commanding general for a stack of weekend passes. Schine's departure meant nothing to McCarthy himself. "You can post him to Korea as far as I'm concerned," he told Stevens at one point. But Cohn became frantic. He made regular telephone calls to Secretary Stevens, requesting that "our young friend" be posted close to New York City or at least be permitted extended leave to finish his work with the subcommittee. (What that was never seemed very clear.) He suggested that Schine be commissioned as a captain in order to avoid basic training. In a weak moment, Stevens promised to see what he could do; he even spoke to CIA director Allen Dulles about taking Schine under his wing, but Dulles refused.

Cohn dragged McCarthy into the negotiations. He called Stevens. "For God's sake," he exclaimed, "don't put Dave in service and assign him back to my committee. . . . One, I couldn't get away with it. . . . The newspapers would be back on us." He said Schine was "a good boy but there is nothing indispensable about him." He realized Cohn was being unreasonable: "He thinks David should be a general and work from the penthouse of the Waldorf." Maybe Stevens could arrange for Schine to join the committee in New York in weekends. But he asked that Stevens not say anything to anyone about their conversation since it would probably get back to Cohn.[19]

Meanwhile, Eisenhower was slowly winding himself up for action. On December 1, he publicly supported John Foster Dulles's position that the United States would not pressure its allies to suspend trade with China and urged that in combating subversion, "it is imperative that we protect the basic rights of loyal American citizens." McCarthy avoided being combative. He simply told reporters that when it came to red china trade, "I have deep convictions on this subject," and that he would urge Secretary Dulles to reconsider. He then urged all Americans to show their support for ending the "blood trade with the enemy" by sending a wire or letter to the White House, which they did, by a comfortable two-to-one margin in support of McCarthy.[20]

Eisenhower was still discovering the depth of the mess that Truman and the Democrats had left behind. First there had been the Harry Dexter White case. Then on December 1, the same day that Ike repeated his belief that Communist subversion would soon be a forgotten issue, he learned that the FBI had considered Robert Oppenheimer to be a major security risk during his work for the Manhattan Project, but was ignored by officials. Eisenhower was deeply shaken. C. D. Jackson fumed in his diary, "The foolishness and/or knavery of past Administration . . . unbelievable." Yet Jackson and the others were still pushing Eisenhower to join battle with McCarthy. They believed that McCarthy was on the brink of subpoenaing Defense Department loyalty board members and records. "Roy Cohn thinks we're going to collide on this issue this week," the Army's chief lawyer, John Adams, wrote to Attorney General Brownell.[21]

During David Schine's first month of active service at Fort Dix, he received four weekends off, as well as four weeknight passes. Then the commanding general decided that Schine's weekend passes had to begin on Saturday at noon, not Friday night, and no more weeknight passes were to be issued. Cohn rang up John Adams. "The Army has double-crossed me for the last time," he screamed. "The Army is going to find out what it means to go over my head."

"Is this a threat?" Adams slowly asked.

"It's a promise," Cohn replied, "I always deliver on my promises. . . . We are not going to stop this. Joe will deliver, and," he added menacingly, "I can make Joe do whatever I want."

The next day McCarthy had lunch with Secretary Stevens to smooth things over. He raised the possibility of a special duty assignment in New York for Schine, then quickly dropped it. A week later things suddenly flew out of control. Adams had gone to New York to attend the Monmouth hearings. He met McCarthy, who at first seemed nonchalant and resigned to leaving Schine at Fort Dix. But when Roy Cohn joined them for lunch, McCarthy's mood suddenly changed. As they dined at Gasner's, a famous East Side Jewish restaurant, McCarthy fell uncharacteristically silent while Cohn berated Adams and the Army for making Schine "eat shit," as he put it, and breaking their promise to assign him for special duty to New York. Finally Adams told them he had to get to Pennsylvania Station to catch a train back to Washington. Cohn drove, with McCarthy in the front and Adams and Frank Carr in the back.

Cohn, a notoriously bad driver, began ripping into McCarthy, while McCarthy meekly tried to cajole Adams into doing something for Cohn's friend. Adams observed that if they continued driving in this direction, he'd miss his train. Cohn stopped the car in the middle of Park Avenue and whipped a U-turn. "Get out and get to the station however you can," he snapped at the Army's general counsel. Mustering what dignity he had left, Adams stepped out, and Cohn drove off.[22]

Juvenile business, to be sure, but Cohn's obsessive desire to rescue Schine from basic training now became entangled in bigger questions—about the future of PSI, not to mention the future of the Republican Party. At four o'clock on January 21, 1954, there was a meeting at Herbert Brownell's office in the Justice building. John Adams, Brownell, Deputy Attorney General William Rogers, Henry Cabot Lodge, Sherman Adams, and Jerry Morgan all attended. A Gallup poll was about to be released showing McCarthy's approval ratings at their highest ever—at 50 percent. He had bested Eisenhower on the red China trade issue. In two weeks, the Senate would vote new appropriations for his committee by 85 to 1 (William Fulbright was the lone dissenter). The men in Brownell's office were worried but confident they occupied the high ground. All agreed that the clash with McCarthy had moved into the constitutional orbit and that his efforts to have loyalty board members subpoenaed for questioning should be refused. They also asked John Adams to draw up a chronology of the pressure Cohn and McCarthy were bringing to bear on him and Secretary Stevens to give Schine preferential treatment. They were beginning to suspect that the Schine issue and the Army investigations were related. If they could prove that some sort of collusion was at work . . .

On January 22 Adams had a long, final meeting with McCarthy at his apartment. We have two entirely different versions of what happened and of who tried to apply pressure to whom.[23] The upshot was the same: the administration was now determined to halt any further investigations into the Army, and that McCarthy just as determined to press forward. He had meanwhile found the perfect case for his purposes: that of Major Irving Peress.

When the Korean War broke out, the Army, in desperate need of doctors and dentists, had begun drafting civilians, regardless of their background, to fill the gap. One was Irving Peress, a forty-year-old dentist from Queens who was inducted into the Army on October 15, 1952, with the rank of captain in the reserves. When he was asked on his application form whether he had ever been a member of "any organization seeking to alter the form of government . . . by unconstitutional means," he answered no.

In fact, this was a lie. Irving Peress had been a member of the Communist Party since 1948 and a leading activist in the Communist-dominated American Labor Party. An undercover policewoman working inside the party later unambiguously identified Peress and his wife as "active comrades." Later, when he filled out a more detailed questionnaire on membership in Communist organizations, Peress invoked the Fifth Amendment to avoid answering—a tip-off to alert investigators. He reported for active duty to Fort Sam Houston on January 3, 1953.

Within a month, Army intelligence, or G-2, had put Peress under surveillance and kept careful track of his activities. By April G-2 dispatched a letter to Peress's superiors at his new base at Camp Kilmer, New Jersey, advising them that they had him under investigation, followed by a second letter in April alerting them that Peress belonged on a list of "suspects and restrictees." The G-2 officer at Kilmer recommended that Peress be dismissed from the service. The months dragged on. Peress proved to be a less than successful soldier. His Officer Efficiency Report for the latter half of that year, now declassified, considered him to be a "very disloyal and untrustworthy type of officer." He was "an individual who works only for his own personal gains irrespective of his obligations to the Military Service" and "his very presence creates an uncomfortable feeling." Peress, in the view of his superiors, "is trusted by no one" and "his main efforts have been directed toward the seeding of dissatisfaction."[24] There were also rumors that Peress was trying to organize a Communist cell on the base. Finally, on October 18, 1953, G-2 had prepared a confidential report detailing Peress's Communist connections and concluding that he constituted a clear security risk.

Yet less than a week later, on October 23, the Army approved Peress's formal request for promotion to major—even though Peress's own camp commander, Brigadier General Ralph Zwicker, had seen his file and recommended in writing that Peress be dismissed at once. Again, nothing happened. It was not until January 18, 1954, that the Department of the Army finally decided that Peress would be allowed to leave the Army, with an honorable discharge effective March 31, 1954.

What mattered to McCarthy and to the anonymous officer who brought the Peress case to his attention in early November was not who Irving Peress was, or the possibility of a Communist dentist's extracting classified secrets from his patients at Camp Kilmer. What mattered was that the Army bureaucracy and its own loyalty board had totally botched Peress's case—not only permitting him to stay in the Army, in clear violation of the law, but actually promoting him. McCarthy even wondered if Peress had had inside help. Who was responsible for this foul-up? That was what McCarthy wanted to know, and what inspired the rallying cry, "Who Promoted Peress!"

Now recently declassified Army files supply the answer. In late August 1953, Peress had stopped by the First Army's Medical Section to ask about promotion to major. Two Army bureaucrats, Major Van Sickle of the Officers Procurement Branch and Major Curtis Kirkland, chief of the Promotion Branch of the First Army's Reserve Forces, jointly okayed the request. Neither was aware of the G-2 reports, even though the First Army's Medical Section had noted them in Peress's file. Neither man bothered to check. Even more amazingly, Kirkland later told investigators he would have approved the request anyway, since he believed Peress should have been appointed major, not captain, in the first place. From his perspective, the request had been part of an Army-wide retrospective "reappointment" of officers who had been brought in at the rank of captain and should have been majors (there were more than six hundred others at that date). Technically not a promotion at all—hence, said Kirkland, no problem.

The inspector general's investigators were flabbergasted. Their report concluded that "the information that an investigation was being conducted by G-2 was available to, and should have been known to, both Major Van Sickle and Major Kirkland." It condemned their actions and admitted that there was a serious "lack of dissemination of information" between Army security and Army personnel sections.[25] But by the time a serious investigation got under way, in November 1953, the Pentagon was already feeling the heat from McCarthy. When he learned about Zwicker's letter and the Peress situation, General Murphy warned his colleagues there would be hell to pay "if the Senator who has been investigating at Fort Monmouth finds out that the Army is promoting that type of fellow." That senator was, of course, McCarthy.[26]

McCarthy was mistaken in assuming that Peress's promotion was the result of Communist collusion within the Army, but he was right in assuming that the Army's own security procedures were inadequate to the task. Pentagon officials wanted the snafu to go away as quietly as possible.* The last thing they were going to do was to help McCarthy get to the bottom of it.

Nor was Peress himself going to be very forthcoming (the Army warned him to keep his mouth shut). McCarthy was incredulous to learn that Peress had never been questioned about his background by a board of inquiry or a superior officer. He could not know that the Army had not asked because it already was aware of Peress's past, and the Army was not going to enlighten McCarthy. He wrote a formal letter to Stevens asking for background information.

But Secretary Stevens had another soldier on his mind: Private David Schine. He was beginning to see a way out of his dilemma. On February 1 he asked the inspector general of the Army to begin an inquiry into whether Schine was receiving undue preferential treatment, a slightly absurd request because if it were true, it would have be due to Stevens's and the Army's own spineless inability to say no to Roy Cohn and his relentless campaign to protect the hapless Schine.

As it happened, the next round of hearings on the Peress case were scheduled for February 18, in New York City. McCarthy was not in a good mood. He had learned on February 2 that the Army had decided to give Peress his honor-

---

*Both Major Van Sickle and Major Kirkland were removed from their posts, and Kirkland left the Army.

able discharge almost two months early, thus washing their hands of the whole affair. "When they want to move fast, they can shuffle those papers faster than you can see them!" he raged to a staffer. The evening before, a car had collided with the taxi he and Jean were taking to their New York hotel. McCarthy had been knocked unconscious, and his wife had to be taken to the hospital for a broken ankle. He had spent the night with her at the hospital and arrived at the hearings in sad shape. He also decided to skip lunch and confronted his first witness of the afternoon, General Zwicker, hungry and with a splitting headache—and probably after several drinks.[27]

Earlier, Zwicker had been forthcoming and promised to be cooperative. He was as outraged and embarrassed as anyone else at Peress's ability to evade standard security and made that clear to McCarthy. However, a telephone call to the Pentagon that morning had turned him stiff and uncommunicative. As the questioning began, McCarthy became more and more impatient, and he accused his witness of "hedging and hemming," while Zwicker refused to disclose any information about Peress's promotion that he thought might violate rules about confidentiality. McCarthy jumped to the conclusion that Zwicker's reluctance was in fact part of a cover-up; he finally asked him point-blank how he felt about rooting Communists out of the Army.

Zwicker asked, "Do you mean how do I feel about Communists?"

McCarthy exploded, "I mean exactly what I asked you, General, nothing else. Anyone with the brains of a five-year-old child can understand the question." McCarthy asked him if a general who gave an honorable discharge to a Communist, knowing he was a Communist, should be relieved of duty. Zwicker (who probably did not grasp the import of the question) said no.

Flushed with rage, McCarthy now lashed out: "Then, General, you should be removed from any command. Any man who has been given the honor of being promoted to general and who says 'I will protect another general who protected Communists' is not fit to wear that uniform, General."[28]

Roy Cohn, who was sitting beside McCarthy, later said, "He should never have uttered those words." Zwicker later swore to his superiors that he remembered that McCarthy had called him a "Fifth Amendment general" because of his reluctance to testify, and accused him of shielding traitors and Communists.[29] Secretary Stevens gave the affidavit to the press, although the official transcript of the hearings, which Senator John McClellan had checked with official Senate stenographers to establish as complete and accurate, revealed no such exchange. But anti-McCarthy newspapers had a field day. They quoted McCarthy as saying that Zwicker, a war hero and intrepid field commander during the battle of the Bulge, was unfit to wear a uniform (ignoring the fact that McCarthy had posed the issue as part of a series of hypothetical questions). The *New York Post* editorialized, "General Zwicker endured McCarthy's vilest abuses to uphold the fortress of executive authority in the Pentagon."[30]

When the news reached the White House, Eisenhower was livid. Yet this was actually good news for the administration. The ground was now cleared for taking their case to the other members of PSI, who were amazed and embarrassed by this latest flap (none of them had been present). The plan was now to shift attention away from the Army, loyalty boards, and Peress's promotion and onto McCarthy and Cohn.

The White House now had a powerful and a convincing weapon on its side: John Adams's painstakingly arranged, thirty-four-page report on his and Stevens's dealings with McCarthy's staff, listing every separate occasion on which Cohn, McCarthy, or Frank Carr made requests on the behalf of David Schine. At first glance, it looked pretty damning. Adams showed how each demand for hearings and subpoenas had been preceded by Cohn's importunations regarding David Schine. The final incident was on February 16, when Frank Carr had telephoned John G. Adams to ask Zwicker to appear before the committee. Adams expressed his worry that this might help to undermine public confidence in the Army's security procedures, just as the Fort Monmouth case had. Carr then told him that "if the Army would be reasonable, probably the committee would be reasonable." Adams asked him what that was supposed to mean. According to the transcript, Carr answered: "If the Army would only do all that had been suggested of it, the Army's problems would be at an end."[31] Adams assumed, and readers were supposed to assume, that Carr was referring to David Schine; however, that was left unstated, and a less suspicious reader might wonder if something else was being referred to: letting McCarthy talk to the Army's security board members and seeing the relevant documents on Peress as well as Fort Monmouth.

In any case, Adams leaked the document to reporters from a trio of anti-McCarthy papers: the *Washington Post*, the *Baltimore Sun*, and the *New York Herald-Tribune*. As the first hint of what was to come crept out to the public, the Eisenhower forces were ready to unleash it on the Hill.

They found Senate Democrats interested but reserved. As one former White House aide put it, "They opposed McCarthy but they also wanted Republican blood on the floor."[32] However much they hated Joe McCarthy, they were not going to make the first move. Then Stevens and Adams approached Dirksen and Mundt. They were willing to see Cohn removed, but noncommittal on reining in McCarthy himself. It was not until the Pentagon spoke to Charles Potter on March 8 that they realized they had their man.

Charles Potter had been elected to the Senate in 1952. He was a conspicuous figure in the corridors of the Senate, since he had to make his way along without any legs: they had been blown off during fighting in the Ardennes in 1944—not far, in fact, from the site of the Malmédy massacre. Mild-mannered, balding, and bespectacled, he looked more like the popular television character Mister Peepers than a war hero. The White House considered him "weak" but with "decent instincts," and believed they could turn him to their purpose. When Secretary of Defense Charles Wilson showed Potter the Army's chronology on Schine, detailing when and how Cohn had tried to pressure Stevens into giving Schine preferential treatment, Potter immediately agreed that Cohn had to go.[33] He hastened to show it around to other Republicans in the Senate and to beard McCarthy in his throne room.

When Potter presented it to McCarthy, however, McCarthy became enraged. "It's blackmail," he told Potter. "The Army wants to stop digging out Communists. The report is not true." Potter pointed out that many of the calls between Cohn, McCarthy, and Stevens had been monitored, that the report detailed forty-four specific instances of "unusual activity" on Shine's behalf, and often quoted McCarthy's conversations with Secretary Stevens word for word. McCarthy pleaded, "If I get rid of Roy it would be the greatest victory the Communists have scored up to now. He's indispensable."[34] As Potter left, he noticed a framed motto over McCarthy's desk:

> Oh God, don't let me weaken. Help me to continue on. And when I go down, let me go down like an oak tree felled by a woodsman's ax.

That moment was coming sooner than anyone thought. Arthur Krock's column in the *New York Times* of February 28, 1954, began the countdown. Krock, an intimate of Eisenhower, detailed how the Army-McCarthy conflict was injuring the Republican Party. He revealed that the consensus in PSI and the Senate was that Cohn had to be dismissed and that McCarthy himself had to be curbed, even disciplined. Krock quoted Edmund Burke's advice: "Cure the condition by removing the cause."[35] On March 3, Eisenhower mildly rebuked the senator from Wisconsin (not by name), and McCarthy let him, Zwicker, and his critics have it with both barrels. Willard Edwards of the *Chicago Tribune* warned him not to issue the reply. McCarthy ignored him. "It was all downhill for him from that day," Edwards later remembered.[36]

Potter and Wilson had met on March 8. That next day, Ralph Flanders, Republican senator from Vermont, went to the Senate to deliver a sneering, stinging attack on "the junior senator from Wisconsin." "He dons his warpaint," Flanders went on in his clipped, nasal New England accent, "he emits his war whoops. He goes forth to battle and proudly returns with the scalp of a pink Army dentist." He accused McCarthy of dividing the Republican Party and running a one-man party; "its name is McCarthyism." On March 10, the same day that the Pentagon sent the Adams memo to Potter,

Eisenhower in his press conference singled out Flanders for praise and for attacking what Ike called "the divisive elements" in the Republican Party. McCarthy tried to laugh it off, calling Flanders "one of the finest old gentlemen I've ever met" and pointing out that the Vermonter had voted against more Republican legislation than almost any other Republican in the Senate. It did no good. The tide was now running against him.

It had been raised further by a program that aired the previous night on CBS's *See It Now*, called "Report on Senator McCarthy." Host Edward R. Murrow had spent two months putting together what he described as a "report on Senator Joseph R. McCarthy." Murrow and his staff had meticulously cut and edited film clips to put McCarthy in the worst possible light: The result was appalling. Murrow showed him belching, picking his nose, ignoring or berating witnesses in front of his committee (there were no clips of McCarthy being restrained or business-like), and giggling at his own "Alger—I mean Adlai" remark. At times he seemed to sway in front of the camera, obviously under the influence of alcohol. Murrow threw in his own clipped and sardonic commentary: "Upon what meat does Senator McCarthy feed?" he asked. The answer: "Two of the staples of his diet are the investigations (protected by immunity) and the half-truth." McCarthy's antics, Murrow insisted, "have caused alarm and dismay amongst our allies abroad and given considerable comfort to our enemies. . . . We cannot defend freedom abroad by deserting it at home."

Despite CBS's pretensions, *See It Now* was not a report at all but a full-scale assault, employing exactly the same techniques of "partial truth and innuendo" that critics accused McCarthy of using. McCarthy's most consistently hostile Catholic critic, John Cogley of *Commonweal*, sharply attacked Murrow and his producers for their distorted summary and selective use of video clips. "A totally different selection of film," he pointed out, "would turn Senator McCarthy into a man on a shining white steed—infinitely reasonable, burdened with the onus of single-handedly cleaning out subversives in the face of violent criticism." Cogley warned that the power of television to project a single, simplistic view in defiance of a more complicated truth was not a very encouraging sign for the future. "Television is dynamite," he concluded. "Combined with selectivity it could explode in any person's or any group's face." He and an anti-McCarthy critic in the *Saturday Review* agreed that it was not a proud moment for television journalism.[37]

However, most liberals loved it, and Murrow became a hero. At last someone was willing to expose Joe McCarthy publicly for who he was, however crudely. The audience response was overwhelmingly favorable: calls to the CBS switchboard ran almost 15 to 1 in support of Murrow. The network called it the heaviest favorable response to any *See It Now* broadcast.[38]

McCarthy hit back as best he could in a radio broadcast, calling Murrow an "extreme left-wing bleeding heart" with links to Moscow University's summer exchange student program, but no one was listening anymore. From then on, everything McCarthy said was automatically a lie and everything his opponents said was automatically true.

Murrow had concluded that evening with the admonition, "This is not the time for men who oppose Senator McCarthy to keep silent." That was now the last thing they were doing. The condemnations were pouring out thick and fast. Doctor (soon to be Bishop) James Pike called McCarthyism "the new tyranny," and Reverend Francis Sayres called it "only another of the devil's disguises." Walter Lippmann wrote that McCarthy "has netted no spies but only a few minnows at the cost of terrible injustice . . . and the filling of our air with poison and stink." The editor of the Wisconsin *Sauk-Prairie Star* called McCarthy a "menace" to the country and the Republican Party and organized a Joe Must Go campaign to recall him from the Senate.[39]

Defenders of McCarthy were increasingly dismissed as reactionaries, morons, or worse. One reporter even claimed to observe that the pro-Murrow mail at the CBS studios was invariably neatly typed and signed, while pro-McCarthy letters were "scrawled and abusive." When the *Saturday Review* ran the article that criticized Murrow's half-truth and innuendo methods even though it applauded his aims, the editors decided to publish it with a disclaimer. The liberal line on McCarthy was hardening. McCarthy was evil, pure and simple; any criticism of the campaign against him, however justified, was not going to be permitted.

Early on the morning of Friday, March 12, Roy Cohn was awakened by someone pounding on the door. It was his friend Anthony Lewis, then a reporter for the *Washington Daily News*, who presented him with a copy of the *New York Times* bearing the emblazoned headline:

ARMY CHARGES MCCARTHY AND COHN
THREATENED IT IN TRYING TO OBTAIN PREFERRED
TREATMENT FOR SCHINE

The Pentagon had released its report on the Schine controversy, charging that McCarthy and his staff had tried to destroy the Army's reputation for their own private purposes. Cohn immediately called Lawrence Spivak of *Meet the Press* and demanded he be put on the air to tell his side of the story. He called the accusation "ridiculous on the face of it." Far from being threatened or blackmailed, the Army and Stevens had always cooperated in their investigations, he said. He also insisted that he had never tried to get special favors for Schine at any time.

Cohn passed around memos showing how Secretary Stevens had volunteered to help the committee and to assist Schine. The campaign against him did not even break stride. The Democrats on PSI, backed by Charles Potter, had now seized the initiative and were overruling McCarthy, Mundt, and Dirksen on every point. Two particularly detested Cohn and wanted him gone. One was Stuart Symington, the handsome and self-assured freshman from Missouri, who ripped into Cohn for appearing on *Meet the Press* without the subcommittee's permission. He had earlier clashed with Cohn over the Annie Moss case (see Appendix B) and had warned him several times that he was getting in over his head, that he would be, in Symington's words, "caught in the crossfire." Symington's real target was McCarthy, whom he considered a phony and a blowhard—not unlike many other people's view of Symington himself.

The other was Democrat John McClellan, PSI's chief representative of the Senate's southern old guard. Lean, tough, and wiry at age fifty-eight, he respected McCarthy's energy in pursuing "Commo-nists," as he pronounced it. But he had been disgusted by Cohn's and Schine's antics ever since the Information Bureau investigations.[40] He now used his position as ranking minority member to force the issue and, after a protracted series of gut-wrenching negotiations, McCarthy finally had to yield.

On March 16 at 10:30 in the morning the committee met in secret executive session. What happened there has remained a mystery until now.[41] McCarthy spoke first, vehemently denying that he or any members of his staff had ever pressured the Army to do anything for David Schine. However, he acknowledged that he would certainly have to be a material witness in any investigation of the Army charges, and so he agreed to hand over the reins of the committee to the next-ranking Republican, Karl Mundt of South Dakota. The transcript of the proceedings reveals that Mundt and Everett Dirksen were very anxious that the issue be handled as unobtrusively as possible; like their senior Republican colleagues, they sensed that the situation could blow up in everyone's face. Dirksen proposed as a compromise that Cohn quit, Adams quit, and that be the end of the matter.

Symington countered that this was now a matter that went beyond just Cohn and Adams. "I think the morale in the Army and the Air Force has been badly hurt," he said, and only a full, complete investigation would finally dispel any doubts. Mundt urged passing "this very tasteless job" on to another committee, such as Armed Services, while McClellan and Potter strongly argued that if the Army's allegations against Cohn were true, "then the committee has a responsibility to clean its own house." In the end, McCarthy and the others agreed, and by a unanimous vote (Mundt, the one remaining doubter, voting "present") PSI decided to investigate the Army's charges against its own chairman.

Two ticklish questions remained. The first was hiring a legal counsel to conduct the investigation—since both Cohn and Carr were implicated in the Army's accusations, they would have to recuse themselves. Robert Morris's name came up, but everyone agreed he was too close to McCarthy personally to be a good choice. McCarthy himself proposed Bobby Kennedy, a choice that Stuart Symington strongly seconded. However, Mundt's view prevailed—that the chief counsel should be someone completely outside the committee ("you can see what Bob's position is" having to pass judgement on former fellow staffers, he reminded his colleagues). The man they eventually hired was Ray Jenkins, a tough, taciturn criminal lawyer from Tennessee whom Dirksen had met on a trip to Knoxville and who, as Roy Cohn remembered, was supposed to have "tried some 500 cases without once losing a client to the electric chair."[42] Jenkins was a Taftite Republican but a Washington outsider; afterward all sides agreed that Jenkins had been an impartial, if somewhat bleak, overseer of the proceedings.

The other issue was whether the proceedings should be public and televised, or behind closed doors. Here Senator McClellan held a card he did not show his colleagues. He and minority leader Lyndon Johnson had secretly discussed the possibility of televising the hearings, with Johnson urging him to turn the cameras and lights on McCarthy and his team. Johnson believed that by focusing public attention on the man himself, McCarthy's credibility would crumble under the merciless glare of television, and the man who had bedeviled Democrats for the past four years would finally come a cropper.[43]

McClellan, however, simply presented the issue in terms of the need to reassure the public that the PSI could take care of its own problems without fear of scrutiny or favor. "The charges are out in the open, and open to the public," the Arkansas senator argued. "I think the public will react with a measure of suspicion if we start holding executive sessions to take testimony." Again, Karl Mundt had his doubts. "I don't like to see this thing get to be a public brawl." He worried about the presence of all those television lights and newsreel cameras, which show only edited excerpts instead of the entire proceedings—"this is something where the country should have the full picture and get the full text and no expurgations." Mundt was also concerned that public hearings would tend to drag things out, and while McClellan and Potter assumed things could be cleared up inside of a week, Mundt predicted it would take ten days to two weeks at a minimum (in fact, the hearings took more than a month).

However, McClellan's proposal carried the day. He told Mundt, "I am not here, brother, to defend the army. If they have dirty linen in this thing, or anything else . . . God knows we had better clean it up now." But his argument was the same as the one against handing it on to someone else: "I think this is our baby, and it is our linen, and we have got to wash it, and I favor washing it in public."[44]

Not seeing the trap, McCarthy enthusiastically agreed. He was genuinely convinced that any fair investigation would pin the blame on the Army, not on him. As he told his colleagues, he and Robert Stevens had had several lunches together in the presence of other witnesses, including prominent newsmen. *They* would be able to dispel any notion that undue pressure had been brought to bear. He did urge his colleagues to examine all the evidence and question the witnesses before deciding to proceed. If the committee decided that his staff members had acted improperly, then Cohn and Carr would have to go. But that was not going to happen, McCarthy believed. And so it was McCarthy rather than McClellan who offered the final motion to make the hearings open to the public, to which the other members of PSI consented unanimously.

Afterward, the senator stepped outside to announce their decision and talk to reporters. McCarthy was beaming and confident, almost ebullient. However, the trap was set; it would only require a major McCarthy misstep to spring it.

Chapter 14

McCarthy Against Himself

We are led to Believe a Lie
When we see With not Thro' the Eye.

—William Blake, *The Everlasting Gospel* (1818)

I f you lived in New York City and owned a television set and happened to be home in the late morning of April 22, 1954, you had a choice of what to watch. You could tune in to Channel 2 and catch Arthur Godfrey at 10:00, or *Ding Dong School* on Channel 4. You could also catch the Senate Subcommittee on Juvenile Delinquency, which was holding hearings in the Manhattan Federal Court House at 10:30. Or, if juvenile delinquents and social workers seemed too tame, you could stay on Channel 4, or Channel 5, or 7, and watch the first day of the Army-McCarthy hearings, broadcast live from Washington on ABC, NBC, and the Du Mont television networks.[1]

There was nothing new about televised hearings. What was new was the public buildup and the political drama that surrounded this one. For millions of Americans, it was an opportunity to finally see the man who, in Walter Lippmann's words, had become "a national obsession"— or more accurately, a Washington obsession. From their television screens, they were able to see Joe McCarthy in the flesh, and see him destroy himself. To this day many, perhaps most, of the people who watched have no idea what the hearings were

258

actually about. All they knew was that Joe McCarthy behaved in a way that seemed to confirm everything liberals had been saying about him for four years. A bully, a demagogue. A liar. A gargoyle of evil.

Few bothered to notice that this time Joe McCarthy was not the accuser but the accused. The new PSI had set itself the sensitive task of finding out whether McCarthy and his staff had unfairly pressured the Army to give special treatment and privileges to David Schine at Fort Dix (and who had since been transferred to Georgia), as the Pentagon charged, and whether they had used the threat of further investigations to bend the Pentagon to their will. McCarthy had been forced to step aside not just as PSI's chairman but as a committee member during the investigation (Henry Dworshak of Idaho, a sometime McCarthy ally, took his place). But his personality would dominate the proceedings from the first day and would eventually expand until it seemed to fill the television screen.

All the people and all the techniques McCarthy had used to boost himself into national prominence were now useless to help him. Republican allies like Mundt and Dirksen proved wavering and impotent. His allies in the press fought in vain to counter the disastrous images that appeared on the television screen. His "Kennedy connection" now belonged to the opposition. The Democrats had taken Robert Kennedy on as their minority counsel, and although he was still sympathetic toward his old boss, he was prepared to go to the limit to destroy Roy Cohn (at one point the pair almost got into a fistfight in the hearing room). The acute physical sense of embarrassment and discomfort other senators felt in dealing with him directly, which had kept them from trying to rein him in until now, suddenly disappeared under the glare of the public eye. They had finally found a forum in which they could strike back at McCarthy by challenging and cross-examining his witnesses, rebutting his arguments, and overruling his objections. By contrast, his standard responses—flares of temper, angry insinuations about a person's bias or even loyalty—served to goad them on.

But it was television—which he had helped to pioneer as an effective way to broadcast congressional hearings—that finally did him in. On television, his skill in probing and exposing hostile witnesses made him look like a bully. His sardonic sense of humor looked heavy-handed, his invocation of the Communist threat stilted and out of place. His ability to simplify issues, reduce them to flesh-and-blood terms that his audiences could feel in their guts, as with the Bob Smith speech, sounded tinny and melodramatic. At one point, he even exclaimed to John Adams, "We caught you red-handed!" as if he were in a Western or a Dick Tracy episode. Yet he could not control himself once the searching, restless, and relentless attention of the camera's eye was on him. As James Reston noted, "When the red lights of those TV cameras go on, the Senator automatically produces sound." Like an addict, McCarthy was drawn irresistibly to the medium that would destroy him.[2]

The most insightful commentator on the effect of television on the Army-McCarthy hearings was, curiously enough, the *New Republic*'s Michael Straight. He realized at once that the real issue would not be the merits of the case but which actor "possessed enough power to take command of the stage."[3] For all his heavy-handed bluster and upstaging interruptions, that would not be McCarthy. It was instead the Army's chief counsel, Joseph N. Welch. A longtime partner of the old-line Boston firm of Hale and Dorr, Welch hid a burgeoning ego and a cold instinct for the jugular behind a facade of old-fashioned courtesy and elegance. Decked out in three-piece tweed suits and bow ties, he was twice the lawyer McCarthy was and understood the visual impact of television far better.

Welch showed his acumen on the very first day as the committee met in the third floor Senate Caucus Room, in front of four hundred spectators, over one hundred reporters, and a dozen whirring television cameras. Suddenly, just as chairman Mundt was about to call the session to order, in marched an impressive array of top military brass, of generals and colonels in full array, to take their seats. McCarthy's claim that the "Pentagon politicians" attacking him did not have the support of the real men in uniform was visually and dramatically belied by the row of glittering medals and stern faces seated behind Welch and Secretary Stevens at the head table.[4] The television camera teaches us to see with, not through, the eye. Its overpowering superficiality left McCarthy floundering from the start.

Welch also understood another important aspect of television: its bias toward intimacy, not public declamation. Its real power is not in electrifying the masses but in addressing the individual; paradoxically, you can command more attention by lowering your voice than raising it. Throughout the proceedings, in Michael Straight's words, "Welch seemed to be conversing respectfully with one individual, and so he gained the audience's devotion to the end."[5]

Of course, Welch's skills did not operate in a vacuum. For a long time the American "public sphere," that universe of discourse among public officials and journalists and intellectuals and politicians and those whose living is words and images affecting civic life, had been resolutely anti-McCarthy. In the hearings every mistake his opponents made would be forgotten and buried; every mistake he made would be magnified and made representative of McCarthy and McCarthyism. Once his opponents realized that McCarthy no longer enjoyed the support of his own party, they were free to bring the full weight of their odium to bear. Their long nightmare of four years of being made to look negligent, even complicit, in dealing with the Soviet threat would soon be over.

Yet almost without knowing it, their attacks had also elevated him to the status of an icon. Repentant ex–New Dealer Raymond Moley had warned them about the dangers of this back in 1953. He wrote that McCarthy was the product of the fright and anger of "a deceived and injured public," who had been lied to regarding the Soviet threat both at home and abroad. Despite the hysterical protestations to the contrary, Moley doubted whether any innocent person had ever been actually harmed by McCarthy's investigations—except, Moley wrote, "those who entered the Communist party before 1939," and "I do not think we should bemoan the fact that their foolishness has found them out." But, he warned, "to elevate 'McCarthyism' to a national or international issue does nothing to diminish him." By doing so, "his enemies may make him think he is the savior of the nation."[6]

And in fact, he did. The drumbeat of attacks fed McCarthy's capacity for self-dramatization, even martyrdom. "This committee," he exclaimed at one point during the Army hearings, "this committee's activities may well determine whether this nation will live or die!"[7] He had come to identify his own fate with that of the country: to yield, to compromise, even to behave sensibly, would be to let down not just his supporters but the nation. He was confident that truth was on his side. His inner circle still believed in him. But then even they slowly began to realize that this was the end of the road.

One of the newer additions was William F. Buckley, Jr. Buckley had made a splash in conservative circles with his *God and Man at Yale* in 1951 and had been hired by the staunch McCarthy defenders at the *American Mercury*. He and a lawyer friend, L. Brent Bozell, had decided to undertake a detailed defense of McCarthy's record as an anti-Communist crusader and worked closely with McCarthy on the book that would eventually become *McCarthy and His Enemies*. McCarthy gave them access to materials and files, but when they tried to get interested in the larger political and ideological issues being raised in his defense, he seemed unable to focus any longer. "You could see his attention wander," Buckley later recalled. Buckley and Bozell also faced the resistance of McCarthy's wife, Jean Kerr. She wanted McCarthy not to endorse the publication of *McCarthy and His Enemies* because she thought it too critical of some of his actions, such as the Marshall speech; Joe himself was inclined to let the chips fall where they might. But he confessed to Buckley's sister Patricia that he really didn't understand the book; its themes were too intellectual for him.[8]

Buckley and Bozell came to admire McCarthy's charm, his down-to-earth affability, and flashes of his anti-Communist zeal, even when it took bizarre forms. Buckley stayed over at McCarthy's house one evening, and was awakened at one o'clock in the morning by his host in a bathrobe and waving a map of red China, which he laid out on the floor. If American bombers could cut the

Shanghai railway line, McCarthy said, jabbing the map with an emphatic fore-finger, then their supply lines into Korea would be cut and then. . . . But then Buckley began to doubt whether McCarthy was still focused on the issue that brought him to public notice, that of domestic communism. When the Associated Press interviewed him in early April, McCarthy appeared to rely on Roy Cohn to feed him his answers. McCarthy seemed, Buckley said later, "drugged by the velocity of events" and more preoccupied with himself and his own problems than with the cause he had come to represent. McCarthy's congressional staffers, like Don Surine and Ed Nellor, believed his campaign against the Army was a huge mistake. "You can't beat these people," Nellor pleaded with him. But McCarthy was no longer listening. He was on the road Cohn and Schine had set for him, and he would follow it down to the end.[9]

Physically he was in terrible shape. He was suffering from constant stomach complaints and sinus headaches, which tortured him throughout the hearings. Then there was the drinking. Alcohol has always been the proper province of the unhappy Irish male. As George Bernard Shaw explained, "An Irishman's imagination never lets him alone, never convinces him, never satisfies him. . . . It makes him so that he can't face reality . . . without whisky."[10] What had been a shot of bourbon at work was now a tumbler. Where he had once relied on a surreptitious drink to get through a public speech, he now needed several to get through a morning of normal work. His schedule during the Army-McCarthy proceedings only made things worse. When the hearings adjourned at 4:30 P.M. he would gather with his aides for several hours, then eat a hurried dinner before returning to the office to look at more files and plan strategy for the next day. While Carr, Cohn, and the others would go home at eleven and Jean went to bed, McCarthy would often sit up all night, shifting papers and sipping straight vodka until 6:00 A.M. After a brief catnap, he would be off to a breakfast meeting and then, incredibly, be back before the committee and the television cameras.

Under these circumstances, it is no wonder McCarthy performed as badly as he did or lost track of reality. He now took seriously the many death threats he was receiving, whereas before he had laughed them off. Two bodyguards followed him in and out of the hearing room every day. He began carrying a gun. When the Republican National Committee chairman visited him at home, McCarthy came to the door with it cradled in his hand.* The man confided to

---

*Actually this was more than just paranoia. J. Edgar Hoover had received reliable information that the same Puerto Rican nationalists who had tried to assassinate Harry Truman in November 1948 and later fired shots in the Capitol were targeting McCarthy. He passed the information on to Joe. The gun and bodyguards were the result. Oshinsky, *Conspiracy Immerse*, 412, n. 2.

Richard Nixon that he thought McCarthy was not ready to face a single day of hearings before the camera, let alone several weeks.

There is no evidence that McCarthy was ever an abusive or violent drunk. He always treated his wife, and later her mother when she moved in with them in their house on Capitol Hill, with a docile and doting kindness and old-fashioned courtesy. The ex-Marine never permitted himself to use four-letter words or repeat off-color jokes in front of any woman. On the surface, the drinking fed his natural garrulousness and good humor. An observer noted that McCarthy's favorite gesture after he had a few drinks was to haul out the telephone and start calling friends, colleagues, and reporters, regardless of the hour or the distance. However, the openness and hilarity were on the surface. McCarthy was like other so-called closet drinkers who rely on alcohol to quell an ever-present sense of insecurity. He needed it now to gird himself for an increasingly steep upward battle with his enemies. He believed it steadied him. In fact, it made him less steady. The protection and shelter it had once provided had now became a tomb.

"He was always alone." That was what Edwin Bayley had noticed about McCarthy as a teenager, and in a profound sense he never changed. McCarthy had always been a loner; his status as an outsider, a pariah, was largely self-inflicted. Other politicians of the same generation who suffered from the same loneliness, like Lyndon Johnson and Richard Nixon—the solitude of a person who has severed old ties in order to enter the hard, charmed circle of public life—either adjusted to the strain or found a substitute in the exercise of power. McCarthy never did. The very nature of the destiny he had chosen—to be the people's tribune, forever despised by those he professed to despise in turn—now came back to haunt him.

Who was he? A man made miserable by what he had become and what was being said about him. To insiders in Washington and to millions on television, he was an ogre. In Herblock's cartoons, he was a hairy, unshaven animal crouching in the shadows who fed on the blood and pain of others. The truth was that he was the opposite of an ogre. Nothing mattered more to him than to be liked and admired. His appetite was not for blood or scalps but the battle itself. Like the prime minister in Anthony Trollope's novel, he did not weigh every blow like deliberate prizefighters do, but "struck right and left and straightforward with a readiness engendered by practice, and in his fury might have murdered his antagonist before he was aware that he had drawn blood."[11] McCarthy prided himself on not bearing a grudge after the fight. It did not occur to him that others did not the feel the same—and that they considered themselves, and their friends and their cause, the truly abused parties.

For all his outrageous behavior, his martyr's complex, his self-destructive impulses and gestures, thus far he had escaped genuine ruin. His enemies

263

had had him on the ropes three times—in the Tydings hearings, the Benton flap, and the Hennings report—and each time he had survived. Now Cohn, Schine, and their antics had given his enemies their best opportunity. For them, it was payback time. In the end, the forces aligned against him were more than he reckoned for and more than he could measure.

Meanwhile, the Army had taken stock of their opponent before the committee met. Staffers had prepared separate background files on both Cohn and McCarthy, which are now declassified and make fascinating reading. Cohn's file included his records as a member of the National Guard and his draft deferment (about which more later), his law school records from Columbia, and even a copy of his birth certificate. McCarthy's included published derogatory material such as the Wisconsin *Progressive*'s pamphlet entitled *McCarthy: A Documented Record*, *New Republic*'s special reprint on McCarthy's financial affairs (which rehearsed the same old charges about Pepsi-Cola and Lustron), as well as Hank Greenspun's columns from the *Las Vegas Sun* alleging McCarthy's homosexuality. However, a lawyer they spoke to who had served on Benton's team advised them against pursuing the last line of inquiry, since, given the large number of reporters and columnists looking for dirt on the senator, "he thinks something would have been turned up by now if there was any real substance behind them." He also recommended not challenging McCarthy on the issue he was most identified with, communism in government, and for a very revealing reason: "The attorney feels it is almost impossible to counter McCarthy effectively on the issue of kicking Communists out of Government, because he generally has some basis, no matter how slight, for his claim of Communist connection."[12]

Another anonymous informant, however, gave them more substantive help.[13] He was evidently a friend of Roy Cohn's father, with inside information on how the son was organizing his defense, so that he could give Welch and his legal team a preview of their opponent's playbook. He warned them that Cohn, McCarthy, and Carr would make John Adams, not Secretary Stevens, their principal target. They would accuse him of offering to open up the Air Force and Navy for their investigation in exchange for laying off the Army and offer written evidence to prove it. They were also going to try to suggest that Adams was fishing for a job offer with the Schine hotel chain once he left government service. The informant urged them to get a "friendly" senator, meaning Jackson, Symington, McClellan, or Potter, to pull a copy of Cohn's tax returns, and that they find out the real story on how David Schine got his draft deferment. He also urged them to find a Jewish aide for Welch in order to dispel any notion that the Army was "trying to salt away two Jewish lads," meaning Cohn and Schine.

Then he made a final suggestion. If McCarthy or Cohn presented any typewritten memos to back up their claims against Adams or Stevens, the Welch team should subpoena the stenographers and their notes as well as the typists who made the copies. They should also check the watermarks on the memos, to make sure that they were typed as part of the same batch of papers as other PSI memos, and inquire whether they were typed on PSI typewriters. The results, he evidently believed, could be revealing.

On the first and second days of the hearings the Pentagon laid out its case against McCarthy. It was on the face of it implausible: that McCarthy had pursued his investigation of the Army for the sole purpose of forcing Stevens, Adams, and Assistant Secretary of the Army Struve Hensel to give David Schine special treatment at boot camp. Anyone who knew McCarthy knew that no personal concerns could have halted him if he believed he was on the trail of lax security and hidden Communists. On the other hand, any sensible person would also have realized that the confluence of those two issues, of the Fort Monmouth–Major Peress investigations and David Schine's status in the Army, created at least the appearance of impropriety, if not a conflict of interest.

However, McCarthy was not going to be sensible and there was no one in a position to advise him otherwise. At the last minute, Roy Cohn had made one final, and disastrous, suggestion to McCarthy and Carr. Since they were all lawyers, he argued, they should dispense with hiring a defense counsel, and instead each would serve as his own counsel in any forays with either Jenkins or Welch.[14] How typical of Cohn to recommend so shortsighted and arrogant an approach to the proceedings, and how typical of McCarthy to agree to it! Left to his own devices, McCarthy unveiled his strategy in the first fifteen minutes of the hearing: to use a steady stream of objections (his famous "point of order") to disrupt the proceedings, question the motives of witnesses, and engage in the sort of hard-hitting cross-examining techniques any defense attorney would use. But he forgot that it was being broadcast to more than twenty million people. They assumed it to be a typical, rather than extraordinary, role for the PSI chairman, and, like television audiences ever since, assumed that the image they saw on their television screens was the man he really was.

McCarthy appeared sullen and flabby. Since his heavy beard gave him an unattractive afternoon shadow (which cartoonists like Herblock exploited), he had himself shaved again every day after lunch. It didn't help. Michael Straight described his "freshly shaved face caked with a cream-colored makeup which from nearby gave a startling aspect to his jowls." When McCarthy leaned across the table to speak, "a roll of flesh beneath his black eyebrows came down over his upper eyelids, making slits of his eyes, and giving his face an almost Satanic look."[15]

Thus handicapped, McCarthy made his first sortie with the first witness against him, General Miles Reber. Reber testified that he had been on the receiving end of solicitations on David Schine's behalf as early as July 1953, from both Senator McCarthy and Roy Cohn. McCarthy interrupted. Did the general know, he casually asked, that his brother Sam Reber had been acting high commissioner in Germany during the Cohn-Schine overseas tour in 1953 and that he and Cohn had repeatedly clashed? And did he know his brother had had to resign as a security risk soon afterward? Reber angrily denied any knowledge of this and denied that it in any way biased his testimony. The other members of the committee shifted in their chairs. It was going to be a long road.

Secretary Stevens then took the stand. He reviewed the highlights of Cohn's efforts to help David Schine and insisted that "there exists no record that matches the persistent, tireless effort to obtain special privileges for this man." He called McCarthy's effort to blackmail the Pentagon "a perversion of power."[16] But he also revealed that the Pentagon had secretly recorded all its telephone calls with McCarthy and his staff, by keeping a stenographer listening in on an extension, as well as with other senators on the committee. McCarthy was aghast: "It's one of the most indecent and dishonest things I've ever heard," he raged. The audience just laughed at his discomfiture. Whatever violation of confidentiality or invasion of privacy the monitored calls represented troubled no one. The victim, after all, was Joe McCarthy.[17]

To make the Army's case stick, Stevens had to prove three things: first, that McCarthy and Cohn had relentlessly hounded him to give Schine special treatment; second, that they had used the threat of investigations as a lever to force him to do so; third, that Stevens and his assistants had fought hard to deflect or resist this blackmail until finally they were forced to go public. But over the course of days, under the steady, relentless grilling by counsel Ray Jenkins, the substance of those claims began to wear away. Jenkins established that McCarthy's investigations at Fort Monmouth had not been prompted by ulterior motives and that even the Pentagon had agreed that the probe had been "vindicated" by their results. As observer Straight put it, Jenkins "affirmed that McCarthy was the man who went in with a hose . . . while the Army was puttering around with a watering can."[18] Stevens also had to admit that he had been more than willing to cooperate on many matters, including Fort Monmouth. Despite his claims about black-

mail, under direct questioning he couldn't remember many specific instances of this "persistent, tireless pressure." McCarthy summed up the gist
of his testimony this way:

> You make the charge one day that Frank Carr did something improper, and
> then you appear under oath and you say he did nothing. And then three days
> later you say, yes, maybe he said something, and maybe he didn't, and you
> don't know, and you think maybe he did, and maybe it was silence.

Michael Straight added, "McCarthy's manner was brutal; but his point was
perfectly fair." General Walter Bedell Smith also testified that he had received a telephone call from Cohn. Did he think it unusual or improper? No.
Any suggestion he was under pressure? None. The Army's case was starting
to look a little thin.[19]

Welch quickly acted to save the situation. He seized on a photograph
Cohn and McCarthy had entered into evidence showing Secretary Stevens
visiting David Schine at Fort Dix. If this meeting occurred at the height of the
tension between them, went their argument, then why were Stevens and
Schine looking so charming and friendly? Welch triumphantly presented to
the committee the original photo, which revealed a third figure standing to
their right, the camp commander, who had been cut from the McCarthy-
Cohn picture. The implication was clear to the audience in the room and on
television: McCarthy and his staff had doctored the evidence.

But in fact the picture had been already altered by *Army photographers*
when they sent the copy on to McCarthy staffer James Juliana for mounting
and public display. The missing portion changed nothing; it still clearly
showed Stevens and Schine beaming at each other in the same good spirits.
But the press began talking about the "faked" and "cropped" photograph and
nothing else. Welch, not the truth, had won.[20]

The same thing happened with the famous "purloined letter" on May 5.
To back up their claims about the need for an investigation at Fort Monmouth, McCarthy offered up a letter from the FBI warning Army officials
about various security risks on the base. Welch immediately shifted everyone's attention from the contents of the letter to its provenance. Where, he
demanded, did McCarthy get this confidential Army document? McCarthy
had to admit that it came from a source inside the Army but insisted it was a
genuine FBI report. Then someone brought in a statement from director
Hoover stating that the letter was not the original he had sent or even an
exact copy, since it did not bear his signature—although he did *not* say that
the contents had been altered or distorted from the original. Welch's claim
that the letter was "a carbon copy of precisely nothing" was false and misleading. But that was not what the press, or the television audience, under-

stood. They heard: *McCarthy and Cohn are using fake documents, just like they use fake photographs.*

But Welch had just started. With just the right amount of skepticism in his voice, he urged McCarthy to reveal the source of this "spurious" document. McCarthy refused. But as Welch continued to press him on it, he made McCarthy look as if he were hiding something—when in fact, as chairman Mundt pointed out "unhesitatingly and unequivocally," congressional investigators, like law enforcement officials (or for that matter, like reporters), were not required to reveal their sources. The press seized on this, too: *Mundt is saying McCarthy should have the same powers and immunities as the police.* All in all, a bad day for the McCarthy team.[21]

These sideshows enabled his enemies to maintain the offensive even when their own plays misfired. First, there was the inadvertent revelation that White House staffers had met with the attorney general to plan their strategy against McCarthy as early as January 21, and that it was not the Pentagon that ordered John Adams to draw up his chronology, but White House chief of staff Sherman Adams. Then it came out that the Pentagon had approached Senators Mundt and Dirksen and implied that if PSI did not stop its investigations and subpoenas, the Cohn-Schine imbroglio might be made public. The threat had been indirect, Dirksen and Mundt had to acknowledge, but it was obvious that Pentagon officials had been more willing to play hardball with Cohn than their tone of injured innocence implied.

Nor did John Adams help matters when he had to testify that far from being browbeaten into submission by the evil Cohn, he had had several meals with him and happily accepted tickets for the theater and prizefights at Madison Square Garden. "They were repaid," Adams tried to point out. Jenkins lost his temper. "Mr. Adams, you didn't pay back that money until you knew the jig was up!"[22]

The biggest mistake, and McCarthy's best opportunity to save the day, came when Senator Symington asked Adams for more details about the January 21 meeting in Brownell's office. Obviously uncomfortable, Adams had to announce that he had been ordered by the White House to say nothing further about the meeting or any other high-level meetings between administration officials. Symington and others, Democrats and Republicans alike, were stunned. "Does this mean we are going to get the information about low-level discussions but not about high-level discussions?" Symington asked incredulously. "I think maybe this testimony may be damaging to the Administration," said Scoop Jackson. "Those conversations have been coming in when they have been favorable. Now that they are unfavorable, are they to be excluded?"

Then, on May 17 Eisenhower sent a letter explaining his conduct and introducing a new phrase into the vocabulary of American politics: *executive privilege.* The letter asserted that it was "not in the public interest" for high officials of the executive branch to have their confidential conversations and communications made public knowledge. The doctrine of separation of powers required that these conversations be privileged, and "this principle must be maintained regardless of who would benefit by such disclosure." No one would answer questions about the nature of the January 21 meeting or why it had been called.

McCarthy told his colleagues, "I must admit that I am somewhat at a loss as to know what to do at the moment." That meeting in Brownell's office was obviously crucial but "at this point, I find out there is no way of ever getting at the truth. . . . The question is . . . how far can the President go? Who all can he order not to testify?" If the principle of executive privilege sticks, McCarthy warned, "then . . . any President can, by an executive order, keep the facts from the American people."[23] Everett Dirksen added, "I do not see how this committee sitting as investigators and judge and jurors could finally make a finding and make a report with the proof incomplete." McClellan and the Democrats agreed. The committee decided to adjourn into executive session to debate what to do.

Closeted together with their staffs and Joseph Welch, the senators seriously contemplated bringing the entire proceedings to a halt. Stuart Symington was the most vocal supporter of continuing but had to admit, "It is my personal opinion, for what it is worth, that an error was made this morning by the White House." McClellan too was miffed. He called Eisenhower's decision "one of the gravest mistakes this administration has made" and expressed his strong sympathy for McCarthy's position, as did Ray Jenkins. McClellan told the gathering, "I am pointing out that the effect of this order, this executive directive, stops these hearings. I mean for all practical purposes, you are plowing through, but you are never going to get the whole truth."

McCarthy did his best to enlist the fellow senator's sympathies. "The whole heart of my answer to the Army's charges," he explained, "is that somebody, some place, conspired, if I can use that word, or planned, call it what you like, to get us in just the hassle we are in now so we wouldn't be exposing Communists in places where it would be embarrassing to certain people in the government." Now he would be unable to question anyone who could substantiate that charge. "At this stage," he complained, "I just can't present my case." Symington urged the committee to go on: "Let's get as much of the truth as we can." McCarthy countered: "There ain't no such animal as part of the truth—we need the whole truth." The other senators agreed and decided to recess for a week in hopes that Eisenhower could be convinced to reverse his order.[24]

The senators weren't the only ones disturbed. An investigative reporter named Clark Mollenhoff was particularly shocked by the wording of the Eisenhower letter. "On the face of it, it seemed to extend the claim of executive privilege to prohibit Congress the access to *any* records or testimony that might involve communications within the executive branch. . . . The thought disturbed me." Both Mollenhoff and Edward Milne of the *Providence Journal* wrote stories that explained to their readers that neither Teapot Dome nor the Truman IRS scandals would ever have come to light if presidential officials had been able to invoke this sort of blanket "executive privilege." Later, with a Pulitzer prize to his credit, Mollenhoff published a book under the title *Washington Cover-Up*, which reminded the public that "a truly thorough investigation of the executive branch can be conducted only in the Congress." Eisenhower's sweeping assertion of executive privilege had seriously undermined that principle. "It seemed strange to me," Mollenhoff wrote,

> that this doctrine would be set forth in the administration of a President who would be regarded as one of the mildest Chief Executives. . . . I was not worried that President Eisenhower would try to use it as a tool for totalitarianism. But with this doctrine in force a man who was inclined toward totalitarian methods might readily administer the laws as he pleased.[25]

Henry Cabot Lodge, Eisenhower's campaign manager, was the next to discover that he, too, could not testify in the hearings because he was an executive adviser. In the end, the Eisenhower administration would invoke its new privilege in front of Congress more than forty times. Raoul Berger noted, "Thus, a claim born of desperation in 1954 had ripened by 1956 into a time-honored principle." In fact, as constitutional experts now agree, a long fuse was being lit that would eventually blow up in the face of American politics in Watergate.[26]

As Mollenhoff admitted, "Seldom had there been more right on the side of McCarthy, but," he added, "seldom had there been fewer people on his side." A clever man would have realized that here was an issue—executive privilege—that might rally his colleagues behind him. Just the day before Arthur Krock had pronounced judgment on the hearings to date: if their purpose was to supply evidence that McCarthy had unfairly pressured the Pentagon or that he pursued his investigations when the Army failed to help Schine, "the testimony so far has not supplied it." McCarthy still had 35 percent of the public on his side; at that point, eighteen days into the hearings, he still could have turned the tables and defied his critics.

But, characteristically, McCarthy blew it. Eisenhower's letter became jumbled with the other issues swirling through his alcohol-sodden brain, including the question of whether covert Communists might be exerting pressure within the White House. He made a wild statement when hearings resumed (McCarthy was now calling them "smearings"), denouncing "the past twenty or twenty-one years of treason" in government, which needlessly alienated Republicans. He maneuvered to keep Frank Carr from having to testify under oath, which reunited the committee's Democrats against him. Then, on May 27 Cohn took the stand. His testimony began the final rout of McCarthy's case.

What were the facts? Starting in mid-July 1953, McCarthy and Cohn first started worrying that David Schine might be drafted, and Cohn began to push for Schine getting a reserve commission in either the Air Force or the Navy.[27] Beginning in late October, Roy Cohn had made almost daily calls to Pentagon officials to try to prevent Schine's induction as an ordinary private. Cohn himself had twice managed to avoid being drafted, and he was determined to do the same for David. When that failed, he tried to get Schine a special assignment. At one point, he even suggested that Schine be assigned to West Point to look for subversive textbooks in the library. He had arranged for Schine's weekend passes from Fort Dix—to enable him to finish his work on the committee, Cohn and McCarthy averred; to enable him to party with Cohn at New York hot spots, critics like Drew Pearson charged.

Pearson published his first column on Private Schine's basic training in December. Unnamed soldiers told the *Washington Post* that officers avoided putting Schine on KP or latrine duty, and that he wore special mittens, special boots, a fur-lined hood, and a heavy down sleeping bag on bivouac (this also played into the "Schine-the-fairy" angle). Some said he had hinted to his fellow draftees that he was at Fort Dix as part of a special investigation. Years later, Schine denied all these stories. "I spent more time doing my duty and working harder than most any other soldier in basic training," he indignantly told an interviewer.[28] But it is very hard to imagine that the officers at Fort Dix did not know they had a VIP in their midst, or that Schine and Cohn did not make it crystal clear that any special favors would be appreciated.

There is also no doubt that McCarthy lent himself to Cohn's campaign in ways that clearly belied his own assertion that he had "an unbreakable rule" not to interfere in matters of military promotion or assignments on anyone's behalf. He had written a letter to Stevens in late December, complaining that Schine "would never have been drafted except that the extreme left wing writers such as [Drew] Pearson et al, started screaming about his case," and wondering whether Schine could have some less demanding assignment to fulfill his military duties. McCarthy added that "the course of this investigation will in absolutely no way be influenced by the Army's handling of the case of any individual"—just the sort of remark that would lead a nervous man like Stevens to conclude that the course of the investigation certainly *would* be influenced by what they did with Schine.[29] McCarthy had also called John Adams and the hapless General Reber on Schine's behalf.

However, evidence also suggests that the pressure on McCarthy to protect Schine did not come just from Roy Cohn. The Schine family chauffeur later remembered coming into the living room in their Florida home when Mrs. Schine was on the telephone. Obviously distraught, she was pouring angry and abusive language into the receiver, and did not even notice the chauffeur come in. She was screaming, "You tell Stevens he has to do this," and "You make sure that they do that," and issuing a series of dire threats if what she wanted wasn't done. The chauffeur testified he did not know who was on the other end—but it was his impression that it was Senator Joe McCarthy. The chauffeur beat a discreet retreat out of the room.[30]

Cohn's own efforts for David Schine went beyond telephone calls. He wined and dined Stevens and Adams, handed out theater tickets, and introduced them to the joys of Jewish cuisine while visiting New York restaurants. They no doubt appreciated the attention, however much they denied it later:

> COHN TO ADAMS: Didn't I get theater tickets for you that no one else could get? Didn't I arrange the little theater party at Sardi's at your request?
> ADAMS: You were always very gracious about that, you always were.
> COHN: And all this after I cursed you and abused you?

However, Cohn shattered his credibility with a countercharge at least as ridiculous: that the Pentagon had used Schine as a "hostage" to get them to stop their investigations. Probably Adams, Hensel, and the rest did realize Schine's induction could be an asset—"a lever," as Michael Straight saw it: "It was a poor lever among ordinary men, for the most Adams could threaten was to treat this private as any other private. But perhaps that was enough to a young man who by then had convinced himself and his friend that they stood above the law."[31]

Cohn did not limit himself to that. He accused Adams of drawing a map and offering up Air Force and Navy installations where homosexual officers could be found in order to steer suspicion away from the Army. He accused Adams of lobbying for a slot in a prestigious New York law firm when he left office. Cohn even released a packet of memos to back up his charges, and when the paper trail was insufficiently clear, Cohn simply made them up.

That, at least, was what Welch and the Pentagon's lawyers, following on the leads provided by their anonymous informant in New York, claimed and attempted to prove. Years later, Willard Edwards told historian Thomas Reeves that he had witnessed the whole thing, with Frank Carr supervising the typing of the counterfeit memos.[32] Still, there was no way to prove definitively that the memos were out-and-out forgeries. But the fact that neither Cohn, who claimed they were merely copies of vanished originals, nor Carr, who had signed six of them, nor McCarthy's secretary Margaret Driscoll, who typed them, could give a coherent account of their origin, makes the claim, and Edwards's account, convincing—as does the fact that the Army's informant knew enough about them to put Welch's investigators on the scent. If Cohn did make up the memos (probably when he learned the Army was planning to go public on the Schine case), and convinced Carr to put his signature on them, then both men faced certain ruin.

So did their boss, Joe McCarthy. McCarthy himself did not know what was happening, and no one has seriously accused him of being privy to the plot. But his closest and most trusted aide had almost certainly fabricated and backdated crucial evidence, and had left a trail of indiscretion and treachery from which McCarthy could not and would not disassociate himself. He believed that by going after Cohn, his enemies were actually going after him. This was true. But it blinded him to the fact that Cohn had misled him and that if Cohn went down for his sins, McCarthy would go down with him.

Cohn's own performance on the stand was, as he admitted a quarter-century later, "a disaster." McCarthy told him he was the worst witness he had heard in his life.[33] The unsympathetic McClellan pressed him on whether there was something "unusual" about his relationship with David Schine. Cohn shifted uneasily and said no. Then Welch had his sport with him. Earlier he had worked in a nasty comment about "pixies" and "fairies" having handled the cropped photograph, which raised gales of laughter from the audience and bewildered irritation from McCarthy. Now he began picking Cohn's story to pieces. Cohn had to fall back on replies like "I have no recollection" and "I don't recall the exact words I used" as the story of the falsified or backdated memos began to come out.

Meanwhile, Gallup polls brought in the bad news for McCarthy. During the first week in May, his unfavorable rating had risen to 49 percent. It was not true, as is often claimed, that the televised hearings undermined public support for McCarthy. His hard-core constituency was unfazed; in June it was still at 35 percent. Besides, very few Americans had seen the hearings. Most of United States west of the Mississippi did not receive any live coverage at all.[34] But the hearings, and the repetition of highlights in news programs and newsreels, did turn many Americans who had been neutral or casually interested observers into doubters and the doubters into McCarthy-haters. The hearings tipped the scales for Americans who were suspicious about Communist subversion but wondered why McCarthy's accusations (or at least the ones they heard about) always involved liberal Democrats and Republicans. And of course, the poll results heartened and mobilized liberals in both political parties.

This public shift regarding McCarthy had little to do with substantive issues, as James Reston pointed out on May 30: "The things that have hurt him and cost him support are his manner and his manners." People continued to debate the charges and countercharges, and the larger question of how to deal with Communists influence; "but on one thing there seems little division: the Senator from Wisconsin is a bad-mannered man."[35] One might call that judgment superficial. But its impact was real for all that.

On June 1 Ralph Flanders gave one of the nastiest, ugliest speeches ever made in the Senate Chamber. It was a full-scale attack on McCarthy on all fronts. It compared him to Hitler and Dennis the Menace and accused him of homosexuality and sowing dissension across the country: "Religion is set against religion, race against race," thanks to McCarthyism. Flanders spoke of Cohn's "passionate anxiety" to protect David Schine and insinuated that McCarthy had his own reasons to keep Schine's "services available." He urged the Mundt subcommittee to investigate the "real issue at stake" in the McCarthy-Cohn-Schine triangle. Flanders wound up by concluding, "Were the junior senator from Wisconsin in the pay of the Communists, he could not have done a better job for them."[36]

If McCarthy had made such a speech, he would certainly have been pilloried on every editorial page and newspaper column on the eastern seaboard. Instead, since it was an attack on the despised Joe McCarthy, there was a deafening silence (although this time there was no letter of congratulations from the White House). Pained and unhappy, McCarthy tried to point out how nasty the speech really was and said he didn't know whether Flanders's problem was "senility or viciousness." But there was no longer any place to turn for cover. He was like a bull in the bull ring, stung and maddened by the attacks coming from every direction, and frustrated by his inability to hit back.

This was the context for the Fred Fisher incident on June 9. No other episode is more important to the McCarthy myth: how McCarthy needlessly maligned an innocent lawyer on Welch's staff in order to wound his chief antagonist, and how Welch rose up in indignation and shamed him on national television. However, the real encounter took place long before the television cameras were turned on. Two days earlier, Joseph Welch and Roy Cohn had reached a deal: Welch would not mention Cohn's avoidance of the draft during his testimony if Cohn did not bring up Fred Fisher's brief membership as a law student with the National Lawyers' Guild, a Communist front. That dirty little secret had already been published in the New York Times two weeks earlier.

Welch had decided to relieve Fisher as his assistant in the hearings; otherwise, he told Cohn, "we would all end up looking like Communist sympathizers." He wanted to make sure the McCarthy team did not bring it up. Cohn told McCarthy; McCarthy agreed.[37]

Then, late in the afternoon on June 9, Welch was riding Cohn hard, as the audience guffawed with appreciation. He had begun to tease Cohn in his deceptively good-natured way to disclose the names of any real Communists as soon as he learned about them—"before sundown," as he put it—whether at Fort Monmouth or anywhere else. "May I add my small voice, sir, and say whenever you know about a subversive or a Communist or a spy, please hurry. Will you remember those words?"

McCarthy listened with growing rage. He had lost almost every throw to the more agile and experienced Welch. The older man had mocked him, insulted him, and teased him to his face; now he was hammering on "one of the finest young men I know," as McCarthy liked to say. He snapped. He grabbed the microphone:

"Mr. Chairman, in view of that question . . ."

"Have you a point of order?" asked Mundt wearily.

"Not exactly, Mr. Chairman," the senator growled, "but in view of Mr. Welch's request that the information be given, once we know of anyone who might be performing any work for the Communist Party, I think we should tell him that he has in his law firm a young man named Fisher . . ."

Cohn writhed in his chair and began to say, "No, no." But McCarthy ignored him. He had forgotten the deal; it is possible, because of his drinking, that he even blacked out on it. In any case, he blundered ahead: "A young man named Fisher whom he recommended, incidentally, to do work on this committee, who has been for a number of years a member of an organization that was named, oh years and years ago, as the legal bulwark of the Communist Party . . ."

The committee and the audience sat aghast as McCarthy wound up his attack. "I have hesitated to bring that up, but I have been rather bored with your phony requests to Mr. Cohn here that he personally get every Communist out of Government before sundown. . . . Whether you knew he was a member of that Communist organization or not, I don't know. I assume you did not, Mr. Welch, because I get the impression that, while you are quite an actor. . . . I don't think you yourself would ever knowingly aid the Communist cause."

Welch paused dramatically, evidently drawing himself together. Then he uttered the words that have become immortal:

> Until this moment, Senator, I think I never really gauged your cruelty or your recklessness. Fred Fisher is a young man who went to the Harvard Law

School and came into my firm and is starting what looks to be a brilliant career with us. . . . Little did I dream you could be so reckless and so cruel as to do an injury to that lad. . . . Let us not assassinate this lad further, Senator. You have done enough. Have you no sense of decency, sir, at long last? Have you left no sense of decency?

The effect was electrifying. However, oblivious to everything, McCarthy blundered on. He tried to enter an article on the National Lawyers' Guild into the record, and continued to press Welch on the point, while the older and wiser lawyer fell silent and let McCarthy rant on. At one point McCarthy said sarcastically, "I know this is painful for you, Mr. Welch," to which Welch responded quietly, "I think this hurts you, too, Senator."

Never were truer words spoke. McCarthy's old friend and former aide Ray Kiermas, who was in the audience, remembered years later, "I was sick to my stomach." Another, Urban Van Susteren, watched on television and said, "It made me sick."[38] He and every other McCarthy supporter knew the senator had just done himself irreparable harm. A shaken McClellan proposed an adjournment; Mundt quickly agreed. As the crowd streamed out, McCarthy tried to be nonchalant and carry on as if nothing had happened, although even he had begun to realize he had gone too far. "What did I do?" he kept asking the people around him.

Outside the hearing room, reporters jammed around Welch, who wept openly in front of the television cameras and photographers and repeated his outrage at McCarthy's brutal action. When he finished, he and another lawyer on his staff walked down the hall, around the corner, and along the far corridor until the last reporter dropped back and the last camera bulb had flashed. The pair turned the corner, all alone. Welch turned to his colleague, the tears still staining his face, and said without changing expression, "Well, how did it go?"[39]

In short, Welch's performance, like the entire Fred Fisher "smear," had been a sham. Nevertheless, the dramatic clash and the image cast by the television camera—the "pseudo-event," as historian Daniel Boorstin might call it—proved indelible, and so much so that even a completely accurate account of what actually happened will probably never completely replace it, no matter how many times it is retold. At the time, of course, the only thing everyone knew was what the cameras had conveyed. Although the hearings had more than another week to run and McCarthy himself was still due to take the stand, conservatives and allies now realized there was no way to save him. The *Wisconsin State Journal*, a former staunch ally, remarked, "It was worse than reckless. It was worse than cruel. It was reprehensible."[40] Fred Woltmann, who had helped McCarthy with his investigations in the early days, began his column for the Scripps-Howard newspapers with the sentence, "Senator Joseph R. McCarthy has become a major liability to the cause of anti-Communism."

What his enemies said need only be imagined. One, Ralph Flanders, wrote to a friend, "I cannot conceive of wanting to live, or wanting my children or grandchildren to live, in an America fashioned in the image of the junior senator from Wisconsin."[41] Two days later Flanders presented a motion to strip McCarthy permanently of his chairmanship of PSI.

There was one final burst of melodrama on June 14 when McCarthy and Stuart Symington got into a shouting match and Symington simply gathered up his papers and left the room, as McCarthy whined with rage, "You can run away if you like, Stu. You can run away if you like. You have been here trying to smear the staff of this committee, the young men who have been working to uncover Communism." The audience filed out, too, leaving McCarthy still pleading and fuming at the head table. The committee concluded its business on June 17, after thirty-six days of hearings and 187 hours of airtime. How many people watched on television is impossible to say, but television ratings gave it a 9 to 12 share, about the same as Arthur Godfrey but far lower than Senator Kefauver's televised hearings on organized crime.[42]

On July 20 Roy Cohn quit before he could be fired. Friends, supporters, and the Joint Committee Against Communism threw a huge testimonial dinner in New York at the Hotel Astor on July 28. Although the event was ostensibly in Cohn's honor, its real purpose was a show of support for the faltering McCarthy. Two thousand people attended, with an estimated six thousand turned away for lack of space. The guest list reads like a who's who of the anti-Communist and conservative movements in New York: Frank Chodorov, Willard Edwards, George S. Kaufman, E. F. Hutton, Alfred Kohlberg, Westbrook Pegler, J. B. and Ruth Matthews, Robert Morris, Archibald Roosevelt, Pat Scanlon of the *Brooklyn Tablet*, George Sokolsky, William F. Buckley, Jr., and various chapters of the American Legion, the Knights of Columbus, and the Catholic War Veterans, among others.

When McCarthy rose to speak, he received a standing ovation that lasted two and a half minutes. He and others paid effusive tribute to Cohn, "one whose unusual knowledge and talents have helped our country expose and fight its internal enemy: communist subversion."[43] Although some may have not have realized it, it was the last hurrah for the McCarthy cause.

Meanwhile, the Committee for an Effective Congress was mobilizing its unusual knowledge and talents to complete McCarthy's rout. The Fred Fischer incident gave them the final opening they had needed. Maurice Rosenblatt set up the "Clearing House" to prepare documents for senators and their staffs on McCarthy's public and personal life, and when Eisenhower's millionaire backer Paul Hoffman gave the group $12,000, they swung into action. They also received help from liberal millionaire Marshall Field and a disparate collection of McCarthy haters: Drew Pearson's lawyer Warren Woods, Kenneth Birkenhead of the Senate Democratic Campaign Committee, and ex-Senator William Benton. Millard Tydings, rising like Lazarus from the political grave, offered them support and copious advice. Meanwhile, Hoffman had lunch with the president and C. D. Jackson at the White House and brought them on board.

Their angle of attack was through Senator Ralph Flanders, who became in effect the Clearing House's stalking horse. They organized his press conferences, drafted his speeches, and provided him with extra staff. On July 30 Flanders offered a resolution of censure against McCarthy, the harshest form of rebuke the Senate can offer one of its own short of actual expulsion. Flanders may not have been the best choice for this: after his speech branding McCarthy a homosexual and comparing him to Hitler, Republican colleagues had carefully shunned him. But the Clearing House now began pressuring key Democratic senators, such as Fulbright, Hennings, and John Sparkman, and liberal Republicans like John Sherman Cooper, to back him up. John McClellan proved an early eager ally and a crucial one: his willingness to ax McCarthy and strip him of his chairmanships may have tipped Lyndon Johnson's hand. Like ice forming on a pond, the anti-McCarthy bloc imperceptibly but suddenly crystallized. The Clearing House figured they already had at least twenty-four sure votes and eighteen probables for a final showdown.[44]

On August 2 the Senate debated the censure resolution as McCarthy himself swung wide and wild: "I assure the American people that the senators who have made these charges will either be indicted for perjury or they will prove what consummate liars they are." The next day his colleagues voted 75 to 12 to submit the resolution, and the various particular articles, to a select committee for consideration.

The end was now almost in sight, not just for Joe McCarthy, but for the cause he had come to represent.

Chapter 15

Censure

Be not afraid, though you do see me weapon'd;
Here is my journey's end, here is my butt,
And very sea-mark of my utmost sail.

—*Othello*, V, ii, 266–268

O
n August 31 the McClellan subcommittee issued its final report. It was as damning to the Army bureaucrats as to McCarthy. If Mc-Carthy had been guilty of permitting Cohn to wage his single-minded campaign to protect Schine, then Stevens and Adams came under fire for pandering to him and for trying to interfere in the Fort Monmouth investigation. The heroes of the hour, McClellan, Symington, and Potter, believed it was time to clear the decks. Cohn was already gone. John Adams and Bob Stevens should be next. McClellan and Symington had already made their feelings toward McCarthy known: that he should quit as chairman of PSI.[1] However, Potter and the PSI Democrats were behind the curve in the press, in cultivated public opinion, and inside the Senate itself. The main issue now was whether McCarthy would be formally censured by a majority of his colleagues.

It was Lyndon Johnson, the Democratic minority leader, who had taken over command of the campaign for censure. Senate liberals had been imploring Johnson to take up the campaign against McCarthy for more than a year.[2] Of course, men like Hubert Humphrey, William Fulbright, and Herbert Lehman wanted to silence a man they considered irresponsible and evil, but they also had another motivation for suppressing Joe McCarthy. As Humphrey explained with his usual unabashed candor, "McCarthy's real threat to American democracy [is] the fact that he has immobilized the liberal movement." Liberals, Humphrey said, "just don't talk about anything else any more."[3] McCarthy's censure would restore their morale and reinvigorate the heirs to the New Deal after their disappointing defeat in 1952.

Johnson had his own reasons to stop McCarthy. By maneuvering the Republican-dominated Senate into voting to censure one of their most popular members, Johnson figured he could split the GOP down the middle. A reunited Democratic Party would grab the legislative initiative, and Lyndon Johnson, not the Eisenhower White House, would dominate the nation's agenda.

There were also personal or professional reasons to dislike the senator from Wisconsin. Johnson was devoted to the Senate as an institution; McCarthy was not. He had treated older, slower colleagues—men who had been Johnson's mentors—with impatience and contempt. In style and personal demeanor, McCarthy had defied the body's folkways, which Johnson respected and admired. Johnson's view of McCarthy was the same as his aide Bobby Baker's: that "he'd do anything for a headline." He would tell late-night intimates as Johnson poured down glass after glass of Cutty Sark, "Joe McCarthy's just a loudmouthed drunk, can't tie his own goddamn shoes." But he did respect McCarthy's ruthless will to win. "He'll go that extra mile to hurt you," he told one aide, and his general advice was "don't get in a pissin' contest with a polecat." Another favorite Texas Hill Country saying Johnson liked to quote when McCarthy's name came up was, "Don't kill a snake unless you've got a hoe in your hands."[4]

Johnson's hoe was the southern Democrats. First, he had urged John McClellan, the chairman of the special subcommittee investigating McCarthy's conduct, to televise McCarthy's ongoing feud with the Army. After McCarthy had mortally wounded himself in public, everyone was clamoring for McCarthy's censure, although they still hadn't agreed on what he should be censured for. The decision to appoint a special committee to investigate charges offered Johnson his opportunity to move the anti-McCarthy effort to its final, critical stage.

Johnson shrewdly understood that if the usual Democrats took the lead in the censure fight—Humphrey, Fulbright, Monroney, and the rest—opponents could dismiss the proceedings as just another liberal smear campaign. He intended to bring members of the Senate's old guard, especially the southerners, on board in order to give the anti-McCarthy effort respectability. Johnson filled his pockets with note cards citing earlier precedents for Senate votes of censure (there had been only three in history) and visited the members of the inner club. The first one he approached was Walter George, who refused to participate unless a similar senior Republican, Ed Milliken, was on the committee. Milliken said no. Then Johnson then went to his old mentor, Richard Russell, who also turned him down.

Frustrated, Johnson complained about George and Russell to his aide Bobby Baker in a late-night drinking session in the minority leader's office. "They say McCarthy's still strong medicine down in Georgia and they've just got no stomach for it. . . . Dick Russell don't want to go to the mat because he's afraid he'll get his hands dirty. You know who they're offering me?" Johnson asked in disgust, as Baker later recalled. "Sam Ervin. The lightweight son of a bitch." Sam Ervin of North Carolina would later gain fame as chairman of the Watergate hearings, but in 1954 he was still a relative newcomer. Despite his doubts about Ervin, Johnson nevertheless decided to go with "the goddamn windbag," as he called him.[5]

Then he brought his attention to bear on the Republican side. He cajoled and bulldozed the Republicans' vacillating majority leader, Bill Knowland, into dropping any McCarthy allies from the committee list. Reporter William White watched it happen. "Johnson would say, 'Now, Bill, I'm sure you want so-and-so.' Knowland would say, 'Oh, no! Good God no, I don't want so-and-so!' And he'd wind up naming the man Johnson wanted."[6] And so Johnson in effect hand-picked every member of the committee in order to ensure a recommendation of censure.

They were an unremarkable group. The chairman was mild-mannered Arthur V. Watkins of Utah, a man with a deeply conventional mind whose chief claim to fame was his sponsorship of federal water reclamation projects and legislation against Mexican migrants. The Democrats were stolid conservatives: Colorado's Edwin Johnson, Mississippi's John Stennis, and Ervin. The Republicans—Watkins, Frank Case of South Dakota, and Frank Carlson of Kansas—were similarly undistinguished. They were also wearing the White House's livery. Like their moderate and liberal GOP colleagues, they were prepared to do its bidding in extinguishing McCarthy.

In the climax of Allen Drury's novel *Advise and Consent*, the Senator casts a vote of censure against one of their colleagues (a character largely based on McCarthy) in a high tide of passion and outrage. The McCarthy censure proceeded in a very different spirit. This was not a job Arthur Watkins wanted. His own sister had called him from Los Angeles and warned him to drop it. He told her, "I've been asked to do this and I can't very well say no," although he admitted, "I'd rather take almost anything" rather than have to chair this committee.[7] But he had been more afraid of backing down than of going ahead. What historian Lewis Namier once wrote an eighteenth-century English peer applies equally well to Arthur Watkins: "His position was pitiful from the outset, and was rendered even more wretched through his sensitiveness and fears, and more ludicrous through the utter lack of judgment he showed in estimating the relative value of things."[8]

Watkins and the censure committee had reluctantly decided to met in open session but voted to exclude cameras and microphones. McCarthy had wanted to fight for public exposure of what he saw as a clear attempt at railroading, but his lawyer, Edward Bennett Williams, persuaded him not to. Williams and other McCarthy supporters did not want to risk another debacle like the Army-McCarthy hearings, but Chairman Watkins did not want the full glare of publicity for what they were about to do either. "Let us get off the front pages and back among the obituaries," he explained.[9]

The Watkins Committee began its deliberations away from the public eye but not out of public reach. The Committee for an Effective Congress and the Clearing House weighed in heavily. Working out of Ralph Flanders's office, a National Committee for an Effective Congress (NCEC) lawyer produced a steady stream of briefs for Watkins and his colleagues, which they acknowledged but did not enter into the formal record. McCarthy had no way of knowing that his enemies were feeding the censure committee material behind his back and that of his lawyer, or that William Benton was working as its unofficial gumshoe. Instead, he found himself trapped in a losing defensive game, of furious rearguard counterattacks and fruitless efforts to have the charges decided on their merits rather than on their intended result: silencing Joe McCarthy. "You have done a fine job," Fulbright told Flanders, "and we all owe you a debt of gratitude." "It is hard to see how a clean bill of health can be given our mutual friend from Wisconsin," Flanders told Benton afterward.[10]

The committee considered five categories of charges against McCarthy, ranging from contempt of the Senate, abusing colleagues (he had once told a reporter that Senator Hendrickson of New Jersey was a "living miracle without brains or guts"), and encouraging government employees to violate the law, to insulting General Zwicker. But around each of the charges swirled doubts and counterarguments. Abuse of Senate colleagues, after all, was a grand and time-honored practice. Every senator could remember when Senator Tom Connally (who had then been majority leader) had said of Michigan's Homer Ferguson that "everything he touches is covered with the vomit of his spleen." Some could even remember when another Wisconsin senator, Robert La Follette, said on the Senate floor that God had given one of his colleagues "a hump on his back" because he was "by nature a subservient, cringing creature."

If colorful attacks on colleagues was a Senate tradition, so was releasing government documents to the press, or what were coming to be known as leaks. In McCarthy's case, those leaks had been the result of his efforts to defend himself against similar leaks of information from the Army and the White House. On May 27 McCarthy had publicly called on government employees to release any classified documents that would help him prove the Army's loyalty program was a sham. Privately Eisenhower called it "the most disloyal act we have ever had by anyone in the Government of the United States."[11] But this too could be seen in a more sympathetic light. Whistleblowers were bread and butter for any congressman who wanted to conduct an investigation in the face of executive branch intransigence, and the committee knew it.

McCarthy faced heavy fire for pleading with federal employees to come forward with information they might have "about graft, corruption, communism, [and] treason," in defiance of Eisenhower's order.* But he had the strength of precedent and constitutional right on his side. Former Senator Burton Wheeler, who had led the Teapot Dome investigations in the twenties, argued that the right of Congress to get information from officials was essential. "Without this, congressional investigations would be crippled. It is disturbing that the President and so many people fail to realize this." McCarthy could even quote liberal icon Felix Frankfurter: "the power of investigation should be left untrammeled, and the methods and forms of each investigation should be left for determination of Congress and its committees."[12] Even Watkins himself, as a member of the Senate Judiciary Committee, had signed a petition along with McClellan and Estes Kefauver urging government workers to come forward and detail any encounters with "subversives." "If these people will come forward," the petition read, "great strides will be made in protecting the security of the country."[13] Watkins was hardly in a position to condemn McCarthy for urging what Watkins himself had done.

So in the end, on September 27, after releasing a sixty-eight-page report reviewing forty-six separate counts, the committee moved to recommend censure on just two: McCarthy's behavior toward Guy Gillette's Subcommittee on Privileges and Elections during the Eighty-second Congress, which it decided constituted "contempt of Congress," and his conduct toward General Zwicker, which it judged "reprehensible."

It must be admitted that McCarthy's case against censure was strong.

---

*This was on May 27, 1954. It was included among the charges for censure but later dropped.

He could point out that the Gillette subcommittee had clearly been out to railroad him, that it had denied him or his legal counsel any power to cross-examine witnesses, and that two subcommittee staffers had resigned because they had qualms about the proceedings against him.[14] Even more, he and Edward Bennett Williams pointed out that the instances of his "contempt" toward Gillette, Hennings, and the others had all occurred during the Eighty-*second* Congress, not the current Eighty-third one. No precedent existed for censuring someone for something he had done in a previous Congress, which had seen fit to do nothing.

From the McCarthy perspective, the Zwicker case was even easier. He and his staff intended to raise the issue "as to whether or not vigorous, hard-hitting cross-examination, necessitated by a witness's evasive answers, is a basis for censure of the interrogator." They argued that Zwicker had provoked McCarthy's outburst by his own sullen and hostile manner. But the heart of their case was that the censure vote "strikes at the basic right of the Congress" to investigate the executive branch and hold officials accountable. McCarthy pointed out that thanks to his battle with the Pentagon and the censure fight, his own probes into Communist subversion had ground to a halt. Most commentators saw this as a matter of celebration rather than regret, but looming up in the background was Eisenhower's May 17 declaration of executive privilege, which made people other than McCarthy supporters uneasy.

Unfortunately, the question of whether McCarthy might be right was swallowed up in the debate over who he was and what he represented. Despite the pretense at fairness and judicious objectivity—Watkins publicly described the proceedings as akin to "a court of law"—the cards were stacked against McCarthy from the beginning. As the *New York Times*'s William White told his readers, McCarthy's censure was "inevitable" the moment the subcommittee had been set up. In the very strictest sense, the debate on the McCarthy censure was a show trial in which, like other show trials, the real charges were not the ones being brought, and his real antagonists—the liberal Washington establishment—were not those accusing him.*

The focus in the press was on McCarthy the cornered beast, who at long last was about to receive his due. When the Watkins Committee released its recommendation for censure on September 27, *Time* magazine pronounced it "a ringing reassertion of the U.S. Senate's dignity." The *Louisville Courier-Journal* said that "these six inoffensive and austere men have by their unanimity and moderation both destroyed the McCarthy myth and elevated the prestige of a senate which has suffered severe blows."[15] When the right-wing

---

*The only one who did speak during the debate was William Fulbright.

Human Events warned that the new Eisenhower doctrine would "if success-ful take the nation a long way toward dictatorial government," liberals across the country scoffed. The liberal press, including the *New York Times* and the *Washington Post*, stoutly defended Eisenhower's stand on executive privi-lege—a striking irony, considering how they would completely reverse them-selves seventeen years later, during the Pentagon Papers case.[16]

They also scoffed at the efforts to rally public support for the senator from Wisconsin. The day after the censure debate began, on November 7, a caravan of McCarthy supporters from Wisconsin arrived at the Capitol. They drew sneers and jeers from journalists, who noted their ramshackle bus, their depleted numbers, and the angry placards that read "MOSCOW HATES MCCARTHY, TOO" and "WHY ALGER HISS WANT TRIAL IN VERMONT?" Rabbi Schultz of the American Jewish League Against Communism organized a rally at Constitutional Hall, while another group of McCarthy supporters ral-lied in Madison Square Garden. Admiral John Crommelin told them that Mc-Carthy "is the one man left who—single-handed—has been able to rouse the people of the United States to the menace of the *hidden force* in their govern-ment." The Catholic War Veterans had put together a quarter of a million sig-natures on a Save McCarthy petition, while a group calling themselves Ten Million Americans Mobilized for Justice tried to collect even more signatures on a similar petition. Senators were bombarded with pro-McCarthy letters and telegrams. Arthur Watkins later admitted he had received over thirty thousand pieces of mail—most of it intensely abusive.[17]

The committee delivered its recommendation of censure on September 27. Its effect on the midterm elections in November is unclear, but to Mc-Carthy's supporters it was easy to infer. Democrats regained control of both the House and the Senate; Lyndon Johnson was going to be the majority leader in the next Congress. Pro-McCarthy candidates lost in Illinois, Mon-tana, Wyoming, Oregon, and Michigan, as well in as his home state. His friend and supporter Charles Kersten lost his seat, while Wisconsin Democ-rats saw the rise to prominence of two new liberals, Gaylord Nelson and William Proxmire.[18] The November 10 special session opened in an atmos-phere heavy with Democratic triumph and liberal vindication.

Meanwhile, McCarthy himself was outwardly calm and confident. "I can go fifteen rounds," he told reporters on the first day of the debate, "I'll be here to the end." He had to squeeze past hundreds of supporters who jammed the hallways and the Capitol's Rotunda to shake his hand and wish him well.

In his opening statement chairman Watkins appeared almost apologetic. He stressed that the committee had acted merely as the instrument of the will of the Senate. It hadn't brought the original charges; individual senators had. It could not offer final proof of McCarthy's guilt, because the Senate was not a court (which seemed to contradict the impression he had tried to give reporters earlier). The committee had no monopoly on wisdom, he said, and "all human judgments are at best fallible." But its members had tried to bring "whatever wisdom, calmness, fairness, courage, and devotion" they could to "so challenging and important a task." The "uncontroverted evidence" had led them to find against their colleague from Wisconsin.

Now McCarthy was on his feet. Pilloried by the press, baited on television in front of millions of viewers, he now stood on the verge of disgrace and oblivion. Ill and with sagging morale, McCarthy lashed out with a savage determination. He challenged Watkins to state that he ought to have remained silent about the Gillette subcommittee's attempt to expel him from the Senate two years before, even though its investigations, in his opinion and that of others, were "grossly incompetent and dishonest." Watkins replied that his committee had merely considered the charge that McCarthy's behavior had been worthy of censure, not whether that behavior was justified. McCarthy was incredulous: "Is it the Senator's position that a member of the Senate cannot criticize the members of a committee, regardless of what they do?"

When Watkins demurred, McCarthy struck at another point. Watkins grew hot and angry, as did McCarthy. The *Congressional Record*, normally a dispassionate transcript, with ugly and cacophonous sounds carefully smoothed out, still manages to catch the tense atmosphere:

WATKINS: I am giving the best answer I can. The Senator may not agree with it.
MCCARTHY: Let us correct it then.
WATKINS: I will do the correcting of my own answers.
MCCARTHY: I will correct the Senator when he makes a misstatement.

Watkins defended the Gillette subcommittee, saying that McCarthy's conduct "indicated very clearly that he was ignoring that committee completely. He was blasting it with letters [and] making denunciatory statements about the very time . . . he should have been helping them."[19]

In fact, McCarthy *had* appeared before Gillette and his Democrat-controlled committee, on July 3, 1952.[20] Then in October, November, and again in December, they "invited" him to reappear, this time in connection with Senator Benton's expulsion resolution. McCarthy saw the subcommittee's actions as pure partisan politics and flatly refused to appear or answer "their insulting questions," as he put it. Yet the subcommittee did nothing. It never subpoenaed McCarthy (which it could have done); its final report denounced his persistent refusal to testify, but it did not recommend he be censured or denied his seat when the new Senate met that January. The report itself had been a tissue of innuendo, exaggerations, and misinformation, supporting

McCarthy's claim that it was all just a partisan vendetta.[21] In other words, a calm and dispassionate presentation of the facts probably could have demolished a crucial point of the censure recommendation.

But McCarthy was anything but calm and dispassionate. Instead, he furiously asked if Watkins, a Republican, knew that the Gillette subcommittee charges had been all prepared beforehand by the Democratic National Committee? Watkins: "I am aware that the Senator made that statement but he did not claim to know personally about it." McCarthy insisted that it was part of the record. Watkins retorted, "I am sure the Senator does not want to be bound by all that is in the record," a clear reference to McCarthy's reputation for playing fast and loose with the truth.

Watkins still had not finished his opening statement. McCarthy defended his aggressive tactics: "The Senator is asking that I be censured, and I am entitled to have the Senator tell the Senate the grounds for such censure." In the same barrage, McCarthy questioned the committee's own impartiality. He asked whether Senator Ervin ought to have continued to sit in judgment when the New York Times quoted him as saying that McCarthy could have had him disqualified for letters Ervin had once written attacking McCarthy's treatments of witnesses before his committee. Ervin now interrupted McCarthy, who was interrupting Watkins, to claim he gave no such quotation to the Times (which was true—he had given it to a local North Carolina paper instead).[22] Watkins weakly added that there was no way to have a perfectly impartial committee in this case. Was McCarthy suggesting that no one who had taken a prior position on him should be allowed to sit in judgment of his censure charges? But McCarthy's point was slightly different: that Ervin *himself* had suggested he could be fairly disqualified, given his prior views of McCarthy. But as usual, then and later, commentators heard not what McCarthy had said but what they wanted to believe he had said.[23]

The wrangling went on for another hour. Watkins insisted that the committee's motives had been clean: "There was never a time when politics entered into this matter in any way, shape, or form." It had been, he said, a "distasteful thing" to sit in judgment of a colleague's behavior, especially for Watkins, who had arrived in the Senate at the same time as McCarthy in the famous class of '46, and with whom he had once been on friendly terms. But their assignment had been to rule "on the evidence on the basis of the best light we could get," and this they had done.

It was now after midnight and William Knowland suggested a recess. Everyone was ready for a break, but just before the Senate adjourned for the evening, McCarthy fired a final shot. Had Watkins, he asked, told a reporter (Constantine Brown of the *Washington Evening Star*) that he hoped no one had any pictures of him shaking McCarthy's hand? Watkins angrily and flatly denied saying it. McCarthy's jab brought the proceedings to a gut-wrenching halt. As Edward Bennett Williams left the chamber (he had sat beside McCarthy throughout the session), a reporter asked, "Your boy sure isn't trying to win friends and influence people, is he?" Williams wearily answered, "That's one book he didn't write."[24]

The battle line had been drawn. Earlier that afternoon McCarthy handed over his own formal statement for the record, which he had released to the press the day before. The speech was written by his young assistant, Brent Bozell: "This week the United States Senate convened in a special session to debate Senator Flanders's resolution to censure me. I take it, judging from declarations of individual Senators—made in most cases without bothering to study the Watkins committee record—that . . . I will be censured." He added: "This means that those who are leading the fight against subversion have been slowed down, and that others who might otherwise have been enlisted in the fight will be discouraged from joining us. . . . It thus does mean that the Communist Party has achieved a major victory."

Talking of himself, he said, "It is not easy for a man to assert that he is the symbol of resistance to Communist subversion—that the nation's fate is in some respects tied to his own fate." But he had to acknowledge that McCarthyism had become "a household word for describing a way of dealing with treason and the threat of treason" from Communists and their sympathizers and supporters. Censure of Joe McCarthy would mean the defeat of what he called "hard anticommunism"—those who opposed Soviet communism because they considered it evil and antithetical to the American political tradition. Instead, the burden of battle would pass to the "soft" anti-Communists, who profess opposition to communism in principle but spend their time attacking hard-liners like himself. "In the press and over the radio, from public lecture platforms and in the classroom" they had spread the message that "McCarthyism somehow represents a greater threat to America than communism itself." He doubted whether any of them were up to the fight to come.

"If I lose on the censure vote," he said, "it follows, of course, that someone else wins. Now I ask the American people to consider carefully: who wins?" McCarthy listed two groups. The first were those who controlled the dominant media—"the opinion-molding machinery of the United States," who wanted him condemned. The other was the Communist Party. He noted how the *Daily Worker* had applauded Senator Ralph Flanders's original resolution of censure in June, and then the Watkins Committee ruling. The Communists, McCarthy said, would add his censure to their list of past successes, from Yalta to Korea.

Since his first speech in Wheeling, West Virginia, in February 1950, when he warned the American people of the presence of Communists in the State Department, "the Communists have said that the destruction of me and what I stand for is their number-one objective in this country." They had fought his work as chairman of the PSI, and his probes into Communist infiltration of the State Department's Overseas Information Service, the Voice of America, defense installations at Fort Monmouth, and the U.S. Army. Now the Watkins Committee had allowed itself to become "the unwitting handmaiden" of the Communist Party's attack on America. "The Communists have managed to have me investigated five times," he concluded. "If they fail to silence me this time—and make no mistake, they will fail—I will be investigated a sixth and a seventh time." But "I will proceed as I proceeded before. . . . I shall take to the American people what evidence I have of Communists and other security risks in positions where they can endanger this Nation."[25]

It was an extraordinarily defiant, if desperate, performance for a man at the end of his tether. McCarthy's enemies had always portrayed him as reckless and dangerous and later would point to this speech, and the charge that the Watkins Committee was the "unwitting handmaiden" of communism, as proof. John Stennis condemned it as "a continuation of the slime and slush," and Watkins in particular was outraged. No man enjoys being called a fool (especially if there is the tiniest possibility that he has been one), and Watkins decided to summon Stennis and the rest of the committee to an emergency session to decide how to make McCarthy pay for it.

But now the other members of the Watkins Committee made their speeches. They appealed not to questions of ideology or partisanship, but the honor and traditions of the Senate. John Stennis of Mississippi remarked how he found McCarthy a genial and friendly man, and thoroughly approved of his hunt for Communists in government, but "the fact that he has done good work in that mission does not give him license to destroy other processes of the Senate or destroy its members." Whom McCarthy had thus destroyed remained unclear, unless it was his old nemesis Millard Tydings, who had lost his Maryland Senate seat back in 1950—but that was not one of the charges under consideration.*

McCarthy did have his defenders. Majority Leader Butler of Maryland and William Knowland spoke on the merits of the case for censure. They insisted that there was no formal basis for proceeding since whatever misdeeds McCarthy had done had been in a previous Congress. If his actions were not considered censurable then, there was even less reason now. Herman Welker

*Since Tydings was now an active member of the NCEC campaign against McCarthy (Griffith, *Politics of Fear*, 228), it remains unclear who was out to destroy whom.

289

of Idaho added that the only grounds the Constitution recognized for censure was "disorderly behavior," a far more serious offense than anything McCarthy had done. And if Senate Rule XIX was to be applied, which forbade senators from imputing to each other "any conduct or motive unworthy or unbecoming a senator," what was going to happen to senators who had gone to the Senate floor to accuse McCarthy of lying under oath (on September 28, 1951), or blackmail (February 10, 1952), or doctoring evidence (May 7, 1954), or of being a homosexual and comparing him to Adolf Hitler (June 1, 1954)? Would those men be subject to the same sanctions?[26]

Another of his defenders grasped what was really going on. Barry Goldwater was forty-six years old, the same age as McCarthy. He was the freshman senator from Arizona and one of McCarthy's closest allies, along with Welker and William Jenner. Jenner had spoken along the same lines as McCarthy: about how a vote for censure would be a victory for communism. Goldwater's analysis was deeper and more penetrating.

"I suggest that Senator McCarthy is facing a censure vote in this body because he has put his finger fearlessly upon the men in high places who, through stupidity or muddled ideology, had stood in the way of an all-out fight against communism both in America and abroad." In his campaign against communism, Goldwater declared, McCarthy had dared to lay his hand on the "sacred cows of Washington," and could expect a devastating counterattack. Contrary to Watkins's denials, Goldwater had no doubt that the censure issue was political. For all their claims to "idealism, high-mindedness, and lofty sentiments," his enemies had gathered here to settle the score. "All the discredited and embittered figures of the Hiss-Yalta period" have "crawled out from under their logs to join the effort to get even." In the process, they had managed to split the Republican Party, which was now so "busily chewing on itself" that it had permitted the Democrats to return to power.

"Of course," Goldwater added, "Joe McCarthy has made mistakes. . . . Let the members of this body search their consciences and say whether or not they themselves have not made mistakes equally regrettable." Goldwater added his voice to those who insisted that McCarthy had done nothing that called for a vote of censure and hadn't broken any rules except those imposed ex post facto.

Goldwater also expressed another concern: that a censure vote would cause the investigative functions of Congress, especially regarding the executive branch, to shrivel away. "And when that censure is voted, not for corruption or malfeasance, not for the breaking of any existing rules, but for excessive zeal . . . it is doubly senseless."[27]

It was a good speech and, from the point of view of the merits of the case, largely correct. However, the final outcome was never in doubt. McCarthy's opponents moved the discussion away from the more technical issue of censure to McCarthyism as a political movement.

Moderate Republican Prescott Bush of Connecticut (father of future president George Bush) denounced McCarthy for creating "dangerous divisions among the American people." William Fulbright read aloud from the abusive mail he had received from McCarthy supporters around the country, denouncing him as "a dirty red rat" and hoping that "you and the rotten Jew, Herbert Lehman," will "suffer the tortures of hell." As he waved the letters aloft, Fulbright declared, "I think they are evidence of a great sickness among our people"—implying that a vote for censure would be a kind of cleansing act, a purification of the wellsprings of American political life.

McCarthy's home on Capitol Hill became a fortress. Night after night friends, staffers, and friendly journalists like Willard Edwards of the *Chicago Tribune* gathered to offer support and advice. Roy Cohn became a constant visitor. Brent Bozell's wife, Patricia Buckley, would watch silently from a corner as the discussions swirled along until the early hours of the morning. McCarthy seemed overwhelmed with the often conflicting suggestions they offered. Edward Bennett Williams offered what was probably the best advice. "Get him to stop drinking," he told Jean Kerr. "I can't," she replied sadly.[28]

Outwardly, McCarthy remained tough and combative. He even had the audacity to compel Senator Watkins to appear before the PSI on November 18, to answer questions about any information he might picked up about who had promoted the hapless Irving Peress. But inwardly he was ill and depressed. Staffers coming to work early in the morning were startled to enter his private office and find him sitting alone and dejected at the window. He had arrived hours earlier without telling them, unable to bear seeing anyone.

The censure debate limped along for twenty-one days, interrupted only when McCarthy had to be hospitalized for traumatic bursitis (his enemies suggested that he was faking). Now the only issue left was whether all the conservative southerners would vote for censure. Barry Goldwater was approached by Senator Daniel of Texas who told him that if McCarthy wrote letters of apology to both Watkins and Hendrickson, he could still save himself.

Goldwater, Williams, and Everett Dirksen rushed to McCarthy's bed at Bethesda Naval Hospital and found him sullen and in pain. Goldwater knew the real reason behind McCarthy's injury: when they were at a rally in Milwaukee, McCarthy had drunkenly slipped and smashed his elbow on a glass tabletop.[29] Goldwater and Williams presented McCarthy with drafts of the letters of apology. He refused to look at them. "I will never let them think I would ever crawl," he said. When Dirksen handed him a pen to sign a letter he had redrafted, he threw it across the room. He caused such an uproar that the nurse finally had to call the admiral in charge of the hospital, who threatened to call the shore patrol if they did not leave. Later, to his friend Robert Lee, McCarthy was even blunter. "Fuck 'em," he said.[30]

McCarthy's stubbornness sealed his fate. Several days later when he was released from the hospital, he appeared in the Senate Chamber to urge his colleagues to speed things up and bring on the final vote. His bandaged arm was in a sling, his jacket draped over his shoulders, giving him a vaguely Napoleonic appearance. He looked bloated and ill. He publicly admitted that "at times I have been extremely blunt in expressing my opinion. I do not claim to be a master of words." But, he added, "in the facts and opinions I held, I am unchanged." It was the closest thing to an apology his Senate colleagues would ever get.[31]

One unexpected obstacle turned out to be a member of the Watkins Committee, Senator Frank Case. At the last minute he decided that he couldn't support the charge concerning Zwicker. He decided the evidence was too tenuous and worried that censuring McCarthy for remarks made in committee would limit the power of other chairmen to question witnesses as they saw fit. (In fact, LBJ himself had warned Watkins that at least fifteen Democrats would vote against that article of the resolution.) However, Watkins and other members dropped Zwicker and swiftly substituted McCarthy's own remarks about *them* as "handmaidens of the Communist Party" as grounds for censure. Sam Ervin growled, "He's saying either we're fools or knaves, one or the other, and either one of 'em's bad. It's certainly contemptible to call a fellow senator a knave or a fool." So in the end nothing had changed.[32]

The censure vote was on December 2. On November 22 Andrei Vishinsky died. As Soviet public prosecutor during the Moscow Trials, Vishinsky had cold-bloodedly sent dozens of former comrades to their deaths for crimes he knew they had not committed. Their executions as "Trotskyites" and "German spies" had triggered the execution of at least one million other Soviet citizens, while millions of others were sent to languish in the Siberian gulag. McCarthy had not sent one person to jail. Yet by a terrible irony of fate, it is his name, not Vishinsky's, that has been universally remembered and reviled as the symbol of an era of terror and suspicion.

"The Taft type of Republican was willing to stand up on this thing and be counted," McCarthy told an interviewer for *U.S. News and World Report*. "I think they will vote for me."[33] In the end, they did, with the exception of

Homer Ferguson of Michigan, but they were not enough to save him. The vote was not even close: 67 to 22. Twenty-two Republicans supported the resolution "condemning" McCarthy; most of them were liberal or moderate Republicans from the urban Northeast and New England. Knowland, the majority leader, and twenty-one other conservative Republicans sided with McCarthy (who voted present). Republican members of the Watkins Committee were furious that their leader, Bill Knowland, had decided to vote against censure—in effect, a repudiation of the men he had helped to appoint. His fellow senator from Wisconsin, Alex Wiley, decided not to vote. All forty-four Democrats present, even the southerners, had voted for censure—a major accomplishment for Johnson.

There was, however, one Democrat who did not cast a vote. That was the junior senator from Massachusetts, John Fitzgerald Kennedy. On October 16 he had entered the hospital for back surgery and stayed there recuperating during the vote. His amanuensis, Ted Sorensen, had drafted a speech supporting censure on narrow technical grounds, but Kennedy never had to deliver it. He believed he had dodged a personal and political bullet. "Do you know what's going to happen if I leave this hospital?" he said to a visiting friend. "Those reporters are going to lean over my stretcher. There's going to be about 95 faces bent over . . . and every one of those guys is going to say, 'Now, Senator, what about McCarthy?' Do you know what I'm going to do? I'm going to reach back for my back and I'm just going to yell, 'OW!' "[34]

There was also some confusion immediately afterward when it turned out that the resolution of censure did not contain the word *censure*, only the word *condemn*. Senators Bridges and Jenner immediately pounced. Did this mean that the vote they had been debating back and forth for the past month was not a formal censure at all but something else? Jenner wanted to know, half-seriously, if this meant they had to do the whole thing over again. However, Senator Fulbright pulled out a dictionary and noted that *condemn* seemed to mean the same thing as *censure*, and that that word obviously covered the case. And there the matter stood: an ambiguous ending to an episode that the Senate had preferred not take place, and wanted to forget as soon as it was done. "The Senate," Eisenhower had told his brother, Milton, earlier, "has to deal with Senator McCarthy." And they had, but not in a way that made many of them feel particularly happy or proud.

Ruth Watt had ridden in the elevator to the censure vote with both McCarthy and McClellan. McCarthy pointed to the Democrat and told her, "Well, Ruthy, here's your new chairman, you've got to start taking orders from him." She didn't say what she was really thinking: "I can't stand it because I'm not going to have you for chairman anymore." But despite her respect and devotion to her old boss, she remembered what McClellan had told her earlier: "I'm fond of Joe, but he's getting out of hand, and we have to do something to control him." Ruth, like millions of other Americans, had ruefully accepted the wisdom of that view.[35]

On his way out, a reporter asked McCarthy what he thought about the final vote. "Well," he replied, "I wouldn't say it was a vote of confidence."

Chapter 16

Extinction

Soft you; a word or two before you go.
I have done the state some service, and they know't.
No more of that. I pray you, in your letters,
When you shall these unlucky deeds relate,
Speak of me as I am; nothing extenuate.

—*Othello*, V, ii, 338–342.

I n the press, and in liberal circles generally, the sense of satisfaction was huge. The *New Republic*'s TRB crowed: "From now on Joe is the man with the Scarlet Letter. He has 'C' written on his coat, put there by men who know him best. . . . Well, well, a good week!" Many anti-McCarthy reporters had suffered horrendous abuse for their stand. When the crowd at the Madison Square Garden discovered a *Life* photographer in their midst, they angrily ordered her expelled. Someone even shouted, "Hang the Communist!" Richard Rovere could sift through a drawerful of letters suggesting that he walk into the Atlantic Ocean until his hat floated or that he apply to win the next Stalin Prize. "I never knew such vituperation," Rovere admitted.[1] For journalists like Rovere or Joseph Alsop or James Wechsler, the censure of Joe McCarthy was as much a matter of personal vindication as of public honor or ideology. For four years, a sizable portion of the American public had dismissed their warnings that McCarthy was an unscrupulous demagogue and that McCarthyism was as serious a menace to freedom as communism. The Senate vote for censure proved (or appeared to prove) that they had been right.

It was not just postwar liberalism that scored a devastating triumph with McCarthy's fall: it was also the anti-McCarthy press. Thanks to *See It Now*, Edward R. Murrow entered journalism's pantheon, where he has remained ever since. The Alsop brothers' column would soon be carried in 190 papers, while McCarthy supporters George Sokolsky and Westbrook Pegler entered a permanent eclipse. Alone of McCarthy's supporters, Fulton Lewis, Jr., managed to stay in the public eye, largely because his national radio program looked for support to local sponsors rather than national ones. At the national level, the conservative voice was gradually being muted.

Rovere, who had written devastating portraits of McCarthy in the *New Yorker* and *Esquire*, bounced back from the McCarthy censure in predictable style. He was the obvious person to do the postmortem biography of "Senator Joe": virtually everyone he spoke to in gathering material for the book was either a reporter or columnist. Perhaps no other single event since World War II did more to confirm the proposition that a pro–New Deal, anticonservative media protected fundamental American values of fairness and freedom than McCarthy's censure vote. "It was a melancholy time," Rovere wrote regarding McCarthy's heyday, "and the Chief Justice of the Supreme Court [Earl Warren] was probably right when he said that if the Bill of Rights were put to a vote, it would lose."[2] America had survived McCarthy by the skin of its teeth, was the implication; and now, right-minded persons had to take steps to make sure it didn't happen again.

For McCarthy himself, descent into oblivion was swift and total. It came in three distinct but overlapping stages. The first was political, as he found himself stripped of his power and public influence. The second was personal, physical, and psychological. The third, and ultimately the most important phase, was ideological, a process that moved on past his death and in effect still goes on today.

Some observers were quick to point out that censure did not technically deprive McCarthy of any actual rights or privileges as a senator. It was not the censure but the Democratic victories in 1954 that cost him his chairmanship of PSI and Governmental Operations. But when Ike invited Arthur Watkins to the Oval Office to congratulate him on the successful censure vote, McCarthy's self-control snapped. On December 7, he wandered into the PSI committee room to fire his final shot as chairman, blasting the Eisenhower administration for its "shrinking show of weakness" in dealing with communism and apologizing for having supported Ike in the past. Too late he realized how the White House had been working against him from the beginning. Eisenhower was confident and unconcerned. "Jim, I'm not at all surprised to see it come," he told aide James Hagerty. "I rather suspected as much, and it's all right with me."[3] He knew McCarthy was now powerless to hurt anyone, even as he was burning his last bridges to his own party.

Although McCarthy still had the right to sit on committees, speak, and vote, in the Senate, his words now meant nothing. He was an institutional pariah. His colleagues now ignored his offered bills and amendments, just as they ignored him in the halls and on the Senate floor. When he entered the cloakroom or went to lunch, other senators would immediately leave. A McCarthy speech on the Senate floor meant an empty chamber. As William White observed, "A door, quite unseen but quite heavy, had been shut before him." For a man who had defied and flaunted Senate conventions and had treated his fellow legislators so badly, the silent treatment pained McCarthy deeply. Others did not enjoy watching it either. One senior senator who had been instrumental in bringing the censure to a vote confessed to a reporter as they watched the silent, solitary figure trudge down the corridor: "He feels caged. In my book he has it coming, but believe me, I don't take pleasure in the sight." Bobby Baker, who had helped Lyndon Johnson achieve his silent coup, admitted, "I felt twinges of guilt each time I caught a glimpse of him." Charles Potter remarked about those final years, "I think he was the loneliest man I ever knew."[4]

At home in their new house on Third Street near Capitol Hill, the McCarthys settled into a new, more peaceful routine. The tension and sense of siege that had prevailed during the censure debate, the constant round of visitors and advisers, vanished overnight. Instead, the main problem became how to keep Joe from drinking and how to sustain his interest in issues beyond his own political demise. Brent Bozell joined his staff as speechwriter and as house guest while he and his wife searched for a place to live in Washington. McCarthy was an amiable, even pleasant host; his guests shared the same bathroom on the second floor and the rooms into which his mother-in-law later moved. Patricia Bozell remembers the practical jokes, the amiable humor, the acts of kindness, including the day when her cat, Kiki, disappeared. Joe McCarthy, who hated and feared cats and tolerated the cat's presence only so long as it remained in the Bozell's half of the house, spent that evening searching through the bushes with a flashlight calling out, "Here Kiki, here Kiki," until the police, who had to protect the McCarthy house from threats against his life, rushed to the scene with wailing sirens, thinking he was a burglar.[5]

The only difficulties arose over issue of drinking—alcohol had become part of the household routine for both Joe and Jean, beginning with cocktails before lunch—and the occasional painful intrusion of the recent past. One day Mamie Eisenhower invited the wives of senators, including Jean Mc-Carthy, to a party at the White House. When Joe got home, Jean expressed her outrage at the invitation. McCarthy reassured her, saying, "You know, she's a nice lady." That night the Bozells could hear Jean crying herself to sleep in the adjoining bedroom, while McCarthy tried unsuccessfully to assure her that everything would turn out all right.

Nothing pained McCarthy, however, more than the effect that the censure vote had on his dealings with the press. Overnight they stopped covering him. The crowd of reporters that had once hovered outside his office door or committee room, and had been there ever since the Wheeling speech, vanished. Editors and news producers across the country decided *nothing* Mc-Carthy said was newsworthy any longer. Stewart Alsop compared it to when "a whole pack of beagles will suddenly and collectively realize the scent is false, stop yelping, break stride, and give up the chase." McCarthy and others called it a deliberate blackout. At one point he told a *Milwaukee Journal* reporter that he had been rereading Thomas Jefferson's works and had come to a conclusion that no one should be persecuted for his beliefs, no matter how unpopular they might be. He also bet another reporter from the same paper that this story about Joe McCarthy's amazing turnaround would be spiked. McCarthy won the bet. The reporter later said, "I remember feeling annoyed. . . . I didn't like McCarthy to be proved right on anything about the *Journal.*"

McCarthy's speeches in the Senate, regardless of the subject, drew the same noncoverage. In October 1955 he gave one warning that the USSR was winning the race in missile technologies and that if they developed sufficient range for their rockets, "Milwaukee or Boston or Washington can be wiped out by pushing a button." Coming two years before *Sputnik*, it was a prophetic speech. But it, like everything else, fell on deaf ears. George Reedy: "It didn't matter how good the speech was. What difference did it make? Who cared?"[6]

He briefly toyed with the notion of challenging Eisenhower for the presidential nomination in 1956. He asked Don Surine to do a private poll on his chances. His plan, he told William Buckley at the time, was to rally conservative sentiment and then throw it behind William Knowland or some equivalent figure in order to prevent Ike from running again. He had no illusions that he was very popular in mainstream Republican circles. Still, he was taken aback when the poll revealed only 3 percent of Republicans would consider voting for him. He stopped talking about a return to the national political stage.

McCarthy had become an embarrassment at home as well. His senior colleague, seventy-year-old Alex Wiley, had arranged to be in South America to avoid the censure vote. Wisconsin Republicans were terrified that his name would taint the state's GOP and cost it administration support. Although Tom Coleman still believed in him (while despairing over his alienation from the Eisenhower administration), many other Republican officials had joined the Joe Must Go campaign. Governor Kohler and Representative Mel Laird both fired shots at him. When Democrat Henry Reuss challenged McCarthy crony Charles Kersten in the primary for the Fifth District, he pointed to Kersten's "slavish" devotion to the senator and challenged him to disavow McCarthy. Kersten's answer was evasive: "I don't think anyone should stand or fall on someone else's record." Reuss beat him handily in the district Kersten had won just two years earlier. After the censure, a senior party official, when asked if McCarthy was still a power in Wisconsin, replied, "If he ever was, he is no longer." Republicans all looked to a reelection campaign in 1958 with genuine dread.[7]

When Boscobel, Wisconsin, sponsored a "McCarthy Day" in the spring of 1955, organizers were shocked at the tiny turnout. Where they had anticipated fifty thousand they found fewer than fifteen hundred spectators, many of them members of the high school bands who had been marched out to greet him. Although Joe put the best face on things and thanked the sparse crowd for their "vast turnout," he suffered agonies from incidents like this. A year later he turned up unannounced, and rather drunk, at a campaign dinner for Vice President Nixon in Milwaukee. After he sat down at the end of the dias, an embarrassed GOP official had to ask him to leave. McCarthy obediently left. A reporter followed him out and was astonished to find him sitting alone on the curb in the alley, weeping with rage and humiliation.[8]

Roy Matson, editor of the *Wisconsin State Journal*, told a group in Madison, "Time and public's good sense have taken care of McCarthy. He's a dead pigeon." In fact, McCarthy's political demise was not inevitable. He was forty-six years old, a ranking member of the Senate, with a shrunken, but still considerable, national following. With a little patience and determination, he could have fought back and rebuilt his reputation. Having weathered the worst, he might have emerged even stronger than before, as censured senators have done since. But his heart had gone out of it. The publicity and the cause had sustained him, rather than the other way around. "A Hitler or a Mussolini," as historian John Lukacs noted, "would have taken sustenance from such a censure" as proof they were on the right course.[9] At a deep psychological level, McCarthy accepted the censure of his enemies and resigned himself to his fate. When a friend urged him to take on the critics, he replied sadly, "No, what you want me to do is become a bitter old man."

He did write an angry letter to Roy Matson, complaining that "while I have not been surprised or disturbed by the opposition of Bill Evjue and others, I have been both surprised and disturbed by your sudden and apparent all-out opposition to me. I cannot understand this."[10] Some people he never forgave, such as Watkins and Richard Nixon. "That prick Nixon," he would say to Urban Van Susteren, "kissing Ike's ass to make it to the White House." Yet when the White House threw a Christmas party and invited every senator except one, McCarthy plaintively asked his staff if perhaps his invitation had been lost in the mail. No one had the heart to tell him the truth.[11]

Even Roy Cohn remained a friend and visitor, in spite of all that happened, and the feeling among McCarthy's closest conservative friends that Cohn had been Iago to McCarthy's Othello. When William Rusher ventured to criticize the role Cohn had played in McCarthy's clash with the Army, he responded simply and firmly, "Well, I like him." "And *that*," Rusher wrote later, "was that." The only time friends saw the other side of McCarthy was one day when Cohn rang up the house on Capitol Hill to announce that he was coming for a visit. Jean passed the message on to Joe, who thought that was fine—until Cohn mentioned he was going to bring David Schine by as well. Suddenly eyewitnesses noticed a visible change in McCarthy, and he shouted, in the same wounded, angry voice he had once used with those who had stood in his way, "Tell that so-and-so if he shows his face in this house, I'll punch him in the nose." Neither Cohn nor Schine visited that evening.[12]

The main problem was finding something constructive for McCarthy to do. Jean, the Bozells, Cohn, and everyone who liked McCarthy and were still loyal to him tried unsuccessfully to nudge him in a direction that would once again catch his interest, move him into action, and stop his drinking—like tugboats trying to push a beached ocean liner out to open sea. Each effort met with McCarthy's polite attention, a half-hearted response, and then was dropped. Patricia Bozell remembers going to a political rally in New York for which her husband had written a speech on some esoteric cold war subject. McCarthy read a couple of pages while his audience dozed. Then suddenly he set aside the speech and tried to improvise on the same old themes as in the old days, with the same grandiloquent gestures and sweeping turns of phrase. The effect was, she later remembered, grotesque. It was an embarrassing caricature of the McCarthy of only six years earlier, of Wheeling and the well of the Senate floor—only six years, and yet already a lifetime away.

As time passed, his sense of abandonment was total. He could barely look at friends in the face. "No matter where I go," he complained to an old Wisconsin buddy, "they look on me with contempt. I can't take it anymore." The man who had exuded physical vigor and breezy confident masculinity became weak and subdued. People noticed he seemed unsteady on his feet, dazed and often confused about where he was or who he was meeting. And no wonder. He was, in the estimation of Urban Van Susteren, drinking up to a full fifth of whiskey a day. When he spoke to Joe's doctor in Washington, the physician confirmed that two-thirds of McCarthy's liver was gone and he would die if he didn't stop drinking at once. Van Susteren found himself screaming at his old friend to stop; he was killing himself. McCarthy's answer was, "Kiss my ass." Once he did tell a pair of senatorial staffers that doctors had ordered him to stop drinking, and that if he touched another drop he would die. They then watched amazed as he filled a glass to the brim with bourbon and drained it to the bottom.[13]

His despair was not just personal. He also realized that the anti-Communist cause was fading away, forever tainted with the label of "McCarthyism," and that liberalism, of the soft, yielding sort he despised was gaining ground. His brief bouts of activity in the Senate all sprang from the need to fight back, even if he had to do it in defiance of his failing health and an increasingly moderate Republican Party. He cast the single vote against the nomination of William S. Brennan to the Supreme Court. He waged a desperate campaign to prevent Eisenhower's four-power summit in Geneva in July 1956, warning of a "sellout" like Potsdam and Yalta. He even introduced a bill requiring the summit to take up the issue of the status of Eastern bloc countries, recently dragooned into the Warsaw Pact. Lyndon Johnson cruelly allowed the bill to go to the floor for a vote in order to show McCarthy once and for all how he stood with his colleagues. It was trounced, 77 to 4. A magazine, *Picture Review*, published a jocular article, "Whatever Happened to Joe McCarthy?"[14]

Yet just the year before, the public had learned much of the sober truth about Yalta when the government released thousands of documents relating to its secret negotiations. They failed to confirm the more heated theories about a deliberate sellout. But they did reveal how much Stalin had taken advantage of a disenchanted Churchill and an insouciant FDR. The public could now see how solemn Soviet promises had turned out to be lies and how the old New Deal establishment belief that one could deal with the Soviets on a straightforward, nonideological basis was fatally flawed. None of it could save the disgraced McCarthy.

He began publishing a newsletter for his constituents, which issued Cassandra-like warnings about disasters ahead if America lowered its anti-Communist defenses. He could point to Senator McClellan's and Bobby Kennedy's masterful reexamination of the Peress case, which had definitively established that the Army's security measures had been hopelessly inadequate, detailing some forty-three separate errors in the handling of the case. In another he pointed out that the Senate Internal Security Subcommittee, under Bill Jenner and James Eastland of Mississippi, had just found confirming evidence of Soviet espionage at Fort Monmouth during the war, a vindication of McCarthy's hearings a year and a half earlier.[15] No one noticed. Fort Monmouth, like Peress and the Army-McCarthy hearings, was old news.

A distinct cold war thaw had set in, and concerns like McCarthy's and the Internal Security Committee now seemed stale and trivial.

The one new friend McCarthy made was a Democrat, James Eastland. On domestic issues like race, the southern segregationist and the post–New Deal Republican were far apart. But as the new chairman of the committee Pat McCarran had founded to follow the trail of domestic Communist subversion and with McCarthy's former bloodhound Robert Morris at his side, Eastland believed McCarthy had been more right than wrong. He came to regret the vote he had cast for censure.[16] Like McCarthy, Eastland was dismayed by the series of Supreme Court decisions under Chief Justice Earl Warren reversing loyalty security laws. One overturned sedition laws in individual states. Another reinstated a New York schoolteacher who had been fired for invoking the Fifth Amendment when asked if he were a Communist, while *Watkins* v. *United States* placed clear limits on congressional investigative powers. "No inquiry is an end in itself," Warren wrote for the majority. "It must be related to or in furtherance of a legitimate task of Congress." McCarthy labeled these rulings "a victory for the Communists" and called *Watkins* "the most outrageous instance of judicial legislation that has ever come to my attention." When Eastland asserted, "What other explanation could there be except that a majority of the court is being influenced by some secret, but very powerful Communist or pro-Communist influence," McCarthy agreed. That was the sort of hard-hitting language he recognized and felt familiar with. But everywhere else in the public sphere, it was fast disappearing.

In May 1953, Judge Luther Youngdahl had thrown out four counts of Owen Lattimore's indictment for lying to the McCarran Comittee about his ties to the Communist cause. The judge said in effect that if Lattimore did not think of himself as a "Communist sympathizer," then he could not have been lying when he denied being one. In January 1955, Youngdahl threw out the remaining indictment. The Justice Department dropped the case. When Roy Cohn came to visit to talk about the anti-Communist issue, McCarthy told him with despair in his voice, "It's like shoveling shit against the tide." Jack Kennedy confided to friends, "Even my Dad is against McCarthy now."[17]

By the summer of 1956, after a pathetic appearance at the Republican National Convention (a startling contrast to his triumphant performance in 1952), his drinking became so self-destructive that even Jean felt she had to take action. McCarthy entered the hospital for periods of detoxification. That autumn he had a major bout with delirium tremens, and doctors diagnosed him with hepatitis and cirrhosis of the liver.

As the new year dawned, Jean Kerr struggled to raise his spirits. She had his war medals and the awards he had received from patriotic groups and organizations like Knights of Columbus and VFW mounted and hung in a conspicuous place. She urged him to announce plans for his reelection in 1958, in hopes that the prospect of campaigning would help him recover the old fire. With the help of Cardinal Francis Spellman, he and Jean adopted a baby daughter. William Rusher remembered going with McCarthy into her bedroom while she lay asleep in her crib, and McCarthy's sense of pride but also shyness at the sight of this delicate infant child: "Those hairy hands were unused to such fragility." But these were momentary breaks in the clouds of depression and gloom that were closing around him. In March he flew to Milwaukee to attend a television quiz show. Friends remembered his sickly yellow hue and the gaunt body that he dragged from place to place. He had dinner with one of them, Ray Dittmore, and as he toyed with his food, he said sadly, "Raymond, I've lived a million years." He made it clear that death no longer had any terror for him.[18]

On April 28 McCarthy entered Bethesda Naval Hospital for the last time. Jean Kerr told reporters he was there for some knee surgery. In fact, his liver had finally given out. On May 2, 1957, at 5:02, he expired after receiving last rites from a priest.

Old opponents were subdued when they learned of his death and avoided sounding too triumphant. After all, they had won their battle more than two years earlier, and most found extended commentary unnecessary. John McClellan said, "I found him to be a man of strong convictions and on occasions when I may have disagreed with him I am happy to say there were never any clash of personalities. He will be missed." Stuart Symington said, "I am deeply distressed." He never spoke about McCarthy again, then or later. Joseph Welch announced, "I never hated Joe McCarthy."

The White House released an awkward statement expressing "profound sympathy" for Jean. Another president, Harry Truman, said he was "sorry" to hear of McCarthy's death. Dean Acheson evidently was not. When reporters asked him for a comment, he replied with the Latin tag *de mortuis nihil nisi bonum*—"about the dead say something good or nothing at all"—and then said nothing at all.

The press allowed itself to be more philosophical. Eric Sevareid told his listeners, "McCarthy had a certain manic brilliance. . . . But his brilliance outran his knowledge, and his ambition outran them both." Another old opponent, James Wechsler of the *New York Post*, admitted it was hard to be objective. "We felt he was cynical, primitive, irresponsible, ruthless; he was bully-boy incarnate, but not unlikeable." But Wechsler also felt he was "an accident of history." McCarthy had been "the creature of a time of national frenzy and frustration over Communist aggression in the world," and while McCarthy himself was now gone, the forces that had fed him and he fed in turn, "McCarthyism," still remained. "It lives on in the excesses of the Senate Internal Security Subcommittee and the House Un-American Activities Committee, in the suave operations of a Robert Morris rather than the crudities of a Roy Cohn. . . . In all the blacklists, taboos, and suppression of 'controversy' that still shadows our society, and hold so many men prisoners."[19]

On Monday, May 6, a funeral service was held in the Senate Chamber—the sort of honor usually reserved for presidents and chief justices of the Supreme Court. The casket sat in the well of the chamber, just in front of the secretary's desk, surrounded by huge banks of flowers. Almost every senator was there, both friends and foes, along with Speaker of the House Sam Rayburn and Vice President Nixon. The White House sent aide Jack Martin as its sole representative. In the gallery were J. Edgar Hoover, J. B. Matthews, and a very subdued Roy Cohn. Arthur Watkins took his usual seat at the desk next to McCarthy's own. A few days earlier committee staffer William Rusher had gone into Watkins's office on an unrelated matter. Suddenly Watkins had turned to him and without any prompting launched into a long, rambling soliloquy about why he had believed McCarthy had to be censured. It was, Rusher felt, half an apology, half a self-rationalization for the role Watkins had played in McCarthy's downfall.[20] Now he sat alone, looking at no one.

After a eulogy by the chaplain of the Senate and a funeral sermon by Jean and Joe's Catholic priest, six Marines in dress blues carried the casket out the door, down the Capitol steps, to a car bound for National Airport. McCarthy's body was being flown by military plane for burial in Appleton, where he used to sell eggs from his chicken farm to Sumnicht's grocery store thirty years before. Jean had been calm through the entire ordeal, until the reception afterward. When Bill Knowland entered the room and went up to her, Jean turned and suddenly collapsed in his arms.

Jean, her infant daughter, and the McCarthy family took a separate flight back to Wisconsin. Three of McCarthy's colleagues, in a final gallant gesture, decided to fly on the military plane back alone with Joe. One was Senator Herman Welker of Idaho, who had quit the Gillette subcommittee to protest its proceedings against McCarthy in 1951 and who had passionately defended McCarthy during the censure debate. The other two were survivors from the Class of '46: George "Molly" Malone of Nevada, from whose office in Reno McCarthy had planned his campaign to bring the State Department to its knees, and William Jenner of Indiana. All three were almost as despised in the liberal press as McCarthy was. During the censure debate, the *New Republic* had called Jenner and Welker the "Men of Hate." "There is one in every mob," it had remarked in a famous phrase, "who gives the scream or fires the pistol that precipitates the holocaust."[21] The end was coming soon for them as well. Herman Welker would be dead of a brain tumor in less than a year (hostile reporters had assumed and reported that his frequent headaches were hangovers from excessive drinking). Jenner decided not to return for reelection in 1958 and left Washington to return to private practice in Indiana. Malone lost that same year. Now they were making their last tribute to their old friend and ideological comrade-in-arms.

When the plane arrived in Green Bay, they were met by a thirty-five-man Marine honor guard. Huge crowds lined the route to Appleton to show their respect. In Appleton itself, banks, businesses, schools, and public offices were shut. "Men drifted out of taverns along the avenue," wrote a reporter for the *Appleton Post-Crescent*, "waiting for Joe and standing for a moment as the hearse passed. Then a few looks, a few remarks—and more of the memories."[22] That evening and the following day more than thirty thousand people from Appleton, Grand Chute, Green Bay, Shawano, Neenah, and other nearby communities filed through St. Mary's Church and past the open casket containing the body of their beloved senator and hometown boy. More than twenty-one senators had flown out for the funeral and followed the funeral cortege as it made its way to the cemetery. There McCarthy's old catechism teacher, Father Adam Grill, read a final eulogy. McCarthy, he said, "saw danger to his country and clothed in the shining armor of zeal and love," had marched "forward into battle with the cry on his lips, 'For God and for my Country.'" Now, Grill added, his voice breaking and tears forming, "he has come to rest." The honor guard fired a rifle volley and then "Taps" was sounded as the pallbearers lowered the coffin into the ground.

Standing to one side of the funeral party, unnoticed by many, was a somber, solitary figure—Robert F. Kennedy. Edwin Bayley, who was covering the funeral for the *Milwaukee Journal*, had recognized Bobby at once at Green Bay Airport earlier that morning. Kennedy had been the last person to get off the plane bearing senators and other Washington dignitaries to McCarthy's burial. "Bobby spotted me and came over to the car," Bayley remembered many years later. "He asked if he could ride into town with me. It was about ten in the morning, and the church services and burial were scheduled for the afternoon. I said, 'Sure, hop in,' and he did. I suspected that Bobby didn't want anybody to see him."

Kennedy was chief counsel on PSI under chairman McClellan, and also deep into his investigation of labor racketeering and the Mafia. Fifth Amendment Communists had been replaced by Fifth Amendment mobsters. In fact, the same techniques McCarthy had perfected in his halcyon days of red-hunting—the freewheeling use of the Senate subpoena, the intimidating glare of television lights and cameras, the badgering, aggressive tone with hostile witnesses (Bobby Kennedy to Sam Giancana: "Do you realize you giggle like a girl?")—were now standard operating procedure, although with the approval of the mainstream press, since these were gangsters, not Stalinists. Kennedy had been working in his Senate office when the news had come of McCarthy's death. He had sent everyone home for the day and went to his private office and shut the door. There he recorded in his journal, "It was all very difficult for me as I feel that I have lost an important part of my life—even though it is in the past."

Now he was in Appleton to pay his final respects. Kennedy and Bayley had lunch together in Appleton. "He was in a somber mood," Bayley recalled. Then, after the funeral and the internment, Bobby walked over to Bayley and said "he would prefer that I didn't say anything about his being there." Bayley didn't; he kept Kennedy's secret for more than three decades. Later Kennedy wrote more about McCarthy in his journal:

> He was a very complicated character. His whole method of operation was complicated because he would get a guilty feeling and get hurt after he blasted somebody. . . . He was sensitive and yet insensitive. He didn't anticipate the results of what he was doing. He was very thoughtful of his friends and yet he could be so cruel.[23]

If McCarthy's political opponents had tried to be restrained after his death, his supporters felt no such need. They believed McCarthy had been "hounded to death by those," according to columnist George Sokolsky, "who would not forget and could not forgive."[24] To many, McCarthy's censure and the campaign against him had been nothing less than a form of public murder—a few on the very fringe were willing to believe he *had* been murdered, although most understood that in the final analysis Joe McCarthy had been too weak a vessel for the tremendous burden he had been forced to bear.

That led Willi Schlamm in the pages of the new journal founded by a circle of ex-McCarthyites, *National Review*, to stress what he called McCarthy's "innocence." It was a term, interestingly enough, that Ralph Flanders had also used in his June 1 attack on him. Schlamm called his essay "Across McCarthy's Grave." He wrote, "What the learned frauds could not stand about McCarthy was his certainty: he knew what he knew, he believed what he believed, and there were no two ways about it." He had been the opposite of a cynic, which was why the Washington insiders had hated him. The true cynic and hypocrite in the McCarthy drama had been Joseph Welch, Schlamm asserted, "the greasy old Juggler" with the "phony sanctimonious creak in his voice," who "more than any other figure from the comic strip of our age, personifies the Establishment."[25]

In Schlamm's estimation, McCarthy's chief "crime" was that he had rejected the moral relativism underlying modern liberalism, which insisted that a person's moral and political choices count for nothing. That relativism had allowed liberalism to sympathize with and protect communism's champions and to profess to find moral worth in a system of absolute evil—again, in Forrest Davis's words, a liberalism that "looks evil in the face and pronounces it half-good." McCarthy had turned his back on all that.

> There he came, from the heartland of America, a tenacious and quite ordinary politician; and in a sudden and lasting moment of recognition, he saw the central truth of his age: that his country, his faith, his civilization was at war with communism, war pure and simple. "This war will not end except by either victory or death for this civilization," he said again and again. . . . It was this hot sense of urgency which he, for a short time, forced upon his country. But the automobiles were too sleek, prosperity much too tepid, Eisenhower much too nice, TV much too amusing: and so the country grew tired of the truth and of the man who kept shouting it, redundantly and at the end, hoarsely. The country went to sleep again. And the man lay down and died.

Meanwhile, Jean spent months after the funeral answering the tens of thousands of letters from well-wishers and admirers. Many contained little cards announcing masses said on behalf of Joe. His secretary, Mary Driscoll, remembered, "I opened three letters in fifteen minutes one day which announced 15,000 masses."[26] Jean also answered letters from people like J. B. and Ruth Matthews and Louis Budenz. "I only wish in some way I could comfort you," she wrote to Budenz and his wife, Margaret, "for we do indeed share a loss." J. B. Matthews sent a letter on June 22: "Jeannie, I believe that Joe lives on and on, and that the saga of Joe will be read with that of Patrick Henry to inspire the patriots of the 21st century and succeeding centuries." Jean agreed, as she wrote to another well-wisher: "The battle Joe fought so fearlessly and with such insight is not over. It will end only as Joe so often said, with victory or death for our civilization."[27]

Someone who might have agreed with her, but for different reasons, was Whittaker Chambers. He had been staying at William F. Buckley's home in Connecticut when word reached them about McCarthy's death. Later, Chambers wrote to Buckley regarding the senator, "He was not my leader. . . . I could not follow him living, I could only pity him." Chambers continued: "He never evolved a strategy, but only a tactic which consisted exclusively in the impulse: Attack. That could never be enough, could end only as it did, or in some similar way."[28]

Robert Kennedy summed McCarthy up this way: "Cohn and Schine took him up the mountain and showed him all those wonderful things. He destroyed himself for that—for publicity." Ambassador Joseph Kennedy was more prosaic: "I thought he'd be a sensation. He was smart. But he went off the deep end."[29]

IV

LEGACY

It is impossible to live in peace with those we believe damned; to love them would be to hate God who punishes them: we positively must either reclaim them or torment them.

—Jean-Jacques Rousseau, *The Social Contract*

Chapter 17

Beyond McCarthy

Our country is still in danger.

—William Jenner, tribute to Joe McCarthy, June 11, 1957

During the censure debate, *Time* magazine had hinted that Mc-Carthy's fall might actually *help* the continuing investigation of Communist subversion.[1] It was a fatuous hope. Interest in investigations in both the House and the Senate plummeted. When the Internal Security committee held its public hearings in the mid-fifties, only two newspapers still regularly sent reporters.[2] Antisubversion lost whatever headline appeal it had ever had, and those who had suffered under its strictures now wanted revenge.

With McCarthy gone, anti-Stalinist liberals found themselves at war again with the old Popular Front mentality, which the cold war had driven from the scene. A host of intellectuals and writers and ex–fellow travelers had chafed under the restrictions about appearing pro-Soviet or too anti-American. Arthur Miller's play *The Crucible*, which appeared to great critical acclaim in 1953, had epitomized their moral self-righteousness as well as their sense of injury. It equated the naming of former Stalinists to congressional committees with the trial and hanging of accused witches in Puritan Salem (although the fact that Miller could bring out such a play at the supposed height of the McCarthyite "terror" seemed to undermine that claim).

311

Alarmed by this, Richard Rovere took time off from his forthcoming biography of McCarthy to write a penetrating critique of Miller's work for the *New Republic*, entitled "Arthur Miller's Conscience." He noted how "naming names" had become the cardinal sin when discussing Communist associations, both past and present, rather than those associations themselves. "One could almost say that Miller's sense of himself *is* the principle that holds 'informing' to be the ultimate in human wickedness"—as opposed to, say, working for or supporting a political cause such as Hitler's or Stalin's (as Miller, a former Communist, had once done). As a liberal, Rovere believed in "a free play to the individual's moral judgements" and affirmed that "in recent years, Congressional committees have posed the single largest threat to this freedom." But as an anti-Communist, Rovere recognized that "not all informing is bad. . . . The question of guilt is relevant." Those who commit real crimes—"a hit-and-run driver or a spy or a thief"—need to be informed against, if the social order is to be preserved. "If any agency of the community," Rovere said, "is authorized to undertake a serious investigation of any of our common problems, then the identities of others—*names*— are of great importance." The question came down to whether or not one took the issue of domestic communism and "subversion" seriously. Rovere, like other anti-Communist and anti-McCarthy liberals, still did. But others increasingly did not.[3]

McCarthy's disgrace allowed the anti-anti-Communists to retake the high moral ground they had lost since the Nazi-Soviet Pact and the Hiss case. The anti-anti-Communist left got its next chance with Harvey Matusow. Matusow had been an FBI informant on Communist Party activities in New York, testifying at trials of CPUSA officials and making a small name for himself as a lecturer and author. His 1951 article on Communist infiltration in the military, "Reds in Khaki," may have helped to steer McCarthy's attention toward the Army. Matusow even worked with him for a time. But then law enforcement officials began to get leery about Matusow's increasingly sensational claims and his emotional instability, and he lost his audience. So Matusow skipped to the other side. With the help of publisher and secret Communist Albert Kahn, he released a startling self-exposé called *False Witness*, which detailed how he had lied about the Communist threat and charged that others were doing the same. Its title was a play on the most famous anti-Communist memoir of all, Whittaker Chamber's *Witness*, with the clear implication that ex-Communists who are anti-Communists are *all* liars.[4] The publisher, and reviewers on the progressive left, touted the book in triumph. Exposure of the "cropped photo" and the "purloined FBI letter" during the Army-McCarthy hearings had suggested that the antisubversive cause relied on false evidence, and now Matusow (who had testified from time to time before McCarthy's committee) confirmed it. Red hunting really was just a phony excuse to attack New Deal liberalism—as the popular slogan had it, Republicans spell "FDR" H-I-S-S.

McCarthy's disgrace had completely vindicated men like Acheson, Marshall, and Jessup in the eyes of the media and opinion makers. Now that vindication rippled out to include hosts of others—not just Owen Lattimore or the China hands or other "innocent victims" of McCarthy's attacks, but those whose guilt had seemed more certain, such as Alger Hiss. If Hiss's disgrace had given McCarthy credibility in 1950, now the dynamic was reversed. *The Nation*, the old standard-bearer of the Popular Front, and its fellow-traveling editor, Carey McWilliams, carried on a decade-long campaign to prove that Hiss had been framed. His assistant Fred J. Cook would later publish a deeply negative and influential account of the McCarthy years, *The Nightmare Decade*. Hiss was released from prison and made his first public appearance in April 1956 at Princeton University, where he received a self-consciously discreet standing ovation.

The new liberal position on Hiss's guilt would be "case not proved," and whatever Hiss had done, what Nixon, McCarthy, and his other accusers had done was far, far worse.[5]* Sidney Hook, Hubert Humphrey, Joe Rauh, and a few others tried to keep the focus on the threat that Communist values posed to a genuinely liberal society, but it was a losing struggle. Paradoxically, McCarthy's fall undermined the intellectual foundations not of conservative anti-communism but its liberal counterpart.

Even more paradoxical, the revelations about Stalin's tyranny in Krushchev's secret speech in 1956 hurt the anti-Communist cause. Instead of rebuking those who defended Stalin during his bloodiest years, a chorus of young liberals and radicals argued that the speech proved that the Soviet Union had changed and that the old assumptions about Soviet ambitions and the subversive threat were obsolete.[6] They were prepared to take Soviet claims about wanting to end the cold war and live in peace seriously. Neither the invasion of Hungary in 1956, the Berlin blockade in 1961, nor the installation of nuclear missiles on Cuba the following year could shake that confidence, since they interpreted these crises as strictly defensive moves by a Soviet Union "in transition."

In official circles, these sentiments had not yet surfaced. Instead, the end of McCarthyism marks the true beginning of what historians usually term the cold war consensus, as conservative and Taftite critiques of containment faded away and bipartisanship reigned supreme. But even there a subtle shift of emphasis was under way as the fifties wound down. Policymakers now fo-

---

*In Nixon's case, this would seem to be confirmed by the revelations regarding Watergate.

cused on containment of the Soviet Union and red China as conventional international powers rather than as standard-bearers of an ideology. Eisenhower, Dulles, and their diplomats dropped language about the "defeat of communism" and began talking about "peace" instead. Before the Geneva summit, Eisenhower had said he would travel anywhere, anytime, to discuss peace with the Soviet leadership (two of the key architects of this approach were McCarthy's bêtes noires, Emmett Hughes and C. D. Jackson). At the summit, he announced, "The American people want to be friends with the Soviet people. There are no natural differences between our people or our nations."[7]

Soon talk about "peace" gave way to the desire for "peaceful coexistence." As Allen Drury was writing *Advise and Consent* in late 1958, some of the fictional senators in his novel still understood this sort of language as a pro-Soviet ploy. But in the real world, attitudes were already shifting. The traditional strategic goal of containment was now merely a short-term holding pattern, a way to force the Soviets toward the longer-term goal of coexistence—and still later of détente.

The result was a double policy. In public, officials pushed for smooth relations with the Soviet Union, emphasizing summits, treaties, and cultural exchanges. In secret, the United States launched covert operations to contain aggression, as the new phrasing had it. The CIA, not the United Nations or NATO, became the cold war instrument of choice under Eisenhower and then under his successors. Part of this, of course, was the result of the growth of nuclear arsenals, which made open conflict with the Soviet Union unthinkable, but part of it too was a desire not to allow partisan passions to disrupt the delicate strategic balance as they had during Korea and the McCarthy era. From Iran to Guatemala (where McCarthy's old nemesis John Peurifoy helped overthrow pro-Soviet President Arbenz in 1953) to Laos, the United States began conducting a series of secret wars that the American people knew nothing about and required no prior justification among insiders and members of Congress admitted to their inner councils. In matters of foreign policy, the public was not invited.

For one thing, the establishment's view of the public changed, thanks to the McCarthy episode. America, they believed, had shown itself vulnerable to a dangerous brand of radical populists who saw the world in simplistic terms and who, if allowed to enter the debate, would irrationally turn on their intellectual and social betters. The new view among sophisticated observers was that McCarthy had revealed the ugly face of mass democracy on a scale analogous to Hitler and Mussolini. Sociologists stressed the similarities between McCarthy and other American rabble-rousers like Huey Long and Father Coughlin, and Columbia's Richard Hofstadter stressed McCarthyism's "paranoid style" and the anti-intellectualism of his supporters. Professor Hofstadter even denied them the label "conservatives." They were "pseudo-conservatives" in his view, the products of "the rootlessness and heterogeneity of American life." And, he asked plaintively, "why do they express such a persistent fear and suspicion of *their* own government, whether its leadership rests in the hands of Roosevelt, Truman, or Eisenhower?" Taken together with the damning picture of McCarthy and his followers in Richard Rovere's *Senator Joe McCarthy*, which appeared in 1959, the entire period seemed to prove to liberal intellectuals that "the mass of people could not be relied on to defend civil liberties and democratic rights."[8] America, they agreed, had just dodged a political bullet: the specter of right-wing dictatorship led by goose-stepping ranks of the American Legion and the Knights of Columbus.

Fear of right-wing extremism did not fade with McCarthy's passing. A parade of claimants to the McCarthy mantle had appeared, starting with William Jenner. After the censure, he and others worried about how to reunite the anti-Communist right. Jenner tried briefly to sustain the faithful by speaking out on the "hidden revolution" in American government that elite liberal bureaucrats were carrying out and that provided an "ideal shelter for Communists in our government," but then he too dropped off the stage. Instead, exposure of the international Communist conspiracy fell to increasingly marginal types, like John T. Flynn, Robert Welch and the John Birch Society, Willis Carto's Liberty Lobby, John Beaty of the anti-Semitic and racist *Iron Curtain over America*, and John Stormer of *None Dare Call It Treason*. To sophisticated observers, this disparate group of men summed up the New American right, which posed a far greater danger (despite their diminutive numbers) to American freedom than a battered and discredited Communist Party.

Any attack on liberal conduct of the cold war, insofar as it echoed "McCarthyism," automatically implied a paranoid and dysfunctional view of reality. In the cold war movie *Fail Safe*, the right-wingers all push for nuclear apocalypse (one of them, played by Walter Matthau, even looks like McCarthy), while liberal president Henry Fonda and his elite private school chum, played by Dan O'Herlihy, remain calm and manage to contain the crisis by putting their faith in their Soviet counterparts—who end up looking more human and less ideological than their hard-line American opponents.

The only alternative to the liberal cold war consensus, the conventional wisdom implied, was mass destruction. At every step policymakers insisted on narrowing the range of their options, believing that America's global commitments were too vital to be handled through normal political channels or to be exploited in a "reckless" or "partisan" manner. As liberal Chester Bowles put it, Republican anti-Communist crusades had allowed "Congressional investigations and individual senators . . . to dictate day-to-day policy on foreign affairs; to make a political football of the military establishment; to punish by adverse publicity those men who were guilty of no crime punishable by law; and to divide the president from his subordinates in the Administration."[9] The cold war required instead creative presidential leadership, with a carefully picked coterie of advisers and executive branch officials, all groomed for power and "strategic thought," the new *arcana imperii* of the nuclear age. The last thing anyone wanted were old-style "primitives" like Joe McCarthy or Kenneth Wherry wading in to insist on public debate or scrutiny, and mucking up the clean, cool dispatch of policy.

Congress by and large acquiesced. Unpleasant episodes like the Wherry resolution, or the Bricker amendment, or McCarthy's taunting of State or Defense Department officials were past anomalies, while the Tonkin Gulf resolution became the future norm. As the sixties dawned, the new cold war ideal was of a circle of Ivy League–trained advisers sitting around a smooth, polished table with the president and coolly dealing with each crisis and Soviet move in turn, as an admiring public breathlessly waited on the results— which is precisely what the public got, first in the Cuban missile crisis and then in Vietnam.

The election of John F. Kennedy in 1960 marked the culmination of another political trend McCarthy had started, but which, despite his ties to the Kennedy family, very few noticed: the emergence of American Catholics in the political mainstream. Jack Kennedy, like his brother, never quite turned his back on McCarthy despite their divergent paths to political power. Now, in 1960, he discovered that his Irish Catholic roots, which he had taken such great pains to hide, served him well at the ballot box. As Michael Barone puts it, Kennedy learned that "being a Catholic was worth votes"— and in the same places, such as Massachusetts, working-class New York, and the Fox River valley of Wisconsin, where McCarthy had found his bedrock support. The Catholic vote, in fact, may have been the margin of victory in 1960.[10]

Shrewd, conservative, and cautious, Kennedy had strong doubts about getting involved in Indochina. It was his liberal advisers who did not. Later historians would blame the Vietnam debacle on McCarthyism.[11] In fact, just the opposite is the case. The Best and the Brightest who constructed it— Acheson protégés William and McGeorge Bundy, Henry Cabot Lodge, Marshall protégé Dean Rusk, Harvard's Walter Rostow and John McNaughton—were the very people McCarthy, Jenner, and Taft would have had locked in their sights. Recently released documents reveal that the planners of the Vietnam debacle never seriously worried about a congressional reaction if they failed, or about a repeat of the debate on "who lost China." Instead, they used this fiction to convince liberal doubters, such as George Ball or Arthur Goldberg, to go along with their dubious policy of limited intervention on the grounds that those irrational "right-wing extremists" might push for a nuclear apocalypse.[12]

These heirs to the Wise Men also brought on a new generation of liberals, men like Robert McNamara and Daniel Ellsberg, who would prove in different ways psychologically incapable of handling the strains of fighting a real war against a real opponent. In the final analysis, Vietnam was a war of liberal containment, planned and executed by liberals and ultimately betrayed by them. Lyndon Johnson, McCarthy's old antagonist, became caught up in their toils, and it destroyed him.

Of all the architects of the Vietnam War, Dean Rusk came closest to the old faith. But while he was at State in the early fifties, Rusk had detested Joe McCarthy and all his works, and considered the rout of the China hands a foreign policy disaster.[13] He saw the Vietnam conflict through Achesonian eyes: America's quarrel was with "aggression" rather than the system that spawned it, and its policy should be to stop aggression rather than defeat an enemy and win a war. The fighting "could end literally in twenty-four hours," Rusk was fond of telling people, "if these people in Hanoi should come to the conclusion that they are not [able] to seize Vietnam and Laos by force."

Critics pointed out correctly that this passive view of containment allowed the enemy to decide how and where the war would be fought. Rusk had to agree but shrugged, "It is in the nature of aggression, Senator, that the initiative lies with the aggressor." He added, "If it were left up to us, there wouldn't be any shooting out there at all." He angrily rejected any notion that America's strategy was conservative or counterrevolutionary. Rusk asserted in 1966 that "we are stimulating ourselves very sweeping revolutions in a good many places. . . . The whole effort of the Alliance for Progress is to bring out far-reaching social, economic changes." He even suggested that if the war in South Vietnam were a genuine civil war and the Vietcong a genuine liberation movement, American troops would not have to be there. Bourke Hickenlooper, relic of the Taftite past, wondered whether America did not face an ideological struggle here as well, which made it necessary to stand up to communism wherever it appeared. But Rusk and the others demurred. "Communism today is no longer monolithic," he reminded the senators, "it no longer wears one face but many." One of the illusions that haunted Rusk and other policymakers was that they could count on the Soviets to help force the Chinese to stop the war—when in fact the Soviets would be the prime beneficiaries of North Vietnamese victory.[14]

Far from being inspired by McCarthyite ideology, the Kennedy-Johnson cohort fled from its basic assumptions. They were not fighting for Western

civilization or man's moral stature but to protect America's global commitments. Their opponent was not the Communist octopus but China and its
puppet Ho Chi Minh; the North Vietnamese were not fanatics with whom no
compromise was possible, but rational political leaders who could be forced
to the bargaining table. Rusk, McNamara, and the rest all avoided the sort of
hot, strident anti-Communist rhetoric McCarthyites loved. They preferred to
play it cool and understated—and to play it alone. They kept Congress out of
as many decisions as possible, and when the war turned against them, McNamara and Johnson did not hesitate to lie to the Hill about what was going on.

Vietnam broke the back of the liberal establishment. Stunned by their
own children's revolt against the war at Harvard, Yale, Columbia, Cornell,
and other elite universities; battered by the pounding waves of media criticism; and bemused by the radical restlessness of their intellectual protégés,
the Best and the Brightest lost their nerve and folded. Liberal anticommunism ceased to be a viable political category. Instead, all the anti-anti-Communist propaganda of the post-McCarthy years, from Arthur Miller's *The
Crucible* to Fred Cook's *Nightmare Decade* and Walter Goodman's *The Committee* (which pilloried HUAC), came home to roost. The old discredited Popular Front perspective suddenly became the conventional wisdom, and "the
rigid anticommunism of the Cold War" and containment appeared as the
root of all evil. Out of the resulting chaos emerged the new left, the direct biological and intellectual heirs of the "old" (that is to say, the Communist) left.
Nearly every one of the architects of the Port Huron Statement, the manifesto
of the new left student movement, was a child of former Communists or fellow travelers (one notable exception being Tom Hayden)—"red diaper ba-
bies," as they were called, and as they called themselves with a certain shy
pride. As one of them, David Horowitz, now freely admits, "From its beginnings, the New Left was not an innocent experiment in American utopi-
anism, but a self-conscious effort to rescue the Communist project from its
Soviet fate."[15]

The Port Huron did blast "ultraconservative movements" such as the one
McCarthy's heir, Barry Goldwater, was launching in the Republican Party.
"It is a disgrace of the United States that such a movement should become a
prominent kind of public participation in the modern world," it opined. But
at the same time it welcomed the Goldwater right as a polarizing influence.
Radical students hoped that it would drive the liberals out of the GOP and
destabilize the bipartisan consensus that reigned over foreign and domestic
policy. It was liberalism, not conservatism, that headed the new left's hit list.

This radical shift in political mood in the academy and on the fringes of
the media did not go unnoticed among those insiders who had also distrusted
the old consensus. In 1966, William Fulbright published a stinging critique of

America's role in the cold war, *The Arrogance of Power*. He warned that "this view of communism as an evil philosophy is a distorting prism through which we see projections of our own minds rather than what is actually there." Fulbright even conjectured, "Some countries are probably better off under communist rule. . . . Some people may even want to live under communism."[16] For the first time since the forties, anti-anticommunism had become institutionally respectable.

At the same time, anticommunism's institutional support was fading fast. John Henry Faulk and Dalton Trumbo had broken the media blacklist years earlier. The Warren Court had pulled the teeth from most antisubversive legislation and the government's loyalty security program lapsed into desuetude. In 1950, at the height of the red scare, KGB field officers complained to their superiors about the difficulty of recruiting new agents in the "current fascist atmosphere" of a security-conscious America.[17] Then things began to slacken. Since 1956 only four government employees and twelve applicants had been dismissed or denied employment on grounds of "reasonable doubt" regarding their loyalty to the United States. After 1968 there were none.[18] Dismissal on security risk grounds also fell sharply. At the same time, perhaps coincidentally, there was also a steady, discernible rise in the incidence of espionage involving federal employees (particularly in the U.S. Army), culminating in the Walker family and Aldrich Ames spy cases.[19]

In his sobering analysis of the collapse of the government's security efforts, historian Guenter Lewy is driven to conclude, "Perhaps the greatest damage that Senator Joseph McCarthy has caused this nation is that he succeeded in casting doubt upon the need for a serious and responsible concern with Communism and domestic security."[20] Yet this argument is misleading. McCarthy was discredited and destroyed by those who claimed that his brand of anticommunism was *not* serious and responsible, while the liberal brand was: as the cliché had it, "We agree with McCarthy's aims, but not his methods." Yet very soon after overthrowing his methods, within a decade of his death, in fact, they had lost interest in the aims as well.

No one, especially in liberal circles, seemed particularly concerned by this rise in espionage cases. On the contrary, one influential liberal lobbying group after another was now admitting Communist Party members into its ranks. The civil rights movement had done so in 1964 after two decades of trying to keep Stalinists from exploiting the segregation issue for their own purposes.[21] The next to go was SANE (the Committee for a Sane Nuclear Policy), which opened its doors to Communists in 1967, after a long and ugly fight over the issue six years earlier. The American Civil Liberties Union followed suit, although Norman Thomas pleaded with the ACLU board to keep its 1940 provision banning Communist members, arguing that "those who favor

Chinese or even Russian standards of state control which make any measure of civil liberty a gift of a totalitarian government, not a right, do not belong on our governing boards."[22] The Americans for Democratic Action's anti-Communist provisions were a dead letter by 1970. A series of articles in the *New York Times* in 1972 made Alger Hiss a new liberal hero and martyr, and HUAC fell into deep disfavor. The Senate abolished its Internal Security subcommittee in 1977, and HUAC died an unlamented death in 1975.

The man who had insisted on the changes at SANE, Doctor Benjamin Spock, was also an avid opponent of the Vietnam War. He and William Sloane Coffin openly urged young men to burn their draft cards, which most Americans would have labeled as incitement to treason but now drew sympathy, if not support, from the mainstream media. Spock was the most famous pediatrician in the world; Coffin was chaplain at Yale and pastor at the prestigious Riverside Church in New York. (Who now remembered J. B. Matthews's claim that communism found some of its strongest supporters among the ranks of the Protestant clergy?) In fact, support for the Communist Vietcong among the antiwar protesters was open and unashamed. Student activists made regular trips to Hanoi and Havana to ask North Vietnamese officials how they could help them win the war. Their followers waved Vietcong flags and pictures of Ho Chi Minh at antiwar rallies, while the pacifist Fellowship for Reconciliation shipped food and supplies to North Vietnam. Peter Collier later recounted how the editorial board of the radical newspaper *Ramparts* met every Friday night to watch the CBS evening news and stand up and cheer when Walter Cronkite read the weekly death toll of Americans killed in Vietnam.[23]

It was the nightmare McCarthy and Jenner had conjured up more a decade earlier, of American liberals and radicals allying themselves with domestic Communists on one side and with foreign totalitarians on the other. But in 1968 no one dared to say a word; that would have smacked of McCarthyism. When Congress finally did act, with the War Powers Act in 1973, it was specifically to *prevent* the president from salvaging what was left of anti-Communist forces in Indochina. And so in 1975, American radicals could celebrate the twin victories by the North Vietnamese and the Khmer Rouge while the liberal political establishment, distracted by their infatuation with Mao's "New China," said nothing.* As helicopters scooped the last Americans off the embassy roof in Saigon, abandoning millions to their fate, there would be no congressional investigations, no cries of "who lost Vietnam," not even a squeak of public outrage.

---

*They had already applauded the expulsion of Taiwan from the United Nations and the Security Council and the installation of Communist China in its place.

Epilogue

*McCarthyism is a very old American custom. It is an age-old American
determination to get rid of traitors and grafters and disloyal servants*

—Alfred Kohlberg

McCarthy and McCarthyism had not been entirely laid to rest. Even
as its last gleanings were being swept out of the American public
sphere, the McCarthyite idiom was making an interesting double
reappearance. At one end of the political spectrum, it fed the rebirth of
American conservatism. At the other, and more unexpectedly, it found its
bizarre doppelgänger in a host of new conspiracy theorists, this time from
the far left rather than the right.

The first saga begins in October 1952 as the editorial staff of *the Freeman* split up over the issue of supporting McCarthy. Three of its editors, led
by Forrest Davis, toyed with creating a new journal of conservative opinion,
one that would appeal to a modern, less traditionalist, audience. A year later
the catalyst for their efforts turned up in the person of McCarthy's youthful
defender in his final days, William F. Buckley, Jr. Over the next year Buckley
managed to persuade, bully, and cajole a diverse group of intellectuals, journalists, and financial backers into founding *National Review*, whose first
issue appeared in November 1955.

Buckley's biographer notes that "support for McCarthyism, if not Mc-
Carthy himself, bound together the senior editors and shaped the list of con-
tributors."[1] Willi Schlamm, James Burnham, and Max Eastman had all at one
time or another spoken up for McCarthy in the press. Editors Buckley and
Brent Bozell had worked for him. Another McCarthy admirer, former Internal
Security subcommittee staffer William Rusher, later joined them as publisher.

Although his name did not appear in the magazine's first issue, Mc-Carthy's presence was tangible from the start. The editors of *National Review* firmly rejected the liberal axiom that the red scare had been unnecessary or a threat to civil liberties. They argued, much as McCarthy had, that the struggle for America had to be as much a struggle against modern liberalism as it was against communism. But at the same time, they banished conspiracy theorists like Robert Welch of the John Birch Society to the lunatic hinterlands. Modern conservatism's battle was going to be openly political and ideological, even dialectical. It would be waged in the public sphere and eventually at the ballot box rather than through surveillance cameras, wiretaps, affidavits, and loyalty programs. "Ideas have to go into exchange to become or remain operative," Buckley wrote in their first issue, "and the medium of such exchange is the printed word."[2]

Buckley and his editors also rejected the claims of sociologists and political scientists that America's public culture in the fifties was conservative or even "pseudo-conservative." Everywhere they looked, including the Republican Party, they saw the automatic, often unthinking adoption of liberal assumptions and standards. "There *is* a liberal point of view on national and world affairs," they insisted, which fostered the spread of Communist influence instead of hindering it. Buckley wrote: "I happen to believe that if there were not a single Communist spy in America, we'd still be losing the Cold War—because the classrooms of Harvard are simply no substitute for the playing fields of Eton."

National Review also severed its connections with the old right, which had predated McCarthyism and now seemed out of touch. It gave up on the campaign to revoke Social Security or undo the New Deal. It did not seek to refight World War II or to explain Franklin Roosevelt as an agent of communism—or the Jews. In fact, several of *National Review*'s senior editors were Jews. Anti-Semitic outbursts, worries about maintaining America's racial purity, and not diluting the "Anglo-Saxon stock," were banned from its pages. On ethnic issues, it reflected the same assumptions that McCarthy had brought to the anti-Communist crusade. It did not matter whether you were a Jew, or a Catholic, or black or white, or Democrat or Republican—what counted was whether you were willing to take a stand as an American in a great moral struggle against international communism and its sympathizers.

In 1958, in the pages of *National Review*, Frank Meyer insisted that McCarthyism had established four key truths:

- That communism and modern liberalism share the same basic goal—socialism

- That the key difference between them is not the end but the means to get there
- That both regard "all inherited value," such as church, family, and national traditions, as invalid and without binding authority
- That modern liberalism has shown itself unfit "for the leadership of a free society"[3]

For Meyer, Buckley, and *National Review*, the liberal establishment had lost its legitimacy as a political class, a judgment that would soon be confirmed by the events in Vietnam.

National Review also touched a new upwardly mobile conservative audience, particularly among urban Catholics, many of whom had discovered an interest in politics through Joe McCarthy. Like McCarthy, their roots were working class. Like McCarthy, they saw no contradiction between their Catholicism and their commitment to the American proposition. One was Kieran O'Doherty, who later founded the Conservative Party in New York; another was Pat Buchanan. They and their generation would be the foot soldiers in a sixties cultural revolution at least as important as the one launched by student radicals: the Goldwater revolution in the Republican Party.

By 1960 McCarthy's old ally and friend Barry Goldwater had assumed the role as spokesman for a wholesale rejection of "modern" Republicanism, symbolized by Nelson Rockefeller. That year Brent Bozell ghost-wrote Goldwater's manifesto, *The Conscience of a Conservative*, which became an instant best-seller. The book heralded the reemergence of a political movement that owed its ideology to Robert Taft but found a much broader social and geographic base, running from the traditionally Democratic South to the West and the American heartland. By 1968 a farsighted political analyst named Kevin Phillips was already dubbing this "Southern, Western—and Irish—backed" antiestablishmentarian movement the New Republican Majority.[4]

The truth was that it was not ordinary middle-class and working-class Americans who had been terrorized by McCarthy and the red scare, but the liberals and the intellectuals. "Whatever else Senator McCarthy did," Buckley had written in 1959, "he brought liberalism to a boil." It was they, even more than the Communists, who perceived him as a threat. In trying to undo his political legacy, they in fact unraveled themselves. Liberals used the specter of McCarthyism as a stick with which to beat back this conservative insurgency. That tactic worked in 1964 as Goldwater went down to a humiliating defeat. But below the waterline the movement had stuck fast, an increasingly heavy barnacle on the ship of state despite every attempt to scrape it off.

It may be true, as Michael Paul Rogin and others have claimed, that Mc-Carthy failed to set off a populist revolt. But his ideological heirs did. When Ronald Reagan assumed the leadership of a reconstituted conservative GOP in 1980, it had a distinctly populist appeal. It was Republicans, not Democrats, who could now claim to represent "ordinary working Americans," while liberalism slid deeper and deeper into division and self-doubt.

In the end, then, McCarthy was always a more important figure to American liberals than to conservatives. The nightmarish image of his heavy, swarthy, sweaty features haunted the imaginations of thousands of anti-anti-Communists throughout the sixties and seventies. It appeared and reappeared in documentaries like *Point of Order* and *Seeing Red* and helped to set off the backlash that brought liberal anticommunism crashing to the floor. However, the next development in the political culture of the American left suddenly and very unexpectedly incorporated one of the ingredients of McCarthyism that sophisticated observers had most despised: the so-called paranoid style resurfaced with a vengeance.

At its center was an intense and charismatic university professor named William Appleman Williams. He also came from America's heartland, born in Atlantic, Iowa, and even taught at the University of Wisconsin in McCarthy's home state. Williams was also a World War II veteran who saw action in the Pacific, but unlike McCarthy, he really had suffered injuries there that tortured him the rest of his life.[5] The pain of physical suffering and the bitterness associated with his experiences served to feed a resentment and an angry will to resist the prevailing liberalism in American intellectual life. However, he expressed this by moving not to the political right, as McCarthy had done, but further left. In 1959 he published *The Tragedy of American Diplomacy*. That year was a watershed year for American liberalism. It saw the publication of John Kenneth Galbraith's *The Affluent Society*, which enshrined Keynesianism as the new orthodoxy in liberal domestic policy, and Michael Harrington's *The Other America*, which inspired the war on poverty. It was the publication date for Richard Rovere's dark portrait of Joe McCarthy, which seemed to bury the senator's credibility once and for all. Then, all at once Williams's book shook the dirt from McCarthy's mangled remains and resurrected the old fears of corruptions of empire, this time with a distinctly Marxist coloring.

The Tragedy of American Diplomacy argued that America's relations with the outside world in the twentieth century had been guided by a single objective: "imperial expansion." By comparison, the geopolitical aims and efforts of Stalinist Russia had been more limited. The notion that America's foreign policy was traditionally isolationist was a myth. "Classical economics led to an expansionist foreign policy," Williams wrote, with Americans prepared to take direct action to keep their markets open. To make the world safe for American capitalism, Williams asserted, its corporate and political leaders had taken the United States to war not once but three times: in 1917 (including an expeditionary force to suppress the Russian Revolution), again in 1941, and then during the cold war. Far from being an effort to contain Stalinism, the cold war had been a huge frame-up, an effort by Wall Street and Washington insiders to deter socialist revolutions around the world under the guise of deterring "Soviet aggression."[6] Publication of the book left orthodox diplomatic historians confused and baffled. However, Professor Williams trained a whole generation of influential radical historians at Wisconsin, including Walter Le Feber, Gar Alperovitz, Lloyd Gardner, and Ronald Radosh. When Williams and his disciples mixed his idea of a corporate elite pushing an informal American empire with sociologist C. Wright Mills's notion of an American "power elite" which secretly controlled the nation's institutions, the result was a kind of intellectual Molotov cocktail, ready to be hurled at the prevailing liberal consensus on the cold war and Vietnam. It was the birth of what came to be called cold war revisionism.

In 1965 Gar Alperovitz published *Atomic Diplomacy*, a book that claimed to show that the real target of the dropping of the bomb at Hiroshima was not Japan but the Soviet Union, and that President Truman and his advisers engineered the death of hundreds of thousands of innocent Japanese in order to intimidate Stalin. Despite the book's many flaws and misrepresentations,[7] Alperovitz's thesis was greeted with rapture and relief by left-leaning intellectuals obsessed with the escalating war in Southeast Asia. The cold war was America's fault all along, they could now proclaim, the egregious product of a foreign policy directed by a privileged power elite, "the American mandarins," the title of an influential essay by a professor of linguistics at MIT named Noam Chomsky. America, in other words, was run by a corporate-government *conspiracy*, one as malign and manipulative as anything being dreamed up by the John Birch Society.

Williams described the revisionist as "someone who sees basic facts in a different way and as interconnected in a different way"—again, not unlike the John Birch Society. However, revision took its basic form from old left propaganda that had been circulating for years about capitalism's endless vendetta against the peace-loving and progressive Soviet Union.[8] Yet, significantly, some of the old anti-internationalist writers who had warned about America's degenerating into a "military state," like John T. Flynn, enjoyed a brief vogue among new left revisionists.* In addition, the revisionists now shifted

---

*So did Dwight Eisenhower, for coining the term *military-industrial complex* to describe the institutional underpinnings of cold war liberalism.

discussion of the red scare away from Joe McCarthy to Harry Truman, Dean Acheson, George Kennan, and George Marshall. The very figures McCarthy had accused of being soft on communism suddenly turned out to be rabid *anti*-Communists (the revisionists' own hero was Henry Wallace).

No one ignored McCarthy's role in encouraging the red scare, but he now turned out to be a minor figure in comparison with real villains, the architects of the American "national security state," a massive militarized totalitarian edifice that radicals like Noam Chomsky and Michael Parenti even compared to Nazi Germany. Every diplomatic alliance, every counterinsurgency, every brushfire war, was carried out to protect American corporate capitalism, while America's domestic institutions, from Congress to the media and universities, had been carefully corrupted in order to disguise what was really happening.

As the Vietnam debacle ran its bloody course, the revisionist thesis captured the hearts and minds of antiwar intellectuals and academics. Its central thesis, which had originally been McCarthy's, now proved irresistible: the cold war, like history, "does not just happen." As Williams himself wrote, unconsciously echoing McCarthy, "one can never forget it is people who act—not the policy or the program."[9] It is planned and executed by a small but powerful group at the top. Loyalty programs (ruthlessly deconstructed by historian Athan Theoharis), Hoover and the FBI, secret wars and the CIA, nuclear power, the assassination of JFK, the illicit drug trade, were all swept into the theory's all-devouring maw.[10] Like a good conspiracy theory should, it explained everything, including its own contradictions.

When Joe McCarthy had complained that America was being led to self-destruction by a "conspiracy on a scale so immense as to dwarf any previous such venture in the history of man," he had provoked catcalls and howls of derision, just as Robert Welch did when he repeated it. But by 1980 the radical left's version of that same conspiracy had gained widespread acceptance, thanks in large part to the machinations of Watergate. Conspiracy and cover-up suddenly became the secret dynamic of all Washington governance, although driven by the capitalist right rather than the Communist left. It still leaves its trace today, in stories like *October Surprise* or Navy missiles shooting down a TWA airliner, in TV programs like the *X-Files*, and films like Oliver Stone's *JFK*.

JFK is the McCarthy story told in a mirror, where left is right and right is left. An ordinary government prosecutor in Louisiana, played by Kevin Costner, discovers that John Kennedy was murdered in order to perpetuate a secret foreign policy run by the Establishment, built around covert operations and mass murder in Vietnam. His revelatory encounter with a Washington insider, so redolent of McCarthy's mythic meeting with James Forrestal, lifts the scales from his eyes on the size and immensity of the conspiracy he faces. The hero needs to ask himself a simple question: Who has the power for a cover-up of JFK's assassination? Answer that, his informant tells him, and you will also know who did it.

The forces arrayed against him are formidable. They include the CIA, the Pentagon, and the FBI, as well as the press and the media, who try to discredit him by garbling his stories and generally making him look like a kook. Like McCarthy, he suspects they are bugging his office and discovers that his private conversations are no longer so private. A cabal of homosexuals even puts in an appearance, as ultimate symbols of the corruptions of empire. One of them, absurdly named Fairey, used to work for the CIA. He tells Kevin Costner: "Man, you don't leave the agency; once they got you, they got for life"—words that in an earlier time and place Elizabeth Bentley or Whittaker Chambers would have uttered about the Communist Party.

Like McCarthy, Stone's hero finds his bedrock of support from the little people. They are Louisiana Cajuns in this case rather than Boston Irish or Wisconsin farmers, with plain features and short, dumpy bodies, and twangy down-home southern accents. But the effect is the same. They believe "Jim" and rally to him because he is, in the end, "one of us."

At the same time, knowledge has changed him. He carries a burden that will haunt him until he dies. When the hero's wife complains that the discovery of this vast conspiracy, secretly undermining and destroying everything he believes in, has changed him, he angrily replies, "Of course, I've changed. My eyes have opened. What used to seem normal seems insane."

Later Costner's character says, "Telling the truth can be a scary thing. If you let yourself be scared, then the bad guys'll take over the country." He adds, "Somebody's gotta try, somebody."

It might have been the motto of Joe McCarthy.

Appendix I

McCarthy and the Doctors

Was Joe McCarthy a manic-depressive? There is no way to be certain now, more than forty years after his death. However, any psychiatrist today who confronts the available evidence might well conclude that McCarthy's behavior fits somewhere within the diagnostic spectrum *of bipolar disorder*. If using the terms *hypomania* and *bipolar illness* fails to excuse what McCarthy did or became, it does give some insight into *why* he did what he did and *when* he did it.

Experts now agree that bipolar personality disorders come in different sizes and intensities. At the high extreme are the classic manic-depressive psychoses, which eventually require medication or hospitalization; at the low extreme are cyclothymic or periodic mood swings, such as "the winter blues," which affect behavior but don't normally adversely affect our lives or careers. *Hypomania* refers to "highs" that touch the upper register but fail to cross the line into truly irrational behavior. These highs come slow but hard. They involve feelings of power and self-importance, fidgeting and restlessness, rapid-fire speech and thought, and long bursts of frenzied energy—as described by nineteenth-century German poet Hugo Wolf (who himself suffered from hypomania), "the blood becomes changed to streams of fire."[1]

The hypomanic person is often unusually productive and creative at work and charming and intense in his social life. To outsiders he seems unstoppable, even admirably so. Underneath, however, there is a sense of irritation, suspicion, and emotional volatility, which a lack of sleep and the abuse of alcohol or drugs make worse. That insecurity can lead finally to outbursts of anger and rage—which may mark the onset of the "low" to which the hypomanic type often returns. In McCarthy's case, his flare-ups and temper tantrums had little to do with the issue at hand, as puzzled and alienated friends and colleagues learned—and as the American public discovered live on television during the Fred Fisher episode. Contrary to critics, McCarthy's notorious "cruelty" and "insensitivity" had little to do with the political cause he espoused—and may have had everything to do with a man's simply not being in control of himself.

The best-known expert on bipolar disorders, Kay Redfield Jamison, writes,

> Hypomanic or manic individuals usually have an inflated self-esteem, as well as a certainty of conviction about the correctness of their ideas. This grandiosity can contribute to poor judgment, which, in turn, often results in chaotic patterns of personal and professional relationships.[2]

In other words, Joe McCarthy to the letter.

The hypomanic individual drastically cuts back on sleep: McCarthy was famous for his ability to skip one or two nights in a row. The hypomanic individual works impossible hours: everyone noted McCarthy's chaotic workaholic life-style, which amazed and exhausted his associates. Ed Nellor remembers having to put in seventy- to eighty-hour workweeks as a staffer and speechwriter to keep up with McCarthy, often staying at the office past 4 or 5 o'clock in the morning. "It almost ruined my health," Nellor complained.[3] The hypomanic individual is subject to sudden mood swings: although McCarthy was an unusually kind and considerate boss (see, for example, Ruth Watt's remarks about him as chairman of PSI), on certain days people learned to keep clear of his private office. "Stay away from him today," Don Surine would tell other staffers. "He's angry."[4]

The hypomanic individual often becomes an alcoholic or a compulsive gambler: McCarthy became both. The conventional myth, that McCarthy drank himself to death as a result of the Senate censure, is untrue. In fact, friends noted that his very heavy drinking started much earlier, in 1952, and actually *increased with his rise to success and prominence*, that is, as his "high" took hold. Indeed, McCarthy's notorious drinking may have been one of the ways he tried to take command of his manic moods, a form of self-medication, as it were. "As a matter of course," another self-destructive alcoholic, Edgar Allan Poe, explained, "my enemies referred [my] insanity to the drink rather than the drink to the insanity."[5] The same may have been true for McCarthy; although for both men, the alcoholism contributed directly to their mental and physical collapse.

If McCarthy's rise to prominence was accompanied by a hypomanic

"high," by the same token, it is not hard to see McCarthy's long personal decline after his censure in 1954 as a prolonged "low" or mental depression.
Clinical depression, of course, does not necessarily mean being visibly sad or
upset. Instead, a loss of energy, an inability to concentrate, a slowing of thinking processes and body movement, "a deep sense of futility" accompanied by
"a loss of pleasure in normally pleasurable events," are all standard symp-
toms of depression[6]—and incidentially of McCarthy's last years, from the
censure until his death. Most people who met him during that period, such as
William Rusher and Patricia Buckley, remarked on McCarthy's low energy
levels, but also his easygoing placidity and gentle courtesy. This could hardly
be the same man liberals reviled as a monster and a brute, they would say to
themselves. In a clinical sense, they may have been right.

McCarthy's mental decline was, no doubt, reinforced by his physical
problems, including hepatic liver failure.[7] But until McCarthy's medical
records are made public, we will never know exactly how much of Mc-
Carthy's problems were physical or psychological or a combination of both.

Appendix II

The Strange Case of Annie Lee Moss

Annie Lee Moss plays a minor, if intriguing, part in the myth of Joe McCarthy: how he and Roy Cohn hounded a middle-aged black woman for being a member of the Communist Party, when they had the wrong person all along. According to Thomas Reeves, the Moss case "blackened Cohn's reputation as an investigator, and helped shatter Joe's nationwide popularity." Walter Lippmann even credited it with "breaking the spell" cast by McCarthy over public opinion.[1] Like the earlier Anna Rosenberg fiasco (see chapter 11, note 8 above), the Moss case encouraged the view that McCarthy's pursuit of communism was driven by prejudice rather than by the evidence.

In fact, the documentation shows that Cohn and McCarthy did not have the wrong person, although the truth about Annie Lee Moss's connection with the Communist Party will always remain a mystery.

In 1951, FBI director J. Edgar Hoover offered the Army and the Civil Service Commission information from one of his informants, regarding an employee of the Army Signal Corps named Annie Lee Moss. That information was that Mrs. Moss had been a Communist. At that time, Mrs. Moss had worked in the Signal Corps cafeteria. The Army turned him down and Mrs. Moss, aged forty-five, stayed with the Signal Corps, eventually landing a job in the Pentagon coding room. Someone at the FBI leaked the story to McCarthy's staff (almost certainly Don Surine) and they were off and running; according to Surine years later, the FBI even had a photostat of Mrs. Moss's Communist Party card.[2]

We move on to February 1954. The context is crucial. The feud between McCarthy and Robert Stevens and, by implication, between McCarthy and the United States Army—and by implication, between McCarthy and the White House—was building to a climax. First Fort Monmouth, then Peress and Zwicker, and now . . . Mrs. Annie Lee Moss. On Washington's Birthday in 1954, McCarthy called a press conference to announce that he and his staff had found another "red link" in the Army. "This is primarily for [Bob] Stevens's benefit," McCarthy told the gaggle of reporters. But everyone knew it was really for McCarthy's benefit as well as for Roy Cohn's reputation as an eagle-eyed investigator.

According to Cohn's own account, he had taken a personal interest in the Moss case from the start.[3] On February 23, 1954, he summoned Hoover's original informant, Mary Markward, to appear, first in executive session, then in public. Markward had infiltrated the Communist Party in Washington for the FBI from 1943 until 1949. At one point she had even become membership director. She swore to having seen Annie Lee Moss's name and address on a list of CP members in the Washington region in the 1940s. "Did you ever have information that she attended a meeting or was active in the Communist Party?" asked Senator McClellan. "No," she answered, "I don't specifically recall that I do know her as a person." Nor could she swear that she had seen Moss at a Party meeting. But about Annie Lee Moss's identity, she was in no doubt. McCarthy opined, "This woman, Annie Lee Moss, who is handling the encoding, decoding, the routing of classified work, has been an active member of the Communist Party."

So far, so good. But then things began to turn sour: The Army announced that Mrs. Moss had no access to the cryptographic room or the codes themselves, that she was merely a relay machine operator, "who feeds into or receives from automatic machines unintelligible code messages," some classified but others unclassified. The press began to take notice, and interviewed Mrs. Moss, who said she knew nothing about communism and had "never been in a code room in my life."[4] Cohn then announced that two corroborating witnesses would testify to Moss's membership; however, of the two who were summoned, one pleaded the Fifth and the other, Mrs. Catherine Oram, denied knowing Mrs. Moss or even seeing her before.

Cohn now decided that the one card left to play was to summon Mrs. Moss herself before the committee. She finally appeared on March 11 before television cameras and a standing-room-only crowd.[5] Cohn imagined this would be a moment of triumph; instead it turned into his own Gethsemane.

To begin with, there was Mrs. Moss's appearance: shy, shambling, dressed in a shabby overcoat, and barely able to speak, she did not look much like a security risk. Everyone knew she had been suspended from her job at the Pentagon after the McCarthy revelation, so sympathy immediately gravitated to this pathetic, unemployed black woman. Then, after she denied membership in the Communist Party and said she had not known anything about communism before she heard about the Hiss case on the radio, McCarthy left the room (he had a meeting with broadcaster Fulton Lewis, Jr).[6] With McCarthy gone and Cohn left alone to run the show, the committee Democrats became overtly skeptical. They asked Mrs. Moss to read her suspension notice aloud; she turned out to be barely literate. Stuart Symington asked, "Did you ever hear of Karl Marx?" "Who's that?" she answered, obviously bewildered. The hearing room exploded with laughter as Cohn twisted and fidgeted.

Then she innocently repeated a point she had made earlier: that the committee must have the wrong Annie Lee Moss. "I know there are three Annie Lee Mosses living in the area," she announced. She lived at 72 R Street in Southwest DC, and had been confused with other Annie Lee Mosses before; perhaps that's why copies of the *Daily Worker* kept turning up at her house. Everyone sat stunned, while Cohn looked amazed, startled. "Was this a case of mistaken identity?" Democrats began to ask. Cohn blustered and insisted there was only one Annie Moss FBI file, but Stuart Symington completed his rout.

"Do you need work?" he asked Mrs. Moss.

"I sure do," she replied.

"If you don't get work soon, what are you going to do?"

"I am going down to the welfare."

Symington announced, "I may be sticking my neck out, but I think you are telling the truth. If you are not taken back in your Army job, come around and see me. I am going to see that you get a job." The committee room exploded in raucous applause.

Cohn had been pulverized on national TV— and so had McCarthy. Annie Lee Moss became an instant martyr to McCarthyism. The next week Edward Murrow's team at *See It Now* decided to use the Moss footage as a sequel to their highly successful series lambasting the senator, as "Senator McCarthy Against Annie Lee Moss." Through careful editing they captured the entire scene: the pathetic black woman at the witness table, Cohn blanching and staring, Stu Symington's *beau geste*—and close-up camera shots of McCarthy's empty chairman's chair, the tyrant's throne, the man responsible for this travesty of justice. The program enjoyed the largest audience of any of the *See It Now* shows, with almost 12.5 percent of American homes with TV sets tuning in. The phone calls and telegrams ran almost 9 to 1 in support of Murrow—and Annie Lee Moss.[7] The program inspired the *New York Herald Tribune*'s John Crosby to write one of the most famous quotations of the entire

McCarthy era, a rhetorical blast superseded only by Joseph Welch's "Have you no decency left?" speech: "The American people fought a revolution to defend, among other things, the right of Annie Lee Moss to earn a living, and Senator McCarthy now decided she has no such right."[8]

For some, however, the satisfactions of moral outrage were undermined somewhat by a sense of lingering doubt. One such individual was Stuart Symington. Immediately after his grandiloquent gesture on behalf of Mrs. Moss, as the committee room was clearing, Symington went up to reporter Murray Marder and asked anxiously: "Do you think I was on good grounds?" Murray later recalled, "It suddenly dawned on him that maybe he's going to make an ass of himself. I said, 'On the face of it, it looks good. There's always the off chance that she does turn out to be a Communist.' He says, 'My God, do you think so?'"[9]

Four years later, after McCarthy's death, that off chance suddenly turned up. In 1958 a group representing certain members of the Communist Party called into question FBI informant Mary Markward's testimony in a variety of cases. Then the Subversive Activities Control Board, a government agency created by the McCarran Act, presented the Justice Department with evidence of Mrs. Markward's veracity—including, as it happened, the Annie Lee Moss case. The record read in part:

> The situation that has resulted on the Annie Lee Moss question is that copies of the Communist Party's own records, the authenticity of which the Party has at no time disputed, were produced to it [A.G. Exs. 499–511, inclusive] and show that one Annie Lee Moss, 72 R Street SW, Washington DC, was a party member in the mid-1940s. . . . Consequently, Mrs. Markward's credibility is in no way impaired by the Annie Lee Moss matter.[10]

Vindication came too late for either Cohn or McCarthy, although as Ruth Watt noted, "Senator Symington was sure embarrassed!"[11] Even historian David Oshinsky has to admit that any doubts about Moss's Communist credentials "hardly excused the performance of the Army's security branch, which had known of Mrs. Markward's allegations for several years and never bothered to pursue them." The Army did rehire Mrs. Moss—although they moved her to a "nonsensitive" position in the Finance and Accounts Office. Even in 1955, Secretary Wilson was forced to concede that Mrs. Moss's file contained "certain derogatory information" prior to 1946—before her move to the Pentagon coding room.[12]

What exactly had happened? Was Annie Lee Moss really a Communist, whose appearance before the committee as a barely literate and confused woman was all an act? Had a friend or relative used her house at R Street as an "address of convenience" when he or she joined CPUSA—which would also explain why the *Daily Worker* turned up on her doorstep? We will probably never know the full story. However, even the best-case scenario—the possibility that a relative with Communist connections asked Aunt or Cousin Annie to show them some of the messages she handled for the Pentagon, decoded or not, or even just the contents of each night's wastebasket—constitutes what any professional would call a serious security breach.

Once again, McCarthy and Cohn had a valid case. Once again, through bluster and arrogance, they mangled it out of all recognition. Once again, political opponents turned the missteps of these two to their own advantage. Once again, the press and American public opinion came to believe that the real problem was not the Army, Annie Lee Moss, and communism, but McCarthyism. And as in the Fred Fisher case, their misperception was reinforced by the television image, which presented itself as an "objective eye" that cannot lie—but in fact misled Americans about the real Annie Lee Moss from that day to this.[13]

Notes

Introduction

1. Richard H. Rovere, *Senator Joe McCarthy* (Cleveland and New York: Meridian Books, 1960), 19, 5, 71. Reprint, with Foreword by Arthur M. Schlesinger, Jr. (Berkeley: University of California Press, 1996, originally published, 1959).

2. Rovere, *Senator Joe McCarthy*, 72. The quotation is from Talcott Parsons, in Daniel Bell, ed., *The New American Right* (New York: Doubleday, 1955; expanded and updated, 1963), 189.

3. William L. O'Neill, *American High: The Years of Confidence, 1945–1960* (New York: Free Press, 1986), 154; John Patrick Diggins, *The Rise and Fall of the American Left* (New York: Norton, 1992), 115; Michael Barone, *Our Country: The Shaping of America from Roosevelt to Reagan* (New York: Free Press, 1990), 235; Paul Johnson, *Modern Times: The World from the Twenties to the Nineties* (New York: Harper-Collins, 1991), 459; David Halberstam, *The Fifties* (New York: Villard Books, 1993), 54.

4. Nicholas von Hoffman, "Was McCarthy Right About the Left?" *The Washington Post* (April 14, 1996), C1.

5. Harvey Klehr, John Earl Haynes, and Fridrikh Igorevich Firsov, *The Secret World of American Communism* (New Haven: Yale University Press, 1995), 16.

6. George F. Kennan, *Memoirs: 1950–1963: Vol. II* (Boston: Little, Brown, 1972), 220.

7. Ellen Schrecker notes, "Obviously, compared to what happened in places like the Third Reich or Stalin's Russia, the political repression of the McCarthy period seems tame indeed. Only two people—Julius and Ethel Rosenberg—were killed; only a few hundred went to prison or were deported; and only about ten or twelve thousand lost their jobs." Ellen Schrecker, *Many Are the Crimes: McCarthyism in America* (Boston: Little, Brown, 1998), xiii.

8. James Rorty and Moshe Decter, *McCarthy and the Communists* (Boston: Beacon Press, 1954), 23.

9. Griffin Fariello, *Red Scare: Memories of the American Inquisition, An Oral History* (New York: Norton, 1995), 203.

10. Ronald Grigor Suny, *The Soviet Experiment: Russia, the USSR, and the Successor States* (New York: Oxford University Press, 1998), 266.

11. Ellen Schrecker, *The Age of McCarthyism: A Brief History with Documents* (Boston: Bedford Books, 1994), 33.

12. John Lewis Gaddis, *We Now Know: Rethinking Cold War History* (New York: Oxford University Press, 1997), 40–43; Michael M. Sheng, *Battling Western Imperial-*

ism: Mao, Stalin, and the United States (Princeton: Princeton University Press, 1997), 50–56 and passim; Klehr et al., *The Secret World of American Communism;* Harvey Klehr, John Earl Haynes, and Kyrill M. Anderson, *The Soviet World of American Communism* (New Haven: Yale University Press, 1998); Ronald Radosh and Joyce Milton, *The Rosenberg File* (2nd ed., New Haven: Yale University Press, 1997; originally published, New York: Holt, Rinehart, & Winston, 1983); David Holloway, *Stalin and the Bomb: The Soviet Union and Atomic Energy, 1939–1956* (New Haven: Yale University Press, 1994); Allen Weinstein and Alexander Vassiliev, *The Haunted Wood: Soviet Espionage in America, the Stalin Era* (New York: Random House, 1999).

13. Dale T. Knobel, *Paddy and the Republic: Ethnicity and Nationality in Antebellum America* (Middletown, CT: Wesleyan University Press, 1986), 131.

14. Andrew M. Greeley, *That Most Distressful Nation: The Taming of the American Irish* (Chicago: Quadrangle Books, 1972), 26.

15. R. Scott Appleby, "The Triumph of Americanism: Common Ground for U.S. Catholics," in Mary Jo Weaver and R. Scott Appleby, eds., *Being Right: Conservative Catholics in America* (Bloomington: Indiana University Press, 1995), 37–62.

16. Peter Collier and David Horowitz, *The Kennedys: An American Drama* (New York: Summit Books, 1984), 150.

17. Laurence Leamer, *The Kennedy Women: The Saga of an American Family* (New York: Villard Books, 1994), 419–20.

18. Ralph G. Martin, *Seeds of Destruction: Joe Kennedy and His Sons* (New York: Putnam, 1995), 181; 20. Collier and Horowitz, *The Kennedys*, 218; Victor Lasky, *Robert F. Kennedy: The Myth and the Man* (New York: Trident Press, 1968), 77.

19. Thomas C. Reeves, *A Question of Character: A Life of John F. Kennedy* (New York: Free Press, 1991), 441–42 n. 46.

20. On Kennedy and priests, see Donald F. Crosby, S.J., *God, Church and Flag: Senator Joseph R. McCarthy and the Catholic Church, 1950–1957* (Chapel Hill: University of North Carolina Press, 1978), 35. Reeves, *A Question of Character*, 121–122; Thomas C. Reeves, *The Life and Times of Joe McCarthy* (Lanham, MD: Madison Books, 1997), 647.

21. Martin, *Seeds of Destruction*, 181.

22. Jules Feiffer, Introduction to *LBJ Lampooned: Cartoon Criticism of Lyndon B. Johnson*, Sig Rosenblum and Charles Antin, eds. (New York: Cobble Hill Press, 1968), 7.

23. *New York Times* (September 13, 1953).

24. David Halberstam, *The Best and the Brightest* (New York: Random House, 1969), 415.

25. Floyd Riddick, Interview, June 26–February 15, 1979, p. 360; Carl Marcy, Interview, September 21, 1983, p. 66, Oral History Interviews, Senate Historical Office.

26. Halberstam, *The Best and the Brightest*, 30.

27. For example, Jack Anderson and Ronald W. May, *McCarthy: The Man, the Senator, the "Ism"* (Boston: Beacon Press, 1952).

28. Edwin R. Bayley, *Joe McCarthy and the Press* (Madison: University of Wisconsin Press, 1981), 10 n.

Chapter 1. Wisconsin and the Wider World

1. Reeves, *The Life and Times of Joe McCarthy*, 3.
2. Although by the time he was born the McCarthys had moved into an eight-room clapboard house. Michael O'Brien, *McCarthy and McCarthyism in Wisconsin* (Columbia: University of Missouri Press, 1980), 2.
3. See Appendix I, below.
4. Leon D. Epstein, *Politics in Wisconsin* (Madison: University of Wisconsin Press, 1958), 17.
5. Crosby, *God, Church, and Flag*, 11–13.
6. The other image he retained from his rural childhood was of watching a barn cat catch a rat in the family barn, play with it, and then clear-eyed and calmly tear it to pieces. It gave him a permanent aversion to cats. William A. Rusher, *Special Counsel* (New Rochelle, NY: Arlington House, 1968), 249.
7. Barone, *Our Country*, 75.
8. Roger Biles, *The South and the New Deal* (Lexington, KY: University of Kentucky Press, 1994).
9. Epstein, *Politics in Wisconsin*, 41.
10. O'Brien, *McCarthy and McCarthyism in Wisconsin*, 19–21.
11. Rovere, *Senator Joe McCarthy*, 87–88.
12. Anderson and May, *McCarthy*, 38–39.
13. Arthur V. Watkins, Interview, Columbia Oral History Project, p. 87.
14. Anderson and May, *McCarthy*, 45–46; Reeves, *The Life and Times of Joe McCarthy*, 36; Urban P. Van Susteren, Interview, January 15, 1976, State Historical Society of Wisconsin, p. 2.
15. George Washington, Farewell Address, 19 September 1796, in John C. Fitzpatrick ed., *The Writings of George Washington from the Original Manuscript Sources, 1745–1799* (Washington, DC: United States Government Printing Office, 1940), 231.
16. Samuel Lubell, *The Future of American Politics* (New York: Harper & Row, 1965), 131–36.
17. David A. Horowitz, *Beyond Left & Right: Insurgency and the Establishment* (Urbana: University of Illinois Press, 1997), 170, 178.
18. McCarthy quoted in Reeves, *Life and Times of Joe McCarthy*, 33.
19. La Follette Form Letter, October 1940, quoted in Horowitz, *Beyond Left & Right*, 178.
20. John Morton Blum, *V Was for Victory: Politics and American Culture during World War II* (New York: Harcourt Brace Jovanovich, 1976), 90–92, 331–32.
21. Van Susteren, Interview, November 17, 1975, State Historical Society of Wisconsin, p. 5; Reeves, *Life and Times of Joe McCarthy*, 48–49.

22. David M. Oshinsky, *A Conspiracy So Immense: The World of Joe McCarthy* (New York: Free Press, 1983), 32.

23. Robert Dallek, *Lone Star Rising: Lyndon Johnson and His Times, 1908–1960* (New York: Oxford University Press, 1991), 238–41; Halberstam, *The Best and the Brightest*, 449.

24. Reeves, *Life and Times of Joe McCarthy*, 50.

25. Reeves, *Life and Times of Joe McCarthy*, 55–56.

26. O'Brien, *McCarthy and McCarthyism in Wisconsin*, 52.

27. Reeves, *Life and Times of Joe McCarthy*, 54.

28. Harvey Klehr and Ronald Radosh, *The Amerasia Spy Case: Prelude to McCarthyism* (Chapel Hill: University of North Carolina Press, 1996), 3–6, 50–51, 64–65.

29. Barone, *Our Country*, 155.

30. Roy Hoopes, *Americans Remember the Home Front: An Oral Narrative* (New York: Hawthorn Books, 1977), 374.

31. For example, Frank Kofsky, *Harry S. Truman and the War Scare of 1948: A Successful Campaign to Deceive the Nation* (New York: St. Martin's, 1993).

32. Seymour Martin Lipset, *American Exceptionalism: A Double-Edged Sword* (New York: Norton, 1996), 31.

33. When McCarthy came to see Coleman at the prestigious Madison Club in the capital, he showed up in his old Marine khaki shirt and Coleman had to lend him a coat and tie. O'Brien, *McCarthy and McCarthyism in Wisconsin*, 61.

34. Reeves, *Life and Times of Joe McCarthy*, 82, 84.

35. La Follette quoted in Horowitz, *Beyond Left & Right*, 217.

36. Anderson and May, *McCarthy*, 112. Anderson and May charge (and Oshinsky repeats) that McCarthy also received money from the group. If he did, the amount was insignificant, and no close attachment formed then or later. Reeves, *Life and Times of Joe McCarthy*, 98–99.

37. Horowitz, *Beyond Left & Right*, 218.

38. James R. Boylan, *The New Deal Coalition and the Election of 1946* (New York: Garland Publishing, 1981), 151–52.

39. O'Brien, *McCarthy and McCarthyism in Wisconsin*, 80.

40. McCarthy quoted in Reeves, *Life and Times of Joe McCarthy*, 108; *Milwaukee Journal* (November 6, 1946) quoted in Reeves, 107–108.

Chapter 2. The Class of '46

1. David Brinkley, *Washington Goes to War* (New York: Alfred A. Knopf, 1988), 21.

2. Harry McPherson, *A Political Education* (Boston: Little, Brown, 1972), 3–4.

3. *Historical Statistics of the United States*, Part 2 (Washington, DC: Bureau of the Census, 1970), 1102.

4. "Venona Historical Monograph #3: The 1944–45 New York and Washington-Moscow KGB Messages," Center for Cryptologic History (http://www.nsa.gov:8080/docs/venona/monographs/monograph-3.html), 2; Weinstein and Vassiliev, *Haunted Wood*, 274–275, 265.

5. Ruth Watt, Interview, July 19, 1979, Oral History Interviews, Senate Historical Office, 30.

6. *U.S. News and World Report* (November 15, 1946), 19, 34.

7. Joseph W. Martin, *My First Fifty Years in Politics*, as told to Robert J. Donovan (New York: McGraw-Hill, 1960), 190; *U.S. News and World Report* (November 15, 1946), 34; *Time* (November 18, 1946), 24.

8. Barbara Sinclair, *The Transformation of the U.S. Senate* (Baltimore: John Hopkins University Press, 1989), 2–11.

9. For example, in 1957 there were only 17 Democrats versus 36 Republicans with experience in owning and running a business. Donald R. Matthews, *U.S. Senators and Their World* (New York: Vintage Books, 1960), 19–20.

10. "Freshman Senator" quoted in Matthews, *U.S. Senators and Their World*, 94. William Smith White, *Citadel: The Story of the U.S. Senate* (Boston: Houghton Mifflin, 1968), 100.

11. Matthews, *U.S. Senators and Their World*, 102.

12. Allen Drury, *A Senate Journal: 1943–1945* (New York: McGraw-Hill, 1963), 33–34.

13. The most important exception was Henry Cabot Lodge, scion of a distinguished political dynasty, who had already served in the Senate before going to war and a confirmed moderate.

14. McCarthy and Nixon never met, although they served in the same theater; however, McCarthy did later claim that he met and befriended John F. Kennedy while on duty at Bougainville. Kennedy never denied the story. Roy Cohn, *McCarthy* (New York: New American Library, 1968), 16.

15. John Bricker quoted in Horowitz, *Beyond Left & Right*, 216.

16. George Malone in *Congressional Record*, Daily Edition (July 18, 1956), 12079, quoted in Matthews, *U.S. Senators and Their World*, 77.

17. Reeves, *Life and Times of Joe McCarthy*, 112.

18. Walter Isaacson and Evan Thomas, *The Wise Men: Six Friends and the World They Made* (New York: Simon & Schuster, 1986), 493. The poll appeared in an issue of *Pageant Magazine*.

19. Reeves, *Life and Times of Joe McCarthy*, 113.

20. This was according to the Political Committee of the CIO. Oshinsky, *A Conspiracy So Immense*, 73.

21. David M. Oshinsky, *Senator Joseph McCarthy and the American Labor Movement* (Columbia: University of Missouri Press, 1976), 65–79.

22. O'Brien, *McCarthy and McCarthyism in Wisconsin*, 84; Oshinsky, *A Conspiracy So Immense*, 73.

23. The State Supreme Court later ruled that McCarthy was guilty of a technical violation but recommended against disbarment. *The Capitol Times* called the decision "astonishing." Reeves, *Life and Times of Joe McCarthy*, 188–90.

24. McCarthy quoted in Reeves, *Life and Times of Joe McCarthy*, 194. The evidence regarding Parker is summarized in O'Brien, *McCarthy and McCarthyism in Wisconsin*, 91–98.

25. Reeves, *Life and Times of Joe McCarthy*, 121–23.

26. For example, Anderson and May, *McCarthy: The Man, the Senator, the "Ism,"* 163–164, 309.
27. McCarthy quoted in Robert Griffith, *The Politics of Fear: Joseph R. McCarthy and the Senate* (1970, reprint, Amherst: University of Massachusetts Press, 1987), 164.
28. Jack Anderson quoted in Oshinsky, *A Conspiracy So Immense*, 58.
29. Pat Holt, Interview, Oral History Interviews, Senate Historical Office.
30. J. Edgar Hoover, House Committee on Un-American Activities, *Investigation of Un-American Activities and Propaganda*, (March 26, 1947), 37, 43.
31. Louis Budenz, Committee on Expenditures in the Executive Departments, Hearings, *Export Policy and Loyalty* (August 2, 1948), 158–59.
32. Joseph McCarthy, *Congressional Record* 93, part 4 (May 9, 1947), 4882.
33. Robert Taft, quoted in Russell Kirk and James McClellan, *The Political Principles of Robert A. Taft* (New York: Fleet Press, 1967), 117.
34. Forrest Davis, "The Treason of Liberalism," *the Freeman* 1 (February 12, 1951), 307.

Chapter 3. Fatal Attraction: Liberals and Communism

1. According to one version of this story, Roosevelt told Berle to go f——himself. Rusher, *Special Counsel*.
2. Allen Weinstein, *Perjury: The Hiss-Chambers Case* (1978, reprint, New York: Random House, 1997), 63–67.
3. Rebecca West, *The New Meaning of Treason* (New York: Viking, 1964), 236–37; Leslie Fiedler, "Hiss, Chambers, and the Age of Innocence," *Commentary* (August 1951), 119.
4. Theodore Draper, *American Communism and Soviet Russia: The Formative Period* (1960, reprint, New York: Vintage Books, 1986), 15.
5. Klehr et al., *The Secret World of American Communism* 72.
6. Richard Gid Powers, *Not Without Honor: The History of American Anticommunism* (New York: Free Press, 1995), 32–34. That assumption prompted, among other things, the founding in 1920 of the American Civil Liberties Union, which at that time included several Communists and Communist sympathizers.
7. Harvey Klehr and John Earl Haynes, *The American Communist Movement: Storming Heaven Itself* (New York: Twayne, 1992), 28–29.
8. Powers, *Not Without Honor*, 95.
9. Or, more precisely, that Sacco had pulled the trigger while Vanzetti acted as his knowing accomplice. Vanzetti was willing to go to the electric chair rather than snitch on his comrade. For a definitive overview of the case, see Francis Russell, *Sacco and Vanzetti: The Case Resolved* (New York: Harper & Row, 1986).
10. David A. Horowitz, *Radical Son: A Generational Odyssey* (New York: Free Press, 1997), 400.
11. Herbert Croly quoted in Frank A. Warren, III, *Liberals and Communism: The "Red Decade" Revisited* (Bloomington: University of Indiana Press, 1966), 9.
12. Sherwood Eddy quoted in Paul Hollander, *Political Pilgrims: Western Intellectuals*

in Search of the Good Society, 4th ed. (New Brunswick, NJ: Transaction Publishers, 1998), 122. (Originally published, 1981, as *Political Pilgrims: Travels of Western Intellectuals to the Soviet Union, China, and Cuba.*)

13. Lewis A. Coser, *Men of Ideas: A Sociologist's View* (New York: Free Press, 1965), 256.

14. Eugene Lyons, *The Red Decade* (1941, reprint, New Rochelle, NY: Arlington House, 1970), 191.

15. Stuart Chase quoted in Frank A. Warren, III, *Liberals and Communism: The "Red Decade" Revisited* (Bloomington: University of Indiana Press, 1966), 16.

16. Quoted in Warren, *Liberals and Communism*, 28, 18.

17. Frederick L. Schuman in *The New Republic*, quoted in Lyons, *The Red Decade*, 314.

18. Harvey Klehr, *The Heyday of American Communism: The Depression Decade* (New York: Basic Books, 1984), 76.

19. See articles by James Basset in *The Washington Post* (June 4–6, 1951), and Kenneth L. Billingsley, *Hollywood Party: How Communism Seduced the American Film Industry in the 1930s and 1940s* (Rocklin, CA: Forum, 1998).

20. Lyons, *The Red Decade*, 192.

21. Guenter Lewy, *The Cause that Failed: Communism in American Political Life* (New York: Oxford University Press, 1990), 172.

22. Lewy, *The Cause that Failed*, 174–75.

23. Elia Kazan, *Elia Kazan: A Life* (New York: Knopf, 1988), 112–13.

24. Charles E. Bohlen, *Witness to History, 1929–1969* (New York: Norton, 1973), 51–52; *New Republic*, quoted in Sidney Hook, *Out of Step: An Unquiet Life in the 20th Century* (New York: Harper & Row, 1987), 231.

25. Warren, *Liberals and Communism*, 198–99.

26. Hook, *Out of Step*, 240–41.

27. Lyons, *Red Decade*, 346–51.

Chapter 4. The Forties: Democrats and Communists

1. This thesis was originally proposed by Salvador de Madriaga, in *The Anatomy of the Cold War* (Belfast: M. Boyd, 1955).

2. Lewy, *The Cause That Failed*, 180.

3. Herbert A. Philbrick, *I Led Three Lives* (Washington, DC: Capitol Hill Press, 1972), 44.

4. Klehr et al., *The Secret World of American Communism*, 254.

5. John Colville, "How the West Lost the Peace in 1945," *Commentary* (September 1985), 41–47.

6. Quoted in Lyons, *The Red Decade*, 182.

7. Weinstein and Vassiliev, *Haunted Wood*, 240–43. In fact, Lee's comments about his boss come from one of his secret reports to his Soviet superiors.

8. Christopher Andrews and Andrei Gordievsky, *KGB: The Inside Story* (New York: HarperCollins, 1990), 287.

9. Colville, "Peace," 43–44.

10. Pavel and Anatoli Sudaplatov, with V. and L. Schechter, *Special Tasks: The Memoirs of an Unwanted Witness, a Soviet Spymaster* (Boston: Little, Brown, 1994), 227. According to Sudaplatov (229), at least one other GRU officer believed that Hiss had been deliberately chosen as a confidential contact with Russian diplomats and security officers because Roosevelt and Hopkins knew Hiss's true colors.

11. George F. Kennan, *Memoirs: 1925–1950: Vol. I* (Boston: Little, Brown, 1967), 240–43.

12. Colville, "Peace," 46.

13. Robert James Maddox, *From War to Cold War: The Education of Harry Truman* (Boulder, Colo.: Westview Press, 1989), 70.

14. Quoted in Richard J. Walton, *Henry Wallace, Harry Truman, and the Cold War* (New York: Viking, 1976), 63–64.

15. On the Canadian network, see John Costello, *Mask of Treachery: Spies; Lies, Buggery and Betrayal* (New York: Morrow, 1988), 492–93. Nonetheless, Elizabeth Bentley's revelations and FBI surveillance forced the NKGB to shut down its Washington networks at the end of 1945. Weinstein and Vassiliev, *Haunted Wood*, 230–231.

16. Randall Woods and Howard Jones, *The Dawning of the Cold War: The United States Quest for Order* (Athens: University of Georgia Press, 1982), 115; Bert Cochran, *Harry Truman and the Crisis Presidency* (New York: Funk & Wagnalls, 1973), 182.

17. A year earlier, the American Communist Party had asked their Soviet controllers whether they should join the Democratic Party in the next election or form an independent third party. In the absence of a clear answer, they took Soviet sponsorship of Cominform in 1947 as an indication that they should go the independent route. They jumped on the Wallace bandwagon, and soon were driving it. Klehr and Haynes, *The American Communist Movement*, 109–115.

18. Lewy, *Cause That Failed*, 202; Weinstein and Vassiliev, *Haunted Wood*, 234–35. Kramer's NKGB code name was Mole.

19. John Earl Haynes, *Dubious Alliance: The Making of Minnesota's DFL Party* (Minneapolis: University of Minnesota Press, 1984), 141.

20. E.g., Walton, *Henry Wallace*, 319–21.

21. The most famous example occurred when Dies complained about Communist influence in Hollywood and pointed out how Shirley Temple's name had been evoked during a front function. Liberals crowed that Dies had accused Shirley Temple of being a Communist. The falsehood stuck—even historian Thomas Reeves repeats it as if it were fact. Reeves, *Life and Times of Joe McCarthy*, 208.

22. Quoted in William F. Buckley, Jr., ed., *The Committee and Its Critics* (New York: Putnam, 1962), 97.

23. William Gellermann, *Martin Dies* (New York: Johnathan Day, 1944), 287.

24. Ironically, Dies's most vocal critic in the House, Representative Samuel Dickstein of New York, was a secret Soviet agent—although no one would know this until more than half a century later. Compounding the irony was the fact

that Dickstein had led the committee that partly inspired the creation of HUAC: the MacCormick-Dickstein hearings had probed fascist and pro-Nazi activities in the United States (though not, of course, pro-Soviet groups like the Communist Party). Dickstein was, it seems, a venal rather than an ideological spy: money was his top priority (his code name was "Crook"). He broke off relations with the NKVD in 1940. Weinstein and Vassiliev, *Haunted Wood*, 140–50.

25. Joseph R. McCarthy, *America's Retreat from Victory* (New York: Devin-Adair, 1951), 104.

26. Leo P. Ribuffo, *The Old Christian Right: The Protestant Far Right from the Great Depression to the Cold War* (Philadelphia: Temple University Press, 1983), 178–79, 183.

27. Peter Irons, *Justice at War* (New York: Oxford University Press, 1983).

28. Ribuffo, *Christian Right*, 189.

29. Powers, *Not Without Honor*, 216–17.

30. Martin, *My First Fifty Years in Politics*, 196.

31. Klehr and Haynes, *The American Communist Movement*, 123–25.

32. Barone, *Our Country*, 230.

33. Melvyn Leffler, *A Preponderance of Power: National Security, the Truman Administration, and the Cold War* (Palo Alto: Stanford University Press, 1992), 326.

34. Sam Tanenhaus, *Whittaker Chambers: A Biography* (New York: Random House, 1997), 92.

35. The networks are described in detail in Weinstein and Vassiliev, *Haunted Wood*.

36. According to Allen Weinstein (*Perjury: The Hiss-Chambers Case*, [New York: Knopf, 1978], 351), these charges were first brought as a result of a HUAC investigation.

37. Weinstein, *Perjury*, 362–63.

38. The truth about White would emerge five years later. See Chapter 12, below.

39. This last allegation turned out to be partially true. See Tanenhaus, *Whittaker Chambers*, 344–45.

40. Weinstein, *Perjury*, 365.

41. Summarized in Tanenhaus, *Whittaker Chambers*, Appendix, 515–20.

42. Sally J. Taylor, *Stalin's Apologist: The Life of Walter Duranty, the New York Times's Man in Moscow* (New York: Oxford University Press, 1990).

43. Steven W. Mosher, *China Misperceived: American Illusions and Chinese Reality* (New York: Basic Books, 1990), 63. As editor at *Time* in the early forties, Chambers had to deal with what he considered to be similar misconceptions in reporting from Russia from such luminaries as John Hersey.

44. Cf. Gaddis, *We Now Know*, 63.

45. Ellen Schrecker, *No Ivory Tower: McCarthyism and the Universities* (New York: Oxford University, 1994), passim.

46. Young Republicans Club speech, June 29, 1951, in Matthews Papers, Box 621, "McCarthy" file, Duke University.

47. Leslie Fiedler, "Hiss, Chambers, and the Age of Innocence," *Commentary* (August 1951), 111, 119.

Chapter 5. The Enemy Within

1. Nancy Bernkopf Tucker, "China's Place in the Cold War: The Acheson Plan," in Douglas Brinkley, ed., *Dean Acheson and the Making of U.S. Foreign Policy* (New York: St. Martin's, 1993), 109, 114. Tucker concludes, "In actuality, although Acheson filled the role of cold warrior in policy making toward Europe, McCarthy was not so far wrong with regard to China."
2. David R. Kepley, *The Collapse of the Middle Way: Senate Republicans and the Bipartisan Foreign Policy, 1948–1952* (New York: Greenwood Press, 1988), 65.
3. Reeves, *Life and Times of Joe McCarthy*, 221.
4. Buckley and Bozell, *McCarthy and His Enemies*, 12. The largest was the Office of War Information (OWI), with over 7,400 persons—including many secret Communists—of whom only 2,687 enjoyed any form of security clearance by the Civil Service Commission.
5. Buckley and Bozell, *McCarthy and His Enemies*, 15 n. 3.
6. A photostat copy of this letter is in the Matthews Papers, Box 621, "McCarthy" files, Duke University.
7. Buckley and Bozell, *McCarthy and His Enemies*, 14–15.
8. Daniel P. Moynihan, *Secrecy: The American Experience* (New Haven: Yale University Press, 1998), 66–69.
9. Joseph R. McCarthy, *McCarthyism, The Fight for America: Documented Answers to Questions Asked by Friend and Foe* (New York: Devin-Adair, 1952), 2; reprint, 1977, as *McCarthyism: The Fight for America*.
10. Roy Cohn, *McCarthy*, 10.
11. Walsh himself (no admirer of McCarthy) always denied the tale and privately excoriated Pearson as a liar for repeating it. See Crosby, *God, Church, and Flag*, 47–48, 50–52.
12. O'Brien, *McCarthy and McCarthyism in Wisconsin*, 97.
13. Ed Nellor, Interview, May 7, 1977, State Historical Society of Wisconsin.
14. Reeves, *Life and Times of Joe McCarthy*, 227.
15. Edwin R. Bayley, *Joe McCarthy and the Press* (Madison: University of Wisconsin Press, 1981), 18.
16. According to Robert Griffith, there were actually about forty from the Lee list working in the State Department. Griffith, *The Politics of Fear*, 54. Griffith and other hostile scholars think this proves what a liar McCarthy was. It reveals just the opposite. McCarthy was just seventeen off; if he had had the hard numbers, instead of relying on guesswork, the impact of his speech would have been even more devastating because it would have been irrefutable.
17. This was not as absurd as it must have seemed. Later the FBI did discover illegal wiretaps on two of his staff, Don Surine and Ed Nellor. Reeves, *Life and Times of Joe McCarthy*, 290, 718 n. 7.
18. Bayley, *Joe McCarthy and the Press*, 30.
19. Two people *had* been dismissed for being security risks. By contrast, other government agencies from 1947 to 1951 had had to dismiss more than three hundred

employees on loyalty grounds alone. Buckley and Bozell, *McCarthy and His Enemies*, 29. To explain the discrepancy Peurifoy testified that more than two hundred resigned or voluntarily terminated, the suggestion, that is, of a more polite method of removing possible risks. However, this also meant that such risks could be eligible for work in other departments.

20. Oshinsky, *A Conspiracy So Immense*, 112.

21. Vladimir Lenin quoted in Harry Overstreet and Bonaro Overstreet, *What We Must Know about Communism* (New York: Norton, 1958), 62.

22. John E. Haynes, *Red Scare or Red Menace? American Communism and Anticommunism in the Cold War Era* (Chicago: Ivan R. Dee, 1996), 61.

23. On Hammer's covert role, see Harvey Klehr, John Earl Haynes, and Fridrikh Igorevich Firsov, *The Secret World of American Communism* (New Haven: Yale University Press, 1995), 26–30.

24. Klehr et al., *The Secret World of American Communism*, 105 n. 26.

25. Weinstein and Vassiliev, *Haunted Wood*, 343–344.

26. John Earl Haynes and Harvey Klehr, *Venona: Decoding Soviet Espionage in America* (New Haven: Yale University Press, 1999), 31–34.

27. At least according to Peter Wright, *Spycatcher: The Candid Autobiography of a Senior Intelligence Officer* (New York: Viking, 1987), 231.

28. Haynes, *Red Scare or Red Menace?*, 57.

29. Ralph S. Brown, *Loyalty and Security; Employment Tests in the United States* (New Haven: Yale University Press, 1958), 55–59.

30. Sidney Hook, *Heresy, Yes—Conspiracy, No!* (New York: J. Day Co., 1953), 43.

31. The attorney general's list had been instituted during World War II to monitor pro-fascist and pro-Nazi organizations. Beginning in 1947, administrations began to add Communist fronts and auxiliary groups to the list.

32. There was some confusion about just what Duran did do for the United Nations. The State Department claimed he worked as a cultural affairs attaché; McCarthy claimed he had evidence that Duran was in the International Refugees Organization, screening applications for admission to the United States. Buckley and Bozell, *McCarthy and His Enemies*, 140.

33. Michael Whitney Straight, *After Long Silence* (New York: Norton, 1983), 265–72; Gustavo Duran File, Matthews Papers, Box 601, Duke University.

34. Haynes and Klehr, *Venona*, 31–34

35. Pierre J. Huss and George Carpozi, Jr., *Red Spies in the UN* (New York: Coward-McCann, 1965), 42.

36. Klehr and Radosh, *The Amerasia Spy Case*, 58–61.

37. Buckley and Bozell, *McCarthy and His Enemies*, 139.

38. One example among many was the CIA's Cord Meyer. At one point during the war, Meyer joined an obscure pacifist group called the World Federalist Society. He soon left, but the association was enough to keep him off the employment rolls for years. (What was the connection between World Federalism and world communism, one could imagine security officers asking themselves.) Cord Meyer, *Facing Reality: From World Federalism to the CIA* (New York: Harper & Row, 1980).

Chapter 6. The Tydings Committee

1. Scott Lucas, *Congressional Record*, 81st Congress, 2nd session (Feb. 20, 1950), 1981.
2. Joseph McCarthy, *Congressional Record* (Feb. 20, 1950), 1959.
3. Garrett Withers, *Congressional Record* (Feb. 20, 1950), 1973.
4. McCarthy, *Congressional Record* (Feb. 20, 1950), 1967, 1968. Here, of course, McCarthy was deliberately confusing the State Department's earlier security program with the Loyalty Security Board that Truman had instituted. The first one had proved itself deeply flawed (in 1946 it had specifically cleared Gustavo Duran), which was one reason that the second one had been set up. But Peurifoy himself had said that the loyalty board had fired *no one as a loyalty risk*. So McCarthy could claim his point still stuck.
5. David Demarest Lloyd's great-aunt seems to have been a large contributor to the *Daily Worker*, the Communist Party newspaper. Nothing suggested that Lloyd himself was a Communist; but certainly such a "family association" ought to have raised eyebrows around the White House, and Pearson (who ordinarily took a hard line regarding Communists in government) knew it. Anderson made the mistake of showing the raw, unconfirmed story to McCarthy, who immediately used it for his own purposes. Jack Anderson and James Boyd, *Confessions of a Muckraker: The Inside Story of Life in Washington during the Truman, Eisenhower, Kennedy and Johnson Years* (New York: Random House, 1979), 182–85.
6. McCarthy, *Congressional Record* (Feb. 20, 1950), 1968.
7. Herbert Lehman, *Congressional Record* (Feb. 20, 1950), 1958, 1977; McCarthy, 1977; Henry Cabot Lodge, *Congressional Record* (Feb. 20, 1950), 1955.
8. Scott Lucas, *Congressional Record*, (Feb. 20, 1950), 1981; Stewart Alsop quoted in Richard Fried, *Men Against McCarthy* (New York: Columbia University Press, 1976), 54; Senator Lester Hunt to Mrs. Floyd C. Reno (March 20, 1950), quoted in Fried, *Men Against McCarthy*, 55.
9. Bourke Hickenlooper, *Congressional Record* (Feb. 22, 1950), 2135.
10. McCarthy, *Congressional Record* (Feb. 22, 1950), 2143.
11. I owe these and other insights to conversations with Tydings scholar Richard McCulley of the National Archives.
12. Tydings, Senate, Subcommittee of the Committee on Foreign Relations, Hearings on State Department Employee Loyalty Investigation, *Hearings* (March 8, 1950), 6.
13. Buckley and Bozell, *McCarthy and His Enemies*, 70–72; Fried, *Men Against McCarthy*, 61–62.
14. Joe McCarthy, Senate, State Department Employee Loyalty Investigation, *Hearings*, 18.
15. Dorothy Kenyon, *Hearings*, 176–214; 213. For details on Kenyon's front associations, see Buckley and Bozell, *McCarthy and His Enemies*, 80–83.
16. McCarthy did draw material from an article in *Columbia* magazine (published by the Knights of Columbus), attacking Lattimore as a party-liner back in September 1946; Buckley and Pozell, *McCarthy and His Enemies*, 160 n. 2. Robert P.

Newman, in his fiercely pro-Lattimore biography, *Owen Lattimore and the "Loss" of China* (Berkeley: University of California Press, 1992), generally blames the China Lobby (2140). However, who actually put McCarthy on to Lattimore and that article remains unknown; Reeves, *Life and Times of Joe McCarthy*, 713 n. 37.

17. Dean Acheson, *Present at the Creation: My Years in the State Department* (New York: Norton, 1969), 364.
18. This has been confirmed by Venona materials. Haynes and Klehr, *Venona*, 146–49.
19. Klehr and Radosh, *The Amerasia Spy Case*, 39.
20. This meeting is described by M. Stanton Evans in his article on McCarthy and Lattimore in *Human Events* (May 30, 1997).
21. Reeves, *Life and Times of Joe McCarthy*, 264.
22. *Hearings* on State Department employee loyalty, 417–86; 425; 439.
23. Klehr and Radosh, *The Amerasia Spy Case*, 168–69.
24. Reeves, *Life and Times of Joe McCarthy*, 276–77.
25. Robert Morris, "Counsel for the Minority: A Report on the Tydings Investigation," the *Freeman* 1, no. 3 (October 30, 1950), 79–80.
26. *Hearings*, 799–871, 826–27, 828–29, 831.
27. Owen Lattimore, *Ordeal by Slander* (Boston: Little, Brown, 1950), 224, 222, 220.
28. *Hearings*, 425.
29. The complex threads running between the Institute of Pacific Relations, Soviet and Communist Chinese intelligence, and the CPUSA are all to be found in Klehr and Radosh, *The Amerasia Spy Case*.
30. Quoted in Haynes, *Red Scare or Red Menace?*, 151.
31. Cheng Hanseng [Chen Han-Shen], *Sige Shidai de Wo* (translated as "My Life During Four Ages"), (Beijing, People's Republic of China: Chinese Culture and History Press, 1988). I owe my information about this book to the incisive review in the *Wilson Quarterly* by Mao-Chun Yu of the United States Naval Academy.
32. Reeves, *Life and Times of Joe McCarthy*, 245–46.
33. He had even written the two-volume biography of Elihu Root, the mentor to Henry Stimson, who was the patron and spiritual godfather of the elite circle who would come to be known as the "Wise Men," particularly Robert Lovett and John J. McCloy. Walter Isaacson and Evan Thomas, *The Wise Men: Six Friends and the World They Made* (New York: Simon & Schuster, 1986), 493.
34. Oshinsky, *A Conspiracy So Immense*, 124.
35. The Tydings Committee rejected McCarthy's assertions, saying only two, not five as McCarthy claimed, and before they were officially identified as Communist dominated. Buckley and Bozell, *McCarthy and His Enemies*, 101–102.
36. Philip Jessup, *The International Problem of Governing Mankind* (Claremont, CA: Claremont College for the Four Associated Colleges at Claremont, 1947), 38–39.
37. Tucker, "China's Place in the Cold War: The Acheson Plan," 109–10.
38. Since McCarthy made his charges against Jessup public at the same time as those against Lattimore, at the end of March, the counterattacks overlapped.
39. *New York Times* (March 31, 1950), 1, 3.
40. William S. White, "Politics Deeply Color M'Carthy Accusations," *New York Times*

(March, 19 1950), 6E, and White, "McCarthy Stirs Bitter Row Rare for a First-Termer," *New York Times* (March 31, 1950), 3.

41. Fried, *Men Against McCarthy*, 66–75; Tydings memorandum quoted, 74.

42. Address to Midwest Council of Young Republicans, La Salle Hotel, Chicago, May 6, 1950, Matthews Papers, Box 327, Folder 6, Duke University.

43. Buckley and Bozell, *McCarthy and His Enemies*, 168–71.

44. T.R.B., "Washington Wire," *The New Republic* (July 31, 1950), 3.

45. Quoted in Lately Thomas, *When Even Angels Wept*, (New York: Morrow, 1973), 196.

Chapter 7. Failure at the Top

1. The full story of the Rosenberg espionage case is in Ronald Radosh and Joyce Milton, *The Rosenberg File*, 2nd ed. (1983; 2nd ed., New Haven: Yale University Press, 1997).

2. Which was sleazy but not illegal. See Reeves, *Life and Times of Joe McCarthy*, 317–19.

3. Ed Nellor, Interview, May 7, 1977, State Historical Society of Wisconsin, p. 2.

4. Ruth Watt, Interview, July 19, 1979, 95–96.

5. O'Brien, *McCarthy and McCarthyism in Wisconsin*, 102–104.

6. Oshinsky, *A Conspiracy So Immense*, 117–19. Yet when Tydings had launched his personal diatribe, Republicans had called him to order for his insulting behavior toward William Jenner while ignoring the attacks on McCarthy himself.

7. Margaret Chase Smith, *Declaration of Conscience* (New York: Doubleday, 1972), 14, 15; full text, 12–18.

8. *The Tablet* [Brooklyn] (June 17, 1950); originally published, *Washington Times-Herald* (June 9, 1950).

9. McCarthy quoted in O'Brien, *McCarthy and McCarthyism in Wisconsin*, 99.

10. Barone, *Our Country*, 229; Ralph de Toledano, *Nixon* (New York: Henry Holt, 1956), 105.

11. Gaddis, *We Now Know*, 94–95; Viacheslav Molotov quoted in Albert Resis, ed., *Molotov Remembers: Inside Kremlin Politics, Conversations with Felix Chuev* (Chicago: Ivan R. Dee, 1993), 56.

12. Haynes, *Red Scare or Red Menace?*, 63.

13. This was due to some ill-considered remarks Adolph Berle had made in front of the House Un-American Activities Committee in 1949 during their probe of the Alger Hiss case. Berle had identified Hiss as Acheson's principal assistant (in fact, it was his brother, Donald Hiss) and identified all of them as members of the "pro-Russian" faction in the State Department. Weinstein, *Perjury: The Hiss-Chambers Case*, 55–59.

14. For example, Leffler, *A Preponderance of Power*.

15. George F. Kennan, "Excerpts from Telegraphic Message from Moscow of February 22, 1946," in Kennan, *Memoirs: 1925–1950, Vol. I*, Annex C, 1967, 558, 549. The

so-called X-Article made Kennan's position known outside the Truman administration; see "X," "The Sources of Soviet Conduct," *Foreign Affairs* 25 (July 1947), 566–82.

16. Isaacson and Thomas, *The Wise Men*, 383.

17. Kepley, *The Collapse of the Middle Way*, 76.

18. Stewart Alsop, *The Center: People and Power in Political Washington* (New York: Harper & Row, 1968), 303.

19. Hook, *Hersey, Yes—Conspiracy, No!*, 10.

20. James Burnham, *Containment or Liberation? An Inquiry into the Aims of United States Foreign Policy* (New York: Jonathan Day, 1953), 31.

21. Burnham, *Containment or Liberation?*, 35, 78.

22. Burnham, *Containment or Liberation?*, 40.

23. Robert A. Taft, *A Foreign Policy for Americans* (Garden City, NY: Doubleday, 1951), 6.

24. Speech to the National Press Club, "Crisis in China: An Examination of United States Policy," January 12, 1950, reprinted in *Department of State Bulletin* 22 (1950), 111–18; see also Acheson, *Present at the Creation*, 355–58.

25. Gaddis, *We Now Know*, 72–73.

26. Isaacson and Thomas, *The Wise Men*, 542–43.

27. For example, Stanley I. Kutler, *The American Inquisition: Justice and Injustice in the Cold War* (New York: Hill & Wang, 1982).

28. Haynes, *Red Scare or Red Menace?*, 169.

29. Willmoore Kendall, *The Conservative Affirmation in America* (Chicago: Gateway Editions, 1985), 69–70.

30. Reeves, *Life and Times of Joe McCarthy*, 339–40.

31. Richard M. Fried, *Men Against McCarthy* (New York: Columbia University Press, 1976), 137–38.

32. This stemmed from the infamous "midnight ride" of printing business owner William Fedder, who had promised to mail thousands of campaign postcards for the Butler campaign but then failed to deliver. McCarthy staffer (and former FBI agent) Don Surine and another campaign worker demanded the money back and that Fedder retrieve the postcards he had mailed (so that the Butler campaign would not have to pay for them). When Fedder balked, Surine drove the unwilling printer around Baltimore and its suburbs for nearly five hours, forcing him to pick up the cards at various delivery points and return their $500. Fedder later told his story to Drew Pearson, who presented it to his radio listeners and column readers as a virtual kidnapping. Reeves, *Life and Times of Joe McCarthy*, 342–43.

33. Fried, *Men Against McCarthy*, 157.

34. Oshinsky, *A Conspiracy So Immense*, 175.

35. This was the policy of "reasonable doubt," rather than "reasonable grounds," for dismissal, which shifted the burden of proof from the government to the employee. Alan D. Harper, *Politics of Loyalty: The White House and the Communist Issue, 1946–1952* (Westport, Conn.: Greenwood, 1969), 139–40, 164–85.

36. McCarthy, *Congressional Record* (December 1, 1950), 16640.

37. Gaddis, *We Now Know*, 80–81.
38. Costello, *Mask of Treachery*, 539. Information that Burgess passed included reports on American National Security Council meetings, which may have encouraged Stalin to believe the Americans would do nothing to stop South Korea from being overrun. Gaddis, *We Now Know*, 72.
39. Costello, *Mask of Treachery*, 542, 552.
40. D. Clayton James, *The Years of MacArthur* (Boston: Houghton Mifflin, 1970–1985), 520.
41. In fact, Mao would not have acted anyway without the concurrence of Stalin, who still hoped the war would bleed the Americans white. Sergei N. Goncharov, John W. Lewis, and Xue Litai, *Uncertain Partners: Stalin, Mao, and the Korean War* (Stanford, CA: Stanford University Press, 1993), 188–91.
42. Douglas MacArthur quoted in William Manchester, *American Caesar: Douglas MacArthur, 1880–1964* (Boston: Little, Brown, 1978), 639.
43. Kepley, *The Collapse of the Middle Way*, 123.
44. By contrast, a poll of leading American foreign correspondents found that 85 percent believed Truman was correct. James, *The Years of MacArthur*, 607–608.
45. McCarthy, *Congressional Record* (April 11, 1951), 3640; Nixon, 3653, 3652; Wherry on news ticker, 3657.
46. McCarthy, *Congressional Record* (April 11, 1951), 3640.
47. He had made this point earlier, on April 11.
48. Even moderate Republicans like Lodge, Ives, and Wayne Morse voted with the Asia First group. Kepley, *The Collapse of the Middle Way*, 126.
49. Shu Guang-Zhang, *Mao's Military Romanticism: China and the Korean War 1950–1953* (Lawrence: University of Kansas Press, 1995), 152. In March 1951, Mao was telling Stalin, "After we have consumed hundreds of thousands of American lives in a few years, the Americans will be forced to retreat, and the Korean problem will be settled." In truth, it was the Chinese who suffered the most: more than four hundred thousand killed and wounded during the entire war, according to official Chinese sources. Gaddis, *We Now Know*, 81–82.

Chapter 8. Supporters' Club

1. McCarthy, *Congressional Record* 97 (May 24, 1951), 5779.
2. The term "coalition of the aggrieved" comes originally from political scientist Samuel Lubell, according to Rovere. Rovere, *Senator Joe McCarthy*, 21, 20.
3. See, for example, Daniel Bell, *The New American Right* (1955; republished as *The Radical Right: The New American Right*, expanded and updated (New York: Doubleday, 1963).
4. Martin Trow, "Small Business, Political Tolerance, and Support for Joe McCarthy," *American Journal of Sociology* 64 (November 1958), 270–81.
5. Michael Paul Rogin, *The Intellectuals and McCarthy: The Radical Specter* (Cambridge, MA: MIT Press, 1967), 236; 103; 237–38.

6. O'Brien, *McCarthy and McCarthyism in Wisconsin*, 144.

7. May 24, 1954 (interviewing data from 5/2 to 7/4/54), *The Gallup Poll: 1935–1971* (New York: Random House, 1972), 1237.

8. *Gallup Poll*, 1003, 1135, 1204.

9. See, for example, Schrecker, *Many Are the Crimes*, passim.

10. Bella Dodd, *School of Darkness* (New York: P.J. Kenedy, 1954).

11. George E. Sokolsky, Transcript of April 16, 1950, "Weekly Sunday Night Broadcast American Broadcasting Company Stations."

12. Jim Tuck, *McCarthyism and New York's Hearst Press: A Study of Roles in the Witch Hunt* (Lanham, MD: University Press of America, 1995), 30.

13. Harold, Lord Varney, "What Has Joe McCarthy Accomplished?" *The American Mercury* (May 1954), 5.

14. Robert Morris, quoted in Oshinsky, *A Conspiracy So Immense*, 258.

15. Rusher, *Special Counsel*, 242.

16. Athan Theoharis and John Stuart Cox, *The Boss: J. Edgar Hoover and the Great American Inquisition* (Philadelphia: Temple University Press, 1988), 283–85; Robert J. Lamphere and Tom Shachtman, *The FBI-KGB War: A Special Agent's Story* (New York: Random House, 1986), 78–79, 136–37; Cartha DeLoach, *Hoover's FBI: The Inside Story by Hoover's Trusted Lieutenant* (Washington, DC: Regnery, 1995), 351–52.

17. Francis McNamara, interview with author, August 21, 1997.

18. Reeves, *Life and Times of Joe McCarthy*, 462.

19. Tanenhaus, *Whittaker Chambers*, 476–77.

20. Quoted in Ralph de Toledano, ed., *Notes from the Underground: The Whittaker Chambers–Ralph de Toledano Letters, 1949–1960* (Chicago: H. Regnery, 1997), 116.

21. Weinstein, *Perjury*, 537. Later, Chambers wrote to Henry Regnery: "He is a heavy-handed slugger who telegraphs his fouls in advance. . . . It is repetitious and unartful, and with time, the repeated dull thud of the low blow may prove to be the real factor in his undoing."

22. Rusher, *Special Counsel*, 247.

23. Stanley D. Bachrack, *The Committee of One Million: "China Lobby" Politics, 1953–1971* (New York: Columbia University Press, 1976), 5–6. George Sokolsky had worked for the Kuomintang's Bureau of Public Information while in China and conducted a special confidential mission back in 1930. Although a vigorous pro-Chiang supporter, he was not an influential figure in government circles.

24. See, for example, Robert A. Garson, *The United States and China since 1949: A Troubled Affair* (Madison, NJ: Fairleigh Dickinson University Press, 1994).

25. Bachrack, *The Committee of One Million*, 16.

26. Furuya Keiji, ed., *Chiang Kai-shek: His Life and Times*, trans. Sho Kaiseki Hiroku (New York: St. John's University, 1981), 876–77.

27. Dean Acheson, quoted in Johnson, *Modern Times*, 448.

28. See, for example, Sheng, *Battling Western Imperialism*, esp. 30, 56, 92–93.

29. Bachrack, *The Committee of One Million*, 21.

30. Alfred Kohlberg open letter to Philip Jessup regarding IPR, December 8, 1949, "Alfred Kohlberg" File, McNamara Collection, George Mason University, Box 67.

31. The quotation is from Alfred Kohlberg, letter to Tom Dewey, July 13, 1950, "Alfred Kohlberg" File, McNamara Collection, Box 67.

32. Bachrack, *The Committee of One Million*, 44.

33. See, for example, the adulatory biography of Owen Lattimore by Robert P. Newman, *Owen Lattimore and the "Loss" of China* (Berkeley: University of California Press, 1992).

34. Alfred Kohlberg, letter to Elmer Davis, December 7, 1950, "Alfred Kohlberg" File, McNamara Collection, Box 67.

35. Thomas Griffith, *Harry and Teddy: The Turbulent Friendship of Press Lord Henry R. Luce and His Favorite Reporter, Theodore H. White* (New York: Random House, 1995), 215.

36. "Demagogue McCarthy: Does he deserve well of the Republic?" *Time* (October 22, 1951), 21–24.

37. Buckley and Bozell quoted in George H. Nash, *The Conservative Intellectual Movement in America since 1945* (New York: Basic Books, 1976), 111.

38. Leo P. Ribuffo, *The Old Christian Right: The Protestant Far Right from the Great Depression to the Cold War* (Philadelphia: Temple University Press, 1983), 185–89.

39. James T. Patterson, *Mr. Republican: A Biography of Robert A. Taft* (Boston: Houghton Mifflin, 1972), 277–78.

40. Richard Gribble, *Guardian of America: The Life of James Martin Gillis, CSP* (New York: Paulist Press, 1998).

41. Ribuffo, *The Old Christian Right*, 193–96.

42. Burton Wheeler quoted in Ribuffo, *The Old Christian Right*, 193.

43. John Chamberlain quoted in Nash, *The Conservative Intellectual Movement in America since 1945*, 110.

44. William Schlamm quoted in Buckley and Bozell, *McCarthy and His Enemies*, xv.

45. Russell Kirk quoted in Nash, *The Conservative Intellectual Movement in America since 1945*, 116.

46. Crosby, *God, Church, and Flag*, 130, 136. On McMillin, see Bayley, *Joe McCarthy and the Press*, 130.

47. Rogin, *The Intellectuals and McCarthy*, 238.

48. For discussion of Mindszenty case see Tuck, *McCarthyism and New York's Hearst Press*, 54–58, 64–65.

49. Edmund A. Walsh, *Total Empire: The Roots and Progress of World Communism* (Milwaukee: Bruce, 1951), 208–10.

50. Richard Ginder, *Right or Wrong* (Huntington, IN: Sunday Visitor Press, 1959), 6–7.

51. Crosby, *God, Church, and Flag*, 181–82, 19–20.

52. Summarized in John Courtney Murray, *We Hold These Truths: Catholic Reflections on the American Proposition* (New York: Sheed & Ward, 1960).

53. Fulton J. Sheen, *Communism and the Conscience of the West*, 2nd ed. (New York: Garden City Books, 1951), iii.

54. Crosby, *God, Church, and Flag*, 103, 113–14. The only state where McCarthy could claim to have had any discernible impact on Catholic voters was Massachusetts—by not campaigning for Henry Cabot Lodge so that John F. Kennedy could push ahead and win.

55. Cardinal Francis Spellman quoted in Crosby, *God, Church, and Flag*, 134.

56. Flora Lewis, *Red Pawn: The Story of Noel Field* (Garden City, NY: Doubleday, 1965), 57–58.

57. Schlamm quoted in Buckley and Bozell, *McCarthy and His Enemies*, viii.

58. Lately Thomas, *When Even Angels Wept* (New York: Morrow, 1973), 233.

59. Rogin, *The Intellectuals and McCarthy*, 242.

Chapter 9. McCarthy Rampant

1. Richard M. Nixon, *RN: The Memoirs of Richard Nixon* (New York: Grosset & Dunlop, 1978), 137–50; 149.

2. Quoted in Thomas, *When Even Angels Wept*, 213.

3. Fried, *Men Against McCarthy*, 179.

4. For examples see Buckley and Bozell, *McCarthy and His Enemies*, Appendix D, 364–82.

5. McCarthy quoted in *Congressional Record* 97 (1951), 5771–2.

6. Urban Van Susteren, Interview, November 17, 1975, State Historical Society of Wisconsin, 6; Joseph Kennedy quoted in Richard Whalen, *The Founding Father: The Story of Joseph P. Kennedy* (New York: New American Library, 1964), 427.

7. Truman quoted in Frank K. Kelly, *Harry Truman and the Human Family* (Santa Barbara: Capra Press, 1998), 71.

8. Hiram Bingham and members of the Civil Service Loyalty Review Board, from minutes of meeting February 13–14, 1951, quoted Buckley and Bozell, *McCarthy and His Enemies*, 217–18.

9. General Snow had delivered speeches at George Washington University and at the Harvard Club on October 25 and November 17, 1951, respectively, in which he said that the State Department had found no cases of known Communists in its ranks and that all of the "dust . . . is being created by one man, tramping about the nation and making over and over again the same baseless and disproved accusations." Conrad Snow quoted in Reeves, *Life and Times of Joe McCarthy*, 393, 397.

10. By a strange coincidence, that made 57 disloyalty cases—exactly the number, McCarthy crowed, that he had mentioned in his Wheeling speech! However, McCarthy was mistaken—only 18 of his original list of 57 names had actually left as of January 3, 1953.

11. McCarthy quoted in Buckley and Bozell, *McCarthy and His Enemies*, 236.

12. Buckley and Bozell, *McCarthy and His Enemies*, 134.

13. Athan G. Theoharis, "The Escalation of the Loyalty Program," in Barton J. Bernstein, ed., *Politics and Policies of the Truman Administration* (Chicago: Quadrangle Books, 1970), 256–59.

14. See, for example, Fried, *Men Against McCarthy*, 188, and Griffith, *The Politics of Fear*, 150.
15. William F. Buckley, interview with author, August 4, 1997.
16. Patterson, *Mr. Republican*, 455.
17. John Chamberlain, "Men Who Scuttled China," review of Freda Utley, *The China Story, the Freeman* (June 4, 1951), 569–70.
18. Rovere, *Senator Joe McCarthy*, 176–78.
19. Joseph R. McCarthy, *America's Retreat from Victory: The Story of George Catlett Marshall* (New York: Devin-Adair, 1951), 63; 171.
20. Oshinsky, *A Conspiracy So Immense*, 201; Smith, *Declaration of Conscience* 26–27.
21. Reeves, *The Life and Times of Joe McCarthy*, 372.
22. Mao-Chun Yu, *OSS in China: Prelude to Cold War* (New Haven: Yale University Press, 1996), 253–54.
23. Forrest Davis, "The Treason of Liberalism," *the Freeman* (February 12, 1951), 305–307.
24. McCarthy, *America's Retreat from Victory*, 168.
25. Joseph R. McCarthy, "Speech to Young Republicans, Boston, July 31, 1951," in *Congressional Record* 97 (1951), Part 14, A 4349.
26. Patterson, *Mr. Republican*, 455.
27. Thomas Coleman quoted in O'Brien, *McCarthy and McCarthyism in Wisconsin*, 107.
28. Patterson, *Mr. Republican*, 449; Oshinsky, *A Conspiracy So Immense*, 202.
29. Bernard Levin, *Run It Down the Flagpole: Britain in the Sixties* (New York: Atheneum, 1971), 65–66.

Chapter 10. McCarthy Triumphant

1. William Benton on himself, quoted in Sidney Hyman, *The Lives of William Benton* (Chicago: University of Chicago Press, 1969), 591.
2. Dr. Ernest Mahler to Benton, quoted in Hyman, *The Lives of William Benton*, 126.
3. *Congressional Record*, 82nd Congress, 1st session, vol. 97, 868.
4. Fried, *Men Against McCarthy*, 153.
5. Fried, *Men Against McCarthy*, 185.
6. Fried, *Men Against McCarthy*, 203.
7. McCarthy received $12,000 in an out-of-court settlement and a public apology. Reeves, *Life and Times of Joe McCarthy*, 365–69.
8. Anderson and Boyd, *Confessions of a Muckraker*, 256–59.
9. Van Susteren Interview, November 17, 1975, State Historical Society of Wisconsin, p. 6.
10. As Thomas Reeves points out in *The Life and Times of Joe McCarthy*, 413.
11. A copy of the typed manuscript, with handwritten notes by McCarthy himself, resides in the Matthews Papers, "McCarthy" file, Duke University, Box 326, folders 7–9.
12. McCarthy, *McCarthyism, The Fight for America*, 7–8.

13. George Haberman, quoted in O'Brien, *McCarthy and McCarthyism in Wisconsin*, 119.
14. Reeves, *The Life and Times of Joe McCarthy*, 401–402; Oshinsky, *A Conspiracy So Immense*, 231.
15. Oshinsky, *A Conspiracy So Immense*, 70–71.
16. Van Susteren Interview, July 14, 1977, State Historical Society of Wisconsin, 2.
17. McCarthy, *McCarthyism, The Fight for America*, 95.
18. John Robert Greene, *The Crusade: The Presidential Election of 1952* (Lanham, MD: University Press of America), 100–101.
19. See the results in Elmo Roper, *You and Your Leaders: Their Actions and Your Reactions 1936–1953* (New York: Morrow, 1957), 116–17.
20. *New York Times* (September 19, 1952).
21. Reeves, *Life and Times of Joe McCarthy*, 440.
22. Kevin B. Phillips, *The Emerging Republican Majority* (1969, reprint, New York: Anchor Books, 1970), 156–57.
23. *The American Mercury* (October 1952), 16; 4.
24. O'Brien, *McCarthy and McCarthyism in Wisconsin*, 133–46.
25. Reeves, *Life and Times of Joe McCarthy*, 451.
26. Anderson and Boyd, *Confessions of a Muckraker*, 260.

Chapter 11. Republicans Ascendant

1. Robert Ferrell, ed., *The Eisenhower Diaries* (New York: Norton, 1981), 225; Stephen Ambrose, *Eisenhower, Volume Two: The President* (New York: Simon & Schuster, 1983), 41–42.
2. Dwight D. Eisenhower, *Peace with Justice* (New York: Columbia University Press, 1961), 25–33; 28.
3. William S. White, "Joe McCarthy: The Man with the Power," *Look* 17 (June 16, 1953), 30–33.
4. Jean Kerr quoted in Nicholas von Hoffman, *Citizen Cohn* (New York: Doubleday, 1988), 143. See also Chapter 8 on Robert Morris.
5. After graduation, Robert Kennedy worked in the Justice Department's Internal Security Division, which gave him experience in hunting down Communists.
6. Cohn, *McCarthy*, 46.
7. Reeves, *Life and Times of Joe McCarthy*, 464.
8. In December 1950, Anna Rosenberg was nominated to be Assistant Secretary of Defense. Soon afterward, various right-wingers charged her with being connected to four Communist front groups, including the John Reed Club. J. B. Matthews published a sheaf of documents establishing Rosenberg's Communist connections, as did an inflammatory anti-Semitic tabloid called *Common Sense*. McCarthy's people looked into the case—and discovered it referred to the *wrong* Anna Rosenberg. McCarthy could truthfully say he had played no part in the campaign against Anna Rosenberg and, finally, voted for confirmation. However, the case of mistaken identity permitted Drew Pearson, the Anti-Defamation League,

and other interested observers to attack both Matthews and McCarthy as anti-Semites. Reeves, *Life and Times of Joe McCarthy*, 357–59. The Rosenberg case hung, unfairly, around McCarthy's neck from that point on. Rovere, for example, charges him with running a "noisy, sickening campaign" against Rosenberg, a charge that was clearly false. Rovere, *Senator Joe McCarthy*, 162.

9. Oshinsky, *A Conspiracy So Immense*, 257.
10. National Archives, RG 335, Cohn File, Box Three, Army Counsel Files.
11. Athan G. Theoharis and John Stuart Cox, *The Boss: J. Edgar Hoover and the Great American Inquisition* (Philadelphia: Temple University Press, 1988), 284–87.
12. Reeves, *The Life and Times of Joe McCarthy*, 462.
13. Van Susteren Interview, November 25, 1975, State Historical Society of Wisconsin; Ruth Watt Interview, July 19, 1979, Senate Historical Office, p. 158.
14. Joseph McCarthy quoted in *The Compass* (June 27, 1952).
15. John Robert Greene, *The Crusade: The Presidential Election of 1952* (Lanham, MD: University Press of America, 1985), passim.
16. As noted in Weinstein, *Perjury*, 323.
17. Michael A. Guhin, *John Foster Dulles: A Statesman and His Times* (New York: Columbia University Press, 1972), 190–92.
18. James C. Hagerty, *The Diary of James C. Hagerty: Eisenhower in Mid-Course, 1954–1955*, ed. Robert H. Ferrell (Bloomington: Indiana University Press, 1983), 24.
19. Lubell, *The Future of American Politics*, 214.
20. Ambrose, *Eisenhower, Volume Two: The President*, 324.
21. MacLeish had been a prominent Popular Front figure, and Schlesinger's family (particularly his distinguished father) was heavily involved in various fellow-traveling activities. For a summary of these developments, see James Burnham, "The Case Against Adlai Stevenson," *The American Mercury* (October 1952), 13–18.
22. The phrase is quoted from McCarthy, *America's Retreat from Victory*, 104.
23. Thomas, *When Even Angels Wept*, 286–87.
24. Roy Cohn quoted in von Hoffman, *Citizen Cohn*, 140.
25. Libby Marcus quoted in von Hoffman, *Citizen Cohn*, 142.
26. Ruth Watt Interview, 129.
27. von Hoffman, *Citizen Cohn*, 178.
28. Van Susteren Interview, November 25, 1975, State Historical Society of Wisconsin.
29. *Congressional Record* 99, part 7 (July 21, 1953), 9346.
30. *New York Times* (February 4, 1953); Buckley and Bozell, *McCarthy and His Enemies*, 356–57.
31. E.g., Rorty and Decter, *McCarthy and the Communists*, 119 n., 138–39.
32. How ironic, too, that Hiss had been keen to expand the committee's tough investigative powers, including limiting attorney-client contact during questioning. "There is . . . no reason for a legislative committee to respect the attorney-client privilege," he wrote. Alger Hiss quoted in Weinstein, *Perjury*, 144.
33. Klehr et al., *The Secret World of American Communism*, 97–98. The others were John Abt (of the Ware cell) and Charles Flatow.

34. John E. Moser, *Twisting the Lion's Tail: American Anglophobia between the World Wars* (New York: New York University Press, 1999).

35. When Harry Truman had chaired PSI's predecessor in the forties to investigate war profiteering, he stood out as the model of probity and flinty integrity. Yet even he had insisted on seeing the income tax returns of selected witnesses; when McCarthy tried to do the same thing, of course, he was pilloried in the press. Ruth Watt Interview, 153–55.

36. Cohn, *McCarthy*, 51; Ruth Watt Interview, 127.

37. Senate Government Operations Committee, Permanent Subcommittee on Investigations, *Hearings on State Department Information Program*, part 6 (May 6, 1953), 376–77.

38. Ray Kaplan note quoted in Oshinsky, *A Conspiracy So Immense*, 271.

39. This would be General Ralph Zwicker, although McCarthy was hardly on his best behavior when he confronted columnist James Wechsler of the *New York Post*. For a discussion of both incidents, see Chapters 12 and 13 below.

40. Alistair Cooke quoted in Thomas, *When Even Angels Wept*, 357.

41. Drew Pearson, "Washington Merry-Go-Round" column, undated [March 1953?], in Matthews Papers, Box 328, Folder 3.

42. Arthur Krock quoted in Oshinsky, *A Conspiracy So Immense*, 298.

43. Matthews told Roy Cohn the lead sentence was not his and had been reworded by an editor. Ruth Matthews, on the other hand, said the sentence was substantially the same as the one in the original manuscript. Cohn, *McCarthy*, 60–61.

44. Letter from McCarthy to John McClellan, July 15, 1953 (with copies sent to Senators Jackson and Symington), Matthews Papers, Box 621.

45. Crosby, *God, Church, and Flag*, 129.

46. Fried, *Men Against McCarthy*, 267.

47. The story appears in many versions, starting with Emmet Hughes's own memoirs, but the most recent is William Bragg Ewald, Jr., *Who Killed Joe McCarthy?* (New York: Simon & Schuster, 1984), 72.

48. Kennedy letter of resignation, quoted in Lester David and Irene David, *Bobby Kennedy: The Making of a Folk Hero* (New York: Dodd, Mead, 1986), 75–76.

49. One of those with doubts about Conant was John F. Kennedy. He said he would vote for Conant as High Commissioner but added, "it would be a different matter if he were standing for commissioner of education." Reeves, *The Life and Times of Joe McCarthy*, 467.

50. Ambrose, *Eisenhower*, 60.

51. See Chapter Four, above.

52. Bedell Smith quoted in Mark Riebling, *Wedge: The Secret War Between the FBI and CIA* (New York: Knopf, 1994), 118.

53. As noted by Cohn, *McCarthy*, 76.

54. Russell quoted in Sidney Hook, *Out of Step: An Unquiet Life in the Twentieth Century* (New York: Harper & Row, 1987), 367.

55. von Hoffman, *Citizen Cohn*, 148.

56. Cohn, *McCarthy*, 82.
57. Cohn, *McCarthy*, 89.

Chapter 12. McCarthy Against the Press

1. See, for example, the remarks on McCarthy in James Baughman, *The Republic of Mass Culture: Journalism, Filmmaking, and Broadcasting in America Since 1941,* 2nd ed. (Baltimore: Johns Hopkins University Press, 1997).
2. Bayley, *Joe McCarthy and the Press,* 219.
3. Murrey Marder quoted in Bayley, *Joe McCarthy and the Press,* 70.
4. David Schine, Interview, 1971, Columbia University Oral History Project pp. 10–11.
5. George Reedy quoted in Bayley, *Joe McCarthy and the Press,* 69–70.
6. Tuck, *McCarthyism and New York's Hearst Press,* passim; Neil Gabler, *Winchell: Gossip, Power and the Culture of Celebrity* (New York: Knopf, 1995), Chap. 9, especially 454–59 and 468–80.
7. Bayley, *Joe McCarthy and the Press,* 152; Ed Nellor Interview, January 11, 1979, State Historical Society of Wisconsin, p. 10.
8. Bayley, *Joe McCarthy and the Press,* 135.
9. Anderson and Boyd, *Confessions of a Muckraker,* 122–45.
10. Anderson and Boyd, *Confessions of a Muckraker,* 144–45.
11. The staffer at issue worked briefly on McCarthy's staff in 1949 until he was arrested in Washington on a morals charge. McCarthy let him go at once, but Pearson sniffed out the story; William Benton also used it to smear McCarthy.
12. Nixon, *RN,* 138.
13. Reeves, *Life and Times of Joe McCarthy,* 349; Van Susteren Interview, November 25, 1975, State Historical Society of Wisconsin, p. 2.
14. Karr had worked not only on the *Daily Worker* but also in the late thirties for Albert Kahn's *The Hour.* Elizabeth Bentley listed Kahn as one of her espionage contacts when she worked as a spy courier. Another figure at the *Daily Worker,* Howard Rushmore, testified to seeing Karr pull out his Communist Party membership card when he picked up assignments. Senate Judiciary Committee, September 14, 1949, "David Karr" file, Matthews Papers, Duke University. Karr was investigated twice by the FBI, the second time for links to the *Amerasia* case. After his death, a Russian journalist for *Izvestia* called Karr "a competent KGB source." Haynes and Klehr, *Venona,* 244–47.
15. Exchange quoted in Bayley, *Joe McCarthy and the Press,* 143.
16. Venona transcripts, numbers 1313 (September 13, 1944), 1433 (October 10, 1944), 1506 (October 23, 1944).
17. Robert W. Merry, *Taking on the World: Joseph and Stewart Alsop, Guardians of the American Century* (New York: Viking, 1996), 362–63.
18. Oshinsky, *A Conspiracy So Immense,* 310. The *Milwaukee Journal* thought about running the same story but then backed off. Bayley, *Joe McCarthy and the Press,* 134.

19. It was reprinted in *Rave* magazine (June 1954).
20. O'Brien, *McCarthy and McCarthyism in Wisconsin*, 205 n. 10. Oshinsky repeats this story as if it were factual; see Oshinsky, *A Conspiracy So Immense*, 303.
21. John E. Haynes, "The 'Spy' on Joe McCarthy's Staff: The Forgotten Case of Paul H. Hughes," *Continuity: A Journal of History* 14 (Spring/Fall 1990), 21–61.
22. William F. Buckley, Jr., *Up From Liberalism*, 25th Anniversary Edition (New York: Stein & Day, 1984, 1985), 131 (originally published, 1959).
23. Bayley, *Joe McCarthy and the Press*, 73.

Chapter 13. McCarthy Against the Army

1. Radosh and Milton, *The Rosenberg File*, xvii, 107–108.
2. Cohn, *McCarthy*, 166.
3. The FBI had its doubts. Whatever else may have been going on, they concluded Barr and Sarant were actually an extension of the Rosenberg-Greenglass spy ring, not an independent network operating from Fort Monmouth. However, they soon discovered there was no way to persuade Cohn of that. Radosh and Milton, *The Rosenberg File*, 424–25.
4. Roy Cohn quoted in Reeves, *Life and Times of Joe McCarthy*, 517. The number of suspended employees eventually rose to 35. The Army later claimed that the Mc-Carthy committee exposed only one security risk that the FBI had not known about previously, *New York Times* (May 2, 1954). But the point was not where or how the information came from or forward, but what one did with it.
5. Deposition before the Executive Session of the Army-McCarthy Hearings, April 29, 1954, Secretary of the Army, General Counsel, Box 21, National Archives, RG 335.
6. Slattery Affidavit, "Cohn-Army Dispute," Box 3, National Archives, RG 335.
7. For example, Oshinsky, *A Conspiracy So Immense*, 331–32.
8. Rorty and Decter, *McCarthy and the Communists*, 41.
9. Kitty's first husband, Joe Dallet, was a Communist volunteer in Spain who had been killed in action. Strong circumstantial evidence points to Nelson as a member of the Communist espionage network in California. He was also a frequent visitor of scientists at Lawrence-Livermore Laboratory in Berkeley. Klehr et al., *The Secret World of American Communism*, 230.
10. Richard Rhodes, *The Making of the Atomic Bomb* (New York: Simon & Schuster, 1986), 571; Joseph Albright and Marcia Kunstel, *Bombshell: The Secret Story of America's Unknown Atomic Spy Conspiracy* (New York: Times Books, 1997), 106.
11. Quoted in J. G. A. Pocock, *The Machiavellian Moment: Florentine Political Thought and the Atlantic Republican Tradition* (Princeton: Princeton University Press, 1975), 410.
12. Donald H. Riddle, *The Truman Committee: A Study in Congressional Responsibility* (New Brunswick, NJ: Rutgers University Press, 1964), 158.
13. Quoted in Thomas, *When Even Angels Wept*, 432.
14. See note 5, above.
15. Drew Pearson, "Merry Go Round" column, July 17, 1953. Pearson does not seem to have known about the Cohn angle of the story, however. That would come out later.

16. Cohn, *McCarthy*, 96; von Hoffman, *Citizen Cohn*, 182.

17. Tanenhaus, *Chambers*, 479–80. Although Brownell did not and could not say so, it was Venona that supplied the smoking gun. Haynes and Klehr, *Venona*.

18. Ewald, *Who Killed Joe McCarthy?*, 150.

19. Ewald, *Who Killed Joe McCarthy?*, 120.

20. In the end, the White House received over 50,000 telegrams and letters with the "vast majority" (in Oshinsky's words) supporting a China embargo. This was the largest telegram campaign since the Rosenberg execution. For once McCarthy's moderation paid off. He had planned to rip Dulles as a supporter of Hiss with links to IPR, but the Republican National Committee chairman and the postmaster general, both McCarthy allies, persuaded him against this course of action. Oshinsky, *A Conspiracy So Immense*, 353–54.

21. Quoted in Ewald, *Who Killed Joe McCarthy?*, 159, 155.

22. Various versions of this incident exist. The most convincing are von Hoffman, *Citizen Cohn*, 197, and John Gibbons Adams, *Without Precedent: The Story of the Death of McCarthyism* (New York: Norton, 1983), 84–86.

23. Compare Adams, *Without Precedent*, 113–15, and Cohn, *McCarthy*, 116–17.

24. Officer Efficiency Reports (DA Form 67-3), dated March 13, 1953, and January 31, 1954, "Irving Peress File," Box 3, National Archives, RG 336.

25. Inspector General of the Army's Office, "Investigation Concerning Conditions Surrounding the Reappointment to a Higher Grade on One Captain Irving Peress," Army General Counsel, Box 3, National Archives, RG 335.

26. Lionel Lokos, *Who Promoted Peress!* (New York: Bookmailer, 1961), 172.

27. Ewald, *Who Killed McCarthy?*, 192.

28. Senate Permanent Subcommittee on Investigations, *Communist Infiltration in the Army Hearings* (February 18, 1954), 153.

29. General Ralph Zwicker, Memorandum dated February 19, 1954, "Irving Peress" file, Box 3, National Archives, RG 336.

30. *New York Post* (February 25, 1954).

31. John Gibbons Adams, "Chronological Statement," Army-McCarthy Hearings, Box 1, National Archives, RG 335.

32. Ewald, *Who Killed Joe McCarthy?*, 197.

33. Letter from Army Counsel Struve Hensel to Charles Potter, March 10, 1954, in reference to his request for the Adams's Memorandum on March 8, 1954, Box 1, National Archives, RG 335.

34. Charles E. Potter, *Days of Shame* (1965, republished, New York: New American Library, 1971), 29.

35. Arthur Krock, *New York Times* (February 28, 1954).

36. Willard Edward quoted in Reeves, *The Life and Times of Joe McCarthy*, 558.

37. Thomas, *When Even Angels Wept*, 466.

38. Thomas Radeck, See It Now *Confronts McCarthyism: Television Documentary and the Politics of Representation* (Tuscaloosa: University of Alabama Press, 1994), 133–34. Its success was dwarfed a week later when CBS ran its next attack on McCarthy, "Annie Lee Moss Before the McCarthy Committee," 162.

39. Reeves, *The Life and Times of Joe McCarthy*, 584–85.

40. Cohn also believed McClellan hated them because they were Jews. "He likes to see Communists get caught," as Cohn put it years later, "but not by someone named Roy Cohn." von Hoffman, *Citizen Cohn*, 205.

41. Normally, executive sessions of congressional investigative committees are sealed for fifty years. However, a transcript of the March 16, 1954, meeting appears in the Army Counsel's files at the National Archives, which are declassified and available for use. What follows is based on that transcript, in Box 21, RG335.

42. Cohn, *McCarthy*, 134.

43. Rowland Evans and Robert Novak, *Lyndon B. Johnson: The Exercise of Power* (New York: New American Library, 1968), 92–93.

44. Executive Session transcript, 51, 40.

Chapter 14. McCarthy Against Himself

1. *New York Times*, April 22, 1954.

2. Michael Straight, *Trial by Television* (Boston: Beacon Press, 1954), 82; James Reston quoted in Bayley, *Joe McCarthy and the Press*, 202.

3. Straight, *Trial*, 78.

4. *New York Times*, April 23, 1954.

5. Straight, *Trial*, 85.

6. Raymond Moley quoted in Thomas, *When Even Angels Wept*, 383–84.

7. McCarthy quoted in Straight, *Trial*, 94.

8. John B. Judis, *William F. Buckley, Jr: Patron Saint of the Conservatives* (New York: Simon & Schuster, 1988), 108.

9. William F. Buckley, Jr., Interview with author, August 4, 1997; Ed Nellor, Interview, May 7, 1977, State Historical Society of Wisconsin; Judis, *Buckley*, 111.

10. G. B. Shaw quoted in William V. Shannon, *The American Irish* (New York: Macmillan, 1963), 235.

11. Anthony Trollope, *Phineas Redux* (1873, reprint, Oxford: Oxford University Press, 1973), 300.

12. "Memorandum," undated, U.S. Army General Counsel, Army-McCarthy hearings, "McCarthy—General" files, Box 4, National Archives, RG 335.

13. "Roy Cohn—General," Box 21, National Archives, RG 335.

14. Cohn, *McCarthy*, 134.

15. Straight, *Trial*, 80, 90.

16. *New York Times*, April 23, 1954.

17. Reeves, *Life and Times of Joe McCarthy*, 598.

18. *New York Times*, May 4, 1954; Straight, *Trial*, 70.

19. Straight, *Trial*, 65.

20. Reeves, *Life and Times of Joe McCarthy*, 600–601.

21. Senate Committee on Government Operations, Special Subcommittee on Investigations, *Charges and Countercharges Involving: Secretary of the Army Robert T. Stevens . . . , Hearings* (May 5, 1954), 782–84.

NOTES

22. Ray Jenkins quoted in Straight, *Trial*, 108.
23. Symington, Jackson, and McCarthy quoted in Clark Mollenhoff, *Washington Cover-Up* (New York: Doubleday, 1962), 37–41.
24. Senate Committee on Government Operations, Special Subcommittee on Investigations, Executive Session, in R6 335, Army General Counsel files (May 17, 1954), 12–47.
25. Mollenhoff, *Cover-Up*, 11, 49.
26. Mark J. Rozell, *Executive Privilege: The Dilemma of Secrecy and Democratic Accountability* (Baltimore: Johns Hopkins University Press, 1994), 44–45; Raoul Berger, *Executive Privilege: A Constitutional Myth* (Cambridge: Harvard University Press, 1974), 236.
27. Reeves, *Life and Times of Joe McCarthy*, 570.
28. David Schine, Interview, 1971, Columbia University, p. 6.
29. Letter, McCarthy to Robert Stevens, December 22, 1953, National Archives, "Army-McCarthy" file, Box 1, RG 335.
30. "Roy Cohn—General" files, Box 21, RG 335.
31. Straight, *Trial*, 193.
32. Willard Edwards, Interview, January 17, 1976, State Historical Society of Wisconsin.
33. Cohn, *McCarthy*, 181, 183.
34. Bayley, *Joe McCarthy and the Press*, 204, 212.
35. James Reston quoted in Bayley, *Joe McCarthy and the Press*, 208.
36. Flanders quoted in Reeves, *Life and Times of Joe McCarthy*, 624–25.
37. Cohn, *McCarthy*, 202–203.
38. Van Susteren, Interview, November 17, 1975, State Historical Society of Wisconsin, p. 6.
39. The true account is carefully tucked away in the footnotes of Griffith, *The Politics of Fear*, 260, fn. 46.
40. Quoted in Reeves, *Life and Times of Joe McCarthy*, 632.
41. Oshinsky, *Conspiracy So Immense*, 464; Reeves, *Life and Times of Joe McCarthy*, 634.
42. Bayley, *Joe McCarthy and the Press*, 204.
43. Matthews Papers, Box 655, "Roy Cohn" file, Duke University.
44. Griffith, *Politics of Fear*, 285.

Chapter 15. Censure

1. Reeves, *Life and Times of Joe McCarthy*, 637.
2. Robert Dallek, *Lone Star Rising: Lyndon Johnson and His Times* (New York: Oxford University Press, 1991), 265.
3. Hubert Humphrey quoted in Fried, *Men Against McCarthy*, 265.
4. Robert G. Baker, *Wheeling and Dealing: Confessions of a Capitol Hill Operator* (New York: Norton, 1978), 94; George Reedy, *Lyndon Baines Johnson: A Memoir* (New York and Kansas City: Andrews & McMeel, 1982), xv.
5. Baker, *Wheeling and Dealing*, 94.

6. William White quoted in Dallek, *Lone Star Rising*, 457.

7. Arthur Watkins, Interview, 1967, Columbia University Oral History Project, p. 81.

8. Lewis Namier, *England in the Age of the American Revolution* (London: Macmillan, 1961), 284.

9. Cohn, *McCarthy*, 220; *New York Times*, September 12, 1954, quoted in Griffith, *Politics of Fear*, 300.

10. Griffith, *Politics of Fear*, 301–302. Some senators were annoyed by the NCEC's hardball tactics, and some anti-McCarthyites, like John Sherman Cooper, tried to pretend that they knew nothing about its behind-the-scenes maneuvering (see Griffith, *Politics*, 301, n. 89).

11. Eisenhower quoted in Ewald, *Who Killed Joe McCarthy?* 365.

12. Editorial, *Human Events*, June 2, 1954; Memorandum, undated, Matthews Papers, Box 621, Duke University.

13. Column by John O'Donnell, "Capitol Stuff," in Matthews Papers, Box 621.

14. Memorandum, undated, Matthews Papers, Box 621, p. 4. The two staffers were Daniel Buckley (who later worked for McCarthy's staff) and Jack Poorbaugh. For the details on Buckley, see Reeves, *Life and Times of Joe McCarthy*, 394–95.

15. Quoted in Reeves, *Life and Times of Joe McCarthy*, 652, 653.

16. Rozell, *Executive Privilege*, 45.

17. Watkins, *Enough Rope*, 186.

18. Reeves, *Life and Times of Joe McCarthy*, 654.

19. *Congressional Record*, 100, part 12 (November 10, 1954), 15922–15926.

20. As noted by David Lawrence in "Justice to the Memory of Senator McCarthy," *U.S. News & World Report*, June 7, 1957, 140.

21. For details, see Chapter 10 above.

22. In fact, Ervin himself believed it might disqualify him and told Johnson so. As usual, Johnson coaxed him into staying on. Evans and Novak, *Lyndon Johnson*, 95–96.

23. *Congressional Record*, (100, Part 12), 15930.

24. *Congressional Record*, 15931; *Time*, November 22, 1954, 16.

25. *Congressional Record*, 15951–15954.

26. For the best summaries of the anticensure arguments, see Cohn, *McCarthy*, 231–33, and Lawrence, "Justice to the Memory of Senator McCarthy," 139–44.

27. *Congressional Record*, 16002–16004.

28. Patricia Buckley, interview with author, May 10, 1998.

29. Barry Goldwater with Jack Casserly, *Goldwater* (New York: Doubleday, 1988), 130.

30. Robert E. Lee, Interview, March 15, 1977, State Historical Society of Wisconsin, p. 3.

31. McCarthy quoted in *Time*, December 13, 1954, 12.

32. Watkins interview, Columbia University, p. 86. By making themselves the objects of McCarthy's contempt, the Watkins Committee had incidentally disposed of the anticensure argument of opponents that they were charging him with actions under a previous congress.

33. *U.S. News & World Report*, December 10, 1954, 36.

34. Thomas Reeves, *A Question of Character. A Life of John F. Kennedy* (New York: Free Press, 1991), 123.
35. Ruth Watt, Interview, Senate Historical Office, 147–48.

Chapter 16. Extinction

1. Rovere, *Senator Joe McCarthy*, 236.
2. Rovere, *Senator Joe McCarthy*, 23.
3. *Diary of James Hagerty*, 128.
4. Potter, *Days of Shame*, 296.
5. Patricia Buckley, Interview with author, May 10, 1998.
6. Oshinsky, *Conspiracy So Immense*, 496.
7. O'Brien, *McCarthy and McCarthyism in Wisconsin*, 172–73, 175.
8. Oshinsky, *Conspiracy So Immense*, 503.
9. John Lukacs, *Confessions of an Original Sinner* (New York: Ticknor & Fields, 1990), 177.
10. Oshinsky, *Conspiracy So Immense*, 503.
11. Van Susteren, Interview, November 25, 1975, State Historical Society of Wisconsin, pp. 3–4; Ruth Watt, Interview, Senate Historical Office, p. 151.
12. Rusher, *Special Counsel;* Patricia Buckley, Interview with author.
13. Van Susteren, Interview, February 5, 1977, p. 3; Reeves, *Life and Times of Joe McCarthy*, 671.
14. Reeves, *Life and Times of Joe McCarthy*, 668.
15. "Senator McCarthy's Report to the People of Wisconsin," Report No. 7 [no date], 1–2.
16. Rusher, *Special Counsel*, 252.
17. Reeves, *Question of Character*, 124.
18. Rusher, *Special Counsel*, 250; Reeves, *Life and Times of Joe McCarthy*, 670–71.
19. *New York Post*, May 3, 1957.
20. William Rusher, Interview with author, June 1997.
21. "TRB," *New Republic* (December 9, 1954), 2.
22. *Appleton Post-Crescent* quoted in Oshinsky, *Conspiracy So Immense*, 506.
23. Arthur Schlesinger, Jr., *Robert Kennedy and His Times* (Boston: Houghton Mifflin, 1978), 173; Lester David and Irene David, *Bobby Kennedy: The Making of a Folk Hero* (New York: Dodd, Mead, 1986), 76–77.
24. "Joe," in *Washington Post* and *New York Herald Tribune*, May 4, 1957, reprinted in *Congressional Record* 103, 6404.
25. "Across McCarthy's Grave," *National Review* (May 18, 1954), 470.
26. Reeves, *Life and Times of Joe McCarthy*, 674.
27. Letter to "Mrs. Dribble," dated May 22, 1957, and published in the *Detroit Times* on June 11, 1957.
28. William F. Buckley, Jr., *Odyssey of a Friend: Whittaker Chambers's Letters to William F. Buckley, Jr., 1954–1961* (New York: Putnam, 1970), 176–177.
29. Schlesinger, *Robert Kennedy*, 105–106; Whalen, *The Founding Father*, 427.

Chapter 17. Beyond McCarthy

1. *Time*, November 22, 1954, 14.
2. The two papers were the *New York Daily News* and the *Chicago Tribune*, represented by McCarthy's old friend, Willard Edwards. Rusher, *Special Counsel*, 265.
3. Richard Rovere, "Arthur Miller's Conscience," *New Republic*, June 17, 1957, republished in Dorothy Wickenden, ed., *The New Republic Reader* (New York: Basic Books, 1994), 236–41.
4. Harvey Matusow, *False Witness* (New York: Cameron & Kahn, 1955).
5. See the summary of the Hiss-Chambers controversy as it continued during the sixties and seventies in Weinstein, *Perjury*, 449–61, 486–503.
6. See, for example, Norman Podhoretz, *Breaking Ranks: A Political Memoir* (New York: Knopf, 1978), 39–40.
7. Blanche Wiesen Cook, *The Declassified Eisenhower: A Divided Legacy* (Garden City, NY: Doubleday, 1981).
8. Richard Hofstadter, "The Pseudo-Conservative Revolt," in *The Paranoid Style in American Politics and Other Essays* (New York: Knopf, 1967), 41–65, 50; Michael Paul Rogin, *McCarthy and the Intellectuals*, 232.
9. Chester Bowles, *The Coming Political Breakthrough* (New York: Harper, 1959), 170.
10. Barone, *Our Country*, 321, 334–35.
11. For example, David Halberstam, *The Best and the Brightest* (New York: Random House, 1972).
12. See the revealing account in H. R. McMaster, *Dereliction of Duty: Lyndon Johnson, Robert McNamara, the Joint Chiefs of Staff, and the Lies that Led to Vietnam* (New York: HarperCollins, 1997).
13. Dean Rusk, with Richard Rusk, *As I Saw It* (New York: Norton, 1990), 159–60.
14. Senate, Committee on Foreign Relations, *The Vietnam Hearings* (New York, Random House, 1966), 16, 30, 53.
15. David Horowitz, *Radical Son* (New York: Free Press, 1997), 106.
16. William Fulbright, quoted in Lewy, *The Cause That Failed*, 118.
17. Weinstein and Vassiliev, *Haunted Wood*, 299.
18. Lewy, *The Federal Loyalty-Security Program*, 5–6.
19. For details, see George P. Morse, *America Twice Betrayed: Reversing 50 Years of Government Security Failure* (Silver Spring, MD: Bartleby Press, 1995), 9–47. The Army traitors in the fifties included Larry Wu-Tai Chin, a native Chinese translator working with the Army; sergeants Robert Lee Johnson and James Mintkenbaugh; Air Force Captain George French; and Navy Yeoman Nelson Drummond.
20. Lewy, *The Federal Loyalty-Security Program*, 2.
21. See Ronald Radosh, *Divided They Fell: The Demise of the Democratic Party, 1964–1996* (New York: Free Press, 1996).
22. Lewy, *The Cause That Failed*, 158.
23. Peter Collier, "Looking Backward: Memories of the Sixties Left," in John Bunzel,

ed., *Political Passages: Journeys of Change Through Two Decades 1968–1988* (New York: Free Press, 1988), 162–86; 173.

Epilogue

1. Judis, *William F. Buckley*, 130.
2. "Publisher's Statement," *National Review* (November 19, 1955), 5.
3. Frank Meyer quoted in Nash, *Conservative Intellectual Movement*, 150.
4. Phillips, *Emerging Republican Majority*, 77.
5. On Williams, see the introduction by Harry Berger to *A William Appleman Williams Reader*, ed. Harry Berger (Chicago: Ivan Dee, 1992), 12–14.
6. W. A. Williams, *The Tragedy of American Diplomacy* (1959, revised and enlarged edition, New York: Dell, 1962), 89.
7. See Robert Maddox's essay *"Atomic Diplomacy:* Gar Alperovitz," in his *The New Left and the Origins of the Cold War* (Princeton: Princeton University Press, 1973), 63–78.
8. For example, Albert Kahn and Michael Sayers, *The Great Conspiracy: The Secret War Against Soviet Russia* (San Francisco: Proletarian Publishers, 1946).
9. Williams, "Confessions of an Intransigent Revisionist," quoted in *Williams Reader*, 11.
10. Athan Theoharis, *Seeds of Repression: Harry S. Truman and the Origins of McCarthyism* (Chicago: Quadrangle Books, 1971), and *The Truman Presidency: The Origins of the Imperial Presidency and the National Security State* (New York: Coleman Enterprises, 1982).

Appendix I. McCarthy and the Doctors

1. Hugo Wolf quoted in Kay Redfield Jamison, *Touched With Fire: Manic-Depressive Illness and the Artistic Temperament* (New York: Free Press, 1993), 13–15;27. See also Frederick Goodwin and Kay R. Jamison, *Manic-Depressive Illness* (New York: Oxford University Press, 1990), and Roger Horton and Cornelius Kortona, eds., *Biological Aspects of Affective Disorders* (London: Academic Press, 1991).
2. Jamison, *Touched With Fire*, 13.
3. Ed Nellor, Interview, May 7, 1977, State Historical Society of Wisconsin, p. 3.
4. Ed Nellor, Interview, January 11, 1979.
5. Jamison, *Touched With Fire*, 36, 37. Of the many works on alcoholism, two I found particularly useful were Norman K. Denzin, *The Alcoholic Self* (Newbury Park, CA: Sage Publications, 1987), and, from a very different perspective, Richard Stivers, *Hair of the Dog: Irish Drinking and American Stereotype* (University Park, PA: Pennsylvania State University Press, 1976).
6. Jamison, *Touched With Fire*, 18, 261–62.
7. Reeves, *Life and Times of Joe McCarthy*, 671–72.

Appendix II. The Strange Case of Annie Lee Moss

1. Reeves, *Life and Times of Joe McCarthy*, 569.

2. Reeves, *Life and Times of Joe McCarthy*, 548.

3. Cohn, *McCarthy*, 121.

4. *New York Times*, February 24, 1954.

5. She did make a preliminary appearance on February 23. Her lawyer, George Hayes, said Mrs. Moss was too sick to testify, and McCarthy agreed.

6. Reeves, *Life and Times of Joe McCarthy*, 568.

7. Rosteck, See It Now *Confronts McCarthyism*, 162.

8. John Crosby quoted in Rosteck, See It Now *Confronts McCarthyism*, 163.

9. Murray Marder quoted in von Hoffman, *Citizen Cohn*, 205.

10. *Reports of the Subervsive Activities Control Board*, Vol. 1. Washington, DC: Government Printing Office, 1966, 93–94.

11. Ruth Watt Interview, Senate Historical Office.

12. Oshinsky, *Conspiracy So Immense*, 403, note.

13. Rosteck, See It Now *Confronts McCarthyism*, 166.

Bibliography

Archival Sources

Francis McNamara Collection, George Mason University
J. B. Matthews Papers, Duke University
Related Manuscript Collections, Herbert Hoover Presidential Library
Secretary of the Army, General Counsel Files, Army-McCarthy Hearings, National
    Archives
Thomas Coleman Papers, State Historical Society of Wisconsin
Thomas Reeves Collection, Joseph McCarthy Papers, State Historical Society of
    Wisconsin

Published Government Documents

U.S. Congress. *Congressional Record*, vols. 93–102, 1947–1956.
U.S. House of Representatives. Committee on Un-American Activities. *Investigation of Un-American Activities and Propaganda*. 79th Congress, 2nd session, 1947.
U.S. Senate and House. *Memorial Services Held in the Senate and House of Representatives of the United States, Together with Remarks Presented in Eulogy of Joseph Raymond McCarthy*. 85th Congress, 1st session, 1957.
U.S. Senate. Committee on Armed Services. *Malmédy Massacre Investigation. Hearings. . . .* 81st Congress, 1st session, 1949.
U.S. Senate. Committee on Armed Services. *Malmédy Massacre Investigation. Report.* 81st Congress, 1st session, 1949.
U.S. Senate. Committee on Expenditures in the Executive Departments. Subcommittee on Investigations. *Export Policy and Loyalty Hearings. . . .* 80th Congress, 2nd session, 1948.
U.S. Senate. Committee on Foreign Relations. *State Department Employee Loyalty Investigation, Individual Views*. 81st Congress, 2nd session, 1950.
U.S. Senate. Committee on Foreign Relations. *State Department Employee Loyalty Investigation. Report. . . .* 81st Congress, 2nd session, 1950.
U.S. Senate. Committee on Government Operations. Permanent Subcommittee on Investigations. *Army Signal Corps: Subversion and Espionage. Hearings. . . .* 83rd Congress, 1st and 2nd sessions, 1954.
U.S. Senate. Committee on Government Operations. Permanent Subcommittee on Investigations. *Communist Infiltration Among Civilians Workers. Hearings. . . .* 83rd Congress, 1st session, 1953.
U.S. Senate. Committee on Government Operations. Permanent Subcommittee on In-

vestigations. *Communist Infiltration in the Army. Hearings.* . . . 83rd Congress, 1st and 2nd sessions, 1953–1954.

U.S. Senate. Committee on Government Operations. Permanent Subcommittee on Investigations. *State Department Information Program: Information Centers. Hearings.* . . . 83rd Congress, 1st session, 1953.

U.S. Senate. Committee on Government Operations. Permanent Subcommittee on Investigations. *State Department Information Program: Voice of America. Hearings.* . . . 83rd Congress, 1st session, 1953.

U.S. Senate. Committee on Government Operations. Special Subcommittee on Investigations. *Charges and Countercharges Involving Secretary of the Army Robert T. Stevens, John G. Adams, H. Struve Hensel, and Senator Joe McCarthy, Roy M. Cohn, and Francis P. Carr. Hearings.* . . . 83rd Congress, 2nd session, 1954.

U.S. Senate. Committee on Government Operations. Special Subcommittee on Investigations. *Special Senate Investigation on Charges and Countercharges Involving Secretary of the Army Robert T. Stevens, John G. Adams, H. Struve Hensel, and Senator Joe McCarthy, Roy M. Cohn, and Francis P. Carr. Senate Report 2507.* 83rd Congress, 2nd session, 1954.

U.S. Senate. Committee on the Judiciary. Subcommittee to Investigate the Administration of the Internal Security Act and Other Internal Security Laws. *Institute of Pacific Relations. Hearings.* . . . 82nd Congress, 1st and 2nd sessions, 1951–1952.

U.S. Senate. Committee on Rules and Administration. Subcommittee on Privileges and Elections. *Investigation of Senators Joseph R. McCarthy and William Benton. Report.* 82nd Congress, 2nd session, 1952.

U.S. Senate. *Report of the Select Committee to Study Censure Charges.* 83rd Congress, 2nd session, 1954.

U.S. Senate. Subcommittee of the Committee on Foreign Relations. *State Department Employee Loyalty Investigation. Hearings.* . . . 81st Congress, 2nd session, 1950.

Venona Historical Monographs http://www.gsa.gov:8080/docs/venona/monographs/.

Interviews

Thomas C. Reeves. Interviews with Willard Edwards, Charles Kersten, Robert E. Lee, Ed Nellor, and Urban van Sustern. State Historical Society of Wisconsin.

Pat Holt, Carl Marcy, Floyd Riddick, and Ruth Y. Watt interviews. Senate Historical Office, Oral History Interviews.

Author's interviews with William F. Buckley, Jr., Patricia Buckley, Francis McNamara, and William Rusher.

Roy Cohn, David Schine, and Arthur Watkins interviews. Columbia University Oral History Project.

Books and Other Secondary Sources

Acheson, Dean. *Present at the Creation: My Years in the State Department.* New York: Norton, 1969.

Adams, John Gibbons. *Without Precedent: The Story of the Death of McCarthyism.* New York: Norton, 1983.

Albright, Joseph, and Marcia Kunstel. *Bombshell: The Secret Story of America's Unknown Atomic Spy Conspiracy.* New York: Times Books, 1997.

Alsop, Stewart. *The Center: People and Power in Political Washington.* New York: Harper & Row, 1968.

Ambrose, Stephen E. *Eisenhower.* New York: Simon & Schuster, 1983–1984.

Anderson, Jack, and James Boyd. *Confessions of a Muckraker: The Inside Story of Life in Washington during the Truman, Eisenhower, Kennedy and Johnson Years.* New York: Random House, 1979.

Anderson, Jack, and Ronald W. May. *McCarthy: The Man, the Senator, the "Ism."* Boston: Beacon Press, 1952.

Andrews, Christopher, and Andrei Gordievsky. *KGB: The Inside Story.* New York: HarperCollins, 1990.

Bachrack, Stanley D. *The Committee of One Million: "China Lobby" Politics, 1953–1971.* New York: Columbia University Press, 1976.

Baker, Robert G. *Wheeling and Dealing: Confessions of a Capitol Hill Operator.* New York: Norton, 1978.

Barone, Michael. *Our Country: The Shaping of America from Roosevelt to Reagan.* New York: Free Press, 1990.

Bayley, Edwin R. *Joe McCarthy and the Press.* Madison: University of Wisconsin Press, 1981.

Belknap, Michael R. *Cold War Political Justice: The Smith Act, the Communist Party, and American Civil Liberties.* Westport, CT: Greenwood Press, 1977.

Bell, Daniel. *The New American Right.* New York: Criterion Books, 1955. Republished as *The Radical Right: The New American Right,* expanded and updated. New York: Doubleday, 1963.

Berger, Harry. *A William Appleman Williams Reader.* Chicago: Ivan Dee, 1992.

Berger, Raoul. *Executive Privilege: A Constitutional Myth.* Cambridge: Harvard University Press, 1974.

Bernstein, Barton J. *Politics and Policies of the Truman Administration.* Chicago: Quadrangle Books, 1970.

Biles, Roger. *The South and the New Deal.* Lexington, KY: University of Kentucky Press, 1994.

Billingsley, Kenneth Lloyd. *Hollywood Party: How Communism Seduced the American Film Industry in the 1930s and 1940s.* Rocklin, CA: Forum, 1998.

Blum, John Morton. *V Was for Victory: Politics and American Culture during World War II.* New York: Harcourt Brace Jovanovich, 1976.

Bohlen, Charles E. *Witness to History, 1929–1969.* New York: Norton, 1973.

Bowles, Chester. *The Coming Political Breakthrough.* New York: Harper, 1959.

Boylan, James R. *The New Deal Coalition and the Election of 1946.* New York: Garland Publishing, 1981.

Brinkley, David. *Washington Goes to War.* New York: Knopf, 1988.

Brookhiser, Richard. *Founding Father: Rediscovering George Washington.* New York: Free Press, 1996.

Brown, Ralph S. *Loyalty and Security; Employment Tests in the United States.* New Haven: Yale University Press, 1958.

Buckley, William F., Jr. *Up From Liberalism, 25th Anniversary Edition.* New York: Stein & Day, 1984, 1985; originally published, 1959.

Buckley, William F., Jr., ed. *The Committee and Its Critics.* New York: Putnam, 1962.

Buckley, William F., Jr., ed. *Odyssey of a Friend: Whittaker Chambers' Letters to William F. Buckley, Jr., 1954–1961.* New York: G. P. Putnam's Sons, 1970.

Buckley, William F., Jr., and Brent L. Bozell. *McCarthy and His Enemies: The Record and Its Meaning.* Chicago: H. Regnery Co., 1954.

Bunzel, John, ed. *Political Passages: Journeys of Change Through Two Decades 1968–1988.* New York: Free Press, 1988.

Burnham, James. *Containment or Liberation? An Inquiry into the Aims of United States Foreign Policy.* New York: Jonathan Day, 1953.

Caute, David. *The Great Fear: The Anti-Communist Purge under Truman and Eisenhower.* New York: Simon & Schuster, 1978.

Cochran, Bert. *Harry Truman and the Crisis Presidency.* New York: Funk & Wagnalls, 1973.

Cohn, Roy. *McCarthy.* New York: New American Library, 1968.

Collier, Peter, and David Horowitz. *The Kennedys: An American Drama.* New York: Summit Books, 1984.

Cook, Blanche Wiesen. *The Declassified Eisenhower: A Divided Legacy.* Garden City, NY: Doubleday, 1981.

Cook, Fred J. *The Nightmare Decade: The Life and Times of Senator Joe McCarthy.* New York: Random House, 1971.

Coser, Lewis A. *Men of Ideas: A Sociologist's View.* New York: Free Press, 1965.

Costello, John. *Mask of Treachery: Spies, Lies, Buggery and Betrayal.* New York: Morrow, 1988.

Cox, Edward Franklin. *State and National Voting in Federal Elections, 1910–1970.* Hamden, CT: Archon Books, 1972.

Crosby, Donald F., S.J. *God, Church, and Flag: Senator Joseph R. McCarthy and the Catholic Church, 1950–1957.* Chapel Hill: University of North Carolina Press, 1978.

Dallek, Robert. *Lone Star Rising: Lyndon Johnson and His Times, 1908–1960.* New York: Oxford University Press, 1991.

David, Lester, and Irene David. *Bobby Kennedy: The Making of a Folk Hero.* New York: Dodd, Mead, 1986.

DeLoach, Cartha. *Hoover's FBI: The Inside Story by Hoover's Trusted Lieutenant.* Washington, DC: Regnery, 1995.

Denzin, Norman K. *The Alcoholic Self.* Newbury Park, CA: Sage Publications, 1987.

Dies, Martin. *Martin Dies' Story.* New York: The Bookmailer, 1963.

Diggins, John Patrick. *The Rise and Fall of the American Left.* New York: Norton, 1992.

Dodd, Bella. *School of Darkness.* New York: P. J. Kenedy, 1954.

Draper, Theodore. *American Communism and Soviet Russia: The Formative Period.* New York: Vintage Books, 1986; originally published New York: Viking Press, 1960.

Drury, Allen. *A Senate Journal: 1943–1945.* New York: McGraw-Hill, 1963.

Dugger, Ronnie. *The Politician: The Life and Times of Lyndon Johnson, the Drive for Power, from the Frontier to Master of the Senate.* New York: Norton, 1982.

Eisenhower, Dwight D. *Peace with Justice.* New York: Columbia University Press, 1961.

Epstein, Leon D. *Politics in Wisconsin.* Madison: University of Wisconsin Press, 1958.

Evans, Rowland, and Robert Novak. *Lyndon B. Johnson: The Exercise of Power.* New York: New American Library, 1968.

Ewald, William Bragg, Jr. *Who Killed Joe McCarthy?* New York: Simon & Schuster, 1984.

Fariello, Griffin. *Red Scare: Memories of the American Inquisition, An Oral History.* New York: Norton, 1995.

Fried, Richard M. *Men Against McCarthy.* New York: Columbia University Press, 1976.

———. *Nightmare in Red: The McCarthy Era in Perspective.* New York: Oxford University Press, 1990.

Furuya, Keiji, ed. *Chiang Kai-shek: His Life and Time.* Trans. Sho Kaiseki Hiroku. New York: St. John's University, 1981.

Gabler, Neil. *Winchell: Gossip, Power and the Culture of Celebrity.* New York: Knopf, 1995.

Gaddis, John Lewis. *We Now Know: Rethinking Cold War History.* New York: Oxford University Press, 1997.

Garson, Robert A. *The United States and China since 1949: A Troubled Affair.* Madison, NJ: Fairleigh Dickinson University Press, 1994.

Gellermann, William. *Martin Dies.* New York: Jonathan Day, 1944.

Ginder, Richard. *Right or Wrong.* Huntington, IN: Sunday Visitor Press, 1959.

Goldwater, Barry. *Goldwater.* New York: Doubleday, 1988.

Goncharov, Sergei N., John W. Lewis, and Xue Litai. *Uncertain Partners: Stalin, Mao, and the Korean War.* Stanford, CA: Stanford University Press, 1993.

Goodwin, Frederick, and Kay R. Jamison. *Manic-Depressive Illness.* New York: Oxford University Press, 1990.

Greeley, Andrew M. *That Most Distressful Nation: The Taming of the American Irish.* Chicago: Quadrangle Books, 1972.

Greene, John Robert. *The Crusade: The Presidential Election of 1952.* Lanham, MD: University Press of America, 1985.

Gribble, Richard. *Guardian of America: The Life of James Martin Gillis, CSP.* New York: Paulist Press, 1998.

Griffith, Robert. *The Politics of Fear: Joseph R. McCarthy and the Senate.* Amherst: University of Massachusetts Press, 1987; originally published, Lexington: University Press of Kentucky, 1970.

Griffith, Thomas. *Harry and Teddy: The Turbulent Friendship of Press Lord Henry R. Luce and His Favorite Reporter, Theodore H. White.* New York: Random House, 1995.

Guhin, Michael A. *John Foster Dulles: A Statesman and His Times.* New York: Columbia University Press, 1972.

Hagerty, James C. *The Diary of James C. Hagerty: Eisenhower in Mid-Course, 1954–1955,* ed., Robert H. Ferrell. Bloomington: Indiana University Press, 1983.

Halberstam, David. *The Best and the Brightest.* New York: Random House, 1969.

———. *The Fifties.* New York: Villard Books, 1993.

Harper, Alan D. *Politics of Loyalty: The White House and the Communist Issue, 1946–1952*. Westport, CT: Greenwood, 1969.

Haynes, John E. *Red Scare or Red Menace? American Communism and Anticommunism in the Cold War Era*. Chicago: Ivan R. Dee, 1996.

Haynes, John Earl. *Dubious Alliance: The Making of Minnesota's DFL Party*. Minneapolis: University of Minnesota Press, 1984.

Haynes, John Earl, and Harvey Klehr. *Venona: Decoding Soviet Espionage in America*. New Haven: Yale University Press, 1999.

Hofstadter, Richard. *The Paranoid Style in American Politics and Other Essays*. New York: Knopf, 1965.

Hollander, Paul. *Political Pilgrims: Western Intellectuals in Search of the Good Society*, 4th edition. New Brunswick, NJ: Transaction Publishers, 1998; originally published as *Political Pilgrims: Travels of Western Intellectuals to the Soviet Union, China, and Cuba*. New York: Oxford University Press, 1981.

Holloway, David. *Stalin and the Bomb: The Soviet Union and Atomic Energy, 1939–1956*. New Haven: Yale University Press, 1994.

Hook, Sidney. *Heresy, Yes—Conspiracy, No!* New York: Jonathan Day, 1953.

———. *Out of Step: An Unquiet Life in the 20th Century*. New York: Harper & Row, 1987.

Hoopes, Roy. *Americans Remember the Home Front: An Oral Narrative*. New York: Hawthorn Books, 1977.

Horowitz, David A. *Beyond Left & Right: Insurgency and the Establishment*. Urbana: University of Illinois Press, 1997.

———. *Radical Son: A Generational Odyssey*. New York: Free Press, 1997.

Horton, Roger, and Cornelius Kortona, eds. *Biological Aspects of Affective Disorders*. London: Academic Press, 1991.

Huss, Pierre J., and George Carpozi, Jr. *Red Spies in the UN*. New York: Coward-McCann, 1965.

Hyman, Sidney. *The Lives of William Benton*. Chicago: University of Chicago Press, 1969.

Ignatiev, Noel. *How the Irish Became White*. New York: Routledge, 1995.

Irons, Peter. *Justice at War*. New York: Oxford University Press, 1983.

Isaacson, Walter, and Evan Thomas. *The Wise Men: Six Friends and the World They Made*. New York: Simon & Schuster, 1986.

James, D. Clayton. *The Years of MacArthur*. Boston: Houghton-Mifflin, 1970–1985.

Jamison, Kay Redfield. *Touched with Fire: Manic-Depressive Illness and the Artistic Temperament*. New York: Free Press, 1993.

Jessup, Philip. *The International Problem of Governing Mankind*. Claremont, CA: Claremont College for the Four Associated Colleges at Claremont, 1947.

Johnson, Paul. *Modern Times: The World from the Twenties to the Nineties*. New York: HarperCollins, 1991.

Judis, John B. *William F. Buckley, Jr.: Patron Saint of the Conservatives*. New York: Simon & Schuster, 1988.

Kahn, Albert, and Michael Sayers. *The Great Conspiracy: The Secret War Against Soviet Russia*. San Francisco: Proletarian Publishers, 1946.

Kazan, Elia. *Elia Kazan: A Life*. New York: Knopf, 1988.

Kelly, Frank K. *Harry Truman and the Human Family*. Santa Barbara: Capra Press, 1998.

Kendall, Willmoore. *The Conservative Affirmation in America*. Chicago: Gateway Editions, 1985.

Kennan, George F. *Memoirs: 1925–1950, Volume I*. Boston: Little, Brown, 1967.

———. *Memoirs: 1950–1963, Volume II*. Boston: Little, Brown, 1972.

Kepley, David R. *The Collapse of the Middle Way: Senate Republicans and the Bipartisan Foreign Policy, 1948–1952*. New York: Greenwood Press, 1988.

Kirk, Russell, and James McClellan. *The Political Principles of Robert A. Taft*. New York: Fleet Press, 1967.

Klehr, Harvey. *The Heyday of American Communism: The Depression Decade*. New York: Basic Books, 1984.

Klehr, Harvey, and John Earl Haynes. *The American Communist Movement: Storming Heaven Itself*. New York: Twayne, 1992.

Klehr, Harvey, John Earl Haynes, and Fridrikh Igorevich Firsov. *The Secret World of American Communism*. New Haven: Yale University Press, 1995.

Klehr, Harvey, John Earl Haynes, and Kyrill M. Anderson. *The Soviet World of American Communism*. New Haven: Yale University Press, 1998.

Klehr, Harvey, and Ronald Radosh. *The Amerasia Spy Case: Prelude to McCarthyism*. Chapel Hill: University of North Carolina Press, 1996.

Knobel, Dale T. *Paddy and the Republic: Ethnicity and Nationality in Antebellum America*. Middletown, CT: Wesleyan University Press, 1986.

Kofsky, Frank. *Harry S. Truman and the War Scare of 1948: A Successful Campaign to Deceive the Nation*. New York: St. Martin's, 1993.

Kutler, Stanley I. *The American Inquisition: Justice and Injustice in the Cold War*. New York: Hill & Wang, 1982.

Lamphere, Robert J., and Tom Shachtman. *The FBI-KGB War: A Special Agent's Story*. New York: Random House, 1986.

Larson, Arthur. *A Republican Looks at His Party*. New York: Harper, 1956.

Lasky, Victor. *Robert F. Kennedy: The Myth and the Man*. New York: Trident Press, 1968.

Lattimore, Owen. *Ordeal by Slander*. Boston: Little, Brown, 1950.

Leamer, Laurence. *The Kennedy Women: The Saga of an American Family*. New York: Villard Books, 1994.

Leffler, Melvyn P. *A Preponderance of Power: National Security, the Truman Administration, and the Cold War*. Stanford, CA: Stanford University Press, 1992.

Levin, Bernard. *Run It Down the Flagpole: Britain in the Sixties*. New York: Atheneum, 1971.

Lewis, Flora. *Red Pawn: The Story of Noel Field*. Garden City, NY: Doubleday, 1965.

Lewy, Guenter. *The Cause that Failed: Communism in American Political Life*. New York: Oxford University Press, 1990.

———. *The Federal Loyalty-Security Program: The Need for Reform*. Washington, DC: American Enterprise Institute, 1983.

Lipset, Seymour Martin. *American Exceptionalism: A Double-edged Sword*. New York: Norton, 1996.

Lokos, Lionel. *Who Promoted Peress!* New York: Bookmailer, 1961.

379

Lubell, Samuel. *The Future of American Politics.* New York, Harper & Row, 1965.

Lukacs, John. *Confessions of an Original Sinner.* New York: Ticknor & Fields, 1990.

Lyons, Eugene. *The Red Decade.* New Rochelle, NY: Arlington House, 1970; originally published, 1941.

Maddox, Robert James. *From War to Cold War: The Education of Harry Truman.* Boulder, CO: Westview Press, 1988.

———. *The New Left and the Origins of the Cold War.* Princeton: Princeton University Press, 1973.

Madriaga, Salvador, de. *The Anatomy of the Cold War.* Belfast: M. Boyd, 1955.

Manchester, William. *American Caesar: Douglas MacArthur, 1880–1964.* Boston: Little, Brown, 1978.

Martin, Joseph W. *My First Fifty Years in Politics.* New York: McGraw-Hill, 1960.

Martin, Ralph. *Seeds of Destruction: Joe Kennedy and His Sons.* New York: Putnam, 1995.

Matthew, Donald R. *U.S. Senators and Their World.* New York: Vintage Books, 1960.

Matusow, Harvey. *False Witness.* New York: Cameron & Kahn, 1955.

Mayers, David. *George Kennan and the Dilemmas of U.S. Foreign Policy.* New York: Oxford University Press, 1988.

McCarthy, Joseph, R. *America's Retreat from Victory: The Story of George Catlett Marshall.* New York: Devin-Adair, 1951.

———. *McCarthyism, The Fight for America: Documented Answers to Questions Asked by Friend and Foe.* New York: Devin-Adair, 1952; reprinted as *McCarthyism: The Fight for America,* New York: Arno, 1977.

McMaster, H. R. *Dereliction of Duty: Lyndon Johnson, Robert McNamara, the Joint Chiefs of Staff, and the Lies that Led to Vietnam.* New York: HarperCollins, 1997.

McPherson, Harry. *A Political Education.* Boston: Little, Brown, 1972.

Merry, Robert W. *Taking on the World: Joseph and Stewart Alsop, Guardians of the American Century.* New York: Viking, 1996.

Meyer, Cord. *Facing Reality: From World Federalism to the CIA.* New York: Harper & Row, 1980.

Mollenhoff, Clark. *Washington Cover-up.* New York: Doubleday, 1962.

Morse, George P. *America Twice Betrayed: Reversing 50 Years of Government Security Failure.* Silver Spring, MD: Bartleby Press, 1995.

Moser, John E. *Twisting the Lion's Tail: American Anglophobia between the World Wars.* New York: New York University Press, 1999.

Mosher, Steven W. *China Misperceived: American Illusions and Chinese Reality.* New York: Basic Books, 1990.

Moynihan, Daniel P. *Secrecy: The American Experience.* New Haven: Yale University Press, 1998.

Murray, John Courtney. *We Hold These Truths: Catholic Reflections on the American Proposition.* New York: Sheed & Ward, 1960.

Nash, George H. *The Conservative Intellectual Movement in America since 1945.* New York: Basic Books, 1976.

Newman, Robert P. *Owen Lattimore and the "Loss" of China.* Berkeley: University of California Press, 1992.

Nixon, Richard M. *RN: The Memoirs of Richard Nixon.* New York: Grosset & Dunlap, 1978.

O'Brien, Michael. *McCarthy and McCarthyism in Wisconsin.* Columbia: University of Missouri Press, 1980.

O'Neill, William L. *American High: The Years of Confidence, 1945–1960.* New York: Free Press, 1986.

Oshinsky, David M. *A Conspiracy So Immense: The World of Joe McCarthy.* New York: Free Press, 1983.

———. *Senator Joseph McCarthy and the American Labor Movement.* Columbia: University of Missouri Press, 1976.

Overstreet, Harry, and Bonaro Overstreet. *What We Must Know about Communism.* New York: Norton, 1958.

Parmet, Herbert S. *Jack: The Struggles of John F. Kennedy.* New York: Dial Press, 1980.

Paterson, Thomas G., ed. *Cold War Critics: Alternatives to American Foreign Policy in the Truman Years.* Chicago: Quadrangle Books, 1971.

Patterson, James T. *Mr. Republican: A Biography of Robert A. Taft.* Boston: Houghton-Mifflin, 1972.

Philbrick, Herbert A. *I Led Three Lives.* Washington, DC: Capitol Hill Press, 1972.

Phillips, Kevin B. *The Emerging Republican Majority.* New York: Anchor Books, 1970; originally published, New York: Arlington House, 1969.

Pocock, J. G. A. *The Machiavellian Moment: Florentine Political Thought and the Atlantic Republican Tradition.* Princeton: Princeton University Press, 1975.

Podhoretz, Norman. *Breaking Ranks: A Political Memoir.* New York: Knopf, 1978.

Potter, Charles E. *Days of Shame.* New York: Coward-McCann, 1965; republished, New York: New American Library, 1971.

Powers, Richard Gid. *Not Without Honor: The History of American Anticommunism.* New York: Free Press, 1995.

Radeck, Thomas. *See It Now Confronts McCarthyism: Television Documentary and the Politics of Representation.* Tuscaloosa: University of Alabama Press, 1994.

Radosh, Ronald. *Divided They Fell: The Demise of the Democratic Party, 1964–1996.* New York: Free Press, 1996.

Radosh, Ronald, and Joyce Milton. *The Rosenberg File.* 2nd ed. New Haven: Yale University Press, 1997; originally published, New York: Holt, Rinehart, & Winston, 1983.

Reedy, George. *Lyndon Baines Johnson: A Memoir.* New York: Andrews & McMeel, 1982.

Reeves, Thomas C. *The Life and Times of Joe McCarthy.* Lanham, MD: Madison Books, 1997; originally published, New York: Stein & Day, 1982.

———. *A Question of Character: A Life of John F. Kennedy.* New York: Free Press, 1991.

Resis, Albert, ed. *Molotov Remembers: Inside Kremlin Politics, Conversations with Felix Chuev.* Chicago: Ivan R. Dee, 1993.

Rhodes, Richard. *The Making of the Atomic Bomb.* New York: Simon & Schuster, 1986.

Ribuffo, Leo P. *The Old Christian Right: The Protestant Far Right from the Great Depression to the Cold War.* Philadelphia: Temple University Press, 1983.

Riddle, Donald H. *The Truman Committee: A Study in Congressional Responsibility.* New Brunswick, NJ: Rutgers University Press, 1964.

Rogin, Michael Paul. *The Intellectuals and McCarthy: The Radical Specter.* Cambridge: MIT Press, 1967.

Rorty, James, and Moshe Decter. *McCarthy and the Communists.* Boston: Beacon Press, 1954.

Rosenblum, Sig, and Charles Antin, eds. *LBJ Lampooned: Cartoon Criticism of Lyndon B. Johnson, with an Introduction by Jules Feiffer.* New York: Cobble Hill Press, 1968.

Rosteck, Thomas. *See It Now Confronts McCarthyism.* Tuscaloosa: University of Alabama Press, 1994.

Rovere, Richard H. *Senator Joe McCarthy.* Cleveland and New York: Meridian Books, 1960; originally published, New York: Harcourt Brace Jovanovich, 1959; reissued, Berkeley: University of California Press, 1996, with a new foreword by Arthur M. Schlesinger, Jr.

Rozell, Mark J. *Executive Privilege: The Dilemma of Secrecy and Democratic Accountability.* Baltimore: Johns Hopkins University Press, 1994.

Rusher, William A. *Special Counsel.* New Rochelle, NY: Arlington House, 1968.

Rusk, Dean. *As I Saw It.* New York: Norton, 1990.

Russell, Francis. *Sacco and Vanzetti: The Case Resolved.* New York: Harper & Row, 1986.

Schlesinger, Arthur M., Jr. *Robert Kennedy and His Times.* Boston: Houghton-Mifflin, 1978.

Schrecker, Ellen. *The Age of McCarthyism: A Brief History with Documents.* Boston: Bedford Books, 1994.

———. *Many Are the Crimes: McCarthyism in America.* Boston: Little, Brown, 1998.

———. *No Ivory Tower: McCarthyism and the Universities.* New York: Oxford University Press, 1986.

Senate Committee on Foreign Relations. *The Vietnam Hearings.* New York: Random House, 1966.

Shannon, William V. *The American Irish.* New York: Macmillan, 1963.

Sheen, Fulton J. *Communism and the Conscience of the West, 2nd ed.* New York: Garden City Books, 1951.

Sheng, Michael M. *Battling Western Imperialism: Mao, Stalin, and the United States.* Princeton: Princeton University Press, 1997.

Sherry, Michael S. *In the Shadow of War: The United States since the 1930s.* New Haven: Yale University Press, 1995.

———. *Preparing for the Next War: American Plans for Postwar Defense, 1941–45.* New Haven: Yale University Press, 1977.

Sinclair, Barbara. *The Transformation of the U.S. Senate.* Baltimore: John Hopkins University Press, 1989.

Smith, Margaret Chase. *Declaration of Conscience.* New York: Doubleday, 1972.

Straight, Michael. *Trial by Television.* Boston: Beacon Press, 1954.

Straight, Michael Whitney. *After Long Silence.* New York: Norton, 1983.

Stivers, Richard. *Hair of the Dog: Irish Drinking and American Stereotype.* University Park, PA: Pennsylvania State University Press, 1976.

Sudaplatov, Pavel, and Anatoli Sudaplatov. *Special Tasks: The Memoirs of an Unwanted Witness, a Soviet Spymaster.* Boston: Little, Brown, 1994.

Suny, Ronald Grigor. *The Soviet Experiment: Russia, the USSR, and the Successor States*. New York: Oxford University Press, 1998.

Taft, Robert A. *A Foreign Policy for Americans*. Garden City, NY: Doubleday, 1951.

Tananbaum, Duane. *The Bricker Amendment Controversy: A Test of Eisenhower's Political Leadership*. Ithaca, NY: Cornell University Press, 1988.

Tanenhaus, Sam. *Whittaker Chambers: A Biography*. New York: Random House, 1997.

Taylor, Sally J. *Stalin's Apologist: The Life of Walter Duranty. The New York Times's Man in Moscow*. New York: Oxford University Press, 1990.

Theoharis, Athan. *Seeds of Repression: Harry S. Truman and the Origins of McCarthyism*. Chicago: Quadrangle Books, 1971.

———. *The Truman Presidency: The Origins of the Imperial Presidency and the National Security State*. New York: Coleman Enterprises, 1982.

Theoharis, Athan G., and John Stuart Cox. *The Boss: J. Edgar Hoover and the Great American Inquisition*. Philadelphia: Temple University Press, 1988.

Thomas, Lately. *When Even Angels Wept*. New York: Morrow, 1973.

Toledano, Ralph, de. *Nixon*. New York: Henry Holt, 1956.

———. *Notes from the Underground: The Whittaker Chambers–Ralph de Toledano Letters, 1949–1960*. Chicago: H. Regnery Co., 1997.

Tuck, Jim. *McCarthyism and New York's Hearst Press: A Study of Roles in the Witch Hunt*. Lanham, MD: University Press of America, 1995.

Tucker, Nancy Bernkopf. "China's Place in the Cold War: The Acheson Plan." In *Dean Acheson and the Making of U.S. Foreign Policy*, 109–132. New York: St. Martin's, 1993.

Utley, Freda. *The China Story*. Chicago: H. Regnery Co., 1951.

Von Hoffman, Nicholas. *Citizen Cohn*. New York: Doubleday, 1988.

Walsh, Edmund A. *Total Empire: The Roots and Progress of World Communism*. Milwaukee: Bruce, 1951.

Walton, Richard J. *Henry Wallace, Harry Truman, and the Cold War*. New York: Viking, 1976.

Warren, Frank A., III. *Liberals and Communism: The "Red Decade" Revisited*. Bloomington: University of Indiana Press, 1966.

Watkins, Arthur V. *Enough Rope: The Inside Story of the Censure of Senator Joe McCarthy by His Colleagues*. Englewood Cliffs, NJ: Prentice-Hall, 1969.

Weaver, Mary Jo, and R. Scott Appleby, eds. *Being Right: Conservative Catholics in America*. Bloomington: Indiana University Press, 1995.

Weinstein, Allen. *Perjury: The Hiss-Chambers Case*. New York: Random House, 1997; originally published New York: Knopf, 1978.

Weinstein, Allen, and Alexander Vassiliev. *The Haunted Wood: Soviet Espionage in America, the Stalin Era*. New York: Random House, 1999.

West, Rebecca. *The New Meaning of Treason*. New York: Viking, 1964.

Whalen, Richard J. *The Founding Father: The Story of Joseph P. Kennedy*. New York: New American Library, 1964.

White, William Smith. *Citadel: The Story of the U.S. Senate*. Boston: Houghton-Mifflin, 1968.

Wickenden, Dorothy, ed. *The New Republic Reader.* New York: Basic Books, 1994.

Williams, W. A. *The Tragedy of American Diplomacy.* Revised and enlarged edition. New York: Dell, 1962; originally published 1959.

Woods, Randall, and Howard Jones. *The Dawning of the Cold War: The United States's Quest for Order.* Athens, GA: University of Georgia Press, 1982.

Wright, Peter. *Spycatcher: The Candid Autobiography of a Senior Intelligence Officer.* New York: Viking, 1987.

Zhang, Shu Guang. *Mao's Military Romanticism: China and the Korean War, 1950–1953.* Lawrence: University Press of Kansas, 1995.

Acknowledgments

Writing a book like this would have been impossible without the help of scores of people and institutions, so many that I can't possibly list them all. If anyone has been inadvertently left out of this abbreviated list, I hope he or she will understand and forgive.

For a writer, the act of acknowledging involves the public recognition of a debt, whether intellectual, professional, or personal. So I have to begin by recognizing the debt this book owes to a series of recent scholars whose professional, painstaking, and sometimes courageous research has given all of us a much clearer and more accurate picture of the context of McCarthyism, the cold war, and America's role in it. John Earl Haynes, Harvey Klehr, Richard Gid Powers, Ronald Radosh, Herbert Romerstein, Michael Sheng, Allen Weinstein, and Mao Chun Yu stand out in my mind, although I can even include here my predecessor biographers of McCarthy, Thomas G. Reeves and David Oshinsky. I know many, or even most, of them do not agree with all the conclusions I have extrapolated from their meticulous labors; but I do hope they will accept this tribute to their work, without which this book would not exist.

A special thanks goes to Adam Bellow, who put me on the right McCarthy trail after my initial flounderings and false starts, and to my agents Glen Hartley and Lynn Chu, who encouraged me to push on from the very earliest stages and never lost heart or hope.

A special thanks also goes to George Mason University's Fenwick Library and its director of Special Collections, Paul Koda. As a librarian and archivist, Paul is every scholar's dream. He provided me with free and unlimited access to one of his newest acquisitions, the Francis McNamara Collection, as well as other related materials. His enthusiastic support for this project, and our frequent conversations, all helped to keep the book on track. His assistants Bob Vay and Barbara Haase showed the same courtesy and enthusiasm, and their knowledge of the Oliver Atkins Photographic Collection saved me when I faced more than one deadline. I owe a very particular debt of gratitude to everyone in Special Collections, for their help and friendship.

At the same time, the library's directors, John Walsh and John Zenelis, graciously extended the support from my Fenwick Research Fellowship for an extra year to allow me to complete the book. I also want to thank the Fenwick's computer systems librarian, Lara Bushallow, who kept our database up and running at crucial times, as well as Lisa Hampton, and the Fenwick Fellowship Committee for their generous support.

A similar debt of gratitude goes to the staff of the National Archives in Washington, DC, and the Center for Legislative Archives, above all to my old friend and colleague Kenneth Kato. Ken was part of this project from the beginning: helping me find relevant documents, listening patiently to my theories and leads regarding McCarthy, and often passing along documents I did not know existed. Katherine Brasco cheerfully sorted through the Berryman Collection at NARA looking for McCarthy cartoons, while Richard McCulley gave me invaluable insights into the relationship between McCarthy and Millard Tydings.

Thanks are also due to my colleagues, students, and the staff of the history department at George Mason University, who suffered through my obsession with this project over these past three years with patience and tolerance. My chairman, Jack Censer, always allowed me to arrange my teaching schedule to fit with the demands of completing the book, and never seemed to mind that he had hatched a renegade American historian in the department's midst. Rex Wade gave unstintingly of his extraordinary knowledge of Soviet communism and Russian history as I was researching and writing, and patiently suffered through my attempts to turn him into a sounding board for the core ideas in the book.

Then come the helpful people at the State Historical Society of Wisconsin, especially Dee Anne Klodinsky, and Pat Wildenberg of the Herbert Hoover Presidential Library. The library staff at Duke University helped me locate key documents in the J. B. Matthews Papers and did not seem to mind my incessant need for photocopies of so many of the rare items housed in this fascinating and valuable collection.

Thanks also go to the people who graciously agreed to do personal interviews in order to give me their insights into Joe McCarthy and his era: Patricia Buckley, William F. Buckley, Jr., William Rusher, and Frank McNamara. Conversations with Daniel Boorstin, Robert Forster, David Kaiser, Leonard Liggio, John J. Miller, John Moser, John Pocock, Orest Ranum, Joel Smith, Phoebe Stanton, Caroline Turner, and Carol and Fred Warshofsky all helped enormously to shape my thinking about this project, although some of them may have been unaware of it at the time and may be astonished to learn it now.

The following persons also read versions of the manuscript, either in part or in full: M. Stanton Evans, John Earl Haynes, Arthur and Barbara Herman, Leonard Liggio, Betty Lockhart, Jerry Z. Muller, Fred Warshofsky, and Mao Chun Yu. All of them contributed valuable suggestions and criticisms, but four deserve special mention. Stan Evans at the National Journalism Center was extremely generous in sharing the results of his own research on McCarthy and helped me track down sources and materials I otherwise would never have found. John Haynes was never at a loss in answering specific questions, no matter how obtuse or obscure; the same applies to Herb Romerstein. Finally, Jerry Muller took time from his busy schedule to read and comment on an early version of the manuscript. If he reads this now, he will see that I did not take every suggestion he made, but I did take enough of them to make it a far better book.

For my discussion of McCarthy's medical and personality history, I found expert advice and guidance from the following persons: Dr. Jacob Katsow, Associate Clinical Professor of Psychiatry at George Washington University Medical School and Director, Washington Institute of Mood Disorders; Dr. William Pollin, former Chief of Psychiatry at the National Institute of Health and former Director, National Institute on Drug Abuse; Dr. Frank J. Rath, Jr., of the University of Maryland; and Dr. Christopher Wemple.

Then, special acknowledgments for three students who enabled me to complete my research for the book. The first is Bill Carpenter, of the Army Declassification Center in Arlington, Virginia. The second is Robbi Rowley of the University of Maryland, who generously allowed me to examine her research at the National Archives on the Irving Peress case. The third and greatest debt is to my research assistant, Lynn Hopffgarten. His careful attention and unflagging zeal not only helped me to correct errors and uncover new sources, but also gave me new perspectives on the issues this book was meant to address. I owe Lynn a huge debt of gratitude and, in many ways, the final version of this book represents a collaborative effort. Of course, I alone am responsible for any errors or mistakes that remain—a statement that applies to everything else in the book as well.

The people at The Free Press handled matters with their usual professionalism and good will, even under pressing deadlines and trying circumstances. My editor Bruce Nichols; Dan Freedberg and Edith Lewis; and finally Lisa Rivlin, Simon & Schuster's General Counsel, all helped enormously to bring this project to its happy conclusion.

Finally, thanks to my father and mother, who put on a brave show of enthusiasm for a project about which I imagine they were very dubious, and to my wife, Beth, who endured this painful and arduous journey for so long, but who turned out to be a fellow pilgrim in more ways than one.

Index

Bureau of Economic Warfare (BEW), 109
Burgess, Guy, 78, 109, 153, 154*n*
Burke, Edmund, 252
Burnham, James, 146–147, 153, 163, 172, 205–206, 321
Burr, Aaron, 1
Bush, George, 291
Bush, Prescott, 291
Butler, John M., 150–151, 196, 289, 353
Byrd, Harry, 47, 224
Byrnes, James, 76, 94–95, 244

Cain, Harry, 50, 206
Capehart, Homer, 133
Capitalism, 65, 143, 144
Carlson, Frank, 281
Carnegie Endowment for Peace, 86, 89
Carr, Frank, 212, 244, 246, 251, 256, 262, 264, 265, 271–273
Carto, Willis, 315
Case, Frank, 281, 292
Catholics
  as Kennedy supporters, 316
  as McCarthy supporters, 8–9, 160, 176–180
Catholic War Veterans of America, 176, 277, 285
Catholic Worker, 178
Caute, David, 3
Chaffee, Zachariah, 125, 128
Chamberlain, John, 172, 175
Chambers, Esther, 166
Chambers, Whittaker, 83, 97, 105, 139, 169, 179, 180, 213, 327
  Hiss case and, 58, 60, 84–86, 161
  McCarthy and, 162, 165–166, 227, 307
  Witness, 312
Chase, Stuart, 65
Chavez, Dennis, 124, 226
Chen Han-shen, 126, 127
Chennault, Claire, 167
Chiang Kai-shek, 84, 85, 93, 107*n*, 111, 121–123, 129, 147, 148, 166–170, 190, 191
Chicago Sun-Times, 232
Chicago Tribune, 83, 161, 162, 231
Chi Ch'ao-ting, 107*n*, 111, 123, 126
Childs, Marquis, 194, 224, 234
China Lobby, 2, 50, 166–172
Chinese Communists, 34, 94, 98, 107*n*, 121, 130, 143, 144, 167–169, 171, 188–191, 223–224, 244, 247, 320
  Cultural Revolution, 167
  Korean War and, 153–154, 157
  Nixon's visit, 167
  recognition of, 93
  Soviet Union and, 6, 89, 121–122, 168–169

Chinese Nationalists, 111, 121–123, 130, 147, 166–169, 171, 191
Chodorov, Frank, 172, 277
Chomsky, Noam, 325, 326
Christian Century, 184
Christian Science Monitor, 231
Churchill, Winston, 73, 77, 301
  "Iron Curtain" speech (1946), 78–79
CIA (Central Intelligence Agency), 56, 85, 143, 227–228, 314, 326
CIO (Congress of Industrial Organizations), 38, 39*n*, 67, 84, 173
Civil rights movement, 15, 319
Civil Service Loyalty Review Board, 187
Clearing House, 232*n*, 277, 278, 282
Clifford, Clark, 143, 236
Clubb, Edmund, 188
Coe, Frank, 107*n*, 216
Coffin, William Sloane, 320
Cogley, John, 178, 253
Cohn, Roy, 10, 96, 162, 182, 226, 242, 262, 291, 300, 304
  Army background files on, 264
  Army-McCarthy hearings and, 262, 264–266, 271–275
  background of, 217
  as chief counsel of PSI, 210, 211, 218, 221–224, 226, 228–229
  draft deferment, 264, 271, 274
  Fort Monmouth case and, 238–240
  homosexuality, allegations of, 218, 273
  McCarthy, relationship with, 210, 218–219
  Moss case and, 333–337
  Schine and, 211, 218, 243, 245–247, 249, 251, 252, 254, 255, 273
Colby, James, 33
Cold war consensus, 313–316
Cold war revisionism, 325–326
Coleman, Tom, 12, 37, 140, 141, 194, 201, 299
Collier, Peter, 320
Collier's magazine, 190
Collins, Henry, 85, 180
Coming American Revolution, The (Soule), 65
Comintern (Communist International), 77, 103, 127
Commerce, Department of, 183
Committee, The (Goodman), 318
Committee for Cultural Freedom, 70, 184
Commonweal, 178, 184, 253
Communist Control Act, 10
Communist International, 63
Communist Labor Party (CPU), 62
Communist Party of America (CPA), 62
Communist Party of the United States (CPUSA), 3–4
  front organizations for, 67–68, 70, 74, 79